Winner of the Aberdare Literary Prize, awarded by the British Society of Sports History, 1994

Shortlisted for the William Hill Sports Book of the Year Award, 1994

"An American socialist cricket-lover strips back the game's history to reveal venality and racism. The strengths of the book lie in its passion and in the meticulous retelling of cricket's development ... Only an outsider who has come to the game late in life could articulate its peculiarities so well. Cricket is refreshed through his eyes"

Sunday Times

"If you enjoy cricket but despise the stripy tie world of the cricket establishment, Marqusee's book is what you've been waiting for. Its beauty and originality is its insistence that it is possible to love the game while understanding that it is a game, nothing more or less ... here is something for the supporter on the bench, not the executive box"

Mark Steel

"Mike Marqusee is an American, a socialist, and a cricket-lover. The alchemy of this unique combination has contributed to the production of this remarkable book. To call it a book on cricket would be a gross misnomer ... It weaves together the social history of English cricket with the social history of England in a manner which is as unique as it is brilliant. It is doing a sort of CLR James on English cricket ... The book is laced with insightful comments about the relationship between cricket, the nation and the market. Quite fascinating"

Prabhat Patnaik, Frontline (India)

"The most perceptive, challenging and irreverent book on cricket since CLR James' magnificent classic, *Beyond a Boundary* ... Mike Marqusee has studied the game and the political, commercial and racist ramifications with the thoroughness of a social scientist. CLR James started it all. Marqusee is a most worthy successor. *Anyone But England* deserves an honoured place in your library"

Caribbean Times

"The New Cricket Culture's origins can be traced to 1994, and a genuinely different cricket book – *Anyone But England* ... Marqusee used it as a platform to declare his distaste for a whole range of organisations, activities, and methods dear to the conservative English – with a focus on cricket"

The Australian Magazine

"The book's argument is powerful and well-sustained. The cricket bosses do not come out of it well, nor do they deserve to. Unfortunately, it is certain that few of them will read it. County members might just be stirred by its polemic, because after all Marqusee actually likes the damn game! And maybe he likes the English too"

British Society of Sports History

"Mike Marqusee knows and loves cricket and both qualities shine through his brilliant contribution to cricket literature. Neither blinds him to the reality that cricket in Britain is shot through with hypocrisy and a corrupt and vicious nationalism which perverts the supposed ideals of the game. In this, he puts most cricket writers to shame ... His style, while gently ironic, is charged with deadly truth"

Salim Salaam, Race and Class

"Cricket's iconoclast-in-chief"

Simon O'Hagan, Wisden Cricket Monthly

"What English cricket has done to deserve him is anyone's guess"

Marcus Berkman, Wisden Cricket Monthly

"A damning study of the history of the game, sure to rock the very foundations of Lord's. *Anyone But England* is not only a must for cricket fans, but a must for anyone interested in the social fabric of this country"

Irish World

"An unusual and extremely thought provoking book. It is also a unique book which transcends all the known genres of cricket writing ... Even those who do not agree with all that Marqusee has to say on the politics of cricket and the prejudices of the English will accept that he has provided a novel and a much needed perspective on the noblest game of them all"

Rudrangshu Mukherjee, The Telegraph (Calcutta)

"A fine representative of the vibrant but little known tradition linking cricket and the British left ... His perspective is unusual, and he can write"

Matthew Engel, The Guardian

"The national game's meandering voyage down the proverbial corridor of uncertainty is traced with masterly effect by Marqusee, a cricket-loving American leftie ... Better than CLR James on speed, there are thousands of us who've been waiting years for this"

The Modern Review

"*Anyone But England* is written with honesty and serious intentions by an author who wants to see the game escape from its current slough of despond"

Andrew Shields, Time Out

"Funny, disturbing and deeply provocative ... A ruthless analysis of why the English whine"

Hindustan Times

"A transatlantic wowser"

Michael Henderson, The Times

"That splendid American iconoclast"

Robin Marlar, Sunday Times

"For the true believer of the cricket cult, the game is built on articles of faith. The cult has its saints, its heroes, its cathedral at Lord's, and in the shape of Mike Marqusee it has a heretic. ... Mike Marqusee never fails to involve and inform"

Southeast London Sportscene

"Certainly puts the ball tampering affair in its proper perspective. An excellent critical analysis of English cricket"

Imran Khan

"He writes well, if with a warped intelligence"

EW Swanton

"A very intelligent book, very cleverly written, with a lot that provokes thought. But I am uneasy about the way that he has a go at just about everything cricketers hold sacred"

Christopher Martin-Jenkins, Test Match Special

"Mike Marqusee could hardly have made a ruder impact on the summer if he were Keith Chegwyn banging on Ray Illingworth's door at seven in the morning with a film crew in tow ... If this doesn't make them break wind in the Test Match Special oxygen tent, nothing will"

Kevin Mitchell, The Observer

"This is a different kind of cricket book, a very different kind ... Marqusee is withering in his exposure of the racism and hypocrisy prevalent in the English cricket scene"

Indian Review of Books

"Marqusee has immersed himself in cricket and this book is the result of an enormous exercise in assimilating a sporting culture without absorbing an accompanying bias and subjective national cultural value. This is what makes his book unique, the depth of his understanding of the beauty of the action of cricket ... He writes movingly about both the dancers and the dance ... Among books of the world of sport there are few which also express the sport of the world in all its representation of real life and struggle. *Anyone But England* is one, a commentary on our times"
Chris Searle, Morning Star

"The book that everyone's talking about ... The elegant and concise accounts of the origin of the game, its romance with the British empire, are a must for all cricket fans ... the book is an entertaining and fascinating exploration of cricket and it will come as a revelation to many"
Eastern Eye

"Those who love a good moan will be in ecstasy as they plough through these pages ... *Anyone But England* is perceptive and it will instruct and entertain, but it is unlikely to change anything"
David Frith, Wisden Cricket Monthly

"A thoroughly researched, historic class analysis of cricket's origins and recent controversies"
Socialist Outlook

"Marqusee has a keen eye for hypocrisy, the quintessential English vice ... the average reader of the *Daily Telegraph* will find much to agree with in this book. Marqusee has fallen in love with the English game"
Adam Sisman, The Observer

"*Anyone But England* is a book for anyone with an interest in cricket which goes beyond merely the runs scored and wickets taken. It shows that the game cannot be isolated from the political, economic and cultural context that it is set in. The author has done a great job in tying together the diverse themes of cricket, the nation and the market"
Business Standard, India

"The slightly barking but always readable Mike Marqusee"
Tim Rice, Daily Telegraph

"Marqusee's love of cricket shines throughout this book like the floodlights at the Melbourne Cricket Ground ... enlightening, informative, entertaining and controversial"
Labour Briefing

"His book is rich in insight and makes fascinating reading ... a wonderfully invigorating read and a very welcome corrective to an unreflective view of the charms of leather on willow"

John Gaustad, Sportspages bookshop

"The book is on a small shelf with only a handful of others that have criticised our national game. His application to join the MCC would, I am sure, end up in the waste paper basket ..."

Camden New Journal

"A mildly irritating but otherwise challenging book ..."

Martin Johnson, The Independent

"Marqusee is a skilled historian who knows and loves the game and knows, but does not always love, the British. His is a wide-ranging book that is arguably the most important sociological study of cricket since CLR James ... *Anyone But England* is an authoritative account and analysis of the tortured entanglements of English cricket with class, race and empire. It is also stunningly topical"

Ramachandra Guha, Telegraph (Calcutta)

"Best of the Year"

Mail on Sunday sports book review

"Constantly perceptive ... wise, witty and well-written"

Tribune

"The panache of his approach and obvious love of the game challenge the assumption that only those who grow up with cricket can know the game as it should be known ... His thesis is enriched by transatlantic elements ... a book that contrives to be both cerebral and entertaining"

The Times

"The fascinating aspect here is a history of cricket written by an outsider-*l'étranger* ... what makes his history of the game and its early development remarkable is the novel-like quality of the narrative. The case is presented with the felicity of a QC"

R Mohan, The Hindu

"Challenging and highly individual study of the game"

David Hopps, Guardian

"The author's American background enables him to see matters from an unusual perspective; the result is a book which is indeed provocative and controversial, and has proved one of the surprise successes of the summer"
Kettering Evening Telegraph

"The best sports book of the year was *Anyone But England* by Mike Marqusee, an unlikely study of English decline by an unlikely man"
Irish Press

"The book is well worth the read though you may find yourself at serious odds with the author and that's no bad thing"
Cricket Wodd

"As intelligent an analysis of the relationship between a country and its national sport as you are likely to find"
Hampstead and Highgate Express

"A devastating treatise on the various ills plaguing the game in the land of its birth"
Gulu Ezekiel, Financial Express (India)

"There may have been many cricket histories (too many even) but none that I have come across that takes so much perceived wisdom about cricket, England, pastoral idylls and the role of the establishment and gives them a thoroughly good, and richly deserved, kicking ... you should read this book, whatever your politics"
Matthew Lloukes, Johnny Miller 96*

"Surprisingly witty and perceptive (for an American, do we hear you add?) – a fascinating book"
The Good Book Guide

"An entertaining read, full of delightful information ... it peers beneath the romance of the game to examine commercialism, racism and the role of cricket as some kind of epitome of Englishness"
Simon Rocker, Jewish Chronicle

"Marqusee's overall project is trying to understand the relationship between cricket and society in England, especially in a period in which the game has been undergoing far-reaching transformation ... Marqusee's book brilliantly captures the deep racism, arrogance, hypocrisy, elitism and classism which still pervades English cricket ... On England and South Africa his account is fascinating ... highly perceptive ..."
Transformation (South Africa)

Anyone but England

Also by Mike Marqusee

Slow Turn (a novel)

Defeat from the Jaws of Victory: Inside Kinnock's Labour Party (co-author)

War Minus the Shooting:
a journey through south Asia during cricket's World Cup

Anyone *but* England

CRICKET, RACE AND CLASS

MIKE MARQUSEE

Two Heads
Publishing

This revised and updated edition
first published in 1998 by
Two Heads Publishing
9 Whitehall Park
London
N19 3TS

First Published in 1994 by Verso as
Anyone But England: Cricket and the National Malaise

ISBN 1 897850 43 3

Cover Design by Lance Bellers
Cover illustration by Tim Bradford

Printed and bound in the UK by Biddles, Guildford

Acknowledgements

Thanks to the following for providing information or fruitful lines of research, and sharing their thoughts on cricket and related topics: Hussein Ayoob, Jane Barrett, Graham Bash, John Booth, Jeremy Corbyn, John Cryer, Steve Faulkner, Paul Field, Michael Foot, Ramachandra Guha, Peter Hain, Richard Heffernan, Conrad Hunte, Steve King, Kim Longinotto, Khaya Majola, Narendra Makanji, Geoff Mann, Dave Palmer, Chris Parker, Andy Parr, Liz Philipson, Billy Power, Huw Richards, Peter Roebuck, Adam Sisman, Dennis Skinner, Rob Steen, Achin Vanaik, Donald Woods. I would also like to acknowledge the help I received from the late Bob Cryer, socialist and cricketer.

Special thanks to Colin Robinson, for endless encouragement and sound advice, and Liz Davies, my favourite English person.

Author's note on the second edition

I have corrected those errors which have been pointed out to me (thanks to correspondents and critics), and have made minor revisions in the text in the interests of readability and clarity. All the footnotes are new to this edition, as is the final chapter, in which I examine developments in English cricket since the book was first published in May, 1994. Many thanks to Charles Frewin for giving me a second bite at the cherry!

Mike Marqusee, June 1998

Contents

Foreword

There's a breathless hush in the Close tonight –
Ten to make and the match to win –
A bumping pitch and a blinding light,
An hour to play and the last man in.

Is it art? Is it life? Is it a relic of a pre-industrial age, a version of pastoral, a colonial legacy, a continuation of the class war by other means? Is it a trivial pursuit? Cricket is all these and more. Above all, however, it is quintessentially English and quintessentially conservative – or so generations of flannelled fools, brought up on the patriotic verse of Sir Henry Newbolt, have led us to believe.

It must, then, be infuriating for them to realise that two of the greatest books about the game have been written by chaps who were not only foreigners but also socialists.

C L R James, author of *Beyond a Boundary*, was just about acceptable. True, he was a Trinidadian Marxist who had known Leon Trotsky. But in other respects he was a romantic traditionalist. The heroes of *Beyond a Boundary* were Thomas Arnold, the 19th-century headmaster of Rugby, Thomas Hughes, the author of *Tom Brown's Schooldays*, and W G Grace. James was dazzled by the 'grandeur' and 'moral elevation' of Arnold's ideas, apparently happy to overlook the fact these ideas included a contempt for the working class and a terror of universal suffrage. What mattered, in C L R's view, was that Arnold introduced compulsory games for his pupils – "the only contribution of the English educational system of the 19th century to the general educational ideas of Western civilisation".

Mike Marqusee has no such redeeming qualities. Whisper it not at Lord's, but the man is alleged to be an American.

To me, this is one of his many virtues, and is what equips him to write so sharply and revealingly about the game. As an outsider, he sees things which are often overlooked by those of us who were wearing pads and batting gloves long before we were allowed to wear long trousers. You will learn much from this book about the history of cricket – but even more about the evolution of English attitudes to race and class, tradition and modernity.

Unlike C L R James, Marqusee is not in thrall to the Victorian public-school ideology. He is scathing about the quasi-feudal system that governed cricket until well into this century, with its distinction between 'gentlemen' and 'players', and its determination to perpetuate "the myth of an enduring and natural social hierarchy." The game's aristocratic administrators, who pretended to be guided by a sense of 'fair play', were in fact anything but fair to the working-class players whose talents they exploited. "Pray God no professional may ever captain England," said Lord Hawke, Yorkshire CCC's president, as recently as 1924.

All most deplorable. Does Mike Marqusee rejoice, then, that patrician amateurs such as Hawke – who kept vulgar commerce out of cricket, or at least at a safe distance from it – have been replaced by hard-headed professionals? He does not. He winces as he surveys the present sponsor-infested game, whose Sunday League players are forced to cavort like pantaloons in garish pyjamas at the behest of an insurance company. White flannels "were one of the first things that attracted me to cricket," he reveals, "and I mourn their loss on Sunday as much as anyone." As George Orwell once pointed out, some things are true even though the *Daily Telegraph* says they are true; similarly, one should allow that some things in this country are worth conserving even though conservatives happen to think so too. These include cricket whites, leg-spin bowling and uncovered wickets.

Paradoxical as it may seem, my own criticism of the potentates of the MCC – who are usually denounced as fossilised reactionaries – is that they aren't reactionary enough. Given their hostility to almost everybody outside their own magic circle – black people, women, undeferential foreigners – one would expect them also to shun such modern barbarians as PR consultants, marketing whizkids and corporate-hospitality merchants. Go to any county ground and you will see that this isn't the case. While devoting its energies to keeping women out of the Long Room at Lord's, the MCC has done nothing to prevent rich corporations from disfiguring the arcadian scene – the boundaries, the players' shirts, the very pitches themselves – with logos and huckstering slogans. Even the umpires now wear the colours of a privatised electricity company. "There is no doubt," the promotions manager of the Test and County Cricket Board said recently, "that it is primarily the image of the game and its track record of successful association with the business world which continue to attract corporate advertisers."

Silly me. I thought the attractions of the game were its guile and grace, and those other qualities so evocatively described by Mike Marqusee – "the arc of a straight six, the crisp, dismissive sound of a square cut, the sudden savagery of a stump uprooted by pace . . . the solace of an empty county ground on a bright weekday morning . . . the sublime waste of an entire day on something with no redeeming purpose whatsoever".

Just as the United States came to our rescue during World War II, so the salvation of English cricket may lie in another timely intervention by an American. As *Anyone But England* demonstrates, he seems to understand the game rather better than we do.

Francis Wheen

The crowd at the ball game
is moved uniformly

by a spirit of uselessness
which delights them –

all the exciting detail
of the chase

and the escape, the error
the flash of genius –

all to no end save beauty
the eternal . . .

From William Carlos Williams,
'At the Ball Game'

I

Culture Clash

An oxymoron • Baseball, cricket and the movies
• Love and first sight • 1993:the Ashes
• 1993: World Cup Final • Cricket, nation, market

Neville Cardus, self-made snob and cricket sage, once opined: 'Where the English language is unspoken there can be no real cricket, which is to say that the Americans have never excelled at the game.'

Compared with Shaw's concise quip about the Americans and the English being two peoples separated by a common language, this is mere abuse. But what a world of prejudice is revealed in Cardus's smug aphorism. I've lived in Britain well over twenty years (most of my life), and it still astonishes me.

I shouldn't get irritated, but I can't help it. Every time I'm asked, 'How can an American understand cricket?' I do a bad job disguising my impatience. Why shouldn't an American understand cricket? It's a game like any other. Yet, on both sides of the Atlantic, the very juxtaposition of 'American' and 'cricket' has come to seem oxymoronic. Everything that English people take to be 'American' – brashness, impatience, informality, innovation, vulgarity, rapacious and unashamed commercialism – is antithetical to what they take to be 'cricket'. For the English, it is a point of pride that Americans cannot understand cricket. They may imbibe American movies, music, hamburgers and nuclear missiles, but their national sport remains their own. As for the Americans, everything they took, until recently, to be 'English' – tradition, politeness, deference, gentle obscurantism – seems to be epitomised in 'cricket'. The attitude was neatly put by the affable, pizza-eating vigilante Raphael in one of the Teenage Ninja Mutant Turtles movies. Assaulted by a mystery attacker with a cricket bat, Raphael protests, 'Nobody understands cricket. To understand cricket you gotta know what a crumpet is.'

Cricket was definitely not part of the New York suburban culture in which I grew up in the 1950s and '60s, but somehow I knew of its existence from my earliest years. It was, of course, always associated with England, along with bowler hats, bobbies and Big Ben. It was part of a national stereotype - a relatively benign one compared with those applied to Mexicans, Japanese or Italians, all of whom were, in one way or another, closer to home. The English were quaint, in the thrall of arcane traditions, absurdly polite and well-spoken, and cricket, in so far as I knew anything about it, was a ritual in which all these characteristics were displayed.

As a kid, I was a baseball nut. Later I became an all-round sports buff. Track and field, tennis, what I later came to know as 'American' football, ice hockey, basketball - at one time or another I had a romance with each. But it was baseball which got me started. In the sports pages of the otherwise impenetrable *New York Times*, I discovered the joy of batting averages, league standings and box scores. I was an abysmal player (not only of baseball), frustrated by my frequent failures and intimidated by the competitiveness of the fierce middle-aged men who coached our various teams. My parents' gentler, egalitarian approach had not prepared me for this.

Like many others, I took refuge in the facts and figures of sport. I became a dedicated spectator at the age of eight, and was spoiled for life. The first baseball season I followed was 1961, the year Roger Maris broke Babe Ruth's single-season home-run record for the New York Yankees. The Yanks were my side and they had been the dominant team in baseball since the 1920s. I thought all baseball seasons would be as exciting and satisfying as this one. I soon learned they wouldn't be. Being a quondam Yankee fan gave me an insight into Liverpool and West Indian supporters in the 1990s, taking supremacy for granted, baffled by defeat.

I was ten when I first played cricket at a summer camp in the Berkshire hills of western Massachusetts. One day a camp counsellor, a young Australian, set up some stumps, produced a cricket bat and taught us the rudiments of a single-wicket game. It caught on and we played it for most of the summer. I remember liking the defensive aspect of batting. Unlike in baseball, you could stick around for a while even if you couldn't hit the ball very far or indeed at all. I was also intrigued by the sheer foreignness of the game. It seemed to go with the Australian's accent, which I took to be English. To me, as to most Americans then, Australia was merely a subdivision of England. When the summer came to an end, I forgot all about the curious English game.

After that, cricket entered my world through the movies. And the movies confirmed the impression I had already formed: that the game was something so intensely English as to be hopelessly at odds with the modern world. Hollywood historical epics set in sundry bizarre versions of England and the British Empire deployed references to cricket - along with cups of tea, 'chin up' and 'jolly good show' – to give the fantasy an English flavour. Here was my first visual contact with a real cricketer, though I didn't know it at the time. Sir C. Aubrey Smith, Hollywood's favourite English character actor, played upper crust gentlemen or officers in films like *Lives of a Bengal Lancer*, *Wee Willie Winkie* or *Little Lord Fauntleroy*. But Smith not only played the type, he *was* the type. C.A. Smith (Charterhouse, Cambridge, Sussex, Transvaal) had been a leading amateur right-arm fast bowler and lower-order batsman. He had captained what passed for 'England' in one Test in South Africa in 1888 and then settled there, working as a stockbroker for some years before making a new career on the English stage and ultimately departing for Hollywood. Smith, the living embodiment of cricket's Golden Age and the panoply of Empire, was in the end marketed as a second XI film star to a new mass audience in a foreign country that cared little either for cricket or the British Empire.

As a Hitchcock fan I had seen *The Lady Vanishes* many times before I came to England, where I learned there was a lot more to the film than I had suspected. This whimsical thriller is nothing less than an ironic paean to incipient national solidarity in the face of the Nazi menace. Its two cricket-loving, overgrown public schoolboys (played by Naunton Wayne and Basil Radford) are phlegmatic, xenophobic, obsessive, asexual, and intransigently empirical to the point of stupidity. At first they resent the intrusion of such superfluous, foreign things as espionage and politics into their attempts to reconstruct a Test match over a dining table with the aid of sugar cubes. However, when they discover that despite appearances the suave Nazis are not true 'gentlemen', that their duplicitous behaviour is 'not cricket', they rally to the cause. Hitchcock satirized the infantile silliness of the cricket cult while using it as a metaphor for an England complacent under threat, but capable of being roused.

When war came, Hitchcock moved to Hollywood, where his first film was *Rebecca*, in which an austere, emotionally crippled Laurence Olivier chillingly suggests to his innocent new wife, Joan Fontaine, that she 'have a look at *The Times*. There's a thrilling article on what's the matter with English cricket.' Hitchcock already knew his American audience. He knew that they would find the juxtaposition of the words 'thrilling' and 'English cricket' paradoxical and even sinister.

The same idea appears, in comic form, twenty-five years later in Woody Allen's script for *What's New Pussycat?* Peter O'Toole, cricket mad in real life, plays the compulsive Don Juan confessing all to his psychiatrist (Peter Sellers with wig and Teutonic accent). When he mentions cricket, Sellers demands: 'Is there any sex in it?' The joke, of course, is not only that Sellers is himself sex-mad but he is so sex-mad (and so alien) that he does not know, as others do, that 'sex' and 'cricket' cannot be mentioned in the same breath. Cricket, in other words, is definitely pre-Freudian.*

As a teenager I went to see *How I Won the War*, a chaotically avant garde anti-war satire directed by the expatriate American, Richard Lester, who had made the Beatles films. The film was a flop. I went out of my way to catch it because I was anti-war, because I was intrigued by avant-garde chaos, and because it featured John Lennon in a supporting role. Knowing nothing at the time about England, much of the movie's satire was over my head, notably the scene in which the martinet British officers order their troops to construct a cricket pitch behind enemy lines. The film-makers clearly saw cricket as an apt symbol of the warped values of the British ruling class. That view lingers today. In recent years I have probably been asked, 'How can a socialist be keen on cricket?' as often as, 'How can an American ...?' As ever, the incompatibility is in the eye of the beholder.

After 1967, swallowed up in a culture of mass protest which rejected competitiveness and aggression, I lost interest in sport. Like the Pledge of Allegiance, television sit-coms, and short hair, sport (and baseball in particular) seemed part of the straight world we taught each other to despise.

---

*One of the first films I saw on my arrival in England was *The Go-Between*, a meditation on class, sex and memory scripted by Harold Pinter (from Hartley's novel) and directed by a leftist American refugee from McCarthyism, Joseph Losey. One of the highlights of the film is a village cricket match in which the denizens of the great house take on the local plebes. It was clear that this was cricket as a form of sublimated class war, but at the time I didn't appreciate the contrast between the grass-skimming cover-drives of the public school educated upper classes and the leg-side air-born hitting of the untutored locals. I assume credit for this telling detail belongs to the cricket-lover Pinter.

In 1971 I came to England to study English at university. I had no idea I would spend the next two decades here. Indeed, I had no idea at all why I was here or what kind of society I was coming to. The sixties had left me shell-shocked. I was bewildered and jaded by the rapid succession of social and political events – especially as they were superimposed on the ordinary tumult of adolescence. For me, England was a place to run away to. The country of bowler hats, bobbies and Big Ben had become the country of Chaucer, Shakespeare and Milton. It was also the land of the Welfare State and the National Health Service, of strong trade unions, of a Labour Party that called itself socialist. The policemen did not carry guns. Looking back, I can see that what drew me to England was the idea that it would be a place without violent conflict, a place where disputes were settled in a civilised manner. I had swallowed whole my own version of the old English myth, the myth (I was later to see) at the heart of English cricket.

At university I used to hang out with a group of friends who would listen to 'Test Match Special' on the Third Programme. Stoned, these ex-public-school hippies would don cricket flannels and clap straw boaters on top of mountains of long hair. They would stand there giggling with spaced-out grins at a joke I just didn't get. Cricket to them was an object of affectionate ridicule. It was one of those 'English' things, folk-like, druidic, pastoral, evoked by Pentangle, Jethro Tull, the Kinks, and (with irony) the Bonzo Dog Doodah Band. It was part of the world of English childhood, like Winnie the Pooh, a world to which I was very much a latecomer. Like Tolkien's fantasies, which these counter-cultural youth also admired, cricket seemed a gentle drama played out on an eternal village green, a realm beyond history and politics.

As the years went by, I came to see these contemporaries in clearer focus. Many who in those days mocked their middle-class, home counties backgrounds (of which cricket was a part) later went into the City, voted Tory and sent their children to public schools. Some, no doubt, now occupy the elite hospitality boxes at Lord's on Test match days.

It was not long before my illusions about England were shattered. A series of monster industrial disputes, war in Ireland and a mean-minded street-corner racism did the trick. With the cultural revolution definitely on the wane, I returned to sport in the mid-seventies. It seemed a refuge from the grim reality of economic and political struggle. The irony was that in cricket I was to find the same conflicts from which I was seeking shelter. Cricket (along with the labour movement) was one of those things which drew me, against my will, ever deeper into English life.

Because I did not play or even watch much cricket while growing up, I was spared what George Orwell thought a 'good reason for the decline in cricket's popularity ... the extent to which it has been thrust down everybody's throat'. Cricket for me is not tainted by the personal experience of humiliation and failure. (Those painful associations are reserved for American sports). Instead, I made cricket's acquaintance as an adult, during turbulent years when the game was subject to ceaseless change, stress and controversy. This book is an attempt to make sense of those years. But to do so, I first want to try to put aside my later experiences and go back in time to my first encounter with English cricket, not the cricket of movies or undergraduate mockery, but the real thing (or at least, the televised thing).

I fell in love with the game during the hot summer of 1976, when Clive Lloyd's masterful West Indian side blew away Tony Greig's puny Englishmen. I was living in a village in Devon, doing nothing in particular, and I drifted into listening to and watching the Tests on radio and television. This was the first time I had seen an all-black team play against an all-white one. In America, Jim Crow had kept black players in an entirely separate competitive structure until Jackie Robinson broke the colour bar in 1948. I was therefore riveted by the 1976 Test series, not least by the way the evident superiority of the black players caused such anguish among the English commentators.

From the first, I was enchanted by the sheer visual beauty of the game: the vast green fields adorned with immaculate white-clad figures moving in obscure, complex patterns as if in keeping with an ancient ritual. The change at the end of the over, when I first saw it, struck me as magical. It was so arbitrary, yet so precise, like a sorcerer's trick. At this stage, I saw cricket through the filter of baseball. It was a necessary point of comparison. You simply cannot understand one game (or one society) without referring to another. In cricket, I was startled to discover, there was no 'foul' territory. Batsmen could hit the ball anywhere, even paddle or deflect it behind, and then choose whether or not to run. This struck me as both sophisticated and primitive, wonderfully flexible and bizarrely intricate.

Amazingly, both teams wore the same outfit. And the spectators clapped good play on both sides. On occasion, even the players applauded opponents, an act inconceivable in baseball. Strangely, the fielders wore no gloves (and at that time the batsmen wore no helmets). Instead of flat, functional bases, there were stumps and bails, fragile, toylike castles which grown men used all their cunning to topple or protect. *And the ball was hard.* One American myth about cricket was instantly demolished: the idea that it was a 'soft' game, without physical danger. Watching Brian Close peppered by short, fast-pitched deliveries proved that it could be brutal in the extreme. Anyway, what kind of sport was it in which a forty-five year-old played for the national side?

Cricket seemed to me an extraordinarily unnatural game. The bowling motion with its straight elbow and tortuous body swing, the batsman's crouch, the whole 'side on' geometry of the game seemed to defy logic, not to mention human anatomy. Spin bowling intrigued me from the first simply because it was so slow. This was a sport in which speed and strength had their place but not to the exclusion of guile and touch. There was more brain in it than there was in baseball and the delicacy of its arcane, specialized skills took my breath away. It amazed me that someone would be included in a side just because he could make a ball spin away from a right-handed batsman or that there could be such a profound distinction between opening and middle-order bats.

But in another sense, cricket was much less specialized than baseball. Field placings were fluid rather than fixed. A midwicket is definitely not a short stop, not least because while a short stop will stay at short stop throughout a game a midwicket may be reincarnated over after over as a square leg, slip catcher, gully, cover point or even a bowler! I was charmed by the very idea of the all-rounder. Players who could pitch as well as bat had become anachronistic in baseball in the 1920s, just when the game was becoming a truly national mass sport and very big business indeed. In cricket, it seemed everyone had to be a bit of an all-rounder. Unlike baseball, there were no pinch-hitters but as many bowlers as the captain pleased. Within the named XI, permutation seemed almost infinite, and with it, the dramatic possibilities of the game.

I recognized immediately in cricket the highly individualistic confrontation between bowler and batsman I knew from baseball. But in cricket the confrontation was so prolonged. It was not over in three strikes or four balls or a line drive to third base. It had no determinate end – but it could end at any moment. Like the game itself, it could go on and on, interrupted only for those civilized interludes dedicated to 'lunch', 'tea' and 'drinks'.

As an American, I was fascinated by the idea that a single game could take three or five days to complete. The whole World Series took less time to play than a single Test match. Yet there were no substitutes. If someone was injured during the match, he could not be replaced, which seemed to me most unfair. Only later did I come to see unlimited substitution as a peculiarity of American sports. In the meantime, it just seemed another pointless rule, another one of those arbitrary difficulties out of which the English make a religion, like public-house opening hours.

The insistence on using a single ball throughout the course of an innings, or for at least the better part of a day, seemed bizarre. In baseball and all the other sports I knew, fresh balls were provided on demand. I was startled to learn of 'the slope' at Lord's. Why hadn't they levelled it? Cricket was full of mysteries. I began exploring them, and twenty years later, I'm still at it.

In those days, 'Test Match Special' was broadcast on Radio Three, which implied that it was something for the cognoscenti, and I have always been keen to be one of them. The jargon the commentators used was sometimes obscure, but from the first I savoured the game's childlike, archaic Anglo-Saxon idiom. From radio and television, I learned the Laws of cricket and its technical basis. More important, the broadcasters supplied its dramatic context. I soon learned that in cricket even the simplest occurrences are what semiologists call polysemous – signifying many things at one and the same time.

As purveyed by the 'Test Match Special' team in the 1970s, English cricket was a world where the norms of an imagined nineteenth century still obtained. It was a world of deference and hierarchy, ruled by benevolent white men, proud of its traditions and resentful of any challenge to them.

Cricket, as they portrayed it, did not live in the same world as the Welfare State, feminism and giant trade unions, and certainly not the world of sex, drugs and rock and roll.

I remember Brian Johnston burbling over Ian Botham's 'nice, short haircut' and Fred Trueman pontificating about the 'natural' athleticism of West Indian bowlers. At first I found the reactionary nostalgia and English insularity amusing, if rather pathetic. As the years went by, and I saw more clearly what these attitudes meant in English society, I was less amused. I became one of the multitude who listen to 'Test Match Special' because of an addiction to the ball-by-ball drama of big cricket, and in spite of the prejudices of some of the commentators.

John Arlott, of course, was always an exception. He was the outsider who had somehow found his way into the heart of the English establishment, combining love of tradition with hatred of injustice. While I can no longer swallow his belief that the cricket world reflected his own idealism and generosity, I am grateful still that through his rigour and his sympathy, his mastery of light and shade, he helped me to see and enjoy the epic nature of Test cricket. On first acquaintance, it is almost impossible for a newcomer to the game to get hold of the ever-shifting rhythms of a five-day struggle. Arlott's commentary helped me see the whole, not just the parts.

That summer I also discovered county cricket, the strangest of all of English cricket's strange institutions. Like everything else in my connection with cricket, becoming a Somerset supporter was fortuitous. From my village in Devon I could hitch-hike up the motorway to watch midweek matches in Taunton. In 1976, Somerset had yet to win any major honours in more than eighty years of first-class cricket. Taunton was still a tumble-down ground, all peeling paintwork, rickety benches and manual scoreboard, and the only edible items on the ground were the white-bread ham sandwiches served in the members' enclosure.

As it turned out, Somerset was the ideal introduction to the living anachronism that is county cricket. These shire-based membership clubs were a far cry from the big-city commercial franchises of baseball and other sports. For a start, several counties had more than one 'home' ground. The territorial entities they claimed to represent (depicted in the feudal iconography that bedecks the county game) did not, in many cases, even exist any more. Somerset played home' matches in Bath and Weston-super-Mare, both in Avon. Then there was the oddity of a professional sport being managed by earnest amateurs. I was always fascinated by the sight of clusters of county members, middle-aged men and women bundled in tweeds and corduroys, propped in their deck-chairs by the boundary, talking about the team as if they owned it, which, in a sense, they did.

I was also amazed at the casual interchange between the players and the spectators. I remember sitting cross-legged on the grass at Taunton just outside the boundary rope watching a match against the New Zealand tourists in 1978. Play was slow and between overs I tried to make sense of a Maoist tract on pre-Socratic philosophy. The slow left-armer Stephen Boock, fielding at third man, asked to see the book. I handed it to him and he flipped through the pages with a puzzled look, then passsed it back to me just in time to pluck the ball from the grass and return it to the stumps. I hadn't even seen the ball coming our way. Such easy interplay between spectator and player had been banished from American sports, indeed most sports, generations before.

Of course, the sparseness of the crowds has helped to maintain the casualness. One of the things I have always liked about county cricket is the fact that so few people go to see it. And back then, in the late seventies, the spectators seemed a particularly anomalous mix. There were the pensioners (male and female), the chronically unemployed or under-employed men, the social rejects and fanatical statisticians, the pre-pubescent kids, and not a few long-haired remnants of an era that was rapidly vanishing, some of whom had retreated to the West Country in despair of urban civilization. At least one of these sold quarter-ounces of cannabis resin behind the old Taunton scoreboard. I am sure the cricket authorities had no idea how many late-sixties-early-seventies burn-out cases they had ambling around the boundary ropes in those days.

I worked on this book through the Ashes series of 1993, when so many of its themes sprang to life. As England plummeted to a 4-1 defeat at the hands of an Australian side that had not been highly rated when it first arrived, the parallels between the malaise of English cricket and the economic and social malaise of the country itself were drawn by leader writers, stand-up comedians and the millions shadowing them in pubs, workplaces, bus queues and political meetings. At the same time, the England football team were failing to qualify for the World Cup finals. The tabloids encapsulated the national mood by portraying the England manager Graham Taylor as a turnip, soon followed by the transformation of cricket captain Graham Gooch into a potato. The nadir came when Taylor's squad lost to the USA. After all, everyone knew that the Americans had rejected soccer, which was, until the World Cup of 1994, one of the few areas of global popular culture on which the USA had no claim.

Comparing the hapless Taylor and Gooch with the helpless Tory Prime Minister became a commonplace. In the previous year, sterling had crashed out of the European Exchange Rate Mechanism, the Maastricht Treaty had split the ruling party and the pit-closure plan had pushed the Murdoch press into backing the miners. Amid recession, unemployment, homelessness, rising crime, cynicism towards virtually everyone in authority flourished. Politicians were distrusted and disliked almost as much as journalists, and even more than High Court judges and police. Yet this was an electorate that had returned a Tory government for the fourth time in succession only a year before.

Failure in the Ashes became even more resonant because the nation's leader was a certain type of English cricket lover: a little in awe of the game and the players, 'considerably' impressed by its ruling personnel and traditions, acknowledging with arch self-deprecation the frivolity of his eccentric but 'very English' passion. The lodestar of John Major's cricket memory was the golden summer of 1953, Coronation Year, when as a small boy he watched England regain the Ashes at the Oval under Len Hutton's leadership. When he became Prime Minister in 1990, the MCC allowed him to jump the membership queue.

On St George's Day in April 1993, Major gave what was intended to be a patriotic speech to a group of disgruntled Tory Euro-MPs. Echoing George Orwell, with radically different intent, he invoked 'the long shadows falling across the county ground, the warm beer, the invincible green suburbs, dog lovers and pool fillers ... old maids bicycling to Holy Communion through the morning mist'. As the British economy wrestled with the demands of a global market, Major offered the governing party shelter in the cosy old England of county cricket. But this was an England that did not exist, except, powerfully, in people's heads. Major's real audience was in the suburbs, among voters no longer convinced that they were 'invincible'. Here 'the county ground' and the traditions of country life, including cricket, were ideological mantras to ward off the demons encroaching ever more menacingly from the crime-ridden, multi-racial, dispossessed inner cities.

It was not, however, an opportune moment to ask Tory voters to take comfort in the continuity of English cricket. During the previous twelve months, the Test side had been defeated at home by Pakistan and abroad by India and Sri Lanka. Now they were being humiliated by the Australians.

It was not just that England were losing but the way they were losing. The sheer scale of the defeats – by 179 runs at Old Trafford, by an innings and 48 runs at Headingley, by 8 wickets at Edgbaston – told only part of the story. England's bowlers – fourteen were employed during the series – were drubbed. The Australian batsmen knocked up one huge total after another– 632 at Lord's and 653 for 4 declared at Headingley (where the pitch was supposed to favour English bowlers). Altogether, they struck ten centuries, including four that surpassed 150 and one from wicket-keeper Ian Healy. The top seven in the order all averaged over 40 for the series. England could boast three centuries, two by Gooch, and only four averages over 40. In light of the absence for most of the series of Australia's principal strike bowler, Craig McDermott, the failure of the England batsmen seemed abject.

As a deracinated Marxist of American Jewish background, success for 'England' means little to me. But this abysmal humiliation, though carrying a perverse frisson, undermined the theatrical and creative aspects of the game. No one will look back on England's neurotic and joyless performance of 1993, as John Arlott looked back on the Ashes defeat of 1920, and sigh with satisfaction: 'That was a great year. England were murdered by Australia.' In the *Observer*, Scyld Berry described the Test side as 'resigned, exuding non-commitment, misfielding, hoping not expecting, a group of individuals each wanting to do well without common purpose'. The England cricketers seemed bowed down not just by the burden of losing, but even more by the burden of representing their country.

The responses to the Ashes failure of 1993 were bewilderingly contradictory. What gripped me during that summer was the way the innumerable claims and counter-claims, often vehement and extreme, echoed larger arguments over the plight of the nation. English cricket plunged into one of its periodic frenzied mass hunts for scapegoats and saviours. The media, of course, were at the head of the pack. Soon after his arrival in May, Allan Border had declared, 'The English media are pricks.' Unlike the Pakistanis the year before, his Australians were spared the full treatment as the 'pricks' trained their sights on the home side.

As always, the first targets were the biggest and most visible: chairman of selectors Ted Dexter, team manager Keith Fletcher and captain Graham Gooch. The *Mirror* dubbed them 'the three stooges' and *The Sunday Times* 'the Board of Misdirectors'. After the Lord's defeat the *Sun* implored: 'Drop the Ted Donkey'. The Mirror replied with a Cromwellian, 'Go, in the name of God, Go'. There was more to this than the familiar tabloid exercise of 'building them up to knock them down'. It reflected a deeper quest for heroes, for individual solutions to collective problems.

Selection policy was pilloried. As so often in recent English Test history, it had been inconsistent, panic-driven, at times defying any intelligible logic. Announcing his squad for the first Test at Old Trafford, Dexter proclaimed, 'We don't envisage chopping and changing.' By the end of the series, he had called up twenty-four players to represent the country, only just short of the record-breaking twenty-nine he had employed in 1989, his first year at the helm.

The selection of Foster at Lord's and Emburey at Edgbaston (retrograde moves which betrayed a lack of confidence in younger players), the suspicion of spin and reliance on medium pace, the use of Alec Stewart as a-batsman-wicket-keeper, all came in for sharp criticism. However, the selectors, as ever, did respond to the pressure of public opinion, as orchestrated by the media. Lathwell and Caddick were chosen after glowing early-season notices, then dropped. Later, Malcolm,

Watkin and Maynard came in after sustained media promotion. But the selectors were not prepared to give in to popular demands for a recall of David Gower, whose omission throughout the summer seemed motivated mainly by a desire on their part to save face. Spurned by England, at the end of the season Gower announced a premature retirement.

Gower became a martyr in a popular crusade against the Dexter Gooch-Fletcher triumvirate. What drove the press wild was not merely the failure of the England side, but the refusal of any of the triumvirate to acknowledge or take responsibility for mistakes - an uncanny reflection of the Major government's attitude to the country's economic woes. Dexter's supercilious remark after the Lord's defeat was the final straw: 'We may be in the wrong sign or something. Venus may be in the wrong juxtaposition to somewhere else.' In other circumstances the media might have found in Dexter's unflappable complacency the stuff of a typically English national hero. Instead, 'Lord Ted' became a symbol of the unaccountability of the English cricket establishment, sleepwalking, like the government, to oblivion. When his resignation from the £40,000-a-year part-time post was announced during the final day of the fifth Test, the Edgbaston crowd cheered. 'GOOD RIDDANCE,' whooped the *Mirror*, catching the mood. During his regime, England had won 9 Tests, lost 21 and drawn 4.

Gooch, England captain during most of that time, had resigned two weeks earlier. His route to the top had been halting and circuitous. When he finally seized the prize in 1990, after the failure of all the other leading cricketers of his generation, he surprised many by raising his own game and leading England to respectable performances against the West Indies, India and New Zealand as well as the final of the 1992 World Cup. But this was a false dawn, one of many in English cricket since the Packer revolt. After a poor series in India, Gooch was initially appointed captain only for the first three Ashes Tests. After the loss of the first, he insisted to the press, 'I haven't considered resigning and I don't think this is the right time to do so.' The England Committee then extended his appointment to all six Tests. 'It is now up to the rest of the team to learn from his example,' explained Dexter. After defeat in the second Test Gooch spoke of resigning 'if things don't improve'. However, he remained in post, ever more lugubrious, until defeat in the fourth Test, which ensured that the Ashes would stay with Australia. Asked why England kept losing, he replied, 'We are not playing very good cricket.' It was neither stupid nor evasive. It was simply that Gooch, like Dexter, was baffled by failure.

This applied even more to Keith Fletcher, on a five-year contract worth £250,000. Fletcher spent much of the Ashes series (his first summer in charge) complaining about pitches, balls going soft, net conditions and injuries. He seemed bereft of strategy, falling back, in the absence of any other ideas, on the routines which had served him well in county cricket. He had been the chosen successor of Micky Stewart, the first-ever England team manager, who had also schemed to ensure Gooch's succession to the captaincy. For many commentators, Dexter's greatest crime was to have betrayed his own amateur, cavalier heritage by giving free rein to Stewart's hard-nosed professionalism. Obsessed with 'preparation', Stewart had assembled an apparatus of coaches, scouts and fitness trainers never before seen in English cricket. The lax, dilettante days of the old amateurism were declared at an end. On taking up his newly-created post in 1988, Stewart declared: 'Life is competitive. We talk too much about learning to be good losers.' By the end of his tenure in 1992, his main accomplishment, many thought, was to have taught England's cricketers to be bad losers.

The scientific claims of the Stewart regime had been made to look hollow by the technical deficiencies exposed at the highest level of English cricket. Above all, the English bowlers appeared to have forgotten how to swing the ball. Swing, after all, was a great English tradition, as much the hallmark of English cricket as pace was for the West Indies or spin for India. EW Swanton, the conservative doyen of the cricket media, argued that there had been 'too much fitness training and not enough practice in the nets'. Ray Illingworth wanted more and better coaches. Against the leg-spin of Australia's Shane Warne (who took 34 wickets at 25.79 runs apiece in the course of the series), the English batsmen were at sea, as they had been against the spinners in India earlier in the year.

Warne's success only rubbed in the mystery of England's technical inadequacies. The demise of the arcane craft of leg-spin had been lamented for years by pundits who blamed it on flat pitches, the LBW law, the one-day game or lower seams. Here it was being practised, with relentless exuberance, by an overweight, bleach-blond Aussie beach boy. Warne had been kicked out of the much-admired Adelaide Cricket Academy and had spent the previous English summer playing League cricket in the North of England, drinking the Accrington club bar dry. He listed his favourite cricketers as Rod Marsh, Ian Botham and Ian Chappell, his favourite TV shows as 'Get Smart' and 'Gilligan's Island' (both of which he could know only from daytime reruns), his favourite films as *Rocky III*, *Caddyshack* and *Rambo* and admitted to having no favourite books because 'I've never read anything but sports books'. Warne showed that leg-spinners could flourish in all types of cricket and on all types of pitches. The ever-frustrated left-arm spinner Tufnell, who took five wickets for 63.80 in two Test appearances that summer, made a telling contrast to the easy-going Warne, a sublimely uncomplicated maestro of an infinitely complicated art.

Clearly, this crisis required more radical remedies than mere changes in personnel or a technical fix. But there was little agreement about what these should be. The 'England Committee' system associated with Stewart and his retinue came under fierce attack. It was seen as the malformed offspring of the out-of-control monster which the Test and County Cricket Board (TCCB) had become. Tony Greig declared himself 'speechless' after watching England lose the Ashes. 'Who are these people running English cricket?' he demanded. 'The chairmen of the counties should demand that people are made accountable for their actions ... the counties are merely rubber stamping decisions taken by some TCCB committee ... The trouble is the real villains don't show their faces.' They could rail at Dexter and Fletcher all they liked, but Dexter and Fletcher were accountable only to the inner circle of the England Committee. The new-model TCCB had proved as insular and unresponsive as the old-fashioned MCC.

But was the problem with the TCCB that it was too professional or not professional enough? Was it too autocratic or too bureaucratic? For Tony Lewis, the centralized TCCB concentrated too much power in too few hands. 'The county teams are the focus of local inspiration,' he insisted, calling on cricket supporters to 'blow the bureaucratic centre out of the water'. In contrast, the medium-pace bowler and journalist, Simon Hughes, denounced 'cumbersome selection committees ... assemblies of fuddy-duddies mulling over trivialities'. His alternative to the fuddy-duddies was clear-cut central leadership. Not for the first time, national sporting failure had brought out the authoritarian in the English soul. What English cricket needed, it was argued, was 'a supremo'. The current crop of weaklings had to be replaced with a single, strong man enjoying unfettered powers. Geoff Boycott, of course, was an advocate. Make Stewart captain ('he's a no-nonsense type') and get a 'hands-on, full-time supremo' – provided he wasn't Keith Fletcher. The problem for the supporters of the supremo strategy was that none of them could agree on who the supremo should be. Robin Marlar, the former Sussex amateur and *Sunday Times* cricket columnist, went so far as to propose that Trevor Bailey, at the age of sixty-nine, 'should have been called up and

29

charged with recovering national pride'.*

Marlar, a right-wing Tory, saw the crisis in English cricket – 'more serious than any of us can remember' – as a replay of the dark days of the last Labour government. 'The TCCB reminds me of Jaguar in the mid-'70s.' He proposed that Norman Tebbit or Iain MacLaurin, Chairman of Tesco plc, should take over as TCCB chairman, with Ian Botham, of all people, as team manager. The new leadership would then be given *carte blanche* to refashion cricket on a corporate model, as Marlar's party had tried to refashion the country in the 1980s.

Marlar's contempt for the public sector was shared by many of his foes in the TCCB. The decline of cricket in state schools became another of the summer's recurring themes. Left-wing Labour local authorities, it was alleged, discouraged competitive sports and were hostile to individual excellence. Better-informed observers attributed the decline to other factors, not least among them Tory education policies - under-investment, the national curriculum, the steady alienation of the teaching profession and the selling off of local sports grounds.

But for others, the problem was that the money-maddened TCCB had cursed the English game with crass commercialism. Symbolising the sale of English cricket's soul to the highest bidder were the sponsor's logos painted on the outfield grass. 'These logos remain a damn eyesore,' complained Scyld Berry. 'I do wish English tolerance would not extend to letting them get away with it.' Yes, he recognized the financial argument, but cricket's 'whole *raison d'être* is violated by reality's intrusion into the escape world of the play'. He called for a boycott of the sponsors' products.

Along with the critique of commercialism and in reaction against the mechanistic hyper-professionalism of the Stewart regime, there emerged a call for a return to amateurism. Bill Deedes reminded *Telegraph* readers: 'It was the amateur in cricket who showed the young how to play the game for enjoyment and he has gone.' Like Harold Macmillan decrying privatization as 'selling off the family silver', Deedes lamented schools selling off playing fields. But the hankering after amateurism was not confined to the old Tory grandees. Even Brian Close, who had been a victim of the hypocrisies of the amateur brigade twenty-five years earlier,

---

*In 1995, English cricket finally got its 'supremo' when Ray Illingworth was made team manager as well as chairman of selectors. Many were surprised when Illingworth proved capricious and eager to shunt responsibility for failure on to others. But these are and always have been the vices of dictatorship.

joined the chorus. As ever in England, escape from the dilemmas of the present is sought in the past.

But what precisely was meant by amateurism? It was argued that county cricket, like so many other British institutions, was in need of rationalization and modernization. Former Australian wicket-keeper Rod Marsh poured scorn on the English domestic game, which, he announced, was full of 'bowlers who are really no more than pie throwers'. Rubbing it in, he suggested that in future Australia should grant England only three Tests – which was more than England have so far granted Sri Lanka.

Neil Foster, who made his last appearance for England that summer, maintained that the county competition bred 'mediocrity'. There were too many county sides and too many professional cricketers. Echoing the Tory myth about comprehensive schools, he complained that the best players were 'pulled down' by the rest. Over-manned and over burdened with bureaucracy, county cricket, like nationalized industry, could not sustain itself within the free market. Recipes for its reform were abundant. Many favoured introducing a divisional system, with promotion and relegation. At the same time the number of full-time professionals on each side would be reduced and the numbers made up by non-contracted players paid on a match-fee basis. With the new part-time professionals, a kind of amateurism would return to the game, providing a competitive spur to the small elite of full-time players. A casualized workforce would certainly make life easier for the cricket authorities, but it is no more likely to solve the problems of English cricket than it has the problems of the British economy.

At Headingley, Australian spectators were taunted, racist remarks were hurled at the smattering of black people in the stands, there was at least one case of sexual assault and, finally, an attack on reserve wicket-keeper Tim Zoehrer as he entered the team bus. The Yorkshire Committee was compelled to acknowledge what others had observed for years: that a Leeds Test could be a nasty experience if you came from the wrong country, were the wrong sex or colour. Fred Trueman was, as ever, disgusted. 'I've never seen or heard anything like it in my life,' he claimed. This oft-repeated Truemanism was, as usual, a load of bull. What went on at Headingley in 1993 had been seen and heard there many times before. The difference was that this time it was at an Ashes Test, the highest of the many high holy days of English cricket.

At Edgbaston, a packed Eric Hollies Stand pelted Australian off spinner Tim May with bananas and apples – a form of abuse which

English commentators had previously insisted was confined to the 'excitable' masses of the Indian subcontinent. Twelve spectators were ejected. At the Oval, Surrey introduced 'noise police' empowered to remove without warning 'any spectators involved in excessive or inappropriate singing or chanting'.

'Test Match Special' producer Peter Baxter complained that he had to turn down the microphones to keep out obscene chanting. 'The atmosphere is becoming more like football matches and that is not what cricket should be,' he said mournfully. 'Abuse and violence have plagued this year's Test series,' *The Sunday Times* reported. 'England's cricket authorities have been dismayed by the scale of drunkenness and disruption this season.'

Closed-circuit television, life bans for offenders and restrictions on alcohol were among the remedies proposed, as well as crowd segregation – a nightmare prospect at Test matches, raising the spectre of passport checks at the gate and, if West Indies, India or Pakistan are playing, black people herded into special enclosures.

The mild hysteria over crowd misconduct during the 1993 Ashes series was in keeping with the concurrent Tory clamour over standards of behaviour. For some letter-writers to the *Telegraph*, it seemed the end of civilization as Britain had known it. The many-headed hydra, the mob, was invading the stately world of English cricket. All sense of proportion vanished. After all, even the most boisterous elements in a Test crowd would be drowned by a casual groan from the terraces of any Premiership football match. Worse yet, no distinction was drawn between a Mexican wave and a riot, between witty barracking and sexist and racist abuse. The chant of 'Sumo!' that greeted Merv Hughes was good-natured. And 'Waugh! What is he good for ... absolutely nothing!' was sheer delight – though the reference to Edwin Starr's soul classic was lost on the 'Test Match Special' team. On the other hand, 'Sheepshagger, la, la, la' and 'You're just a bunch of convicts' were witless. There is not one, but many cricket publics, and among them an endless tussle takes place over the meaning and ownership of the game.

Contrary to impressions given by most of the commentators, the disorderly elements were not to be found only among the 'football supporters' in the less expensive seats (there are no truly 'cheap seats' any more) but also among the booze-sodden Hooray Henrys and corporate philistines in the pavilions and the hospitality boxes. Nor was it true that unruly behaviour was somehow extraneous to English cricket or its management. Like the Tory government, the cricket authorities blamed everyone but themselves for the collapse of 'law and order', but brewers' logos were plastered on each player on both sides and booze sales at the grounds provided vital profit margins. In Australia in 1992, Ian Botham had described his hosts as 'descendants of convicts' and the England side taunted the baying home crowds by holding up their wrists as if pointing to invisible manacles. No disciplinary action was taken.

Perhaps the most telling reaction to failure on the cricket pitch was the summer-long obsession with the question of qualification for England. Just who was an Englishman - and, more critically, who was not? Chris Cowdrey, one-time 'rebel' tourist in South Africa, protested that the Test side was 'not English enough'. Neil Foster, also a South African 'rebel', noted that 'when you play Australia or the West Indies ... you are battling against their national pride ... we don't have a truly English side. We have lost some of our identity ... At least Lewis and De Freitas grew up here.' Note the damning 'at least' with which Foster brands the two black players as second-class Englishmen.

According to David Frith, cricket historian and editor of *Wisden Cricket Monthly*,* English cricket was suffering 'a crisis of credibility' because the side included players born in the West Indies and Africa. An Anglo-Australian, Frith disapproved of the recent rise of Australian republicanism and the alleged disrespect shown to the Queen by Australian prime minister Paul Keating. England and Australia, he said, were 'of the same blood'. In his case, the 'at least' was applied to white South Africans Lamb and Smith, whose parents were English. In contrast, Devon Malcolm 'acts, thinks, sounds and looks like a Jamaican. This hits the English cricket lover where it hurts.'

Being born in England has never been a required qualification for playing for England. 'Plum' Warner was born in Trinidad, Freddie Brown in Peru, 'Gubby' Allen in Australia, Douglas Jardine and Colin Cowdrey in India. Mike Denness was Scottish, Tony Lewis was Welsh and Tony Greig was South African. Kevin Curran is a Zimbabwean who has taken out an Irish passport which enables him to play English county cricket. The last time an England Test side were all born in England was the third Test against Australia in 1989. As Mike Brearley observed, 'In an era of mobility, place of birth, as a criterion of belonging, seems to be a throwback to the nineteenth century and before.' But when a national side is losing, mere reason flies out the door.

There was heated debate over the presence in the England side during

*For Frith's subsequent misadventures, see Chapter 8.

the summer of a New Zealander – Andrew Caddick – and an Australian – Martin McCague, who, just to make things really complicated for those seeking authentic 'Englishness', was born in the North of Ireland. Caddick had toured England with a New Zealand under-nineteen squad in 1989. He had signed up for Somerset, where he was nicknamed 'Kiwi', and qualified for England. McCague, known as 'Oz' by his Kent county colleagues, had received most of his cricket education in Australia, but insisted, 'I feel English'. Border disagreed: 'To me, he's Australian.' With Caddick at the other end, he said, 'it takes the gloss off an Ashes Test'.

Scyld Berry suggested 'let us ask the man in the street whether McCague is English or Australian' – confident ordinary English people would recognize an impostor when they saw one. Berry wanted the authorities to draw the line between 'genuine immigrants to Britain' and 'adventurers ... who have come to England specifically to play cricket'. It was a worthy attempt to avoid racism by distinguishing between a Devon Malcolm and an Allan Lamb, but it could never be put into practice. How are the cricket authorities to measure motives? Why is the desire to play cricket a less legitimate reason for immigration than the desire to find any other form of work?

There has never been any correspondence between the definitions of nationality held by the Home Office and those held by the English cricket authorities. The TCCB itself demonstrated a cynical attitude when it reduced the residential qualification from ten to seven years in 1987 in order, it was said, to facilitate Graeme Hick's entry into the Test side. Likewise, the British government slapped a British passport on the South African runner Zola Budd so that she could compete in the Olympics under the Union Jack. Those who pose as the guardians of national identity, who stand at the gates keeping the exotic hordes at bay, define that identity at their convenience.

In cricket, all the components of the United Kingdom are supposed to be represented by 'England'. But the excellent form of Glamorgan in the county championship led to protests at the apparent exclusion of Welsh players from the Test squad. Neath's MP Peter Hain introduced an Early Day Motion 'noting the obstinate refusal of the selectors to choose any Welsh players' and calling on the International Cricket Council to designate the Glamorgan v. Australia match at Neath as an extra Test.

Resentment of Dexter, the archetypal Southerner, and his 'Essex men' also festered in the North. At Derby, the public-address system described the announcement of the squad for the third Test as 'news from the South' (Malcolm had been left out again). At Headingley it was noted that

Atherton was the only player from 'north of Watford Gap'. When Nasser Hussain became the sixth Essex player selected that summer, the Glamorgan announcer sneered, 'It is to be assumed that Mr Trevor Bailey was unavailable for selection.'

Clearly, there was little consensus not only over the question of just who was and was not entitled to represent 'England' but over what this 'England' was and to whom it belonged. Amateur or professional, North or South, streamlined or decentralized, modern or traditional ... only who were the modernizers and who were the traditionalists? Keep the good and throw out the bad, people said, but no one could agree which was which.

What made the arguments sharp was the sense of national decline underlying them. Indeed, the only belief that seemed to bind English people together was that the country was going to the dogs. A survey revealed that two-thirds of the population would emigrate if given the chance. In that respect, the English Test side of 1993 was a faithful reflection of the nation. The English looked at this reflection, recognized it as a true one, and despised it. Out of that loathing the media made an industry. The failure of the national sporting sides gave the legendary masochism of the English a new twist. By the end of the summer, the only thing that was certain was that everything that had been tried up till now had failed. The real significance of the victory at the Oval in the sixth Test, against a tired and unmotivated Australia, was that it followed the departure of Dexter. It came under a new captain – the first Oxbridge man to captain England in twelve years – and it owed much to the recall after long injury of Angus Fraser, a classically English seamer.

The 'England Committee' was abolished by the TCCB in December 1993. The triumph of cricket's self-made 'Essex men', like their counterparts in English politics, had proved ephemeral. One after another, the cricket messiahs of the eighties had failed, along with the miracle cures of 'professionalism' and mass marketing. The old gods departed from the international scene – Gower, Botham, Gooch, Gatting, the cricketers of my generation. I was glad to see them go, even Gower. But what would come in their place?

Lord's on a Sunday with the sun shining for a cup final. England had just given up the Ashes at Headingley. Gooch had resigned and Atherton had been appointed. As the crowd trickled in, an MCC member selling score-cards at the Nursery End explained, 'Australia won the toss and elected to field.'

This was rather strange, as Australia were not playing today.

I knew the MCC member in question. For two decades he had been the virtual dictator of an inner-London Labour council. When he abandoned Labour in the early eighties, he lost his seat on the council and his power-base on the local council estates, but he remained a JP, a prison visitor, a governor of schools and colleges, and a member of the local Police Consultative Committee. I hadn't known, until I saw his egg-and-tomato tie, that he was also a member of the MCC, though it came as no surprise. As a mayor, this man had shown an inordinate fondness for the regalia of office. Proud of his working-class background, he none the less wanted above all else to be included among the 'gentlemen'. I had no doubt that as an MCC member he had cast his vote in 1991 against the admission of women - after all, it had been the incursion of feminism that had most appalled him during his last years in the Labour Party. Now, however, he was excited. So excited that he forgot that it was New Zealand, not Australia, whom England's women cricketers were playing in the World Cup Final that day. My former comrade clearly had the Ashes on the brain. But he was not the only man to draw strange comfort from the England women's performance in 1993.

For decades, women had struggled to find a place in English cricket. The Women's Cricket Association was formed in 1926 – a by-product of the suffrage movement. But it had never been granted a voice in the cricket hierarchy, even after the Cricket Council, TCCB and NCA had replaced the MCC in 1968. Women had invented the cricket World Cup before men. The first cup was held in England in 1973 (two years before the first men's cup), followed by India in 1978, New Zealand in 1982 and Australia in 1988. In Australia women's cricket enjoyed commercial sponsorship, but not in England, where appeals for support from Tetley Bitter, official sponsors of the men's Test side, had been rebuffed. Other potential sponsors told the WCA that women's cricket did not receive enough television coverage or that its image was not suitable for their products. At one point the English women were advised that they would get more television exposure if they played scantily clad. Norma Izard, manager of the England women's side, complained, 'In England, women's cricket is regarded as a charity. In Australia, it's an entertainment.'

The 1993 World Cup nearly did not take place. The tournament's hosts, the WCA, were on the verge of cancelling it when, two days before the deadline, the government-sponsored Foundation for Sport and the Arts stepped in with a grant of £90,000, which was still only half the required amount. The gap was plugged by smaller, mostly non-commercial sponsors (individuals, trade unions, voluntary groups and social clubs) and in the end the MCC agreed to meet the costs of staging the final at Lord's.

Australia had been heavy favourites but surprisingly lost to both New Zealand and England in the early rounds. The New Zealand women had recently been admitted to 'New Zealand Cricket', the male dominated governing council of the game; they were fit, enthusiastic, and well-organized. Though initially ignored by the media, the English women, as they made their way to the Lord's final, benefited from popular disillusionment with the sour, spiritless, unsuccessful England men's side. The women were playing with discipline, panache and team spirit. Unlike the men, they were winning. No wonder the erstwhile town-hall tyrant was excited. They might be women, but at least they were English.

The entrance (£4 adults; £2 juniors and pensioners) proved excellent value – something which could rarely be said of men's matches that summer – and the crowd was larger than any drawn to Lord's by the Sunday League all season. There were New Zealanders of both sexes, Dutch and Irish women (their teams had been eliminated in earlier rounds), middle-aged English couples, groups of young girls, lone male cricket lovers, pale and solemn, and sunburnt working-class women with cropped hair and baggy jeans. A handful of MCC members strolled amid women in 'Pride' t-shirts and multiple ear-studs. The hospitality units were mostly unoccupied and the pavilion, from which women are banned, was nearly deserted.

Back in 1989, Lancashire, the last hold-out among the counties, had admitted women to full membership and the right to use the old Trafford pavilion. Apparently, the vote at the AGM was turned when it was revealed that Mr Keith Hull, a long-time member, had had a sex change operation, but had continued to enjoy her full membership privileges.

The MCC was less convinced of the fluidity of gender roles. After it turned down a similar proposal in 1991, its secretary, John Stephenson, observed:

'I rather like the quaintness, the mystique of the place. I really can't see any great advantage in having women in the pavilion. In fact, I can see some disadvantages. This building wasn't built with the modern day in mind. It was built just for people to watch cricket.'

In England, men's cricket clubs outnumber women's by over 1,000 to one. England's women cricketers are therefore drawn from a limited pool of players. This is a small world with a sense of mission. Year in, year out, the top women cricketers play not for the TV or the press, not for the fans, not for the money or the fame – there is little of either – but for themselves and for each other. That Sunday at Lord's, their loyalty to each other and to their band of followers was palpable.

Without aid from the media, the England women had, it was clear, built up a genuine following. Many in the crowd had attended the earlier matches and knew the players well already. There was anger over television's failure to cover the competition and spectators were urged to write to the BBC. Both sides enjoyed good-natured partisan support and players on the pavilion balconies joined in the Mexican wave (from which, as always, the members abstained). The Union Jack, not the England flag, flew over the home side's dressing room.

The cricket itself displayed classical batting, sharp running, thoughtful bowling and tight fielding. England's victory owed much to the patience and precision of the veteran opener, Janette Brittin, to the flamboyant derring-do of the all-rounder, Jo Chamberlain, and the crafty bowling and captaincy of Karen Smithies. Less powerful than male cricketers, the women relied on deliberate stroke placement and tactical bowling to carefully-set fields. Spinners played a prominent role on both sides and, compared to the men's game, the bowlers raced through the overs. At the end, instead of grabbing the stumps and dashing for the pavilion, the victorious English women ran to embrace their supporters spilling on to the turf from the Nursery End.

At the presentations after the match, Dennis Silk, MCC President, told the women that the 'spirit' of their game was 'everything we like about cricket' and chivalrously declared, 'The lady cricketers have supplied us with a day we shall never forget.' But he did so on the grass in front of the pavilion, not on the balcony as usual. Chamberlain's 38 in 33 balls, backed up by two wickets, a split-second run-out and a surreal catch made her the 'man of the match'. For the media, she became a kind of Botham-for-a-day.

Commentators who had ignored the women's competition through most of the summer now flocked to offer praise. It was, they insisted, not merely that England had won, but the way they had won. Frank Keating, who had criticized the male Test squad for 'lack of character', pronounced himself delighted with the women. This was 'what cricket ought to be'. Suddenly, English women, the invisible outcasts of world cricket, were being held up as champions of 'fair play' and the best traditions of English cricket. Christopher Martin-Jenkins praised the cup final as 'a model example of amateur sport, competitive but fun, bringing its own rewards of honour and camaraderie'.

In their obsession with drawing lessons for the male standard bearers of English cricket, these commentators missed the real, joyful message of the World Cup Final: that women are not an adjunct of the men's game or a throwback to a vanished amateurism, but an independent, dynamic source of renewal. The 'England' championed by the women cricketers at Lord's was not the nation represented by Gooch and his men in the Ashes series.

History made English cricket what it is: its joys and absurdities, its complacency and angst. But history is made by us, or rather, in the process of fighting among ourselves over the present, we make the future. After all, this is what happens every time cricketers take the field. The bowler studies the pitch and considers his options. The batsman observes the field and chooses his strokes. They then interact not in total freedom but compelled by everything that has happened to them - personally and collectively - until that moment. Each game is new; its end is shaped in the course of play. Cricket is tradition-bound and often politically gagged, but it is also, as CLR James insisted, supremely creative. He saw West Indians making their own history on the cricket field and he rejoiced. Looking at English cricket at the moment, it's hard to imagine anyone here feeling what James felt. But in the 1993 World Cup Final, you could catch a glimmer of the transforming power that inspired him.

On a British Airways flight from the USA I watched a promo video for tourist Britain. Swans on the Avon, country churches, sheep grazing on green fields, pub signs, Oxford quads, Windsor Castle, Buckingham Palace, Nelson's Column, the Palace of Westminster, Big Ben, the Albert Hall, West End theatres, St Paul's, the Post Office Tower, Les Miserables, red buses and black taxis, Canary Wharf and, inevitably, a village cricket match (in whites, of course). There was no football, no London Underground, no coal mines or steel works or ports, no M25. Like tourist industries everywhere, the BA promo-makers were marketing a myth, and within it cricket had a special place.

However, Americans, like other foreigners, no longer swallow the old imagery whole. The lager lout in Union Jack shorts, the millionaire pop star, the sleazy tabloid journo on the make, the City slicker and the fascist skinhead are replacing the stiff-upper-lips. When Americans come here and take a good look they find a country stripped of empire and world status, a land of low pay, skinflint benefits, social division, economic and political stagnation. A small country which had lost more than just the Ashes in the Test matches against Australia.

I wrote this book in 1993-94, when 'nation' and 'market', those querulous bedfellows, seemed ever-present in the news bulletins. In Eastern Europe, the reintroduction of the market had been accompanied by an explosion of nationalist sentiments. In India, economic 'liberalization' and the rise of Hindu nationalism were the twin topics of political debate. In Western Europe and North America, the tensions between the dictates of an international market and the old prerogatives of nation-states were revealed in the fraught passages of the Maastricht and NAFTA treaties. Inevitably, 'market' and 'nation' imposed themselves on the book, whose subject became the mysterious triangle they formed with cricket.

Back in 1970, a year before I first arrived on these shores, Rowland Bowen, the maverick cricket scholar, observed that 'one of the reasons for the popularity of sport in England' was 'to enable the people to bury their heads in the sand ostrich-wise'. As the seventies and eighties wore on, that became more and more impossible. As the world outside grew increasingly violent and insecure, as global economic and political trends made English people feel punier and punier, cricket itself, washed along in a rip-tide of perpetual change, seemed to have lost its immunity, much to the anguish of traditionalists. These days, if you're looking for a refuge from reality, Test cricket is not for you. History has invaded the pitch, with a vengeance.

Over the last twenty years, as cricket has passed through a period of radical transformation, a new school of revisionist cricket historians has emerged. The scion of Bowen, CLR James and John Arlott have re-examined cricket history with a more critical eye than their predecessors, and less commitment to the *ancien régime*. Previous chroniclers – Warner, Altham, Swanton – were themselves leading cricket administrators, doyens of the MCC establishment, and their views of the sport's singular history were shaped accordingly. Spurred by the rapid changes and the sheer drama of cricket's latest encounter with the market and modernity, the revisionist historians have refused to see cricket history or cricket itself as a refuge from reality, as did so many of their predecessors. Without their researches, this book could not have been written.

Why does cricket generate such angst? In other sports, particularly US sports, rule changes or alterations in competitive structures, in equipment or uniforms or techniques are pushed through with little public dissent.

A team may even up stakes and move to another city. There may be protests but no one claims that the game as a whole, no less the national heritage, is being dismantled. It is widely accepted that every so often games must be modernized. Only in cricket is reform greeted with such popular anxiety - an anxiety which the media do their utmost to foment, for they have long ago appointed themselves the unofficial guardians of the national heritage. In cricket, there is always the fear that something will be lost. Something intrinsic to the appeal and the 'values' of cricket. Something precious and fragile, like childhood innocence.

Is there something 'English' about all this? Is there something English about cricket? Or is that just the old imperial propaganda? Why does English cricket seem such an acute expression of English frustration and self-doubt? Why is cricket so often taken or promoted as a mirror of England - either its best or worst, its great traditions or, increasingly, its current malaise? What does it mean to call cricket the 'national' game? Is there something in cricket that links it to the destinies of English people? And which English people? Which England? Or rather, whose?

In trying to answer these questions it seemed to me that not being English might be an asset. Over the years I have come to take for granted many of the peculiarities of English cricket. Nowadays when I take Americans to a cricket match – or when I go with an English person who has never been before – I find myself taken aback by their inquiries. Why do the fielders change ends after six balls while the batsmen stay put? Why do the players 'appeal'? Why does everyone wear white (except on Sunday)? Why can you polish the ball but not pick the seam? These and so many other products of cricket's history have become invisible to me, a distressing sign that I may be becoming 'English'.

Since my mid-seventies conversion to cricket my interest in the game has been sustained and deepened by a series of accidents. I keep bumping into cricket, blindly led by friendships, jobs, politics, or sheer wanderlust. And I never cease to marvel how a human activity can be so frivolous, so inconsequential, and at the same time so meditative, so complex, so charged with meaning. I do not believe this is an age of lead. I have heard throughout my cricket-watching life that the modern game is desolate, but that is not my experience. Certainly, it is beset with problems and riven by conflict – that is what makes it such an excellent mirror of the time and the place. The stresses and strains of transformation always bring out the essence of a game – or destroy it.

I have been lucky enough to watch and talk about cricket in India, New Zealand and South Africa, though I was never in any of those

countries for that specific purpose. In India, especially, I became aware of
the game's paradoxical mix of the malleable and the durable. Watching
cricket there, I savoured the blend of the familiar and the exotic – though
cricket everywhere, even on a wet weekday afternoon at the Oval, is still
to me exotic. I can retreat, quietly, into a discrete foreignness and watch
the proceedings close up – and from a great distance.

Now when I'm asked 'How can an American understand cricket?' I
am tempted to answer, 'How can an English person?'

2

The Prison of English History

The past ● The novelty of cricket ● The Star and Garter
● Publicans, promoters and the vanishing peasantry
● From Hambledon to Lord's ● Birth of a nation
● Transition and autochthony ● The power of myth

No sport is as besotted with its past as cricket.

The action in Francis Thompson's classic poem 'At Lord's', published in 1898, does not take place in St John's Wood, but at Old Trafford some twenty years before, when Gloucestershire, 'the shire of the Graces', came north to teach a cricketing lesson to 'new-risen Lancashire'. The young Thompson, skiving from his Manchester medical studies, was wont to waste his days watching county cricket. Seven years after the match described in the poem, he abandoned dreams of a medical career and fled to London, where he descended into drug-addiction and bohemian vagrancy before achieving modest notoriety as a poet. Now, years later, his health broken, his poetic wellsprings drying up, his muse consumed by journalism, he was reluctant to visit Lord's ('It is little I repair to the matches of the Southron folk') even when his beloved Lancashire were playing there ('Though my own red roses there may blow'). The sheer hallucinatory power of his recollections of Old Trafford and the past overpower Lord's and the present:

> For the field is full of shades as I near the shadowy coast,
> And a ghostly batsman plays to the bowling of a ghost,
> And I look through my tears on a soundless-clapping host
>   As the run-stealers flicker to and fro,
>   To and fro:
>   O my Hornby and my Barlow long ago!

The elegiac note sounded by Thompson belongs to cricket. From nearly the beginning, people have said the game is not what it used to be.

Standards of technique, sportsmanship, loyalty or patriotism are perennially in decline. Crowd behaviour has always changed for the worse. And money is forever corrupting a noble pastime.

'Since cricket became brighter, a man of taste can only go to an empty ground, and regret the past,' said CP Snow in 1932. In the same year, the *Daily Herald* headlined an article: 'Why isn't cricket fun any more?' That season, Woolley, Hobbs, Hendren and Sutcliffe were all playing first-class cricket. In 1899, at the height of the Golden Age, the England and Middlesex amateur Vyell Walker observed, 'I am sorry to say that I do not think the game has improved. There is more self now than there used to be. Men do not play as much for their side as they did in my younger days ... there is far too much of the business element in it all around.' In 1884, six years before the official founding of the county championship, the journalist Frederick Gale complained that too many county matches ended as tedious draws. 'Cricket is now so common that it is a mere trade,' he fulminated in a letter to *The Times*. 'The heart and will to "play up" and waste no time are not the mainsprings of some of the modern matches.' In the 1860s, the novelist Anthony Trollope observed that 'cricket has become such a business, that there arises doubt in the minds of amateur players whether they can continue the sport'. In 1833, John Nyren, recalling from a distance of forty years the great days of Hambledon, the archetypal village cricket club, proudly asserted, 'The modern politics of trickery and "crossing" were ... as yet a "sealed book" to the Hambledonians; what they did, they did for love and honour of victory.'

This veneration of the game's past, inevitably accompanied by deprecation of its present, may be attributed in part to an association between this past and the individual's own childhood. A personal loss of innocence finds a ready focus in the sense that the gods whom one worshipped on the pitch in one's youth have been replaced by mere mortals, and not very admirable ones at that. The mythic power of childhood (or, in the case of most English cricket writers, public-school boyhood) overrides the discipline of history.

Being an American has spared me this English version of the old mismatch between ontogeny (the development of an individual) and phylogeny (the development of a species or type). But I can see its power. How pleasant to imagine a past where cricket was played with exuberant abandon, without awareness of commerce, of cheating, of national failure, of social tensions of any kind. And how useful for those with a vested interest in maintaining the social order inherited from that past.

For them, the ills of the modern world are always the result of alien intrusions in a lost paradise.

That paradise is the English village green, purportedly the fons et origo of English cricket, bastion of its abiding values, source and mainstay of cricket's unique 'Englishness'. The literature of English cricket was, until very recently, overwhelmingly bucolic. In his book *English Cricket*, published as a morale-booster during the Blitz, Cardus writes, 'In every English village a cricket field is as much part of the landscape as the old church.' Cardus, of course, made a career out of celebrating cricket's traditions and lamenting the passage of its Golden Age. His attachment to the elegance and complexity of cricket was accompanied by an aesthetic rejection of the modern mass society with which cricket, in his eyes, was perpetually at odds.

The most accomplished literary evocation of village-green cricket is Hugh de Selincourt's *The Cricket Match*, first published in 1924, and very much an attempt to reconsider and reassert the values of village green cricket in the wake of the First World War. With great skill and a light touch, de Selincourt employs a cricket match to link together the destinies of the citizens of Tillingfold, his archetypal southern English village. The book ends: 'Night descended peacefully upon the village of Tillingfold. Rich and poor, old and young, were seeking sleep.'

Because I have always seen de Selincourt as a clever Tory propagandist, albeit of the one-nation variety so despised by Margaret Thatcher and Norman Tebbit, I am afraid I have to contradict Benny Green's dictum: 'Even an American could read *The Cricket Match* and find himself profoundly moved.' My problem is that in *The Cricket Match*, as in so much cricket writing, the village green and the cricket played on it are symbols not just of social harmony, but of social hierarchy, a hierarchy that can resist even cataclysms like the First World War.

In the midst of the Second World War, the poet Edmund Blunden published his *Cricket Country*, a celebration of English cricket's rural innocence. Recounting the entry on to a humble village ground of a 'sturdy' blacksmith-batsman in 'working clothes and leathern apron', Blunden praises the principle of 'degree' exemplified in cricket:

> In our country life hitherto, the much execrated principle of grades of society, walks of life, has been maintained not by compulsion but by inclination, and the keeping up of distinctions and of separate worlds in little has been done not just by those at the supposed top but by those, quite as much, who accept fortune and know a thing or two at the other end of the scale. It is a reversible

ladder. And here once again I must bless the powers and the chances of the English love of games ...

This is the myth at cricket's heart, the myth of an enduring and natural social hierarchy, the myth of the village green. It only requires a cursory survey of rural English life today to see that the myth bears little relation to contemporary reality. The village green, certainly as a meeting point of different classes and generations, hardly exists, having been replaced by the limitless suburbia of 'commuter villages' in which car parks take precedence over cricket fields. But the myth of the village green and the cricket played on it is not only a lie about the present. It is an even bigger lie about the past. Cricket is no more the organic outgrowth of the ancient community of the village green than Magna Carta is the work of freedom-loving Saxons.

In 1979, Geoffrey Moorhouse, in his book *The Best Loved Game*, commented: 'Few things are more deeply rooted in the collective imagination of the English than the village cricket match. It stirs a romantic illusion about the rustic way of life, it suggests a tranquil and unchanging order in an age of bewildering flux.'

In fact, not all 'the English' are transfixed by this heritage. For many in the inner cities, the unemployed, the low-waged, the homeless, and all those who are abused because of their race or sex, the village cricket match is a symbol of the England in which they have no part. Cricket's mythology is the product of a vision of social order in which large sections of the population are consigned to inferior rank. Yet it is also true that many who have no vested interest in this social order cannot help but feel the power and pleasure in Moorhouse's 'romantic illusion'.

There are good reasons for this. Cricket's obsession with the past, its status as something of a national relic, its association with the village green are not accidental or even incidental. Yes, cricket boasts a longer history than other sports, but there is more to it than that. Cricket is what it is because of its origin as a modern sport in a particular time and place: late-eighteenth-century England. From that point of origin, everything flows.

These days, commercial spectator sport has spread to every corner of the globe and has become so much a part of our lives, our culture and our economy that it is hard to imagine just what a bold innovation it was in the late eighteenth century. The advent of cricket deserves the epithet revolutionary because nothing less than a revolutionary process could have bridged the gap between what cricket was and what it became.

Cricket historians have tried to trace the game's lineage to the distant middle ages, to a 'Merrie England' of jolly, honest peasants and benign, patriotic lords. Accordingly, they have cited 'club ball', 'stool ball' and all manner of ancient stick-and-ball games as the direct precursors of cricket. The 'creag' mentioned in Edward I's accounts of 1300 is said to be nothing less than cricket itself, simply because it is not clearly defined as anything else (significantly, these accounts were first published in 1787, the year of MCC's formation). On the basis of no evidence whatsoever, the word 'cricket' is said to derive from 'cricc', an ancient Saxon word for a shepherd's crook. Andrew Lang, the late nineteenth-century folklorist, translator and cricket lover, declared that 'like almost everything else, cricket was evolved'. The need to prove continuity – direct descent from old England – has been a compulsion for nearly all the game's historians, even a Scot like Lang. Alas, the word itself seems likely to be French in origin. Certainly the first reference to a game called 'criquet' is in St Omer in 1478.

Attempts to claim the game as a native 'English' product miss the point about the folk games from which cricket, like most modern sports, was derived. *These games were pre-national.* Countless stick-and-ball games existed – every village had its own version – but no one of these was more or less 'English' than any other. The games played in England at this time were clearly part of a pan-European folk culture. Cricket could have been as easily derived from any of the stick-and-ball games played on the continent as any of those played in England. Indeed, these games existed *only* in their innumerable local variations. No one thought what the games would be like if they were not tied to local traditions and topography. As yet the people playing these games did not imagine themselves as part of a larger, national community with a common culture. The games were, literally, parochial, and that was part of their appeal. They were children's games, to be played by adults in times of holiday sanctioned by the agricultural or liturgical calendars.

It seems unlikely that any single one of them would be the model for the game of cricket that became fashionable with the elite some time after the English Revolution. Rather, elements from different local games were incorporated or discarded according to the whims of the patrons, who formed, at that time, the only nationally-integrated social class. The cumulative result of these adaptations was the creation of something quite new: a set of practices that transcended local tradition and enabled people from different parts of the country who had never met before to play cricket together.

The earliest surviving Laws of the game are contained in the 'Articles of Agreement' for a match to be played between the second Duke of Richmond and Alan Broderick of Peperharrow in Surrey. The match was played, not on a village green, but in *London*, in 1727. Around the same time, the infant weekly newspapers began to cover cricket. To the early reporters, the attendance of persons of high social status, not the result of the match, was the main item of interest. By 1730, cricket was being regularly played in London at White Conduit Fields in Islington, the Artillery Ground in Finsbury and Kennington Common.

In 1744, the first full 'Laws of Cricket' were issued *and published* by 'the London Club', whose president was Frederick Louis, Prince of Wales, the father of George III. Perhaps, for the German-born Frederick, playing cricket was a way of proving his Englishness. If so, how piquant that he died in 1751 after being struck by a cricket ball.

One of the matches played under the new Laws ('Kent' against 'England' at the Artillery Ground) is the first for which a full scoresheeet survives. More important, it was one of the first to charge admission (6d). The match was also the inspiration for the first literary exercise on cricket per se, James Love's ode to 'Cricket! Manly British game!' Love praised the social mix of the crowd, which included great lords and humble bricklayers. However, cricket's popularity made some observers uneasy. The *Daily Advertiser* complained of 'great disorder' and the *Gentleman's Magazine* disapproved: 'The time of people of fashion may be, indeed, of little value, but in a trading nation the time of the meanest man ought to be of some worth to himself and to the community.'

The 1744 London rules spread far and wide. Within a decade, people in New York were playing under them. The game was becoming standardized, though it was to be another forty or fifty years before this process was complete. What was happening to cricket was happening at the same time to the English language. The vernacular was being systematized. Johnson published his Dictionary in 1755. The local wrinkles were being ironed out; a single national vocabulary and grammar were becoming standard.

In the 1760s and 1770s, it became common to pitch the ball through the air, rather than roll it along the ground. This crucial innovation gave the bowler the weapons of length, deception through the air, as well as increased pace. It also opened new possibilities for spin and swerve. In response to the demands placed on them by airborne bowling, batsmen employed new techniques. They now had to master timing and stroke selection. For the spectator, this development enriched the game more than any other. There were now many more ways for batsmen to score runs and many more ways for bowlers to get them out. It raised the premium on skill and lessened the fortuitous influence of rough ground and brute force. Scores became higher (John Minshull knocked up the first recorded ton in 1769) and matches lasted longer.

In the 1770s, modern cricket took shape with astonishing rapidity. That decade witnessed the inauguration of the game's first annual series of matches, Sheffield v. Nottingham, and the first giant cricket crowd, the 15,000 reported to have turned out to watch 'All-England' take on 'Hampshire' in Kent. The weight of the ball was limited to between five and a half and five and three-quarters ounces and the width of the bat to four and a half inches. Both sets of limits remain in force to this day. The first printed score cards appeared at Sevenoaks, Kent.

In 1774, the first leg-before-wicket law was published. At this time, a third stump also became common. In the early part of the century, the wicket might be low and horizontal or even simply a hole in the ground. Now, with the wicket upright, with three stumps, and an LBW law, batsmen created the science of the 'straight bat' and all that went with it. By 1780, three days had become the normal duration of a major match. That year, Dukes of Penshurst in Kent made the first six seam cricket ball and presented it to the Prince of Wales (two centuries later, the firm is still in the trade). The Marylebone Cricket Club was founded in 1787. The next year it published its first revision of the Laws, which prohibited charging down or obstruction, though these practices persisted for years in remote areas. Rolling, mowing and covering the wicket were also now provided for by the Laws, evidence that the standardization of conditions was regarded as a necessary feature of the 'modern' game.

For Raymond Williams, an index of the revolutionary character of the late eighteenth century in England was that it saw the first use of the words industry, democracy, class and culture in their modern senses. He might have also cited the first appearance in print, at the same time, of the words cricket field, cricket bat, cricket ball, cricket match, cricket club and cricketer. By 1800, cricket had been transformed from one among a myriad of traditional, rural folk games into the world's first modern spectator team sport. Its rules (or rather, Laws) were standardized and under the control of a single body, the MCC, recognized by cricketers and the general public as authoritative. It had a permanent urban showground, Lord's, dedicated to staging the best cricket in the country. It had a small corps of paid professional players. It had attracted the interest of impresarios who had begun to exploit it commercially. It also displayed a degree of technical sophistication, an emphasis on skill and strategy, which other team sports would achieve only a hundred years later.

In 1784, a 'Committee of Noblemen and Gentlemen' accustomed to meeting at the Star and Garter tavern in Pall Mall (also at that time the home of the Jockey Club) published a new and complete version of 'the Laws of Cricket'. They appended their 150 names to the Laws, clearly believing the list would enhance the authority of the new code. It makes fascinating reading. Many of those whose names appear on it took part in the founding of the MCC three years later. All were men of power and wealth, which in late-eighteenth-century England meant landed wealth.

At its head was the old Etonian George Finch, the ninth Earl of Winchilsea, then thirty-two years old. He had already raised a regiment of infantry to fight the American revolutionaries at a cost to himself of £20,000, which gives some idea of his disposable wealth. Besides helping to found the MCC (and playing, as a middle-order right-handed batsman in its early matches) he devoted himself to his estate in Burley in Rutland (a new addition to the family's vast spread in Kent), where scientific improvements in agriculture went hand in hand with the construction of a cricket ground and the staging of cricket matches involving the most illustrious players of the day.

John Frederick Sackville, the third Duke of Dorset, was also a sponsor of the Star and Garter laws. His appointment as Ambassador to the French court in 1783 was lampooned in the newspapers, one of which depicted a Frenchman saying, 'He no speak in de Senate but he be one bon cricketer.' It is said that Dorset acquired in France the habit of drinking tea in the afternoon and was responsible for introducing it to England – in which case cricket's debt to him is so much the greater. A Privy Councillor and for many years Lord Steward to the Royal Household, Dorset (whose portrait was painted by his friend, Joshua Reynolds) was a convivial aristocrat who set the tone for cricket and defied personal criticism and political satire to insist that it was a perfectly proper pastime for the rich and powerful.

The members of the Star and Garter 'Committee' were at the core of the oligarchy that ruled England. As landowning capitalists, they were the inheritors of the English Revolution and the 'settlement' of 1688 which had secured the supremacy of property over feudal right. As a result of the civil war of the seventeenth century, England, instead of groaning under the heel of absolutism, enjoyed the benefits of a 'constitutional' monarchy financially subordinate to a Parliament run by and for the landowners. In England, money talked – not customary rights or barter or feudal privileges – before it was even whispering elsewhere. It was the world's first market economy on a national scale. And the men who issued the Laws of Cricket from the Star and Garter were its masters. These 'substantial men of the county' appointed the MPs, JPs, tax assessors, Land Tax Commissioners, and even most of the clergymen. This was the 'Old Corruption', which was, in fact, a novel mechanism through which the elite monopolized and plundered the state. The members of the Star and Garter Committee were at its heart.

Dorset's friend, the Earl of Tankerville, was a Privy Councillor and Postmaster General (and, as such, a leading dispenser of political patronage). The Marquis of Graham became Paymaster General. Sir John Shelley, a relative of the powerful Duke of Newcastle, was Treasurer of the Royal Household. Frederick Howard, Lord Carlisle (Eton, Cambridge), was an ally of Fox in the Commons. Earl Spencer (Cambridge) was a parliamentary follower of Burke and later Home Secretary. Lord Charles Fitzroy (Westminster, Cambridge) was MP for Bury St Edmunds and aide-de-camp to George III. Thomas Pelham, who became the third Earl of Chichester (Westminster, Cambridge), was a Whig MP for Sussex and later Postmaster General.

The state machine also served as the engine of colonial expansion, and many of the Star and Garter men were deeply engrossed in the work of empire-building. Carlisle and Graham were both Presidents of the Board of Trade and the latter became a member of the Parliamentary Commission for India. Captain John Willett Payne had served in the recently-concluded American war, as had Colonel Benastre Tarleton, later an MP for Liverpool. Sir Ralph Payne, at this time MP for Shaftesbury and an ally of Fox, eventually became Baron Lavington, Governor of the Leeward Islands, where he took part in some of the earliest recorded cricket matches in the West Indies. William Monson, a Captain in the Indian army, was prominent in the war against Tipu Sultan which gave the English control of southern India.

Significantly, several gentlemen in the Star and Garter list maintained property in the colony closest to home, Ireland. Lord Tyrconnel and his brothers, the Talbots, had vast holdings there. Carlisle became a Viceroy of Ireland. Pelham became Irish Secretary under Pitt. The then twenty-five-year-old Lieutenant Colonel John Fane (Charterhouse, Cambridge), later the Earl of Westmoreland, became Lord Lieutenant of Ireland and a fierce opponent of Catholic Emancipation.

Under the rule of the landed elite, England in the eighteenth century had become known and envied not only as a beacon of commerce and hub of international trade, but also as the country in which the rule of law, as opposed to the dictates of individuals, was most advanced. Throughout the eighteenth century, statute law had been growing as the old customary rights proved inadequate or were simply overridden by the power of money. In particular, there was extensive legislation dealing with crimes against property, including poaching and squatting. The same people who passed these laws in Parliament drew up the Laws of Cricket, and for much the same purpose.

What drove the landowning elite to codify the laws of cricket were the high stakes now riding on many matches. Cricket's two innings (which feature in all the earliest accounts of the game) made the game ideal for gamblers: it made the wagers more complex and the results less arbitrary; and the conclusion of the first innings provided the occasion for increasing the stakes or revising the odds.

In 1751, a £1,500 formal wager plus side-bets totalling £20,000 were at stake in a match between Old Etonians and 'England'. In the Hambledon matches £500 a side was the normal wager. In 1794, the Earls of Winchilsea and Darnley bet 1,000 guineas on a match between their respective sides. Far from being hidden away in shame, this aspect of the game was promoted as one of its chief attractions. All the early versions of the Laws (including the Star and Garter Laws of 1784 and MCC's first revision in 1787) included provisions to ensure bets were fairly settled. What was at stake in cricket in those days was not honour but money. People played for profit – the composition of teams shifted endlessly – and were only expected to play for love of the game or of country or of county much later. What could reflect more accurately the culture of the world's first entirely money-based society?

The substantial sums bet on cricket matches, and the additional sums invested in the development of cricket fields and the employment of professional cricketers, were drawn from the landed elite's vast and growing pool of liquid assets. During the course of the eighteenth century, the great English landowners were investing profits from land in canals and mines, mercantile ventures and government debts (which rose because of incessant warfare in pursuit of colonial expansion). Through the Bank of England (which was owned by titled peers) and the Stock Exchange (set up in the wake of the Restoration 'settlement'), they were acting as capitalist financiers, just as they were in staging cricket matches and placing huge wagers on them.

The men who put their name to the Star and Garter Laws in 1784 were not indolent aristocrats with nothing better to do than rewrite the rules of a children's game. They were men who took for granted their right to rule at home and abroad. They pilfered from the state and plundered other nations. They were bold (that is to say, shameless), enterprising, and overwhelmingly confident. All of this enabled them to create modern cricket – but they did not do so alone.

During the eighteenth century the landed elite began increasingly to rely on a new class of entrepreneurs, among them publicans and promoters, who swarmed around the rich at play just as they do today. Brewing interests were involved in cricket as early as 1668, when the Ram Inn at Smithfield was rated for a cricket ground. Organized matches were almost always played adjacent to a public house or tavern and innkeepers were the principal advertisers of matches in the press. Occasionally, inns would hire players to represent them in matches, though that seems to have become rarer as the landed elite exerted its authority. More and more, the booze-merchants and professional publicists assumed the role of cricket's middle-men, mediating between the aristocrats who controlled the game and the larger public now willing to pay to see it.

Most of the early professionals were personal servants of the great patrons. John Minshull, the first century-maker, worked for the Duke of Dorset as a gardener at eight shillings a week. The second Duke of Richmond retained the batsman Thomas Waymark, immortalized in Love's 1744 poem for dropping a sitter, as a groom. Dorset's stable of cricketers was said to cost him £1,000 a year. Tankerville hired the bowler 'Lumpy' Stevens as a gardener and others as butlers and gamekeepers. Sir Horatio Mann employed a batsman as a bailiff (the 'Old Corruption' reared its head even in cricket). The few itinerant professionals played as temporary servants for whichever great patron was paying their wages on the day. These wages were always modest. There was a huge gap between the profits made by patrons from gambling and the payments made to players.

The history of the poor and oppressed in shaping cricket remains largely hidden. Though the great patrons played with personal servants, tenant farmers and yeomen, they did not admit the landless poor or labourers to the privileged enclosure of the cricket field. However, by the end of the eighteenth century, in Sheffield, Nottingham and Leicester, cricket was being played by self-employed artisans, who controlled their own hours of employment and sought a recreation in keeping with their skilled status. Hosiers in Leicester and lace-makers in Nottingham, both employed on piece-work, took to the game (and were later to provide the nucleus of the pioneering professionals of the early-Victorian era). The Hambledon generation of professionals included potters, shepherds, blacksmiths and small farmers like Billy Beldham, whose footwork was, according to John Nyren, 'one of the most beautiful sights that can be imagined and which would have delighted an artist'.

In England, the peasantry, the numerically dominant class in every other European country, had been virtually eliminated by 1800. The effects of the 'free market' in land were augmented by the highly profitable process of enclosure. Between 1700 and 1845, half the arable land in England was enclosed by parliamentary Acts.

The result of this exercise in dispossession – in which the elite made full use of their unchallenged control of both the market and the state – was a population increasingly dependent on cash wages rather than subsistence farming or traditional rights to fuel and fodder. The cottagers and smallholders who depended on these rights were, in the words of Eric Hobsbawm, transformed from 'members of a community with a distinct set of rights into inferiors dependent on the rich'.

The enclosure movement, along with the Game Acts which restricted access to the countryside, undermined the old folk games. Many a traditional site for an annual parish contest was now deemed private property. In the second half of the eighteenth century, breaking into closes to play cricket was an offence tried frequently in the Court of Common Pleas. Landowners now permitted people to play cricket in areas where they had previously done so as of right.

'Village cricket' developed in the shadow of the modern cricket played under the aegis of the great landowners. Gradually, the old local variations were eliminated and the Laws issued by 'the noblemen and gentlemen' in London were given precedence. Increasingly, 'village cricket' sought to emulate not only the kind of cricket played by the leading patrons, but the mores and hierarchy which they had introduced into the game.

Like most nations, peoples, religions, political parties, indeed nearly all social institutions, cricket has its origin myth. These are tales communities tell themselves about how they entered history. They seek to explain not so much what these communities have been as what they have become. Cricket's myth is no exception.

Throughout the eighteenth century, the English population had been moving at an ever quickening pace from the countryside to the city. By 1760, London was the biggest and richest city in Europe and the world's greatest port and warehouse. It was also the only locus of anything like commercialized spectator sport. Driven from the villages, the landless and dispossessed created a new urban proletariat whose grievances exploded in periodic riot.

This traumatic, early transition from country to city became etched in English consciousness. The world's first largely urbanized society lived on a cultural diet of sentimental ruralism. The patterns and models for upper-class life remained rural, though increasingly the lives led by that class were town- or city-based.

The late eighteenth century discovered the picturesque village and the cunningly landscaped country park. The cult of nature and rustic sincerity was born, and with it what came to be known as the Romantic sensibility. As a folk game played on wide, unmeasured spaces, cricket was gilded by that sensibility early in its history. With residences (and financial interests) in both country and city, it was natural for the landowning elite to bring the country game of cricket into the city and there remake it according to their needs. Modern cricket was thus formed through and continued to represent the link between country and city. Its origin myth, the symbolic journey from the village green of Hambledon in rural Hampshire to Lord's in London, embodies the transition from one to the other.

The persistence of this myth owes a great deal to the sheer charm of John Nyren's *The Young Cricketer's Tutor*, published in 1833. Nyren was the last survivor of the great generation of Hambledon players. His father, Richard Nyren, had been captain and manager of the Hambledon Club in its heyday. 'Young' John Nyren was sixty-nine when he told his story to Charles Cowden Clarke, cricket's first and probably most able ghost writer. Clarke, the son of a schoolmaster, was a childhood friend of John Keats and later a colleague of Charles Lamb, William Hazlitt and Leigh Hunt. As a professional literary man (his lectures on Shakespeare were box-office hits) he was not only author but also publisher, promoter, distributor and retailer. Nyren's cricket book seems to have been one of his most successful ventures.

Nyren and Clarke are at pains to emphasize the moral probity, dignity and 'Englishness' of the Hambledon players. 'Thomas Brett, the fast bowler, 'bore the universal character of a strictly honourable man in all his transactions'. The 'word' of Tom Sueter, the wicket keeper, 'was never questioned by the gentlemen who associated with him'. Collectively, 'no thought of treachery ever seemed to enter their heads' – this in a period when high stakes meant large inducements to players to throw matches. 'Like true Englishmen, they would give an enemy fair play.' Richard Nyren himself, a left handed all-rounder, epitomized the team's virtues:

> I never saw a finer specimen of the thorough-bred old English yeoman than Richard Nyren. He was a good face-to-face, unflinching, uncompromising, independent man. He placed a full and just value upon the station he held in society, and he maintained it without insolence or assumption. He could differ with a superior, without trenching upon his dignity, or losing his own.

Even the punch at the Hambledon matches was 'not your new ponche à la romaine or ponche à la groseille or your modern cat-lap milk punch – punch be-devilled, but good, unsophisticated John Bull stuff – stark! – that would stand on end – punch that would make a cat speak. Sixpence a bottle.'

To read Nyren and Clarke today is to encounter all the old cricket myths freshly minted, unencumbered by the musty air of pretence that they were to acquire later. Strangely though, there is little in the book about the club's patrons, though a contemporary 'Cricket Song' dedicated to Hambledon insists:

> Let's join in the praise of the bat and the wicket
> And sing in full chorus the patrons of cricket.

In the 1760s, the Reverend Charles Powlett, son of the wealthy Duke of Bolton (a descendant of the Whig landlords who backed William of Orange against James II) had secured an ecclesiastical living in a hitherto obscure corner of south-east Hampshire. With several former Westminster schoolmates, he founded the Hambledon Club (in London) and became its first secretary. Over the next decade, the club's members included eighteen titled aristocrats, two MPs, two knights, and sons, brothers and cousins of the above. Its presidents included the Duke of Chandos, with huge estates in Herefordshire, and the Earl of Darnley, a leading Kent landowner whose grandson and great-grandsons were Presidents of the MCC. Among Hambledon's other patrons were Winchilsea, Dorset, Tankerville and Horatio Mann.

The membership fee was three guineas a year, the same price Hampshire CCC were charging for annual membership as late as 1970.

Club meetings and dinners were advertised in the London papers, as well as in Winchester and Salisbury. That this was very much a sophisticated gentleman's drinking, eating and social club is indicated by the notorious Hambledon Club toast, 'To the immortal memory of Madge'. For decades, the identity of 'Madge' perplexed cricket scholars (one opined that it could not be a woman, because women had nothing to do with cricket). However, recent research has revealed that 'Madge' was a slang word for female genitalia. Clearly part of the attraction of cricket clubs, like other elite men's social clubs, was to get away from home, the nuclear family and the pretence of monogamy – and to reassert the predatory sexual freedom enjoyed by the old military-feudal aristocrats.

For all his pride in the 'yeoman independence' of the Hambledon professionals, John Nyren could still boast of 'the style with which we were accustomed to impress our aristocratic playmates with our acknowledgement of their rank and station'.

Old Richard Nyren, who ran the club on behalf of the rich patrons, was one of tens of thousands of yeoman farmers then being squeezed out by market forces. As a cricket promoter and landlord of the Bat and Ball Inn, he found a new niche in the social hierarchy. He administered payments to the players (three or four shillings for a match or practice session). He also ensured they dressed in the livery provided by their patrons: sky-blue coats with black velvet collars, buckled shoes, knee breeches and stockings.

Hambledon was not so much 'the cradle of cricket' as a sophisticated nursery for the training and development of professional cricketers, run by the rich for the entertainment of the rich. Attracted by the prestige of the patrons, and the wages offered, players came to Hambledon from villages and towns throughout Hampshire and from Surrey, Dorset, Sussex, Essex and Kent.

John Nyren described Hambledon as 'the Attica of the scientific art'. In its brief heyday, the club was the scene of rapid technical improvements in all aspects of the game. Hambledon players were the first to exploit bowling through the air and to add jerks, twists and turns to it. Tom Walker pioneered slow bowling; 'The Little Farmer', Lambert, the off-break ('the first I remember who introduced this deceitful and teasing style of delivering the ball'). John Small was 'the first who turned the short hits to account'; Tom Sueter 'the first to depart from the custom of the old players before him, who deemed it heresy to leave the crease for the ball'.

Nyren himself makes clear that the innovations belonged as much to the professionals playing against Hambledon (the bowlers David Harris and 'Lumpy' Stevens in particular) as to the Hambledon players themselves. The technical revolution associated with Hambledon was not so much an expression of native English genius as of the concentration of resources and the incentive to win created by the capitalist patrons.

In 1787, many of the same individuals who had sponsored Hambledon (and who had issued the Star and Garter Laws) created Lord's and the MCC. The architect of this crowning achievement of the eighteenth century cricket elite was, according to tradition, Thomas Lord, whom H.S. Altham (Repton, Oxford) described in his 1921 *History of Cricket* as coming from 'sturdy and once prosperous yeoman stock'.

In fact, Lord's family were Yorkshire Catholic landowners dispossessed because of their support for the Pretender in 1745. Lord turned Protestant and made his way to London where he became a wine merchant and sometime cricket companion of the gentlemen of the Star and Garter, who at that time played cricket in White Conduit Fields. It was the ideal milieu for an ambitious young entrepreneur prepared to make himself of service to the elite.

In June 1785, the *Daily Universal Register*, predecessor of *The Times*, lectured Lord's new acquaintances:

> It is recommended to the lordling cricketers who amuse themselves in White Conduit Fields to procure an Act of Parliament for inclosing their ground, which will not only prevent them being incommoded, but protect themselves from a petition of severe rebuke which they justly merit and received on Saturday evening from some spirited citizens whom they insulted and attempted *vi et armis* to drive from their footpath, pretending it was within their bounds.

After some delay, the 'lordling cricketers' took the advice to heart. Thus, the founding of Lord's and the MCC had at its heart the capitalist drive for enclosure, the compulsion to transform common property into private property. The impatience of the anonymous journalist with the White Conduit cricketers is revealing: what annoys the writer is their assumption of private property rights *without having secured them in law*.

In 1787, the Earl of Winchilsea and Charles Lennox (later Duke of Richmond) guaranteed the thirty-one-year-old Lord against any loss if he would procure for them a new, *private* cricket ground. Accordingly, he leased land in May of that year on what is now Dorset Square. *The first thing he did was to put a fence around the ground.* This not only ensured exclusive use of the ground for the gentlemen but also enabled Lord to charge a 6d entrance fee.

The Star and Garter elite had already issued two revisions of the laws. As they moved their base from the open spaces of White Conduit Fields to Lord's enclosed ground, they carried with them the authority of established lawmakers. They employed all the principal players and they were the biggest betters on the major matches, which were made in their names. Once Lord had provided them with a London base, they formed themselves into a private club, the MCC.

Although the early records of the MCC have vanished, it seems probable that new members always had to be nominated from among existing members and then approved by the rest of the club. This is a form of democracy often favoured by the English upper class: election – or recruitment – from above.

Lord's was, in its early days, explicitly and unashamedly a business. Lord could get 5,000 into his ground, but to cover big-match expenses in advance, he would solicit 'subscriptions' in the fashionable men's clubs, just as county cricket clubs flog hospitality packages today. He also hired out his grounds for foot races, pigeon shooting, hopping matches, ballooning, parades and ceremonies of all sorts. Gamblers of all types flocked to the cricket matches, as did pickpockets.

Lord was forced to move to Lisson Grove when Dorset Square was earmarked for residential development. A few years later he had to move again to escape canal construction. He arrived at the present St John's Wood site in 1813. Lord would have thought 'Plum' Warner was barking mad when he said: 'Cricket is not a circus and it would be far better that it should be driven back to the village green ... than yield a jot to the petulant demands of the spectator.' Lord staged gimmick matches between left-handed and right-handed cricketers as readily as he took on the Eton v. Harrow match in 1805 (it is still played at Lord's).

Lord turned from cricket promotion to property speculation. In 1825, he was eager to sell the lease on his St John's Wood site to a residential developer, a more profitable exercise, at least in the short run, than running a cricket ground. The elite stepped in. William Ward (Winchester, Oxford), a master batsman whose 278 for MCC against Norfolk was the highest score at Lord's until Percy Holmes's 315 not out for Yorkshire against Middlesex in 1925, bought out Lord's interest for £5,000. At this time, Ward was a director of the Bank of England. Later he was to become MP for the City of London. The next year, after the first Harrow v. Winchester match at Lord's, a fire destroyed the pavilion and with it all the early MCC records. From then on, the game's mythologists, uninhibited by recorded history, let their imaginations run wild.

In contrast to the rise of the MCC, the demise of the Hambledon Club is clearly documented. At the club's last recorded annual dinner in 1794, it was minuted that Thomas Paine, 'Author of the Rights of Man', was present – along with only three members (none of them titled) and twelve guests. The landowners had decamped to London and high politics. Paine was the guest of Hambledon's last honorary secretary, Henry Bonham, a radical Whig whose descendants include the Liberal Bonham-Carter family. Clearly, modern English cricket was congenial to the revolutionary democrats of the time. They recognized in it a suitable vehicle for their own aspirations. Yet they could inhabit Hambledon only when the club was a spent force. For all its democratic tendencies, modern cricket remained the creature of the English elite.

Appearing in the Star and Garter list as a humble 'Lennox, Mr C.' was the future fourth Duke of Richmond, Charles Lennox, descendant through an illegitimate line of Charles II, and perhaps the most prominent gentleman cricketer (a batsman and wicket-keeper) of his day. After a brief spell as MP for Sussex, he embarked on a long military career that took him to Ireland as Lord Lieutenant, across Europe during the Napoleonic Wars, to the Leeward Islands and ultimately to Canada as Governor General of British North America. Everywhere he went, he played cricket. On the eve of Waterloo, he organized a match for the English officers. He nearly became Prime Minister in 1809, losing out to his old cricket colleague William Bentinck.

In 1789, Lennox fought a duel on Wimbledon Common with the Duke of York, brother of George IV, who was a keen cricketer long before his dubious exploits in battle won him the immortality of nursery rhyme. Lennox's second in the duel was his Star and Garter companion, Winchilsea. The next year Lennox faced York again, this time at Lord's new cricket ground. Lennox appeared for 'Hambledon' and York for 'England'.

Clearly, this was a ruling class with one foot still in the old ways, a continental-style aristocracy bound by a feudal code of blood and honour. But it was also a new type of elite, a capitalist elite, which mingled socially with the untitled and even on occasion the unlanded, not least on the cricket field.

Cricket, it must be remembered, was the first team game in which the upper classes took part – at least the first one in which they took part on foot, rather than horseback. They *patronized* football and other traditional, festive games, as well as the modern spectator sports of boxing and racing, but they *played* cricket.

This was a reflection of the gradual demilitarization of the English aristocracy, whose war-skills were to be used on seas and overseas in future, while other means were found to sustain their rule at home. Playing cricket was the logical consequence of the elite's role in a society based not on hereditary rank (though that still counted) but primarily on landed wealth, on capital. The primacy of cold cash, and with it the subjugation of all to the rule of law, blurred social boundaries and brought together individuals from different strata of society. All were part of the nationwide market economy. All could play a single game under a single set of Laws.

Overseas, it was regarded as a peculiar foible of the English aristocracy that, despite its fantastic wealth, it disdained much of the culture of conspicuous display indulged in by its foreign counterparts. Stranger still, it often aped the fashions and manners of social 'inferiors', not least by playing cricket. This was an indulgence that French aristocrats, whose privileges rested not on the endlessly transformable power of money but on the rigid enforcement of a 'divine right' absolutism, could never have contemplated.

'If the French noblesse had been capable of playing cricket with their peasants their chateaux would never have been burnt.' This famous dictum appears in G.M. Trevelyan's *English Social History*, published during World War II to buttress national unity in the face of the fascist enemy. In Trevelyan's vision of 'village cricket' in which 'squire, farmer, blacksmith and labourer, with their women and children ... were at ease together and happy all the summer afternoon', the great myth of English cricket was given a Liberal gloss.

The power of this myth derives from a grain of truth at its heart. When the aristocrats came down off their horses to play cricket with the lower orders, they wrought a revolution. They placed themselves at the head of a game whose premises (unlike those of horse-racing or boxing, the other two commercial success stories of that sporting era) were inclusive. It was on this basis that cricket first staked its claim to be a national sport, and it did so in an era that witnessed the birth of nationalist sentiment across Europe. In this too, England was a pioneer. 'Rule Britannia' was first sung in 1740. Within a few years, 'God Save the King' was adopted for royal ceremonials and became the world's first national anthem.

Cricket in this era acquires and at the same time helps to create a national public. Between 1730 and 1740, some 150 cricket matches were recorded in the contemporary press; between 1750 and 1760, 230; between 1770 and 1790, over 500. By the end of the century, cricket was being played in most English counties, though it was still largely unknown in the far North and far West. Several towns had already seen cricket riots.

The first cricket annual, Samuel Butcher's 'List of all the Principal Matches of Cricket' appeared in 1791. The *Sporting Magazine* was founded in 1793. It became possible to compile batting and bowling averages and make comparisons between players one had never seen. Cricket became something strangers could converse about. The newspaper, the novel, cricket: all come of age in this period and all require an impersonal paying public, not merely elite patronage. All address an anonymous, nationwide constituency.

By the end of the century, cricket, which had been seen as a passing aristocratic craze sixty years before, had become respectable, 'manly' and therefore 'English'. In 1786, *The Times*'s report of a cricket match staged by Dorset in Paris made it clear that cricket had become something the English took pride in: 'The French ... cannot imitate us in such vigorous assertions of the body.' When 2,000 spectators packed the new Lord's ground in 1787, *The Times* praised the crowd for 'conducting themselves with the utmost decorum'.

Already, cricket's Englishness was being identified with masculinity, law and order, and social hierarchy. Cricket's social inclusion was innovatory, but highly conditional. The democratic revolution in cricket, as in English society as a whole, was to remain incomplete, truncated by the endurance of feudal rights within the English capitalist order.

In the old times, the lord of the manor would lay on meat and ale on festival days and, for a fixed period, tolerate a degree of disorder and insubordination. The old folk games were always staged as part of these local saturnalia. Things often got out of hand in parish football matches, which came into disrepute with the ruling classes at the very time cricket was in the ascendant. In cricket, at least after MCC's first revision of the Laws in 1787, there was no body contact; violence was mediated by bat and ball, which made it possible for the elite to play in the company of their inferiors. By patronizing cricket they could control the festive spirit and use it to promote the old hierarchy in an age of rapid change.

When the great patrons began playing cricket with the lower orders, they barred women from the game. Byron spoke of 'cricket's manly toil', a phrase which would have been unthinkable a century before, when cricket among the upper classes was merely a fashion and women joined with men in the child's game played to pass the time on the great estates. Of course, the exclusion of women is something cricket shares with other sports. Significantly, the bar on mixed competition is usually enforced only after puberty. The male body of the team must be insulated from threat of female contamination. The body taboo which held sway for so many generations between gentlemen and players and in South Africa between black and white is still practised with rigour between men and women.

Cricket brought the rulers into contact with a cross-section of the ruled, but it allowed them to make this contact within a circumscribed social space, the space of the cricket field, under carefully controlled conditions, embodied in the Laws of Cricket, like the common laws of property prevailing throughout the market economy. It allowed the rulers to participate in sport with others without jeopardizing their social standing. Whatever happened on the field, social distinctions were preserved off it.

Cricket clubs were exclusively for 'noblemen and gentlemen'. Professional players were employees and, in a telling phrase, 'servants' of the clubs. Cricketers were skilled workers, but they retained the mentality of medieval artisans dependent on noble patrons. Though this status has been challenged again and again in cricket history, it remained the norm up till our own time. Some would say it still does.

The inclusiveness of cricket, which gave it its claim to be 'English', was strictly limited, and that 'Englishness' became the property of the elite which ruled the game and the country. For all their innovatory spirit, the English, unlike the French, did not clear the decks of feudal rubbish by declaring a revolutionary 'Year One'.

In 1789, the Duke of Dorset, then serving as Ambassador to France, proposed that an English cricket side visit Paris. His friend and fellow MCC member, the Earl of Tankerville, was in the government and secured approval from the Foreign Secretary, the Duke of Leeds, also a cricketer. What can only be called the first MCC overseas touring party duly assembled at Dover in July, only to be confronted with Dorset travelling post-haste in the opposite direction, fleeing the revolution which had just broken out in the French capital. The world's inaugural international cricket tour was cancelled because of politics.

The French Revolution terrified the English elite. The Whig grandees of the Star and Garter abandoned the democratic heritage of 1688 and rallied to the crusade against Jacobinism. Several joined Pitt's reactionary ministry in 1799, among them Carlisle, Thomas Pelham and Charles Fitzroy, and voted to suspend *habeas corpus* and implement the Alien, Sedition and Treason Acts. Earl Spencer became Lord of the Admiralty, in which capacity he suppressed the Spithead and Nore mutinies with copious hangings and floggings. John Willett Payne became a Rear Admiral. In 1800, William Wyndham, brother of the Earl of Egremont, became Minister of War. Sir Thomas Fremantle served with Nelson in the Mediterranean and became a Rear Admiral in 1810.

The exception that proved the rule was the former Hambledon cricketer, Sackville Tufton, a nephew of the Duke of Dorset and later Earl of Thanet. While so many of his cricketing peers were moving to entrench landlord and colonial power (particularly in Ireland), Tufton was sent to the Tower for 'creating a riot' at the Maidstone trial for 'seditious libel' of Arthur O'Connor, a leader of the United Irishmen who ended up working for Napoleon.

In the struggle against the French and the plebeian forces unleashed by their revolution, the elite invoked the 'English' national identity which had been forged in the course of the preceding century. Cricket was not only a component of that identity; it had helped create it. And the cricket elite, whose willingness to play with the lower orders had given the game such a powerful democratic impetus, now harnessed it to the cause of reaction.

Cricket's pioneering role made it a prisoner of English history. As the creature of an age of transition, it still has a foot in both the past and the present. At times, it seems in danger of being rent asunder as the two pull in opposite directions.

Yet it is the very transitional nature of the game, the way the legacy of the old endures within the new, that accounts for the fascination of cricket. Cricket retains more features from the age of folk games than any of its modern rivals, forged in later eras. These 'under-developed' features are, indeed, the key to understanding the game's angst ridden struggle to adapt itself to the modern world.

The general tendency of organized modern sport is towards standardization of conditions, regularized and systematic competition, and thorough commercialization. In team sports, these are supplemented by both greater specialization and subordination of individuals to the fortunes of the team as a whole. Sports are driven along this course by the need to make themselves more competitive and therefore more attractive to spectators. Against this general pattern, cricket seems a case of arrested development.

The earliest essence of cricket, undoubtedly an inheritance from the folk game, is two sets of wickets with bowling from alternate ends (single wicket cricket is a later adaptation). The early Laws never even mention these arrangements; they are simply assumed. Out of them came not only the complexity of cricket scoring but the mirror-effect of the change in the field at the end of the over, an eerie survival of an age besotted with symmetry and the pseudo-sciences of cabbala and numerology.

It also reflects the origin of the game in a countryside innocent of capitalist enclosure and ensuing industrialization. Boundaries were not written into the Laws until the 1870s; even today, The Laws stipulate only that 'the umpires shall agree with both captains on the boundary of the playing area'. In the early days, all hits had to be run out: there were no fours or sixes. If the ball went into the crowd, the crowd cleared a way for the fieldsman to retrieve it. This is a legacy from the days when land was held in common and seen as unbounded. Cricket fields had a centre – the pitch – but not a periphery. Because of this, both bowling and batting become infinitely various and captaincy and field-placing infinitely subtle.

Where time-limits are the essence of football, rugby, basketball and hockey, in cricket, time, like space, is indefinite. The early matches had to be played out: there was no draw. By the end of the eighteenth century, three-, four- and five-day matches were common – not because that was the time stipulated for them but because that was how long it took for at least one side to bowl the other out twice. The game expanded to fill as much time as was demanded by the skill of the players in conjunction with the state of the pitch. This too was a legacy of a pre-industrial world before time was measured out in inter-changeable units, before labour was a commodity bought and sold in those units. Initially, the draw was simply an arbitrary abandonment of the game. However, the inevitable time-limit – even one as leisurely as five days – did add another dimension to the game, creating the triangle of runs, wickets and time which makes cricket dramatic.

Cricket's open-endedness in time and space gives it the episodic quality which is one of its chief glories. The widely-held belief that the uneven rhythm of the game reflects a slower society in which the boundary between work and leisure was less stark is solidly grounded in history. That history is also reflected in the way batting in cricket carries such potent intimations of mortality: you know your innings will end, but you don't know when; each ball might be your last, but then again it might not. The fall of a wicket, an immediate, ignominious and irreversible end to occupation of the crease, is the sort of sudden death which more advanced sports tend to eliminate.

Already in the eighteenth century, cricket's great attraction is the gladiatorial contest between bowler and batsman. Cricket is the first modern team sport, but it is a team sport whose greatest fascination seems to be the display of individual prowess. Even today, the most fervent partisan will openly admire any piece of fine cricket by an individual, regardless of which side he or she plays for. It is impossible to play cricket of any real drama or skill without a full team; single-wicket or six-a-side are feeble shadows of the real thing. Yet it also seems that the most enduring attraction of full-blooded team cricket is the way it allows diverse personalities to flourish.

Cricket's pre-industrial origins have thus stamped the game with a unique interplay between the individual and collective, derived from its special alchemy of space and time. These qualities have taken the game through the industrial age and may yet take it beyond.

Because it is played out over a longer period of time than other sports, cricket is more susceptible to the vagaries of weather. English cricket skills were developed to cope with these vagaries; the aim was not so much to master the environment as to exploit it. This is why the old conundrum – how could a game requiring five successive days of good weather ever be invented in England? – misses the point. English cricket is not made for relentless sunshine, which may be why touring abroad is often such an ordeal for English cricketers.

Most sports seek to make themselves weather-proof: Americans have taken this to a logical extreme by staging games in domed stadia on artificial turf. Cricket has resisted this process. Its grounds remain astonishingly diverse in size, shape, exposure to the elements, quality of pitch and outfield. This diversity does not reflect mere foot dragging by old-fashioned cricket authorities. It is the product of cricket's *autochthony*, one of the game's inner secrets.

The word comes from the Greek *autochthon*, of the land itself. In pathology, an autochthonous disease is one which is found in a particular locality. In ecology, it pertains to plants or animals indigenous to a particular region. In psychology, it refers to ideas or illusions that seem to originate in some alien, outside reality, like earth, rocks or trees.

Where most modern ball games required a standardized inflatable ball

– and therefore had to await developments in rubber technology – cricket has always been played with a hard, solid ball composed of cork, twine and leather. Its red dye (the balls seem to have been red from the beginning) is merely a heightening and polishing of the natural colour of the leather. Because of their pre-industrial origin, cricket balls have peculiar, irregular, apparently contradictory qualities, many of them baffling physicists to this day. To exploit the ball's primitiveness demands extraordinary skill and cunning, and to influence the behaviour of the ball, bowlers have applied spit, sweat, flannel, earth, sawdust and hair oil. In baseball, as every American child knows, you're out of the game if you spit on the ball – or, at least, you're out if you're caught doing it. Not in cricket.

The oldest surviving measurement in cricket is the length of the pitch, twenty-two yards, or one chain. The chain was a surveyor's device, a by-product of the transformation of land into a capitalist commodity, first used in England in the late seventeenth century. It consisted of one hundred links of equal length, measuring twenty-two yards in total. European Union or no, cricket, because of its early origins, is likely to continue to defy the invincible march of the metric system, that creation of the French Revolution.

In early cricket the ball was rolled ('bowled') along the ground. Pitching it under-arm through the air eliminated much of the arbitrary influence of ground conditions, but an essential contact with the ground remained. This autochthony accounts for the crucial role of the state of the pitch in determining the outcome of the games played on it.

Every time Thomas Lord moved his cricket ground, he dug up and transported his pitch. Up until 1811 the visiting team chose where to pitch the wickets, though always within a specified radius of a point picked by the home team. After 1811, the pitching of wickets was given to the home team's groundsman and the toss for choice of innings became all-important – not least to prevent abuse by home groundsmen, always a topic of heated debate. The toss in cricket is more important in determining the result of matches than in any other sport. It requires cricketers to make complex meteorological and geological calculations which never enter the heads of players in other games.

Standardization has been essential to the development of most sports. By eliminating the arbitrary influence of ground conditions or weather, the players' own skills, strength and state of mind play a greater role in determining results. In cricket, the limits of standardization – in time, space, and the very implements of play – are the key to unlocking its rich store of skill and drama.

Cricket's early Laws are not comprehensive descriptions of the game or even systematic sets of rules covering every eventuality. They often fail even to mention the criteria for winning or losing. The circumference of the ball is not stipulated until 1838. The width of the bat was limited only in 1774 after Shock White walked on to the pitch to commence his innings against Hambledon with a bat as wide as the wicket itself. White was breaking no known Law. He was, however, violating what was already coming to be known as 'the spirit of the game'. The LBW law was brought in, according to an elderly Billy Beldham, because 'one of our best hitters was shabby enough to get his legs in the way and take advantage of the bowlers'.

Cricket's perennial controversy over the supremacy of bat or ball was born with the game itself. Already there was debate over the legitimacy of bowling actions. Jerking, throwing, pitching, pushing are all denounced, but it always proves difficult to define them clearly enough to allow umpires to make consistent rulings. The third stump was added, it is said, because in a 1775 match against Hambledon, 'Lumpy' Stevens, a Surrey player, managed to get the ball between batsman John Small's two stumps three times in an over without dislodging the bails. In 1798, MCC increased the size of the wickets from 22 x 6 to 24 x 7 inches in order to assist struggling bowlers against increasingly dominant batsmen (they are now 28 x 9). From the very start, then, we see the endless tampering with the Laws in a vain quest for the perfect balance between bat and ball. The pendulum had started to swing and was never to stop.

Generally, Laws are added or amended in response to attempts to exploit loopholes or in order to accommodate technical innovations wrought by higher standards of play. In cricket, law always follows practice. Even the early laws are meant to define and to restrict *existing practices*, i.e. practices associated with the folk games from which cricket was derived. Hence they are *laws* not *rules*. They are statutes passed against the broader background of common law and ancient custom, and implicit in them is the existence of unspecified norms to which people are expected to adhere. 'Fair play' is first mentioned in the Laws in 1774. The 1787 revision makes clear that umpires 'are the sole judges of fair and unfair play'. Moreover, 'they are not to order a player out unless appealed to by the adversaries'. Here is the origin of that peculiar cricketing custom, the appeal: in the assumption that both sides, being composed at least partly of 'gentlemen', should always invite the umpire to give an adjudication rather than have him intervene unilaterally.

Cricket's constitution, then, is like England's: unwritten, and therefore open to abuse by those who claim to act in its name.

By the late eighteenth century, cricket had broken free of the liturgical and agricultural calendars. It was no longer an affair of seasonal wakes and parish festivals, but it had not established an independent schedule of its own. There was no cricket season; there were no leagues or championships or integrated competition of any kind. Play was at the whim of the patrons, the bookies and the weather.

The characteristically English arm's-length relationship between the landowning elite and the nitty-gritty of industry and trade meant that the publicans and promoters who assisted the great patrons were subordinate within the hierarchy of the game. The exploitation of cricket as a commercial commodity, path-breaking in its day, remained, for one hundred years, hesitant and spasmodic.

The big matches were either one-offs or once-a-year affairs. A stable, reliable return on investment was not yet possible. In the heyday of fashionable cricket the proprietor of the Artillery Ground, the leading cricket venue in the country, went bankrupt. Despite the economic development of the eighteenth century, at its end there was still not a large and stable enough market to sustain cricket as a commercial venture. Until the 1840s, working-class spending power and leisure time was simply insufficient. Middle-class professionals and small businessmen were neither numerous nor confident enough as yet to provide an alternative. The costs and inconvenience of transport meant that the game could be made profitable only in London.

Representative cricket was haphazard. The teams that played under the names of Kent or Surrey or Hampshire were assembled by rich patrons, the 'leading men of the county'. As landowners, they identified their social status with territorial authority. When they brought teams to London to play for and with them, they logically called these teams by the names of their counties. The cricket historians who refer to the 'beginning of county cricket' in the mid-eighteenth century (and the present-day county members who claim lengthy genealogies for their clubs) mistake the name for the reality. There were few fixed loyalties. The professionals belonged to patrons, not to organized clubs. It was common for teams to supply their opponents with 'given' men to ensure equal competition. 'Hambledon', 'Kent', 'All-England' were transient appellations of convenience. The word county (used in cricket in preference to the Anglo-Saxon 'shire') comes from the Latin *comitatus*, a body of companions or retainers, and later a feudal retinue. This was

precisely what the early 'county' teams were. Out ot that heritage came
the permanent anachronism that is English county cricket.

In the 1820s, the novelist Mary Russell Mitford championed village
cricket against:

> a set match at Lord's ground for money, hard money, between a certain number
> of gentlemen and players, as they are called - people who make a trade of a
> noble sport, and degrade it into an affair of bettings and hedgings and
> cheatings, it may be, like boxing or horse-racing.

Cricket starts believing its own myths early in its history. After all, it
was the gentlemen who placed the bets and suborned the honour of the
players with bribery. It was the gentlemen who had staged the great
matches and the publicans and promoters who charged admission. Why
did the players, the professionals, get the blame? Why were those market
forces which had given birth to cricket so quickly banished from its
ideology?

Cricket becomes the first modern sport at the dawn of the industrial
revolution. Indeed, the same forces that changed a childish folk-game
into modern cricket unleashed that revolution: the spread of the market
economy, the domination of the state by a landowning bourgeoisie, the
triumph of private property and law, the revenues from overseas trade
and colonial conquest, the movement into the cities. But the creation of
modern cricket was nearly complete when the Industrial Revolution was
just beginning to gather pace. Cricket was not a product of that
revolution but a by-product of the conjuncture of social and economic
forces which set it in motion.

Though market relations were widespread in the late eighteenth
century, and critical to the emergence of cricket, cricket was also shaped
in its early years by older, pre-market institutions, notably aristocratic
patronage and a social hierarchy not entirely based on money. As the
tempo of change accelerated in the early nineteenth century, creating
hunger and want as well as new aspirations and new social movements,
people began to see cricket as something with its roots in an earlier, less
predatory, less money-minded age. The argument between cricket and
the market has been going on ever since.

Even as the bonds of the past were being sloughed off, a new
historicism was emerging. Unprecedentedly rapid social change made
people more self-conscious about the past. The era was marked by a

growing fascination with those linked lost paradises: childhood, the countryside and the primeval nation. No wonder cricket began looking backwards almost as soon as it opened its eyes. It was forged in the transition between old and new, between country and city, and stamped indelibly with the date and place of manufacture.

Ever since, *rus in urbe*, the country in the city, has been the leitmotif of the game's mythology. You can feel it any time you step into a major cricket ground in a big city – Lord's, the Oval, Old Trafford, Headingley. Suddenly you enter a world where the clock is ticking with an ancient, irregular rhythm, inflected by hints of the changing seasons and ineffable shifts in the weather. Across the sheer expanse of green, defying the long-term inflation in urban property values, the episodic, elastic, open-ended, earthbound game preserves a pre-industrial world, but preserves it in a form that has existed only in a market economy.

A hundred years junior to cricket, football, with its intense physical and temporal compression and fierce partisanship, is the classic expression of industrial urbanism. In contrast, cricket has come to represent the English pastoral, the dream of an unchanging, natural society in which all conflicts are magically resolved. It is a society outside history, abiding in the eternal world of mythological time, not the world of the wristwatch, the factory punchclock and the football referee's whistle.

Cricket fans who find in the dress, grounds, jargon, ritual, pace and unobtrusive complexity of cricket a whiff of an earlier age are not deluded. That *is* the past they're sniffing. And why shouldn't people get high on this scent? There is more than enough that is ugly in the present to justify taking momentary refuge in an earlier time.

The past shades and highlights, nuances and enriches cricket. Alas, it also sits like a dead weight on the poor game, cutting it off from sources of renewal. The hypocrisy that has long been regarded as one of the chief characteristics of the English takes root early in cricket, and is indeed one of the things that makes English cricket *English* – the way it lies about itself to itself. *The Englishness is in the lie*, in the cult of the honest yeomen and the village green, in the denial of cricket's origins in commerce, politics, patronage and an urban society. The tyranny of mere wealth, on which the English eighteenth-century achievement rested, had to be wrapped in something finer and, at least in appearance, older.

3

The Cathedral and the Cult

*Lord's, 1987: an invented tradition ● William Clarke's pioneers
● Cricket's first ideologist ● The dictatorship of the MCC ● The
great pretenders ● Workers in whites ● The stillbirth of county
cricket ● Empire ● 'Play the game, Lord Hawke!'
● Legacy: the teflon canvas*

In 1987, the MCC marked its bicentenary by unveiling the new Mound
Stand at Lord's. Its post-modernist architecture, applying high tech to
traditional purposes with flair and skill, was admired even by those
normally contemptuous of the style. Certainly, it was a vast improvement
on the Warner and Tavern Stands of the fifties and sixties, with their stark
utilitarian awkwardness. Light and airy, the tented roof and cantilevered
upper tier of the new stand seemed to float over the arena, while at the
base the brick colonnade preserved the ancient circuit of the arena and
rooted the flamboyant structure stoutly in the earth.

The new stand was the creation of Michael Hopkins, who also
designed facilities at Glyndebourne and Cambridge, as well as the
country home of David Mellor. His work at Lord's is celebratory and
festive, evoking a grand marquee at a stately home, a lost world of
prosperity, elegance, leisure and stability. The new stand harked back not
just to Victorian England, but beyond that to the village green and the
original meaning of the word pavilion, derived from the medieval French
for a tent or canopy (related to *papillon*, butterfly) which the feudal lords
pitched on the field of battle. In the course of the eighteenth century it
became a designation for an ornamental building in a park or a temporary
shelter on a playing field. Hopkins's Mound Stand summoned such
images, which seemed the essence of what cricket, especially cricket at
Lord's, was all about.

Back in the forties, Nikolaus Pevsner had found Lord's an
unprepossessing jumble, 'unthinkable in a country like Sweden or
Holland'. Now, at last, Lord's had a structure worthy of its centrepiece,
the high Victorian pavilion, built in 1889-90, at a cost of £21,000, by

Thomas Verity, who was responsible for the terracotta work at the Albert Hall and the redecoration of the State Apartments in Buckingham Palace. Anyone who has spent time at Lord's comes to admire the pavilion, whatever they may think of the people who inhabit it. Its rosy brickwork, ornamental iron and terracotta, vast window space and solid flanking towers combine to produce an effect that is at once lavish but light, substantial without being stolid. It is a cheerful sight, a fitting edifice for an elite that was, at the time, very much in command, and not only of cricket.

By the second half of the nineteenth century the Industrial Revolution had created a new urban England. As the towns and cities grew, they acquired parks, libraries and other amenities, including cricket grounds. Of the ninety-odd venues used for first-class cricket in England and Wales in 1992, sixty were established between 1860 and 1910. At the same time, a new, broader cricket public came into being, served not only by the ever-expanding sports coverage in the daily newspapers but also by a host of specialist publications.

Britain witnessed an explosive growth of mass spectator sport. The first Open Golf Championship was held in 1860. The Football Association was founded in 1863 and immediately banned handling the ball and 'hacking' opponents. The Rugby Football Union, founded by dissidents loyal to the 'handling game', was organized in 1871. Tennis was first devised in 1873; the MCC revised its rules in 1875, then handed authority over to the All-England Club in Wimbledon, which staged the first championships in 1877.

Cricket, as we have seen, had codified its Laws and established itself as a popular modern sport a century before. But it too underwent a transformation in this period. Its ramshackle organization was consolidated. The county championship emerged, as did Test cricket, placing Lord's at the hub of the domestic and imperial games. In these years the phrases 'cricket cap', 'cricket flannels', 'cricket week' and 'duck' (a bit of public-school slang) were first seen in print. The old game was acquiring regalia, rituals and a jargon of its own. Just as cricket was initially created in the era of Johnson's Dictionary, it was re-created, augmented with the authority of the past, in the era of the Oxford English Dictionary ('based on historical principles') and the Dictionary of National Biography.

In 1887, the MCC dared to couple its first centenary with the Queen's Jubilee. Though it masqueraded as a celebration of the past, the jubilee was a modern innovation. For historian Eric Hobsbawm, it is the premier example of the 'invented traditions' which proliferated in the late nineteenth century. Fusing ancient ceremony, national symbolism and political expediency, the 'invented traditions' aimed to bind the new, literate, half-enfranchised public to the old regime, not least through the medium of the popular press. The challenge of democracy forced the rulers to find new ways of cementing national unity around the existing institutions, including the monarchy, which in this era became a symbol of both nation and empire, of ancient right subsumed within bourgeois respectability. Elite domination had to be seen as something more than a mere accretion of wealth and weapons. The rulers learned to pose as the guardians of national values, transcending particular class interests.

It is in this context that cricket consolidates its ideology. In 1867, *Lillywhite* advised young cricketers, 'Do not ask the umpire unless you think the batsman is out; it is not cricket to keep asking the umpire questions.' The 'cricket' in 'it isn't cricket' had already come to refer to a transcendent code of behaviour above and beyond the explicit Laws of the game. By the end of the century the phrase 'it isn't cricket' was being widely applied to all spheres of public and private life. On the eve of World War I, Lord Harris staked the boldest of claims for the old game: 'It is an institution, a passion, one might say a religion. It has got into the blood of the nation, and wherever British men and women are gathered together there will the stumps be pitched.'

Cricket had become a totem for a set of values, a distillation of Englishness. One of the most enduring invented traditions of this era is Britain's 'unwritten constitution', celebrated by Walter Bagehot in 1867. In the bible of public-school ideology, the 1857 novel *Tom Brown's Schooldays*, Thomas Hughes (Rugby, Oxford), MP, barrister and cricketer, made the comparison with cricket explicit:

> 'It's more than a game. It's an institution,' said Tom.
>
> 'Yes,' said Arthur, 'the birthright of British boys, old and young, as *habeas corpus* and trial by jury are to British men.'

Only two years before *Tom Brown's Schooldays*, Karl Marx had scoffed at the British constitution as 'an antiquated, obsolete, out-of-date compromise between the bourgeoisie, which rules not officially but in fact in all spheres of civil society, and the landed aristocracy which governs officially'. The landed aristocracy certainly governed in cricket, both officially and in fact, and continued to do so until our own times. But just as the Victorian monarchy came to stand above party politics, a disinterested embodiment of the national and imperial destinies and protector of the 'unwritten constitution', so the MCC, guardian of 'cricket' and 'fair play', came to stand above the teams and the individuals who played the game.

In so doing it undermined cricket's democracy, the inclusiveness on which it staked its claim to be a national game. The new pavilion epitomised the prestigious institution which cricket had become, but it also increased social segregation at its headquarters. In 1903, Alfred D. Taylor, in *Annals of Lord's and History of the MCC*, mourned the passing of cricket's casual social interchange:

> The cobbler no longer associates with the Duke, or the farmer with the squire. The plebs that pays its shillings is marked off with painful distinction from the patricians who are entitled to higher honour. No longer do the masses mingle with society ... the game is robbed of its old world charm ... Lord's is Lord's no longer ... It is an amphitheatre for gladiatorial contests with its massive and mighty circle of seats, stands, boxes and buildings ... MCC is a club no longer: it is a national institution.

The old protest against enclosure had already been voiced by Lewis Carroll in his poem, 'The Deserted Parks', on the construction of a cricket ground on Oxford's ancient common land:

> The man of wealth and pride
> Takes up a space that many poor supplied;
> Space for the game, and all its instruments,
> Space for pavilions and for scorers' tents;
> The ball, that raps his shins in padding cased,
> Has wore the verdure to an arid waste;
> His Park, where these exclusive sports are seen,
> Indignant spurns the rustic from the green;
> While through the plain, consigned to silence all,
> In barren splendour flits the russet hall.

The missionary confidence of cricket in the Golden Age overwhelmed the voices of opposition. By the turn of the century, the superstructure of English and imperial cricket was in place. It was a magisterial edifice, embodying hierarchy and deference, social stasis and public self-confidence. The natural rulers were in their natural place (the new Lord's pavilion), dispensing cricket to the populace for the good of the nation.

English cricket had become an institution with an ideology, but not without resistance, not without casualties, and not without a host of uneasy compromises.

Cricket in the first half of the nineteenth century was still the cricket of All-Muggleton and Dingley Dell in *The Pickwick Papers*. It was popular, but there was little systematic competition. An air of festive exhibition hung about all the great matches. Single-wicket contests, matches of XI against XX or XXII, 'given' men and handicapping of various kinds gave cricket a circus-like ambience. Results mattered most to the gamblers. People came to see the great champions, Alfred Mynn, Nicholas 'Felix' Wanostrocht, Fuller Pilch. It was a jocular, picaresque pastime, an occasion to eat and drink, romanticized but not yet institutionalized.

Cricket did not acquire its special place in the national culture through an uncontested process of gradual evolution. It did so in reaction to an alien force thrown up by rapid social change, a force that threatened to seize cricket from the landowning elite and remake it in a new image. After 1832, England became, in the words of E.P. Thompson, 'a world in which the working class presence can be felt in every county ... and in most fields of life'. That presence was felt in cricket in the persons of William Clarke and his professional All-England XI.

Both Clarke and the All-England XI were born in Nottingham, a centre of the lace and hosiery industries and a Luddite and later Chartist stronghold. From the ranks of the artisans and piece-workers who had been playing cricket in the area since the late eighteenth century rose up successive generations of labour militants, asserting their right to the vote and to economic security.

In 1838, Clarke, an under-arm slow bowler whose style was considered antiquated but surprisingly effective in his own day, purchased the Trent Bridge pub and adjacent fields. The former bricklayer had acquired the necessary capital through years of hiring himself out to the elite as a professional cricketer. He enclosed the fields, laid out a pitch and charged 6d entrance. Eight profitable years later, he brought together the best professional cricketers in the land to form his travelling All-England XI, the first cricket side run strictly as a commercial concern. Until then, cricket professionals had worked on the ground staff at Lord's, as servants to private patrons, or as practice bowlers and groundsmen for universities and public schools. Now Clarke offered them summer-long employment as independent professionals. His recruits were mostly self-employed crafts- or tradesmen: butchers, tobacconists, glass blowers, cabinet makers, carpenters, braziers, printers, tailors, shoemakers. These skilled workers saw in cricket an opportunity for economic independence. Long before the cricket elite, they saw that there was a new market for the game.

The All-England XI played its first match in August 1846 against 'XX of Sheffield'. The next year they played matches in Manchester (where, it was reported, £30,000 in side-bets were placed), Liverpool, Leeds, York, Stockton, Sheffield, Birmingham and Newcastle. In 1848 they added Derby, Bradford, Walsall, Coventry, Sunderland, Darlington, Chelmsford and Southampton to their itinerary. For the next thirty years they played at least twenty matches a season, bringing top class cricket to growing industrial towns and cities across the country, well beyond cricket's traditional enclaves in the South, the East Midlands and Yorkshire. In their geographical reach and appeal to all classes, Clarke's All-England Xl and its imitators gave cricket's claims to be England's 'national sport' an anchor in reality. Between 1845 and 1875, the touring professional XIs provided the country's principal spectator sport. They certainly dominated gate-money cricket, showing how railways and newspapers could be used to exploit a market which their social superiors had ignored.

Clarke's XI was ostensibly run by a committee of professionals, but in reality it was a small business owned and managed by Clarke himself, and after his death by George Parr, the legside-hitting 'lion of the North'. Clarke distributed payments of three to five pounds to individual players according to his estimate of their standing with the public and their match performance. This was no workers' co-operative. The professionals remained individual freelancers and were paid as such. Newspapers turned them into famous names. Many sought to re-create themselves as entrepreneurs or small traders. Edgar Willsher, the pioneer over-arm bowler, a farmer's son from Kent, managed a cricket ground in Islington and a cricket outfitters in Lewisham. Tom Box, who started off as a cabinet maker, kept a hotel and cricket ground in Brighton while playing for Clarke. He ended up running a pub in Leicester Square.

In 1854, Clarke found himself in dispute with the MCC. Along with several fellow professionals, he declined to play in the Gentlemen v. Players match at Lord's because of a prior All-England commitment in Maidstone. Like the Packer rebels, the All-England men were accused of biting the hand that fed them. Ninety years later, Pelham Warner was still aggrieved: 'It is a pity that Clarke's great services to cricket were marred by an over-tenacity in asserting his rights, real or otherwise.'

The independent, rootless entrepreneurship of the itinerant professional XIs – untrammelled by loyalty to patron, county or club – posed a major threat to the cricket hierarchy. But from the beginning its limitations were apparent. The one-sided contests, the distorted matches against odds, the lack of systematic competition, meant that while they could whet the public appetite for cricket they could not satisfy it. In order to exploit their skills as cricketers in the market place, they had cut themselves loose from the old bonds, the old identities, but they failed to create new ones. The MCC and the ad hoc county clubs run by the local gentry chose all the players for the major representative fixtures. And without representative cricket, the professionals were compelled to compete among themselves in an entirely unregulated market. John Wisden, a Brighton-born fast round-arm bowler, broke with Clarke in 1852 and set up the United All-England XI. Over the next decade, half a dozen touring XIs were formed. Commercial competition was fierce and sometimes bred bitter rivalries.

Because they remained individual freelancers, the professionals were unable to develop a new model of nationwide competition or a means of stable management. In the end, Clarke's professionals had the mentality of the self-employed, and that made them easy meat for the establishment.

As a result of perceived slights and festering resentments, reflecting tensions over the new style of over-arm bowling and a growing divide between North and South, George Parr and his All-England comrades boycotted fixtures at Lord's and the Oval for several years in the 1860s. *The Times* was outraged:

> The cause of this unfortunate position of things is to be found in the too prosperous conditions of the players. So long as they can earn more money by playing matches against twenty-twos than by appearing at Lord's - so long as they can be 'mistered' in public houses, and stared at in railway stations, they will care little for being absent from the Metropolitan Ground, but they are wrong. They may be certain the 'Gentlemen' will not give way in this struggle.

In the 1860s, the MCC came under heavy fire from the press. The *Sporting Life* waged a campaign to replace it with a 'cricket parliament', a representative institution with decision-making meetings held in public. The idea was to prod the MCC into becoming cricket's upper house, something that did not happen for another century.

The MCC Committee was already viewed as an addled coven of old duffers. The Surrey Committee appealed to the MCC as 'the only true cricket club in the country' to 'travel out of their ordinary retinue'. The MCC was charged, even by its friends, with failing to respond to the social changes overtaking the country and the game, changes epitomized in the controversies surrounding over-arm bowling.

Round-arm bowling, legalized by the MCC amid much confusion in the 1830s, had at first reduced batsmen's scoring opportunities. But with so many balls off the wicket, it soon became easy for batsmen to know which ones to leave alone, so wicket-taking was also reduced. Inevitably, as batsmen conquered round-arm, the bowlers raised their arms higher. From at least 1857, Edgar Willsher, one of the stars of Clarke's All-England XI, had been defying the existing Law. No umpire, however, would call him. Then, in 1862, Willsher was no balled six times in succession by his old friend John Lillywhite, standing as an umpire in the England v. Surrey match at the Oval.

It was widely believed that Lillywhite acted at the behest of the amateur Surrey Committee. All the professionals in the England side walked off the field in protest, leaving Vyell Walker, the amateur captain, alone with the Surrey batsmen. Play resumed only the next day when Lillywhite was replaced. The controversy, however, continued to rage.

Bowling at this time was regarded as a form of manual labour, and as such had become a professionals' speciality. Over-arm bowling was a professional innovation, thanks to which cricket became once again a side-on game, in which bowlers and batsmen exploit the wicket-to-wicket axis. It made both batting and bowling more scientific. Along with better wickets and new, spliced bats, it raised the premium on skill.

Yet over-arm was fiercely resisted by members of the old guard. Their pre-eminent polemicist was the Reverend James Pycrott. He had played cricket at Oxford (where he helped re-establish the annual Varsity fixture in 1836) and published his 6d pamphlet *Principles of Scientific Batting* while still an undergraduate. At first he followed in his barrister father's footsteps, but in 1840, at the age of twenty-seven, he abandoned law for the church, taking up a curacy in the West Country.

In 1851, Pycroft published *The Cricket Field*, a compendium of history, lore and technical advice which contained the first printed reference to a specimen of behaviour not being 'cricket' – in this case, the dangerous fast bowling of Etonian and MCC member Harvey Fellows. In *The Cricket Field*, Pycroft sketched out what was to become the Victorian credo of the game:

A cricket field is a sphere of wholesome discipline and good order ... The game of cricket, philosophically considered, is a standing panegyric of the English character: none but an orderly and sensible race of people would so amuse themselves ... the game is essentially Anglo-Saxon. Foreigners have rarely, very rarely, imitated us. The English settlers everywhere play at cricket; but of no single club have we ever heard dieted either with frogs, sauerkraut or macaroni.

The book proved popular, going through nine editions (including an American one in 1859) in four decades. A few years after its publication, Pycroft abandoned his curacy, took up residence in Bath and devoted himself to literature and cricket. He penned popular instructional works on Greek and Latin as well as novels and memoirs. He was much in demand as a lecturer and was well rewarded for talking to middle-class audiences about the virtues and vices of cricket.

In 1864, he brought his recent lectures together in a volume entitled *Cricketana*, which harps repeatedly on the dangers of legalizing over arm bowling. 'We see no check or limit to the rough play that will ensue,' Pycroft argued. 'The ball will often rise as high as the face of the batsman.' He feared that the batsman would soon be forced 'to pad even his elbow' (and so it has proved). In an anticipation of criticisms made of recent West Indies sides, he foresaw 'tall, strong fellows, pelting down most pitilessly, as mechanically as a catapult, with every ball about the same'.

But Pycroft was no champion of the round-arm style, which he regarded as 'unnatural'; it had discouraged batsmen from playing straight and deprived bowling of 'spin and variety'. His answer was to de-legalize round-arm and go back to under-arm, which was 'true bowling' with a 'natural' action. He also wanted to see better-prepared wickets (like those at the Oval and unlike the notorious rough pitches at Lord's).

His opposition to over-arm bowling was part of his wider critique of professionalism. 'The game is becoming too professional or too much a matter of routine and business, and too little a matter of mind and manoeuvre and of every kind of dodge and keen judgement.' He proposed that the MCC and Surrey refuse to select professionals from the major itinerant XIs. In a foretaste of the contempt that was to be heaped on the Packer 'circus' a century later, Pycroft wrote scornfully of the great annual contests between the All-England XI and the United All-England XI: 'Very much like the "four-and-ninepenny hat shop" versus the "true original four-and-ninepenny hat shop" which after months of recriminating abuse to attract partisans for each party proved both to belong to the same smart Barnum of a man.'

'Pycroft feared that what he called 'free trade in cricket' was lessening the powers of the game's traditional rulers. He inveighed against 'a style of cricket which is becoming a very serious nuisance, as superseding those annual contests between rival counties which used to be fought with a degree of spirit and emulation without which cricket deserves not the name'. To Pycroft, the itinerant XIs promoted 'the cheapest kind of immortality' and he hit at their weak spot, the unrepresentative nature of the cricket they played: 'For any men calling themselves cricketers to play with double numbers, year after year, as a match, and to boast of victory, the thing is childish and absurd ... A flat, stale, spiritless game- no honour for the one to win, no discredit to the other to lose.'

As a result of playing too many matches ('he does not play for the score, he plays for the till'), the professional is 'fagged and jaded – stale and over-done ... the powder and the spirit is out ...' Professional cricketers were 'a remarkably respectable set of men' but too often spoiled by 'feasting and flattery and a sudden elevation to a degree of intimacy with those above them - an intimacy unknown save amidst the warm enthusiasms and genial fellowship of the sporting world'.

Pycroft accused the professionals of over-cautiousness in both batting and bowling. Even though they were regularly and heavily beating the amateurs at this time, the Reverend insisted: 'The Players, though decidedly superior on the whole, are not as superior to the Gentlemen in real cricket as the score would represent ... There is more invention in their play and while it lasts it is infinitely better worth seeing.'

Pycroft singled out for praise the young prodigy, EM Grace, then playing as an 'amateur' for the All-England XI. 'He plays for the sport and not for a livelihood,' Pycroft claimed, and this, he believed, was the secret of his willingness to improvise and entertain. The following year, 1865, EM's younger brother WG made his first-class debut.

Not surprisingly, Pycroft was strongly opposed to the cricket parliament:

Men who meet, big with their own importance, and proud of their first suit of 'little brief authority', if they find nothing to settle, will find something to unsettle; so jaw, jar and discord will be the order of the day. As to harmonising fixtures and programmes of matches, 'in the name of the Prophet, FIGS!' a Committee of the whole House will not settle such things by Doomsday.

Pycroft had great faith in cricket's unwritten constitution. 'No laws can comprise everything that should be done or left undone.' Behaviour in cricket would be best restrained by the abiding principles of 'fair play' and the supervision of 'gentlemen'. In this as in so many of his prejudices, he was the spiritual great-grand-father of Swanton and Woodcock, Trevor Bailey and Christopher Martin-Jenkins.

The MCC resisted the calls for a cricket parliament. It wrote to the *Sporting Life* that its members saw no reason 'to depart from the course which they have pursued in the spirit of cricket through all the difficulties since the first year of their existence in 1787'. But, a few months later, in June of 1864, they did agree to legalize over-arm bowling. In so doing they preserved their status as the arbiters and overlords of the game. They knew better than Pycroft that to do anything else would have been to cede control to other forces.

Pycroft called the MCC 'the great central power, the very balance wheel of the world-wide machinery of cricket', but he lamented the fact that it was 'tied to time and place; its circuit is limited'. It was therefore the wrong body to deal with the cricket crisis engendered by the rise of the professionals and their practice of over-arm bowling. 'The exigencies of the country in these railway days required some club of equal strength and standing, but moveable and ubiquitous withal. It wanted an amateur All-England XI.'

Something like that amateur All-England XI already existed in the form of a private, itinerant cricket club called I Zingari ('the gypsies' in Italian). For Pycroft, 'the Zingari are as much entitled to be consulted on cricket law as any club whatever – we think more'. If the MCC was to be the Commons of cricket then Zingari, Pycroft thought, should be the Lords.

I Zingari had been founded at a London dinner party on 5 July 1845 by a group of Old Harrovians. They adopted as club colours black, red and gold ('out of darkness, through fire, into light') and dedicated themselves to the cause of amateur cricket. By pledging themselves to field an all-amateur side they hoped to remedy the dearth of amateur bowlers, which gave the professionals the upper hand in the annual Gentlemen v. Players matches. Harvey Fellows, the Etonian whose round-arm fast bowling had been condemned by Pycroft, was one of the first products of the Zingari regime. In 1907, he was buried wearing his I Zingari tie.

From the beginning, the club was self-consciously exclusive, so exclusive that it banned any formal subscription. Membership was by invitation only. An amazingly enduring organization, I Zingari became an inner circle within the inner circle of the MCC, a kind of freemasonry linking key individuals in the cricket, political and financial elites. Lords Harris and Hawke were members, as were AC MacLaren, the Lytteltons and FS Jackson (who played his Tests for England in an I Zingari cap). Edward Chandos-Leigh (Harrow, Oxford), barrister, QC, Counsel to the Speaker for twenty years and MCC President in the jubilee year of 1887, regularly sported an I Zingari ribbon in his bowler hat. Alongside the famous cricketers, the club has always counted leading bankers, stockbrokers, barristers and Royalty among its members.

In initiating a new, exclusively amateur type of cricket, I Zingari was as path-breaking in its own way as Clarke's All-England XI. In the decades that followed, a host of travelling amateur clubs followed in its footsteps: Quidnuncs, Harlequins, Free Foresters, Incogniti, and dozens of public school Old Boys clubs. Nevertheless, the Zingari must have been a disappointment to Pycroft. Rather than displacing the MCC, they chose to infiltrate it. Rather than expelling the professionals and their innovatory bowling, they chose to incorporate them.

In 1863, a twenty-nine-year-old barrister and Zingari enthusiast, RA Fitzgerald (Harrow, Cambridge), became the MCC's new Honorary Secretary. Fitzgerald had been nominated by one of the founders of I Zingari, Sir Frederick Ponsonby (Harrow, Cambridge), later the Sixth Earl of Bessborough. A barrister who sat as a Liberal in the Lords, Ponsonby, descended from an old Whig family with large holdings in Ireland, later headed Gladstone's Commission on Ireland, which led to the Irish Land Bill of 1881. Throughout his life he was a major patron of cricket, coaching at Harrow and helping to found and fund Surrey CCC.

Frederick's brother, Sir Spencer Ponsonby Fane (Harrow, Cambridge), was also a founder of I Zingari and served for decades as its Honorary Secretary and Governor. Elected a member of the MCC in 1840 at the age of sixteen, he later played for Surrey, Middlesex, the Gentlemen and between 1858 and 1862, for 'Ireland'. As a member of the MCC Committee from 1866 until 1878 and then as Treasurer from 1879 till his death in 1915, he was a key figure at Lord's when it was at the zenith of its prestige and power. The new pavilion, which he formally opened, featured a caricature of him in terracotta on one of the corbels. As a high-ranking civil servant, he served as private secretary to a succession of Foreign Secretaries, including Palmerston, Clarendon (who was MCC President in 1871) and Granville. He also retained a brace of City directorships and kept up family estates in Ireland and Somerset.

Among Fitzgerald's backers at Lord's was another founder member of I Zingari, Robert Grimston (Harrow, Oxford), fourth son of the Earl of Verulam and grandson of the Earl of Liverpool. Grimston gave up his career at the bar to become Chairman of the International Telegraph Company and later a Director of Anglo-American Telegraph. The *Dictionary of National Biography* describes Grimston, MCC President in 1883 and an influential figure at Lord's for over thirty years, as 'a Tory ... averse to change of all kinds'. Another I Zingari founder and key member of the new Lord's elite was William Nicholson (Harrow, Cambridge), a gin magnate who became MCC President in 1879. He also owned land in Hampshire, of which he was High Sheriff, and sat as an MP for Petersfield.

Along with legalizing over-arm, Fitzgerald and his supporters set in train other urgently-needed reforms. When the Lord's leasehold came up for sale in 1860 MCC had not even bid for it. Six years later, Fitzgerald convinced the Committee to purchase the lease, at three times the 1860 price. The money was lent to the club, at 5 per cent interest, by William Nicholson. Lord Suffield, that year's MCC President, argued that the club should model itself on the Jockey Club and become 'a central authority and a playing headquarters' which would 'benefit cricket of all classes'. The Marylebone Professional Cricketers Fund was set up to aid players who 'during their career shall have conducted themselves to the entire satisfaction of the Committee of the MCC'.

In 1868, Fitzgerald was made the MCC's first paid Secretary, at an annual salary of £400. During his thirteen years in charge of the club, MCC hired its first groundsman and installed its first practice nets. The old pavilion was enlarged, a new tavern was built and the first public grandstand rose, courtesy of a private subscription. Press accommodation was constructed. The ground was levelled and returfed. A mowing machine replaced the flocks of sheep which had nibbled the stubble at Lord's for generations. In 1870, the heavy roller was introduced. Club membership rose from 650 to 2,000. Taking a leaf out of the professionals' books, Fitzgerald increased admission charges for the annual Harrow v. Eton and Varsity matches and hired police to control the crowds. Orange and yellow, variants on the Zingari stripes, were adopted as the MCC colours.

Fitzgerald's greatest contribution to the endurance of the MCC may well have been the recruitment of the phenomenal young all-rounder, WG Grace. Fitzgerald thus ensured that WG remained, technically, within the amateur ranks – even as he was touring the country with the professional United South of England XI. Playing for MCC, WG drew crowds to Lord's and boosted the fortunes of the Gentlemen on the field of play. Before WG, they had won seven out of their thirty-five matches with the Players. In the fifty contests which followed his match-winning debut in 1865, they triumphed thirty-one times, with WG scoring fifteen hundreds and taking 271 wickets.

In 1865, the Committee was expanded from sixteen to twenty-four by the addition of ex-officio members, including the five Trustees, the President, the Secretary and the Treasurer. Presidents nominated their successors, who were always drawn from active Committee members. Only four Committee members were elected each year, of whom the retiring President was always one. The Committee became effectively self-selecting and self-perpetuating. Recruitment from above remained the rule.

The cornerstone of this amazingly clubable, unashamedly hierarchical system was MCC's custodianship of the Laws of Cricket. Like the English judiciary, the MCC dressed its authority in the trappings of antiquity. The club was alleged to be 'disinterested', like the Law Lords or the monarchy; on assuming the MCC Presidency in 1873, the Earl of Cadogan described the job as 'the woolsack of cricket'. The club undertook a systematic revision of the Laws in 1883, and for the first time boundaries became a formal requirement. Cricket had travelled far from its origins in common land.

The MCC became more selective about the uses to which it allowed its ground to be put. There were no more pony races, clowns or army drills. Racquet sports such as tennis, which could be practised in private, away from the eyes of the multitude, were preferred. The boys hawking tankards of beer in the open stands were banished, along with the gamblers. No more would bookies roam the boundary shouting the odds. The money changers had been chased from the temple. Soon, all-white clothing became *de rigueur* at Lord's. It was attire befitting a solemn national ritual.

The ramshackle, mismanaged MCC of 1860 had become an embarrassment to the elite. Under Fitzgerald and his successors, it underwent a gradual transformation, similar to transformations taking place at the same time in other English institutions. The church, army and civil service all purged themselves in this period. The old free booting merchants and soldiers of the East India Company were replaced, after the 1857 Mutiny, by the direct rule of the Indian Civil Service and the imperial bureaucracy. Not long after, the haphazard, informal rule of Lord's gave way to a rational MCC structure and the codification of its right to govern. Between 1864 and the end of the century, the average age of MCC presidents and committeemen rose from the mid-thirties to the mid-fifties.

In 1888, proposals to run a railway through Lord's were blocked by cricket's friends in Parliament. The market which had created Lord's was being pushed back. It was becoming inviolable territory. The next year, MCC purchased the Lord's freehold with money advanced by Nicholson and began work on the new pavilion.

In 1898, Francis Lacey (Sherborne, Cambridge), another barrister, became MCC Secretary. He had been nominated for the post by Ponsonby Fane. Lacey set up a system of sub-committees and introduced into the MCC the Civil Service-style culture of officiousness and secrecy for which it became notorious. Within the next decade, the MCC established formal control over both county and Test cricket.

Throughout this period, the landowners remained dominant at the MCC, as they did in Parliament. The Earl of Sefton, one of the MCC's first Trustees, owned 20,000 acres in Lancashire. The Earl of Verulam, MCC President in 1867, owned 14,000 acres in Hertfordshire. The Duke of Beaufort (Eton), President of MCC in 1877, owned 52,000 acres, mostly in Gloucestershire. Lord George Hamilton (Harrow), MCC President in 1881, owned 157,000 acres. The Tory MP, WH Long (Harrow, Oxford), MCC President in 1906, owned 15,000 acres in Wiltshire.

The MCC Presidents and Committee men combined interests in land with multiple directorships in the City and a hunger for speculative profit. They forged a close alliance with booze merchants like Nicholson. The Walker family of Southgate, prominent amateur cricketers and MCC members, owed their fortune to brewing, which sustained a stately home and private cricket ground in Southgate. Vyell Walker (MCC President in 1891) had been the amateur captain left alone on the field at the Oval when the professionals walked out over the no-balling of Willsher. His five brothers also played cricket and several served on the MCC Committee.

The landowners, financiers and alcohol kingpins were joined by an array of professionals, notably barristers. Sir Henry James (MCC President in 1885) was a QC and judge before becoming Gladstone's Attorney General. AL Smith (Eton, Cambridge, MCC President in 1899) was Lord Justice of Appeal and later Master of the Rolls. The England batsman-wicket-keeper, Alfred Lyttelton (Eton, Cambridge, MCC President in 1898), also a QC, served as private secretary to James when he was Attorney General and later Recorder of Hereford and Oxford. Lyttelton was also Gladstone's nephew and successively brother-in-law of Asquith and Balfour. From 1900 until 1913, Viscount Alverstone, an MCC Committee member, presided as Lord Chief Justice.

Although there were few clergy on the MCC Committee, large numbers played as amateurs and maintained MCC membership. One in three Oxbridge cricket blues between 1860 and 1900 (209 amateur cricketers) took holy orders. Fifty-nine of these played county cricket. Seven became bishops. Catholics or non-conformists were rare. This was the Church of England at play and it provided English cricket with ideologists and missionaries. Among the latter was the England cricketer, CT Studd (Eton, Cambridge), who served the church in China and India and played for the Gentlemen of India in 1902. As a vicar in Kennington, HH Montgomery (Harrow, Cambridge) praised the Oval's 'vast, good-humoured, happy crowd impartially cheering successes and failures'. Later, he took the gospel of cricket to Tasmania, where he was bishop for nearly twenty years.

The cricket elite was well placed in both the military and colonial hierarchies. Hamilton, Earl Spencer, and WH Long became First Lords of the Admiralty. Hamilton also served as Secretary of State for India. Long and Alfred Lyttelton became Secretaries of State for the Colonies. Lord Lansdowne (Eton, Oxford, MCC President in 1869) served as Governor General of Canada, Viceroy of India, Secretary of State for War and Secretary of State for Foreign Affairs. Viscount Downe (Eton, Oxford, MCC President in 1872) was a major general who served in India and fought in the Zulu and Boer Wars.

Like the Ponsonbys, many of the cricket elite had interests in Ireland. Spencer was twice Lord Lieutenant of Ireland, in which capacity he helped suppress the Fenians in the 1880s. Long was Chief Secretary for Ireland. Lansdowne's Irish house was burnt to the ground by Republicans in 1922. Perry Anderson has remarked that Britain's military officers and colonial officials tended to come from 'the neediest and least reputable branch of the ruling class, its Anglo-Irish extension, which provided most of Britain's leading commanders down even to a century later'. Among the latter was Field Marshal Montgomery, son of HH, the Bishop of Tasmania, who had played cricket for Ireland in 1867 and 1868 and who died on the family estate in Donegal in 1932.

In every respect, including the Irish connection, the cricket elite of the late nineteenth century was the direct descendant of the clique that met at the Star and Garter in 1784. It was also an uncannily precise mirror of the broader elite which ran the country as a whole, knitted together by a shared public-school culture. Forty-nine per cent of MCC Committee members in this period went either to Eton or Harrow and 57 per cent to Oxford or Cambridge. Among the presidents, secretaries and treasurers, these proportions were even higher.

Obviously, the MCC spurned workers of all kinds, not to mention trade unionists or radicals, and there were few industrialists. The rare exceptions prove the rule. They were tradesmen who had remade themselves as gentlemen of landed leisure. Marcus Samuel explained that he had sold his Shell oil company to the Dutch because he preferred 'horses, gardens, angling and watching cricket in comfort' to the trials of business.

In characteristically English fashion, the MCC managed during this period to increase its overall membership without compromising its exclusivity or social status. In 1877, 330 of the club's 2,300 members were titled; ten years later, there were about the same number of titles among a membership of 5,000. Yet at least 30 per cent of the MCC Committee remained titled throughout the 1860-to-1914 era. Thus MCC always retained an aristocratic ethos, no matter how many parvenus it admitted. Money itself was never the decisive factor. The £3 annual subscription was unchanged from 1856 to 1948. To join the MCC, you had to have *connections* (public-school connections).

Though cricket develops in and through an industrial society, it does so under the aegis of non-industrial classes. These classes made English cricket in their own image – and that image was never one of market-supremacy. Unlike industrialists, they remained at a safe distance from the market's vicissitudes. Their fortunes were, of course, entirely dependent on it, but their relation to it was an institutional one, mediated through the City. This profit-at-one remove experience provided the elite with the model on which they ran English cricket. Their hands-on approach to ruling the country and the empire meant that they rarely let slip MCC's control of the game; their hands-off approach to the market meant that they rarely intervened to organize the game at the base of society.

Between 1860 and 1914, 57 per cent of the MCC Committee members were Conservatives and 37 per cent Liberal. Nearly all of the latter became Liberal Unionists following the break-up of Gladstone's coalition in the 1880s. Significantly, it was Irish Home Rule that precipitated the split. Clarendon, Lansdowne, Nicholson, Lyttelton, James, Wenlock and Suffield, all MCC Presidents and prominent politicians, opposed Home Rule (many had land in Ireland) and moved over to Liberal Unionism and in some cases ultimately to the Tories. As with the movement of the rich Whigs into Pitt's ministry in 1792, the rightward shift of the cricket elite following 1885 mirrored a broader recomposition of the English ruling class, which faced an increasingly assertive working class. By the end of the century, the MCC had become overwhelmingly Conservative, dedicated to the Tory truisms of constitutional royalism, the supremacy of private property and the expansion of empire.

The aim of the Zingari clique which had assumed control of the MCC in the 1860s was to resist the take-over of the game by the professionals. To do that they had to ensure cricket remained a game, not a business. Paradoxically, that meant they had to insist it was 'more than a game', and therefore above the exigencies of the market. In 1904, Andrew Lang declared: 'Marylebone is the Omphalos, the Delos of cricket.' Cricket had become a cult. The MCC Committee were its priests and Lord's was its cathedral.

AN Hornby, one of Francis Thompson's immortal 'run-stealers', forever flickering 'to and fro', was a free-scoring amateur batsman in the classic mould. His father, whose cotton-manufacturing family had married into Lancashire land, sat as the Tory MP for Blackburn until removed from Parliament following a bribery charge. His brother, EK Hornby, who played for the Gentlemen of the North in 1862, immediately reclaimed the seat with an increased majority, and later became the first Baronet Hornby.

Coached by Frederick Ponsonby, the young AN was a star bat at Harrow. Pycroft watched him play at Lord's against Eton in 1863, and foretold that he and the other 'successful batsmen' of the day would 'remember their score – aye, and not be above talking of it, however high their honours at the bar or the senate, till their dying day'. Hornby went on to captain the England side that lost the famous Oval Test to the Australians in 1882. Against Spofforth, the world's first complete over-arm fast bowler, England were unable to make the 85 runs needed to win. The next day the famous notice appeared in the *Sporting Times* announcing the death of English cricket: 'The body will be cremated and the ashes taken to Australia.' Thus, one of cricket's most celebrated traditions was invented as a sour comment on an English cricketing failure.

At the newly-formed Lancashire CCC, the neatly moustachioed and brilliantined Hornby was, in the words of the 1879 *Lillywhite*, 'the life and soul of the team'. He was a hard hitter with strokes all around the wicket, but his calling for quick singles sometimes confused his batting partners. *Lillywhite* noted that Hornby's 'impetuosity' had often cost the team the wicket of his fellow opener, 'the patient Barlow'. For fifteen years, off and on, Hornby captained Lancashire, and was elected club President in 1894, while still playing. At old Trafford in 1899 he whipped a reporter who had dared to criticize his tactics. He retired from active cricket that year at the age of fifty-two, but remained President of the club for another twenty-two years. In 1903 he forced the amateur fast bowler Walter Brearley out of the side after the latter had aired opinions with which Hornby disagreed. 'The press have been against me,' he complained, but insisted, 'As long as I am President of this club I will not tolerate bad behaviour on or off the cricket field by any player.'

The gospel of amateur cricket which Hornby had imbibed at Harrow became the theology of the public schools. As the nineteenth century progressed, the transition from childhood to adulthood was elongated. 'Puberty' became a 'problem'. The upper and middle classes contracted this 'problem' out to the public schools. Games, especially cricket, were a means of preserving some of the non-utilitarian pleasures of the child's world in the brusquely utilitarian world of the adult. For the burgeoning public schools, they formed a bridge spanning the mysterious gulf separating the two. In the 1870s, the old-school tie and old boys' rituals first appear: a proud and novel projection of adolescent loyalties into the adult world.

Cricket became an exercise in character-building, which was rated more highly by the public schools than mere academic excellence. JEC Welldon, Harrow headmaster between 1881 and 1895, explained:

> The pluck, the energy, the perseverance, the good temper, the self-control, the discipline, the co-operation, the esprit de corps, which merit success in cricket or football, are the very qualities which win the day in peace or war ... In the history of the British empire, it is written that England has owed her sovereignty to her sports.

Cricket was seen in England as a preparation for the greater games of war and empire. Elsewhere, sport was seen as play, as childish indulgence, and the belief that it was a serious affair was regarded as characteristically English. CB Fry declared: 'cricket is a cult and a philosophy inexplicable to the *profanum vulgus* ... the merchant-minded ... and the unphysically intellectual'. The ugliness of Fry's public school philistinism was starkly revealed by his later attempts to organize paramilitary-style youth training and his dalliance with Nazism. 'The Nazi ideal of education,' he noted admiringly, 'definitely places health and character in front of mere intellectual learning.'

In emphasizing 'character', the amateur elite played down the virtues of competitiveness and partisanship, and often presented them as vices peculiar to professionals and the lower orders. They feared that a cricket meritocracy would make ability, rather than social status, the dominant value of the 'national' game. The free market of sport and the democratic premises of cricket were curtailed and compromised by an amateur code that claimed to embody values transcending mere winning and losing.

The Victorian ethic of team sport was deeply paradoxical. The individual was subordinated to the team but the team itself was subordinate to the overriding dictates of 'fair play'. Winning was not all-important, even if the game itself was. 'Playing the game', submitting to the Laws and the authority of the umpire, giving the benefit of the doubt to opponents, had nothing to do with not caring about winning or about personal success, both of which remained the driving forces in every game of cricket, then as now. Losing graciously was a way of saying not only that there were higher and more important games to win but that those who lost in those higher and more important games – economics, politics, empire – must also accept the verdict of the system. In this way a savagely competitive and unequal domestic and world order was cloaked in the mystical raiments of 'fair play' and the rule of law.

In becoming 'more than a game' under the aegis of the amateurs, cricket acquired not only a moral, but also an aesthetic justification. In 1897, Fry's great friend Ranjitsinjhi declared, 'There is much more in a fine on-drive or a well-bowled ball than the resulting four or wicket.' In the 'Golden Age' of 1895-1914, style was supreme. The model amateur batsman combined elegance and power. His play appeared 'effortless', a telling adjective. The off-drive, transmuting the pace of the bowler into its opposite through timing and footwork, was the consummate expression of this aesthetic. How you looked became as important as how many you scored. And the counterposition of the aesthetic to the utilitarian was frequently seen as a question of class.

Off-side play became an amateur fetish in the 1880s. A generation of public-school batsmen were taught that hitting the ball for runs on the leg side was not the done thing. These 'bread-and-butter' strokes were for professionals; gentlemen were expected to disdain such vulgarity. Fry and other amateurs railed against this bizarre taboo (not least because of the advantages it gave professional bowlers). And in the next generation Ranji's leg glance came to sum up the delicacy, ease and elegance of the Golden Age. But the on-side taboo endured in folk memory. In a county match in the 1990s, a promising young Yorkshire batsman, Michael Vaughan, played a shot to midwicket. Dicky Bird, the umpire, asked him cheekily if he could balance that with a shot to the off side. Vaughan obliged and turned to Bird: 'Posh-side, all right, ump?'

The sheer irrationality of the on-side taboo tells us a great deal about the nature of the divide between gentlemen and players. Dressing rooms were strictly segregated. There were separate entrances to the field (the grand entrance through the pavilion's central gate was reserved for amateurs), separate travel, accommodation and dining arrangements, even separate tables and menus for meals taken during lunch intervals. These facilities were not only separate, but unequal in every respect. They symbolized the static hierarchy which the amateurs imposed on the democratic fluidity of cricket.

From the 1880s, county and Test captaincy became the preserve of amateurs, even when it meant appointing as captain the least experienced, least effective player on the field. In cricket, mental labour, and with it the exercise of leadership, were made the prerogatives of those who exercised leadership off the field. Amateurs were addressed by professionals as Sir or Mr at all times. Omitting this courtesy could result in a fine or dismissal. The amateurs, in turn, addressed the professionals by their surnames alone. Match reports and score cards denoted amateur status by placing the cricketer's initials before the surname. As with the taboo against on-side hitting, the sheer arbitrariness of the distinction hints at the reality of the gentleman/player dichotomy: that it had little to do with whether or not you made your living from cricket.

Indeed, for many decades, the distinction was ambiguous, and not of great concern to anyone, perhaps because it was considered self evident in a society so sharply divided between the haves and the have nots. The Earl of Aboyne, for instance, appeared for the Players against the Gentlemen at Lord's in 1819, for the simple reason that he had bet on them. A direct financial investment obviously made the Players 'his' side. But that did not stop him from becoming MCC President in 1821 or playing for the Gentlemen in 1827.

Defining and enforcing amateur status became a concern only in the 1860s and '70s, when the elite were reasserting their old authority against the professionals. GF Grace was excluded from the Gentlemen's side at Lord's in the 1870s because he had received money for playing with the United South of England XI. In 1878, the MCC at last defined amateur status: 'No gentleman ought to make a profit by his services in the cricket field, and that for the future, no cricketer who takes more than his expenses in any match shall be qualified to play for the Gentlemen against the Players at Lord's.'

But the 'expenses' allowed gentlemen cricketers – the costs of the first-class travel, hotels, drink and dining which they regarded as appropriate to their social status – could cost promoters a pretty penny. Touring Australia in 1887-88, Arthur Shrewsbury, the greatest professional batsman of the day, complained that 'the expenses of each amateur member of Lord Harris's team was more than double those of any one of the professionals'.

As fixture lists grew and competition increased, it became harder for amateurs to dedicate sufficient time to the game to keep pace with the professionals. In order to preserve the gentlemen/players dichotomy, 'shamateurism' grew up.

It was widely observed that the leading amateur captains were actually 'professionals in disguise'. The Lancashire captain, AC MacLaren (Harrow), regarded by many as the incarnation of swashbuckling amateur batsmanship, was employed by his County Committee as a 'cricket instructor' and 'Assistant Secretary' at £450 per annum, twice what the club's leading professionals received. MacLaren also stipulated that he was to play in all the county's first-class fixtures, a guarantee denied professionals. When he threatened to move to Hampshire, Lancashire improved its terms, making him the club's 'Assistant Treasurer'.

Though an amateur, the England batsman and Surrey captain WW Read was the best-paid cricketer on the county's staff, thanks to the salary he received as the club's Assistant Secretary. In 1884 the Surrey Committee voted to pay the stock exchange entrance fee for MP Bowden, their nineteen-year-old amateur batsman-wicket keeper. Bowden went to South Africa with CA Smith's side in 1888-89 and stayed there. He tried his hand at liquor running and died in Rhodesia in 1892 after falling from a cart.

All the leading amateurs enjoyed testimonials which were often more profitable than the benefits staged for professionals. Lord Harris himself was presented with a 400-guinea candelabra in 1882. In 1895, the Surrey Committee donated £200 to Read's testimonial, but only £50 to professional Bobby Abel's benefit. Fry received a motor car from Sussex in 1904. Lord Hawke was given jewellery worth £1,842 in 1908.

The most flagrant and successful of all shamateurs was WG Grace, who was estimated to have earned £120,000 (equivalent to more than £1 million today) from the game during his forty-three-year career. Gloucester paid him £50 a match, plus handsome expenses. He received £1,500 plus expenses for the 1873-74 Australian tour (the professionals got £170 plus expenses). Eighteen years later he asked for and received £3,000 for going back. In 1895, at the age of forty-seven, he hit 2,346 runs, averaged 51 and became the first man to score a thousand runs in May and the first to hit a hundred hundreds. That year the *Daily Telegraph* raised £4,000 for him though a National Shilling Testimonial, an MCC appeal raised another £3,000 and the Duke of Beaufort's Gloucestershire appeal a further £1,500.

The Graces were a middle-class professional family seeking respectability through cricket and its association with the elite. But WG himself attended neither public school nor university. He took ten years to qualify as a doctor – long after he had achieved fame as a cricketer. Respectability demanded that a gentleman cricketer maintain an outside profession. But the expense of this profession was borne by WG's cricket patrons, who had to pay a locum to run his medical practice.

Wisden described his case as 'an anomalous one': 'The work he has done in popularising cricket outweighs a hundredfold every other consideration ... nice customs curtsey to great kings.'

WG was indeed an anomaly, but not in his shamateurism, which was only an extreme example of common practice. Unkempt, unwashed, gluttonous, exuberantly competitive and a notorious cheat, WG brought into the urban world of the late nineteenth century a rural, yeoman aura a hint of a past that was vanishing before people's eyes. For that, the elite patronized him and the public adored him. However, he was never invited to join I Zingari, did not captain England until his tenth Test appearance in 1888 and was not asked to captain the Gentlemen at Lord's until the 1890s.

Amateur status was clearly not simply about having money. The great fear of penurious amateur cricketers was that if they turned professional they would lose social status and the privileges that went with it. As a result, very few crossed the line. County clubs were usually willing to make discreet arrangements to enable their amateurs to stay amateur. Being an amateur implied having 'private means', that is, access to capital without recourse to labour. The model for all affluence was landed leisure. No matter how you had accumulated your wealth, you were still expected to behave as if it was inherited and unearned.

For the cricket amateur, to play cricket for a living, to turn the game into a species of labour, was demeaning. The trappings of amateurism – the emphasis on 'style', the muffling of the competitive strife of the game in 'fair play' – were attempts to redefine the 'manliness' associated with the game (and the English) in ways that suited those who did not work with their bodies. Talented young amateurs could while away whole summers as country-house guests with unlimited access to a cornucopia of food, drink and tobacco. Their only expenses would be fares, tips to servants and cricket-bat oil. All this left the amateurs, in the end, as dependent on the patronage of the rich as the professionals.

The hypocrisy that sustained amateur status was affectionately but knowingly satirized by EW Hornung in his tales of Raffles, the England slow bowler and 'amateur cracksman'. In one story, Raffles takes umbrage at being treated by his country-house hosts as if he were a *professional* cricketer. In revenge, he breaks his code of honour and steals their jewels. Hornung's friend and fellow cricket devotee, Arthur Conan Doyle (who played for MCC), was distressed that a thief should be portrayed in fiction as a gentleman cricketer and a hero, but in Raffles Hornung captured the parasitism of amateur cricket, and the cleavage between appearance and reality which propped up the national institution which the game had become.

In keeping itself at a safe distance from the stresses and strains of industrial life, the elite contrived a cult of ruralism which was (and still is) mimicked by the middle and professional classes in the suburbs. From at least the 1860s, cricket was seen by these classes as a refuge from the new hordes in the cities. Amateurism was part of a wider revolt against industrialism and its extreme division of labour.

> It is not, truly speaking, the labour that is divided, but the men – divided into mere segments of men-broken into small fragments and crumbs of life ... the great cry that rises from all our manufacturing cities, louder than their furnace blast, is all in very deed for this – that we manufacture everything there except men.

Thus Ruskin, whose books sold in large numbers to a middle-class audience seeking escape from the crassly commercial world which had spawned it. But the more Ruskin thought about it, the more convinced he became that only co-operative socialism could make human beings whole again. The cricket elite had other ideas. Through the amateur code, it seized control of the 'national' game. The virtues of a protected masculinity – encased in pads and gloves and 'fair play' – became national virtues. The national character, as embodied in the cricket cult, became the property of a particular type of English person: the 'gentleman', whom Ruskin scathingly defined as 'a man living in idleness on other people's labour'.

Cricket was unique among the gate-money sports of the late-Victorian era in encompassing amateur and professional in one competitive structure. By 1900, top-class football had been taken over by professionals. Rugby suffered a schism over the issue. Hockey, tennis and athletics were strictly amateur. Cricket's origins in an earlier age enabled it to house both amateur and professional within a single stately home, but they also ensured that within this mansion, 'upstairs' and 'downstairs' remained strictly demarcated.

Hornby's opening partner, the stonewalling RG Barlow, was for twenty years a model Lancashire professional, a teetotaller and non-smoker. Bolton-born, he worked as a moulder in the Staveley ironworks in Derbyshire, where he played against the All-England XI and thus came to the notice of the Lancashire Committee. As a defensive batsman, he was the perfect complement to the stroke making Hornby. Twice in county matches he occupied the crease for two and a half hours for only five runs. In 1876, *Lillywhite* observed: 'It is constantly said by spectators that they do not care to see Barlow play. To our mind, they are thereby paying him a great compliment, for if the onlookers are wearied, what must be the feelings of opposing bowlers?'

He was also a crafty left-arm medium-pacer who took 5 for 19 in the 'Ashes' Test at the Oval in 1882. For a time, he was second only to WG as the country's outstanding all-rounder. But in 1892, Lancashire decided Barlow was past his best and dropped him from the side. Barlow protested. The Committee then dismissed him for 'lack of courtesy'. At their next Annual General Meeting, Lancashire members voted by 200-4 to support the Committee's action. Barlow repaired to the Lancashire League and played as a professional there for another seven years. He also worked for many years as a first-class umpire. In 1908, Lancashire, under Hornby's presidency, appointed Barlow ground manager at £200 a year 'with house, gas and coal'. But the great stonewaller left the job after nine months, tired of the peremptory demands of the amateur Committee men.

The contrasting fortunes of the most famous opening partnership in poetry neatly illustrate the obscene gulf between the gentlemen and the players on which the triumphs of the Golden Age were predicated. The containment of the working class, the repression of the haughty professionals, went hand in hand with the rise of county and Test cricket. One could not have happened without the other.

During this period the rules governing qualification for county sides were gradually tightened. These measures were in part an attempt to make the county competition more meaningful to spectators. There had to be some sense in which the personnel of a team 'belonged' to the county. But where football evolved a transfer system in which 'belonging' was defined by a business-style contract, cricket preferred to define it by birth or residence, tying players to the land and wrenching them from the national market. Their freelance status was undermined and their bargaining power reduced. County cricket became a cartel: an agreement among ostensibly rival employers.

The professional cricketer was left at the mercy of his county committee. Out of his match fees (£4 or £5 for a county match, £10 for a major fixture like Gentlemen v. Players), he had to meet the costs of bed and breakfast, third-class rail fares, meals and drinks. Tips, talent money and bonuses made up the living wage. Taking the hat around the ground following an exceptional performance became common practice. In each match, amateur captains would award points to professionals according to their own recondite marking systems and, as often as not, their mood on the day. Bonus payments would be issued accordingly.

The strictly amateur county committees regarded any attempt by professionals to secure even a modicum of independence as treacherous. At Gloucestershire, WG dropped the county's veteran bowler, William Woof, because Woof had taken a coaching job at Cheltenham College, which might make him unavailable for some of the county's early-season fixtures. Woof said he would give up the job if the club guaranteed to play him in (and thus pay him for) all matches. Otherwise, he argued, 'they could not expect me to leave a certainty for an uncertainty'.

In 1880, seven Nottinghamshire professionals, among them Arthur Shrewsbury and the medium-pace bowler Alfred Shaw, petitioned the County Committee to pay them £20 each for playing in the match against the visiting Australians, the most popular and profitable of the season. The county met the demand – but awarded £21 to those professionals who had not signed the petition.

By common consent, Shrewsbury was one of the finest batsmen of the era. His 164 against Australia (and Spofforth) at Lord's in 1886 was described by Lord Harris as 'the finest innings I ever saw'. The son of a draughtsman in a Nottingham lace factory, he had little time for the MCC and was contemptuous of amateur hypocrisy. In a letter to the Surrey all-rounder George Lohmann, he complained bitterly of amateurs 'who get a nice round cheque each season out of cricket'. With his friend Shaw, an astonishingly economical bowler who sent down more overs than he conceded runs, he organized commercial cricket tours to North America and Australia, and built a sporting-goods business. These assertive, aspirant descendants of William Clarke were the most independent force in first-class cricket, but they proved no match for the MCC cartel.

In 1881, the Nottinghamshire seven, again led by Shrewsbury and Shaw, decided to organize a Nottinghamshire side to play a one-off match in Bradford, as had been customary in previous years. But times had changed. The county was now asserting its monopoly. It could not allow Shaw and Shrewsbury to do what Clarke had done. The Committee demanded that the players make themselves available for all county matches that season, which meant no freelancing in Bradford. In response, the seven asked for a contract for the whole season and the guarantee of a benefit after ten years. The Committee refused and the seven were dropped. At the end of the season, five of them backed down and retracted their demands. Shaw and Shrewsbury held out until the following May, then gave in and issued the apology required by the Committee.

The 1882 *Lillywhite* accused the Nottinghamshire seven of engaging in 'a deliberate combination against a recognised administration':

> In county cricket the professional, who is the labourer, makes a profit: the committee, who is the capitalist, does not, but merely seeks to encourage and support the game ... Professional cricketers ought to remember that their relation with County Committees is not the ordinary commercial relation of labour and capital.

In 1886, Lord Harris proposed reducing the qualification period from two years to one. 'I have been called a cricket socialist,' he observed wryly. 'I do not know what a cricket socialist is, but if it means I have the interest of professional cricketers at heart, then I am one.' In the same year, there was a resolution which would have prevented players moving counties as long as their current county wanted them, seconded by WG himself. Harris opposed it, saying he could not accept 'anything that had any suspicion of interfering with a working man from selling that which was his property – his labour'. Both proposals were rejected and the qualification rules remained as before.

Professionals sought compensation for their lost freedom of movement in benefit matches and funds. Prior to the rise of the counties as their chief and ultimately exclusive employers, players organized their own benefits on their own initiative. Under the county regime, benefits were awarded strictly at the employer's discretion.

Benefits are exempt from tax because they are supposedly *ex gratia*, uncontracted payments. This anomalous status was confirmed by the courts in a test case in 1927. Lord Harris used all his influence to secure this decision, ostensibly to protect professional cricketers from the Inland Revenue. But if benefits had been treated as contracted payments and taxed accordingly, the players would have had a powerful argument to back their long-standing demand that benefits be awarded according to length of service, not the whim of the County Committee.

County clubs often insisted on retaining half the income from a player's benefit and guarding it on his behalf until the player's retirement. Johnny Briggs, a popular Lancashire and England slow bowler, requested a benefit after his fourteenth year with the county, but was told it was too early. A few years later, he suffered an epileptic seizure on the field and was committed, penniless, to Cheadle Asylum, where he died at the age of thirty-nine.

In the 1890s, in response to demands made by their highly successful professional corps, the Surrey Committee agreed to pay the county's best players thirty shillings a week during the winter. Lancashire and Yorkshire followed suit. However, in Yorkshire, half the winter pay (plus 4 per cent annual interest) was retained by the county until a player's retirement.

Ponsonby Fane found the idea of 'paying a man to idle away eight months out of twelve' distasteful. Winter pay also caused alarm among the weaker counties, who feared Yorkshire and Surrey would snap up all the talent. But Yorkshire already had its Yorkshire-born policy (ruthlessly enforced by the Lincolnshire-born Lord Hawke). And *Wisden* calmed the counties' fears by reminding them that 'the law of supply and demand can be trusted to keep things tolerably straight' – *as long as the informal amateur quota in county cricket was preserved*. Without that, the players would gain the whip-hand. Many counties reserved playing places for amateurs, especially during university holidays. Amateurs comprised on average between a third and a half of county sides in the two decades before World War I. These amateur sinecures limited the number of professional berths available and forced professionals to compete against each other, but not the amateurs, for a place in the side.

Winter pay was never meant to be a full wage but a supplement to other earnings. Professional cricketers were expected to belong to the 'respectable' working class and to maintain a trade other than cricket. The amateurs expected them to reproduce, in modest form, their own part-time approach to the game, and to reflect in their demeanour an appreciation of their place within the social hierarchy.

Professional cricketers in the era of the itinerant XIs were noted for their enjoyment of food, drink and merriment. But under the aegis of Harris, Hawke and others within the MCC elite, the image of the professional was reformed. In Yorkshire, 'professionalism' became tantamount to teetotalism. Lord Hawke proclaimed, 'the man who is a pernicious example ought to be sacked, no matter how skilled he may be as a cricketer'. The county was purchasing more than the professional's labour; it was appropriating his body and soul.

The players were expected to be well-attired, proud of their appearance, but never showy. Where amateurs donned multi-coloured blazers, caps, boaters, and ties, professionals, who had once taken the field in stripes, spots and checks, were forced into a uniform of starched white shirts and flannels, ornamented only by the official county blazer and cap. Their duties included preparing the pitch and bowling in the nets to county members. They also maintained equipment and served drinks. Thus, county cricket institutionalized the ethos of aristocratic patronage even as it was dying out in the rest of society.

In 1896, prior to the third Test at the Oval, Test players Gunn, Lohmann, Richardson, Abel and Hayward had the temerity to submit what they called a 'demand' to the Surrey Committee (which staged and organised the Test). They wanted £20 each for the fixture, doubling the existing fee, which, despite the boom in cricket, had not changed for two decades. The Committee rejected the 'demand', dropped all the players from the side named to play the Test, then hauled up the four Surrey players involved for a personal dressing-down. Three withdrew their 'demand' on the spot, placed themselves 'in the hands of the Committee' and were promptly reinstated to the Test side. The other two, Lohmann and Gunn, were excluded from the match.

In an interview in the *Daily Mail*, Lohmann explained: 'The enormous crowds which now follow the game benefit the clubs and, in fact, everyone but those who have done at least their fair share towards bringing the game to its present state – the professional players.'

The Times took a different view: 'Loyalty to the Surrey Club and patriotism for English cricket should have been a sufficient incentive to the players to have practised self-denial for a while longer.'

The crowds at the Oval backed the dissident players. According to the *Star*, 'the voice of the people in this instance is unmistakably in favour of the professionals'. Nevertheless, Surrey punished Lohmann by dropping him from county matches. To get back into the side, he issued an apology to the Committee in which he stated that he had made a 'request', not a 'demand', which expression, he claimed, 'was inserted against my wish and better judgement'.

'The players were right in principle, but their action was ill judged and inopportune,' said *Wisden*. Following the 1896 dispute, Surrey and the other counties hosting Tests raised the match fee, quietly, to £20. In 1898, Lord Harris, having abandoned his 'cricket socialism', proposed that the residential qualification period be increased to three years. He also suggested that professionals should not be allowed to move unless released by their current counties. To enforce these regulations, he called on the MCC to establish a central register of county cricketers.

Though the qualification period remained two years, Harris's other proposals were gradually adopted. At all levels, professionals, by the end of the century, were dependent on amateur selection committees for any and all opportunities to ply their trade. The only way to challenge the MCC cartel would have been through trade-union action, but this the professionals spurned. They served their counties in the hope of securing a benefit, the only way they could see to achieve the financial independence that would preserve them from the factory or the poorhouse. Like the amateurs, they were in flight from an industrial society.

However, not everyone was prepared to cede the ownership of English cricket to the elite. While few unskilled labourers took to cricket, it was immensely popular among skilled workers. Before the 1880s, Yorkshire cricket was dominated by framework knitters, lace workers, fitters and turners. As their crafts were undermined by industrial development, a Yorkshire supporter lamented, 'Fast looms have destroyed our fast bowling.' That was before the miners emerged. Like their piece-worker forebears, and like most cricketers in the North, they lived in semi-rural industrial villages. Major urban areas lacked the space for cricket and most factory workers lacked the time and money.

Though industrialism curbed the development of cricket in some areas, it created new markets for it in others. Twenty thousand now attended the big matches. In London, Birmingham, Manchester and Leeds, county cricket was keenly followed by working-class boys who filled the sixpenny seats to ogle their heroes, who were usually professionals. It cost no more to spend a whole day watching cricket than it did to watch ninety minutes of football. But watching the cricket required a full day off work. County cricket remained largely a mid-week affair for the benefit of amateurs who had social engagements on the weekends. For the working class, cricket remained a holiday entertainment, while football was a weekly staple. This reinforced ruling-class governance of the game. Since the cricket holiday was seen as a special dispensation, suitable behaviour and respectable attire were required. But among these working-class supporters, debates about cricket were keenly pursued, and sometimes with a conscious class perspective.

Cricket was covered regularly in the pages of Robert Blatchford's *Clarion*, the most popular socialist newspaper of the time. Blatchford had worked as a reporter on *Bell's Life* (a sporting paper) and the Manchester *Sunday Chronicle* before converting to socialism (and losing his job) at the age of forty. He started the *Clarion* in 1890 and within a few years its circulation had risen to 60,000. Blatchford and his contributors celebrated the dignity, skill and intelligence of the professionals and lampooned the pretensions of the amateurs. A faux-naif *Clarion* columnist commented:

> Gentlemen dont get payed nothin for playin except their expenses. This is wye they looks down on the perfeshernals who has to call em sir, an go in at the bak door. You coodnt tell witch was the gentleman if it wasn't for this ere. That is wye it is. You see you cant tell by there close nor there maners so they does it this way.

Blatchford described Shrewsbury as 'the Andrea del Sarto of cricket: the perfect batsman ... He never slogs and he never funks. He is no more capable of swiping at a good ball than of tamely blocking a bad one ... He is a cricketer and a man ...' In other words, he possessed all the 'Golden Age' virtues which the amateurs claimed for themselves. Blatchford concludes his paean to Shrewsbury with a vignette from the Trent Bridge Test:

> Outside the gate, a small, poorly dressed boy, not above ten years of age, came

up to me and said, 'What's the score, mister?' I said, 'England 300 for 4 wickets.' 'O-o,' said the urchin, then turning up the tail of his eye and turning down the tail of his mouth, he asked, "ow many's Arthur got?' I gave him sixpence and told him to go in and see 'Arthur' for himself.

In 1893, after eighteen years' service to Nottinghamshire, Shrewsbury received a benefit of £600. He was still playing in 1902, when he topped the first-class batting averages, for the sixth time, at the age of forty-six. A small, shy, unmarried man with a streak of hypochondria, he grew melancholy during the following winter, complaining of kidney pains, and visited doctor after doctor. In May 1903, he died after shooting himself in the chest and head. The obituary in *Wisden* explained: 'The knowledge that his career on the cricket field was over had quite unhinged his mind.'

English cricket inherited the county unit, with so much else, from the eighteenth century and the landed elite. But the county championship itself emerged only in the late nineteenth century. Unlike the great football or tennis competitions which came into being at the same time, county cricket did not enter the late-Victorian scene as something novel, an internally coherent creation of the age. It was, from the outset, a compromise – between professional and amateur, local and national, tradition and the market.

The modern county organizations were formed out of patchwork quilt of pre-existing clubs and associations. In most counties, there was tension between the old market towns and new urban industrial areas, between county-based aristocracy and town-based bourgeoisie. Usually this was resolved by making the landowners president and vice-president of county clubs, while local professionals, clergy and businessmen undertook the administrative tasks. All of them were united in their loyalty to amateurism and the overlordship of the MCC. The formation of the modern county clubs in the second half of the nineteenth century was very much the work of the elite at the centre of English cricket, which helps explain why county clubs have always been dependent on the Lord's apparatus and never established their own equivalent of the Football League.

Unlike football clubs, cricket clubs were (and are) membership organizations. The former were dominated by industrial proprietors with an admixture of skilled workers; the latter by landowners, professionals and high-street traders. County secretaries were accountable not to shareholders but to members, and they were slow to respond to the growing press and public interest in county cricket.

In 1873, inspired by the recently-inaugurated FA Cup, the MCC proposed to organize an annual competition to determine the Champion County Club. Only two counties entered. The rest rejected the idea, fearing 'it may have a tendency to introduce a speculative element into cricket'. Ten years later, the county secretaries at last agreed to meet together annually – at Lord's. It was a natural choice of venue. They were all MCC members.

Not everyone was pleased by the rise of county cricket. In *The Times* in 1887, Frederick Gale, styling himself 'Old Buffer', declared grumpily: 'Cricket is a game and not a business.' He objected to the press's habit of categorizing counties as first- and second-class, which, he reminded readers, was against 'the dictum of the MCC'. He detested 'the new fad about "champion counties"' and urged MCC not to award any championship – because under such competitive conditions, the professionals would always play for the draw. 'Exit old English cricket, enter the betting ring.'

A cricket reporter replied: 'Cricket is played for honour, and will so continue; but honour implies renown, and how is renown to be gained except in a defined and eager competition among rivals of approximately equal skill and ability?'

The echoes of Pycroft in Gale's protest are clear, but once again the MCC was wiser – or more adaptable – than its moralistic counsellors.

In July 1888, on the MCC's initiative, delegates from the counties met at Lord's during the Gentlemen v. Players match. Lord Harris chaired the meeting, which received a report recommending the formation of a County Cricket Council. Delegates were most concerned that nothing they did should undermine MCC's right to make the Laws of Cricket. The thorny questions were the qualification rules and the determination of first-class status. Harris wanted to leave both questions in abeyance so that the Council could be set up at once. As usual, he got his way. The Council was established on the basis of equality among all counties, including several 'minor' or 'second-class' ones. The subscription was £1 per county per year, which indicates the modesty of the new body's ambitions.

Harris was made its chairman and immediately announced that 'there was room for improvement' in the 'working rules of cricket'. The bowler needed help to be 'placed on more equal terms with the batsman'. He suggested a change in the LBW Law to prevent stonewalling. The

Yorkshire delegate warned that spectators in the North would drift away unless something was done to make the county games more exciting. Changes in the hours of play were mooted. Even the elimination of boundaries was contemplated. It was thought that 'a cricket match now was rather a tame thing to watch'. Something had to be done to spice it up.

At its inception, county cricket was already struggling with the dilemma that haunts it today: how to fit the old game into the new marketplace. When a formal county championship was finally inaugurated in 1890, it was barely noticed by the press or the public. It seemed merely a belated codification of what had been happening for years. As so often in cricket, where others innovated, the authorities consolidated - and reaped the rewards.

A stalemate over the question of which counties were or were not first-class led to the collapse of the County Cricket Council in 1890-91, when Harris was out of the country on imperial duties. In 1894, the county secretaries, having given up on any kind of self-government, asked the MCC to intervene. The MCC obliged. In future, its Committee would decide which counties were worthy of joining the select band. First-class counties would be those which played a sufficient number of first-class matches! This was, at best, an abstract, not a competitive standard of excellence. At the same time the MCC decided there would be no 'second-class' counties: there would be first-class cricket and there would be the rest of cricket. In the absence of a system of promotion and relegation, a gulf opened between first-class and club cricket. It became rare for a county cricketer, amateur or professional, to play at lower levels.

In the following years, the established county clubs used MCC's control of the game to see off potential rivals. Five new counties were granted first-class status between 1895 and 1900. A total of three more were admitted in the following ninety-two years.

In 1899, WG ended his thirty-year association with Gloucestershire to spend the remainder of his career as captain and secretary of the newly formed London County Club, based at Crystal Palace. For his services, he was paid £600 per annum, twice as much as the professionals in the side. The London County side was a forerunner of celebrity cricket (one of its attractions was the fast bowler Walter Brearley, whom Hornby had dropped at Lancashire). It shamelessly exploited famous names to get paying customers through the gate. As such, it was deeply distrusted by the MCC and the established counties, which repeatedly refused to admit it to the county championship and even stripped it of first-class status, despite the proven high standard of its cricketers.

CLR James observed of WG: 'Like all truly great men, he bestrides two ages.' As a transitional figure between the agrarian past and the urban present, he epitomized cricket's perpetually arrested development, its incomplete accommodation with the modern world. But WG was also a prophetic figure. His London County Club, based on a modern identity (the metropolis of London, not the pseudo-counties of Surrey and Middlesex) and aimed squarely at the mass market, pointed the way to a different form of domestic cricket. Thanks to the MCC, it was frozen out of the market and folded after eight years in business.

In 1904, the Advisory County Cricket Committee was set up under the aegis of the MCC, which thus became at long last the undisputed ruler of county cricket. It had less direct financial or bureaucratic power than either the FA or the League or, for that matter, its ancient cousin, the Jockey Club, but it was seen by the counties themselves as a higher authority, independent of partisan interests, embracing the whole of English and ultimately imperial cricket.

MCC policy was that 'all counties are equal'. In reality, this meant preserving the extreme inequalities among current county sides. The Football League provided a stable basis for systematic competition and a ladder whereby teams rose or sank in the hierarchy according to their performance on the field. In contrast, MCC did little to promote closer competition among the counties. There was no central subsidy, no pooling of gates and no transfer fees. No county has ever been relegated from the county championship. Even after MCC took over the championship, the county clubs retained control over their own fixture lists and were not required, in the beginning, to play all other first-class counties. The total number of fixtures varied from year to year as the MCC and the counties tried and failed to iron out anomalies. Between 1890 and 1993, the points system for the county championship was altered more than thirty times.

Although attendance at county matches grew throughout the 1880s and '90s, most county clubs led a perilous hand-to-mouth existence. Rain always made it difficult for counties to secure a stable income from the gate, as did the large number of meaningless draws and abbreviated one-sided wins (a consequence of the MCC's failure to promote equal competition). All this meant that county clubs relied on membership subscriptions and donations from the local elite.

In keeping with cricket's rarefied ethos, few counties allowed their grounds to be used for anything else (football was banned from the Oval in the 1890s). Fixed assets therefore lay dormant for most of the year - as they still do. It was always accepted that the game could not survive in the marketplace unaided. County committees emphasized the social obligation of members to maintain the county side. County ties became symbols of social status. But the local chauvinism that motivated the football clubs was largely absent. County cricket was seen as a national institution and supporting it a public duty.

Unlike urban football clubs, county cricket clubs did not compete against each other for spectators. Their roots in an earlier age left them with clear territorial monopolies. However, their boundaries were anachronistic even then. Successive reform acts had eroded the counties' political significance. The new counties wanted and needed an urban base (hence Old Trafford, Headingley, Edgbaston and Bramall Lane) but couldn't tear themselves away from the old landed loyalties.

Many among the elite shared CB Fry's contempt for 'the artificial interest of the County Championship', regarded as inferior to the annual Gentlemen v. Players fixture or the Test matches. Because MCC's governance of county cricket was an act of *noblesse oblige*, little effort was made to capture a mass audience for it. In contrast, league cricket shamelessly catered to its working class audience, spreading rapidly through the North and Midlands in the 1880s and '90s. Admission fees were low. Because competition was local, it cost less to travel to matches. And a result was guaranteed, which was vital to highly partisan paying customers. The wickets were rough and therefore unsuitable for classical amateur strokeplay. Everyone had to pull his weight in the field. The crowds were boisterous. The middle-class-dominated, socially exclusive Southern clubs held aloof: In the 1920s their Club Cricket Conference prohibited affiliates from playing in any league or knock-out competitions. Among these clubs, all matches were 'friendly' until the 1960s.

Like black baseball in the USA, league cricket was derided as a backwater and its achievements largely ignored. League clubs were the first to introduce overseas professionals to English cricket. Nelson hired the Australian fast bowler EA McDonald in 1922 and the West Indian all-rounder Learie Constantine in 1929. Basil D'Oliveira too made his start in English cricket in the leagues.

From the beginning, the leagues offered a refuge for disgruntled county professionals. Bobby Peel, thrown out of Yorkshire by Hawke for alleged indiscipline, continued his career at Accrington. SF Barnes, blunt and never deferential, left Lancashire in 1903, at the age of thirty, to spend the rest of his career in the more congenial atmosphere of the leagues, though he appeared in England Test sides until 1914. More recently, Johnny Wardle found shelter in league cricket after falling out with the county hierarchy, as did Viv Richards, under different circumstances.

Disdaining partisanship, county cricket guaranteed no results. As pitches and batting techniques improved, draws became more common and spectators fewer. In 1902 a noisy campaign to change the LBW Law to aid beleaguered bowlers failed. The MCC always found it hard to adopt new Laws solely for the benefit of first-class cricket because its Laws applied to all cricket, including club cricket, where the pitches already aided the bowlers more than enough. Its claims to universal governance hampered its ability to improve the county game.

By the turn of the century, critics of county cricket regularly decried the excessive number of draws, the domination of bat over ball, the dull and defensive play. At the apogee of the cricket cult, all the discontents of the modern English game were being voiced. The pathology of English county cricket, its ceaseless struggle for survival in a hostile world, cannot be blamed, *pace* Pycroft, Gale and a thousand latter-day pundits, on 'professionalism'. Cautious play and uncompetitive, pointless matches, still the bane of the county game, are the result of its gerrymandered structure. 'Professionalism', long seen as an English disease, is a creature of the amateur-dominated hierarchy.

The *Clarion* lost much of its audience when Blatchford became an enthusiast for the South African War at the turn of the century. The jingoism which mortally infected him, as it has so many socialists in times of war, was then in its heyday, as was the British Empire. What had begun as piracy on the high seas and sharp practice by English businessmen in foreign lands had become a cause to fight and die for.

The imperial caste carried cricket across the globe, but once again, the professionals, more sensitive to the market, took the commercial lead. In 1859 Parr and a squad of professionals (accompanied by Fred Lillywhite and his printing press) made the first overseas tour – to North America, then second only to England itself as a cricket capital. The first English visit to Australia, three years later, was sponsored by a Melbourne cafe, which netted £11,000 profit from the tour and promptly moved to London.

Test cricket, the supreme form of the game, was pioneered, like county cricket, by the market and the media. The Melbourne Cricket Club, every bit as establishment as MCC itself, began sending representative

Australian sides to England in 1886. But for years MCC left overseas touring in the hands of private entrepreneurs and patrons. In 1887-88, two rival England teams – one led by Hawke and one by Shrewsbury – toured Australia at the same time. Only in 1893 did MCC officially invite and host an Australian touring side – the eighth to visit these shores. In 1899, MCC finally set up a Board of Control for Test matches, composed of the MCC President, five others from the Committee and one from each first-class county. The Board appointed a Selection Sub-committee to replace the separate panels at Lord's, Old Trafford and the Oval. (This system remained unchanged until the – ultimately disastrous – reforms of 1989.) It was not until 1903-04 that MCC selected and sponsored its own England side to tour Australia.

Soon requests for MCC tours were pouring in from the colonies. English cricketers, professional and amateur, were in demand and the MCC had once again cornered the market. Its power of patronage was now global. Lord's was the HQ of both English and world cricket. The red-and-yellow club colours were no longer sufficient. From 1903, MCC touring sides sported the national emblem – the lion rampant.

The first proposal for an 'Imperial cricket contest' between England, Australia and South Africa was mooted in 1907. One of its aims was to foster South Africa's integration into the empire. The Australians, however, were not keen on coming all the way to England to play South Africa, nor were they prepared to divide with South Africa the profits of an England tour. A compromise was reached. The Australians were invited to tour England alone, as usual. At the same time, a conference was called 'to discuss arrangements' for matches between the three Test-playing countries. In 1909, a meeting at Lord's, with Lord Harris in the chair, established the Imperial Cricket Conference (ICC). The MCC President became the new body's ex-officio chairman and the MCC Secretary its ex-officio secretary. It was not a governing bureaucracy, but a forum for private negotiation. After much wrangling, it organized the Triangular Tournament in England in 1912, a commercial flop that put an end to multi-sided international contests until the World Cup of 1975.

Under the aegis of the ICC, cricket was formally linked to empire. This was no help to the game in the USA, which was excluded from the ICC, as South Africa was to be when it left the Commonwealth in 1960. In practice, the 'internationalism' of the ICC was restricted to bilateral relations between the MCC and the colonial cricket authorities.

This was in keeping with the world view of the Tory imperialists ruling at Lord's and Westminster. Chief among them was the Trinidad-born

Lord Harris (Eton, Oxford). He toured Australia in 1878-79, at the age of twenty-seven, and despite some rough treatment by the Australian crowds arranged the 1880 return tour to England and the first Test at the Oval. His family, with 3,000 acres in Kent as well as substantial interests in the City, boasted four generations of colonial military service. His grandfather was Archdeacon of Trinidad. As Governor of Madras, his father helped put down the 1857 Mutiny. Later, he became Governor of Trinidad, as well as Chairman of the London, Chatham and Dover Railway, a position which his son inherited. To that, the Fourth Baron Harris added the Chairmanship of Consolidated Goldfields (founded by Cecil Rhodes) and a Directorship of the Naval Construction and Armaments Company in Barrow.

Harris reformed in order to conserve. He was the ideal figure to preside over the marriage of cricket and empire because he was a central figure in both. He served as Under-Secretary for India and then Governor of Bombay, where he organized the first visit by an English cricket side. In the South African war he served as an Assistant Adjutant General. Later, he was an ADC to Kings Edward and George. Harris was also 'Chancellor' of the Primrose League – a kind of Tory popular front – which stood for the 'True Union of the Classes' and the 'Imperial Ascendancy of Great Britain' and claimed over a million members.

The Primrose League was the Tory response to the challenge of an extended franchise. Through it, the Tories aimed to link the middle classes with the upper classes against the menace of the proletariat. They did so by propounding a higher national interest – which, by an amazing sleight of hand, became an *imperial* interest. The similarities with cricket are obvious and were not lost on Harris himself, who declared frequently that 'cricket has done more to consolidate the Empire than any other influence'.

Harris's principal disciple was Sir Pelham 'Plum' Warner (Rugby, Oxford) whose father was Attorney General of Trinidad. Trained as a barrister under Alfred Lyttelton, Warner dedicated his life (with occasional interruptions for stockbroking in the City) to playing, reporting and administering cricket. When the England side arrived in Australia in 1932 for what was to become the 'Body Line' series, Warner, the tour manager, declared that the aim of the MCC in 'sending teams to all parts of the world' was 'to spread the gospel of British fair play'.

The imperialists left English cricket with a peculiar legacy. It became a symbol of both nation and empire, as English as 'habeas corpus', and as universally applicable. Under the jurisdiction of the empire, everyone, it was said, was subject to the same laws. It was an extension of cricket's old mythology of social inclusion – wed, as ever, to rigid hierarchy.

'High and low, rich and poor, greet one another practically on an equality, and sad will be the day for England if Socialism ever succeeds in putting class v. class and thus ending sports which have made England.'

Thus, Lord Hawke in 1924, during the first, short-lived Labour government. The next year, at the Yorkshire CCC annual dinner, Hawke, having been reconfirmed as club President for the twenty-seventh year running, made an off-the cuff remark about the professional cricketer Cecil Parkin, who had publicly criticized the way the amateur, AER Gilligan, was captaining the England side in Australia. Hawke sniffed: 'If he had been a Yorkshire player, I do not think Parkin would ever step on another cricket ground in Yorkshire. Pray god no professional may ever captain England.'

The Labour-supporting *Daily Herald* saw this as a declaration of class war and struck back: 'Is it cricket, Lord Hawke?' a headline demanded. The newspaper went on to impugn the great lord's patriotism. 'He would rather see England's prospects at Test cricket imperilled than allow a professional to captain the side.'

From Adelaide, Hobbs, Sutcliffe and other professional Test players wired London: Hawke's remarks were 'disparaging to professionals'. The *Herald* praised their 'moderate and dignified protest' and noted that in Australia, where all cricketers were considered amateurs and paid the same expenses for each match, the English division between gentlemen and players was seen as backward. Denouncing Hawke's 'snobocratic' views, the paper demanded, 'Play the game, Lord Hawke!' It argued: 'The best interests of cricket are imperilled by these snobbish class distinctions. What is the MCC going to do about it?'

An Independent Labour Party branch secretary from Harlesden wrote to the *Herald*: 'If anyone were to tell Lord Hawke that he was preaching the class war, he would be horrified, yet that is what he is doing.' The *Herald* warned readers that Hawke's 'stone age views' were not merely 'funny old survivals' but 'representative' of many in the upper classes who believed 'it is a mark of inferiority to be obliged to earn your own living'.

Sir Home Gordon explained that his friend Hawke had never meant to be inflammatory. All he had been trying to say was that amateurs, as well as professionals, should have their reserved places in the game. 'If first-class cricket has not the leaven of amateurs with professionals,' Gordon argued, 'it would lose its national character.'

Both parties to the debate claimed to be speaking on behalf of the nation and both claimed the mantle of 'fair play'. The *Herald* was right to insist that the 'cricket' in 'it is not cricket' referred to a spirit of equality and universal human respect. Hawke was right to argue it was also about people knowing their places. That paradox was the creation of English cricket's transitional nature, a legacy of its early origins and uneasy accommodation with modern society.

The integration of world cricket under the English landed elite coincided with the beginnings of that elite's decline in domestic and international politics. Even as the county championship was finally coalesced, the old county gentry were losing their monopoly over the bench and local government in the countryside. From the 1880s, the landed presence in the House of Commons began to dwindle. In 1895, Oscar Wilde had Lady Bracknell complain of the burden of land ownership: 'It gives one a position, and prevents one from keeping it up.' When WH Long narrowly lost the leadership of the Conservative Party to the Ulsterman, Bonar Law, in 1911, it was seen by many as the eclipse of the old landed elite within the party.

Rival imperial powers were emerging. German and US industry had taken off in the 1860s and by the 1890s both were making overseas claims. At the same time, anti-colonial movements appeared. The Indian National Congress was founded in 1885. A new Irish national movement took shape. Australia and New Zealand achieved dominion status.

For a hundred years, English cricket has been struggling with the consequences of the prolonged decay of its patron class. The inauguration of Hopkins's new Mound Stand in 1987 invoked past glories, but could not revive them.

At the start of its bicentenary year, MCC had gone through a severe internal crisis over its relations with the marketeers of the TCCB, leading to the resignation of its long-serving Secretary and Treasurer and a contentious Extraordinary General Meeting. The cost of the new Mound Stand had put the MCC under more pressure than ever to do business with the TCCB, and in order to stage a bicentenary match it had to compensate the counties for the revenue they lost from a normal Lord's Test. In the end, JP Getty, the billionaire American, bailed out the old club. His name was inscribed in a stone plaque in the new stand. Getty thus joined WG Grace, Lord Harris, Plum Warner, Gubby Allen, Compton and Edrich among the select benefactors of cricket commemorated at Lord's.

Having survived a tycoon father, the University of San Francisco, a stint in the US navy and a hellish period managing the family interests in Italy, Getty moved to England, where he fell in love with cricket at the age of forty. He purchased a complete set of *Wisdens* from the estate of Robert Maxwell and a stately home at Wormsley in Buckinghamshire from the Fanes, the aristocratic family of a former England Test captain. There, at considerable expense, he attempted to re-create country-house cricket (with help from TCCB pitch-master Harry Brind, various BBC commentators and that personification of Golden Age strokeplay, David Gower). Getty disapproved of his fellow magnate, Kerry Packer: 'There should be limits to commercial exploitation,' he insisted. The world's most famous American cricket fan has recast himself as an English gentleman, one of the old amateurs, enjoying a style of life which few of their contemporary descendants can afford.

The anomaly of Getty is impressive testimony to the endurance of landed wealth as a touchstone of elite status in English cricket. But, of course, Getty is an expensive copy, not the real thing. In this respect, the new Mound Stand is his perfect memorial. Its billowing tents are not made of canvas, but of a teflon-coated synthetic fabric. No gentle summer breeze can rustle them. Beautiful as it is, the Mound Stand is ersatz, like the mock-Tudor McDonald's in Stratford-upon-Avon. In leaning so heavily on the past, it reminds us that English cricket has yet to come to terms with the present.

4

Permanent Revolution

Cricket's anti-christ ● *1968* ● *The Packer charade* ● *The war between the TCCB and the MCC* ● *A peculiar political economy* ● *The Murray Report and the end of civilization: county cricket, the one-day game and coloured clothing* ● *Modernization without end?*

When the cricket historian Rowland Bowen died in 1978, *Wisden*, in a brief obituary, praised the original research published in his *Cricket Quarterly* but could not refrain from observing that 'his views were often highly controversial'. It was referring not only to his opposition to playing cricket with South Africa, but, perhaps even more, to the conclusion he had reached ten years before his death: 'There is no real future for highly organised cricket at Test match or first-class level, nor, in the long run, for cricket annuals, periodicals or literature.'

When Bowen started his magazine in 1963, he had asked the MCC for permission to circulate members with a prospectus. It had granted the same facility to *The Cricketer* only months before, but this time it demurred. The Committee men already knew Bowen, a long-standing member, all too well.

Back in the early fifties, he had submitted a memorandum warning that long-term economic changes would make the current structure of the English game unworkable. He proposed radical reform: a shift to two-day county cricket played at weekends and on holidays and a two divisional county-championship structure. When he argued for an end to Tests with South Africa at the MCC AGM of 1960, he was a lone voice, opposed by that year's MCC President, HS Altham, a public school master and author of one of the game's standard histories. Ten years later, in the midst of the campaign to stop the South African tour, Bowen offered to train the young anti-apartheid protesters in sabotage techniques he had learned in counter-insurgency work in India and Malaya.

Major Rowland Bowen was the worm that turned. His upbringing in the public-school tradition and his experience as a British army officer turned him into a caustic critic of English cricket, the British Empire and their linked hypocrisies.

In 1970, he published *Cricket: a History of Its Growth and Development Throughout the World*. Like Ruskin's *Stones of Venice*, Bowen's History is a tale of the 'rise, life and decline' of a peculiar civilization, laced with puritanical disgust and high aestheticism. The book is by turns cranky, obsessive, pedantic and prophetic, like its author. Bowen's aim was to debunk the cult of cricket and above all its teleology: the assumption that the supremacy of the MCC was the desirable end towards which all cricket history tended. 'The rise was an accident of geography and social history,' he insisted. 'Its esteem during the best part of its healthy life was something quite definitely accidental as it became a hand maiden of the British Empire; and its decline was as inevitable as was the decline of that Empire.'

World War II, Bowen believed, had offered English cricket a unique chance to rationalize, modernize and nationalize itself, on the model of other public services. But that chance had been spurned, leaving English cricket unable to cope with the spread of the motor car and the television, full employment, higher wages, and long-term inflation.

For Bowen, the decline of the Eton v. Harrow match at Lord's, once the high point in the English social calendar, was symptomatic of the post-war displacement of the old upper class. The match was 'no longer felt by English "top people" to be an appropriate focus for a gathering'. The new meritocracy bred by the post-war Butskellite consensus had little time for the old games ethic. Cricket was: 'too much identified with an outmoded social division in the country, with a now powerless but still moneyed class which does not reflect the general outlook of the country in its perpetual half-strangled appeals for "proper behaviour" and "good form" and the rest of it'.

Noting the failure of the MCC (in contrast to the athletics authorities) to make cricket metric, he denounced those in charge of the game as 'men of little intelligence and little status' whose actions smacked of 'venality, of self-interest, and of straightforward vanity'. The result of their refusal to move with the times was that 'all over the country, in almost all grades of cricket, matches are now played before a mere handful of spectators, sometimes even none at all'. In 1946, 2.3 million had attended first-class cricket; in 1960, one million; by 1970, fewer than 500,000.

Bowen believed there had been a 'great falling off in batting and bowling ability' and that the 'defensive cricket' of the modern county game was 'putting people off even attempting the more enjoyable game'. Like others, he blamed the LBW Law for breeding 'the really dreaded double-shuffle-cum-forward-defensive pad'. He despaired of 'the ubiquity of seam bowlers, depending on the new ball for their effect'. One hundred years on, he echoed Pycroft: 'The modern game is dreary.' But the reforms he proposed would have appalled Pycroft. 'Any scheme based on counties is a non-starter,' he declared, and he was scathing about plans for four-day mid-week county cricket: 'There is no prospect of that kind of competition doing any good at all.' Nor did he have any time for the recently-introduced one-day game: 'A wholly artificial element is brought into a small number of matches in an attempt to save from bankruptcy seventeen often ill-run and un-representative clubs.'

But Bowen agreed with Pycroft that the basic problem in English cricket was 'over-professionalism'. Like so many others, Bowen associated 'the aesthetic influence' with the 'true amateur' presence. His charge against the self-styled amateurs who ran English cricket was that they had forgotten that cricket 'is a game and not an ethic'. If the love of play for its own sake was to be restored to its proper place at the heart of the game, the whole apparatus of cricket would have to be dismantled.

Unlike other commentators, Bowen welcomed the social changes which he believed were making English cricket obsolete. 'England as a whole started to grow up,' he said of the post-war era. 'Keenness on sport and games is part of childhood: so it ceases.' One of Bowen's favourite themes was the collective immaturity of the English (he believed Americans were even worse). In the new society, the upper classes 'are forced to be more equal - more to the point, they are forced to grow up'. It was 'the essential childishness' of the English upper class which made the army, the institution with which, apart from cricket, he was most familiar, 'too often even now but school writ large'.

What, he asks, is the meaning of the epithet 'manly', so frequently applied to cricket? In cricket, as in public school, 'it is manly to stand up and receive physical punishment'. Appalled at such barbarousness, he adds: 'Oddly enough, real manliness (which is surely sexual prowess) was thought distasteful and even in an odd way womanish. To such an extent were the characters of a century and more of this country's youth perverted!'

Bowen was the first cricket historian to introduce adult (if idiosyncratic) references to sexuality and gender. In his indictment of South African cricket, he observes: 'Afrikaner Boers thought nothing of taking Hottentot women to themselves, whence the large South African coloured population ... and whence also the coloured strain in almost every Boer family. Such nonsense is Apartheid.' Chronicling the exclusion of women from cricket, he notes, 'It is an interesting speculation what might happen if sexually unsegregated cricket were to ever be introduced at a serious level.'

Bowen examined cricket's claims to embody a set of 'values' and found them not only fraudulent but against the game's own best interests. Yet he himself was one of cricket's many missionary zealots. He judged the game by a moral standard, albeit an unconventional one, and found it deficient. Throughout his book, there is a note of bitter disillusionment. He mocks the shallow illogic of English cricket's pretensions, but he has the impatience of a convert and the stridency of a prophet in the wilderness. Bowen, the anti-christ of English cricket, was as English a figure as you will find.

'This is not a trough into which the game has fallen. It is decline into the grave.' Bowen issued this prophecy of doom at the end of a long period of stability in English cricket, a stability which had bolstered the game's long-held mythology of social stasis, class harmony and rural purity. Ironically, the more cricket fell out of step with a changing society, the more potent this mythology became. The stage was set for cricket's clash with modernity – a clash that begins in the 1960s and has yet to end. One thing, however, is already clear. The result of this clash was not the apocalypse which Bowen foretold.

In 1946, Plum Warner wrote to *The Times* to condemn the newly appointed British Ambassador to the United States, who had confided to the American public that he found cricket 'the dullest game ever invented'. Warner was outraged that the national representative 'should see fit to make a pronunciamento so at variance with the feelings of the majority of his countrymen'.

But not everyone shared Warner's view of cricket's place in the national heritage. In the same year, film-makers Michael Powell and Emeric Pressburger released *A Matter of Life and Death*, a fantasia on the dilemmas facing those who had survived the Second World War, not least among them the nature of relations between the USA and Britain. Airman David Niven – the embodiment of the old-school tie now keen to take a productive place in an egalitarian world, 'Conservative by instinct, Labour by experience' – is on trial before a heavenly court. If he wins, he may return to earth and pursue a new life, with his American lover, in the post-war world. If he loses, he must join the dead. His prosecutor, an

Anglophobe hero of the American Revolution, throws all the sins of the British Empire in Niven's face. Finally, in order to demonstrate that the English are simply unfit for a place in the modern community of nations, he produces a wireless and tunes in the Test match commentary. It is slow and obscure, like an old man mumbling in his sleep. For the American prosecutor, cricket is the final indictment of a nation obsessed with the past and incapable of renewal.

In the fifties and sixties, commentators often blamed cricket's decline on the advance of an American-influenced youth culture which seemed to lack the patience for the game. Wally Hammond despaired of the modern generation: 'All they do is go to the cinema and see rubbishy crime films.'

Turning its back on the nascent youth culture, English cricket, like many of its traditional patrons, embraced a quaint cult of genteel poverty. Its resistance to change was legendary. 'I have been a member of the Committee of the MCC and of a Conservative Cabinet,' observed Viscount Monckton in 1968, 'and by comparison with the cricketers, the Tories seemed like a bunch of Commies.' On this question, if few others, Monckton (Harrow, Oxford) was authoritative. Before becoming President of the MCC, he had served as Attorney General, confidant of Edward VIII, adviser to the Nizam of Hyderabad, Chairman of Midland Bank, and Director of the Iraq Petroleum Company.

The problem for the MCC was that the material base for amateur rule was being steadily eroded. The old rentier section of the upper classes – the backbone of empire and of county cricket – had been squeezed by higher taxes and rising wages. In 1929, there were 205 amateur players in county cricket. In 1959, there were only-thirty nine, of whom a number received payment as county 'secretaries'.

In 1958, the Duke of Norfolk chaired an MCC sub-committee on the amateur question. It concluded that 'the distinctive status of the amateur cricketer was not obsolete, was of great value to the game and should be preserved'. However, it recommended that amateurs be allowed to accept 'broken time payments' for overseas tours, which in rugby union, athletics or rowing would have been a serious breach of the amateur code. It seemed that the only way the MCC could preserve amateurism was to discredit it further with shamateurism. The ancient bifurcation had become untenable. A meeting of the Advisory County Cricket Committee in November 1962 resolved (by a vote of 11 to 7) to abolish the distinction between professionals and amateurs entirely. In early 1963, the day after Plum Warner's death, the decision was ratified by the MCC.

The last ever Gentlemen v. Players match took place at Lord's in 1962. Rain on the final day saved the Gentlemen from going down to their sixty-ninth defeat in the 137 matches played there (twenty-eight were drawn) since the fixture had begun over 150 years before. Among the Gentlemen were Ted Dexter, Tony Lewis, Mike Smith, Trevor Bailey, Alan Smith and Ossie Wheatley. All were to play leading roles in the highly professionalized English cricket of the eighties and early nineties. Among the Players were Micky Stewart, Fred Titmus, Fred Trueman, Keith Andrew, Norman Gifford and Tom Graveney. They also found niches in the TCCB's modern game.

The significance of the demise of the amateur cricketer was not lost on Harold Wilson, then waging war against the 'elegant anachronisms' of Alec Douglas-Home's crippled Conservative government: 'At the very time when even the MCC has abolished the distinction between amateur and professional, we are content to remain, in science and industry, a nation of gentlemen in a world of players.'

It was easy for Wilson to draw parallels between cricket and the country as a whole. Both Home and his predecessor, Harold Macmillan, were strongly linked to the old landed elite; both were members of the MCC (Home, who appeared for Oxford and Middlesex in the 1920s, became MCC President in 1966). This was an aristocratic, old-school-tie government. It offered the perfect demonstration of Wilson's claim that the country, like English cricket, needed to be 'modernized'.

Voters gave Wilson several chances to cure the British disease, but the symptoms always recurred. However, one of Wilson's innovations was to have a profound impact on English cricket, though no one at the time would have guessed just where it would lead. The creation of the Sports Council, with a remit to supervise all government assistance to sport, was one of the Labour administration's attempts to make Britain more like other European countries. The MCC, like other venerable institutions, including the monarchy, was hungry for state hand-outs. But the Labour government, through the Sports Council, refused to give public funds to a private members' club. It urged the MCC to establish an all-embracing, representative governing body.

In response, the MCC set up the Cricket Council in 1968. Its constituent bodies would be the MCC itself and two new organizations, both created by the MCC: the Test and County Cricket Board, responsible for the first-class game, and the National Cricket Association, responsible for the recreational game. The TCCB was composed of representatives of the first-class counties, minor counties and MCC. Despite anomalies, English cricket seemed to be acquiring, at last, the rudiments of a democratic structure. The TCCB's first act was to agree an automatic annual share-out of Test match revenue to the counties. Previously, such hand-outs had been given by the MCC as a matter of grace and favour. The change gave the counties greater security, but it also tied them financially to the new Board.

The National Cricket Association, under whose wing club cricket, schools cricket and youth cricket were forced, was really just a new name for the old MCC Youth Cricket Association. Initially, all administrative functions for the Cricket Council, the TCCB and the NCA were performed by MCC assistant secretaries. The MCC and all it stood for remained dominant within the game. So while the barricades went up in Paris, English cricket was quietly remodelling itself to accommodate to the winds of social change. The purpose, however, was not to replace but to preserve the old order.

Another new cricket body came into being that year, but, significantly, it found no place on the Cricket Council. At the first Annual General Meeting of the Professional Cricketers' Association (at that time claiming 130 members, one-third of all professional cricketers), trade unionism made its belated entry into commercial cricket. Professionals in the sixties were still denied freedom of movement, collective bargaining and grievance procedures and were still dependent on the whims of amateur committees. They could see that trade unionism was a power in the land. Skilled workers were now making more money than cricketers and enjoyed far greater job security. And they were not treated as serfs by their employers, who had learned to fear their industrial muscle. For the first time, professional cricketers banded together to protect their collective interests. In the decade that followed, the PCA grew to enjoy nearly 100 per cent membership among county cricketers. The union won a group retirement scheme to replace the old MCC-administered benevolent funds, a minimum wage and representation on TCCB registration and disciplinary committees.

Of all the changes in the 1960s, the advent of the John Player League in 1969 was perhaps the most momentous. The Gillette Cup had introduced the one-day format to county cricket in 1963. The addition of Sunday play now put an end to what Trevor Bailey once called 'the tranquil continuity' of English county cricket. For the players, it became a regime of ceaseless travel and constant alteration between the one-day and first-class games.

For years, Rothman's Cavaliers, a mix of overseas stars and English professionals, had played Sunday benefit matches, many of which were broadcast on BBC2. As ever, the authorities followed safely after others blazed the trail. Their problem was that no sponsor would come in behind the proposed Sunday League unless television coverage was guaranteed. BBC2 was happy with its coverage of the star-studded Cavaliers and could see no reason to switch to the new league, in which so many of the players would be unknown to a wider audience.

MCC Secretary Billy Griffiths and Assistant Secretary Jack Bailey decided that the only way to get the Sunday League off the ground was to convince the counties to ban cricketers from playing for the Cavaliers – leaving BBC2 no alternative but to cover the official League if it wanted to show Sunday cricket at all. The authorities used the cartel to wipe out the competition. There was a stumbling block, however, in their dealings with another cartel. The BBC would cover the Sunday League only as part of a package including the Gillette Cup. London Weekend Television owned the rights to the latter but was in ill odour with Lord's because it had switched to its regular programmes when the 1968 final ran late, thus missing out the crucial final overs. The MCC signed the deal with the BBC and John Player (looking for new outlets because of restrictions on cigarette advertising) paid £75,000 to sponsor the first year of the forty-over competition.

ITV and LWT sued the MCC for breach of contract, but before the MCC could get into the dock its place was taken by the TCCB. In a High Court hearing in February 1969, the plaintiffs were represented by Geoffrey Howe QC (later Thatcher's Chancellor, Foreign Secretary and, ultimately, nemesis) and a junior barrister named Robert Alexander. The court found in favour of the cricket authorities.

With regular television exposure now guaranteed, the county cricket clubs, hesitantly at first but with ever-increasing confidence, began selling advertising space on their grounds. The boundary, which had evolved almost by accident, now became English cricket's most marketable asset.

For years the MCC had been a soft touch, practically giving away the catering franchise at Lord's (to Watney's, whose chairman, FG Mann, was on the MCC Committee) and under-selling the television rights. The new TCCB set up a sub-committee on public relations and promotions, chaired by ex-Surrey amateur and PR specialist Raman Subba Row and administered by MCC Assistant Secretary Jack Bailey, a former Essex amateur and journalist. The BBC, hoping to resecure the television rights for Test matches at the old knock-down prices, tried to go behind the sub-committee's back by appealing to MCC Secretary Billy Griffiths in the name of the old-school tie. But Bailey and Subba Row stood their ground and forced the BBC to double its payment.

Cricket was learning to live in the modern world. The first one-day international was played in Melbourne in 1971 and became a regular fixture in England the following year, which also saw the birth of the Benson & Hedges one-day cup competition, introduced at the behest of the sponsor. In less than a decade, English county cricket had acquired three new competitions, after making do, for generations, with one. In 1974 the bookmakers, after an absence of nearly a century, were readmitted to Lord's. And with the staging of the first World Cup in England in 1975, English cricket seemed to have come to terms with the new global media marketplace.

What, then, was all the fuss about Kerry Packer?

The Lord's Test against the Australians, 1977. Fast bowler Jeff Thomson takes the ball to warm applause from the English crowd. It has just been announced that Thomson has withdrawn from his contract with Packer in order to play for his country.

Why on earth should an English cricket crowd take to its heart a man who was about to unleash extreme physical violence against English batsmen? A man who had boasted of wanting to 'hurt batsmen'? Stranger still, why should it take delight in the prospect of a Packer-free Thommo battering English batsmen in future Ashes Tests? In the end, Thommo, always a volatile character, played for Packer anyway. But he had given the crowd at Lord's a chance to show its feelings about Kerry Packer's World Series Cricket.

I had already watched more than one sport mutate under pressure from the all-powerful media. Even tennis had emerged from the cocoon of well-mannered amateurism to flutter through the airwaves as a gaudy professional spectator sport. Why should cricket be any different? The old regime at Lord's was clearly out of touch. Their ritual references to the 'values' of English cricket meant little to me. If they fell to Packer, why should I care?

And yet, like most cricket fans in England, I found myself shaking my head in disapproval at the idea of cricket being purchased by a media millionaire and recast as prime-time entertainment. I had had enough of that in the States. England, I had thought, and cricket especially, would be a haven from all that, if only by virtue of its increasing economic backwardness. The things in cricket that had seemed alien and arbitrary only two years before had already come to seem natural, and even worth fighting to preserve.

The World Cup of 1975, staged under the aegis of the Duke of Edinburgh, that year's MCC President and ICC Chairman, had alerted Packer to the commercial potential of international cricket. It also made 'stars' of Ian Chappell's 'ugly Australians', the first true TV-age cricketers. Swaggering, rude and crude, they epitomized a strongly anti-Pom Australian national identity, and they bitterly resented the fuddy-duddies of the Australian Cricket Board telling them how to behave. It was Packer's ability to recruit nearly the whole lot of them that made it possible for him to mount his challenge to the cricket authorities.

Thus, modernity and the market were imported into English cricket from abroad. At least, that was how many in England chose to see it. Packer was portrayed not merely as a commercial rival but as a cultural adversary. Where Americans used to see Australians as junior Brits, English people tended to see them, equally myopically, as half American. Hence the repeated charge that Packer was going to 'Americanize' cricket. Ironically, only two years before Packer, the American CIA had effectively staged a coup d'etat in Australia. Gough Whitlam's Labour government, the most radical and independent minded in Australia's history, had fallen victim to a classic destabilization campaign. The *coup de grace* was administered by the Queen's representative, Governor-General Sir John Kerr, who used his ancient prerogatives to strip Whitlam of office.

The Australian Board had incurred Packer's ire by rebuffing his bid for exclusive television rights. He had offered the authorities more money than the Australian Broadcasting Corporation, who nevertheless retained the contract. The Australian Board, like its cousin, the MCC, was loyal to precedent, not profit. Packer could not understand how traditional loyalties could be elevated over the dictates of the market.

The Board promised to let Packer bid in open competition with ABC in the future. But Packer turned the tables by declaring that from now on *the Board would have to bid against him in open competition for the services of the players*. The Board offered to stage special matches for Packer (at this stage its objections to him were apparently not as profound as was later claimed), but he wanted the Tests. When the ICC met Packer at Lord's in June 1977, the aim was to negotiate a compromise. But the Australian Board was adamant and forced nervous ICC colleagues to back its stand. Leaving the meeting, Packer was positively gleeful. 'Let the Devil take the hindmost!' he chortled. From then on, the struggle against Packer became a matter of high principle. The former Kent amateur captain, DG Clark (Rugby), that year's MCC President and ICC Chairman, declared: 'Wars are not won by appeasement.'

Jack Bailey recalled the mood of the authorities:

> We were protecting cricket: part of the English heritage, now the world's heritage, a game in which honour was a byword ... cricket was one of the constant bastions of the ideals we hoped the world would one day live by ... it was too precious not to preserve as we had tried to preserve it ... the honour of representing your country could not be surpassed by all the money in the world.

The nation stood above the market, and cricket stood for the nation. 'Loyalty' became the watchword of the hour. The cricket authorities were outraged to find that they had nursed a viper in their bosom. Not long ago, the South African-born Tony Greig had been hailed as the saviour of English cricket. Now, as Packer's adjutant, he was sprayed with vitriol. Packer's other English recruits – Knott, Underwood, Snow, Amiss – were treated more gently. Greig was singled out because he held the England captaincy, and because he was a foreigner. 'What has to be remembered,' John Woodcock reminded Times readers, 'is that Greig is English only by adoption, which is not the same as being English through and through.'

Greig answered his critics by claiming allegiance to a higher loyalty: 'I have sacrificed cricket's most coveted job for a cause which I believe could be in the interests of cricket the world over.' He became Packer's prophet, and still works for Packer's Channel 9 TV. He has never been granted the honorary life membership which the MCC has bestowed on every other England captain.

Greig's apostasy created two unlikely defenders of the faith. When Geoff Boycott had absented himself from Test cricket two years earlier, Greig had questioned his courage and 'loyalty'. Now Boycott denounced Packer, returned to the England fold, scored his hundredth hundred at Headingley and became, for a moment, a champion of the establishment. Stranger still, at his side was the new England captain, Mike Brearley, a former academic who clearly believed that cricket was not the only rewarding activity in life. His high-minded liberalism was mistaken by some (including the Australian press) for the old English amateurism. But Brearley was a pragmatic modern professional with little time for nationalist pieties. 'His clarity of mind,' Arlott wrote, 'enabled him to pierce the woolly romanticism and anachronistic feudalism which for so long obscured the truth of cricket.'

Having eschewed 'appeasement', the cricket authorities decided to fight fire with fire. Within a month, Cornhill Insurance became the first sponsors of Test cricket in England. Cornhill, which had never before advertised outside the trade and whose name was largely unknown to cricket fans, was feted as a national saviour. Until then, the TCCB had insisted that Test cricket was too prestigious to sell to a commercial sponsor. Doug Insole, the former Essex amateur who chaired the TCCB Cricket Committee, told the insurers: 'There is no way we'd accept your sponsorship if you were selling Kentucky Fried Chicken.' But there was no escaping the fact that the TCCB needed sponsors' cash to win a bidding war with Packer for Test players' services.

The authorities' stand against Packer was popular in England and backed by most of the media. But not everyone took their case at face value. The *Economist* welcomed Packer's challenge to the stale monopoly of 'authorized cricket', a behemoth which had been shielded from the realities of the marketplace for too long. The magazine's support for Packer was part of its late-seventies ideological war against over regulation, nationalized industries and Britain's 'uncompetitive' culture. The magazine's proto-Thatcherism enabled it to grasp the irony of the Cornhill signing: 'The English cricket authorities are preparing to defend in court the restrictive practices by which they have been seeking to prevent the entry of Mr Packer into a sort of competition which has now proved to be their salvation.'

The *Economist* explained the commercial advantages Packer enjoyed in his war with the TCCB, especially the fact that he did not have to pay wages to the non-stars of domestic cricket. But here it noted a disadvantage: Packer would be unable to mobilize the 'patriotism' which the *Economist* considered one of cricket's prime assets. As early as August 1977, the magazine predicted the ultimate result of the contest between the seemingly implacable opponents: 'between the disciplining gentlemen and the commercial operators there is being waged ... a war which must eventually be settled by compromise'.

But before compromise came cricket's day in court. The ICC and TCCB had attempted to ban the Packer players from county and international cricket. All those currently under contract to Packer were given until 1st October to withdraw from World Series Cricket. The West Indies warned that the courts would not swallow it, but the ACB and TCCB were intent on asserting their traditional prerogatives. Packer argued that his World Series was not an alternative, but a supplement to traditional Test cricket. The authorities, however, were not willing to share. They were promptly challenged in the courts by Greig, John Snow and Mike Procter, all backed financially by Packer.

In the High Court, Insole and Bailey claimed that 'authorized cricket' had special responsibilities and therefore special powers. English cricket was one, from top to bottom, county to county. Through this unitary system, the weaker benefited from the stronger, the amateur from the professional. Packer only wanted to cream off the best without helping the game as a whole. Packer stood for nothing but himself; the TCCB stood for cricket.

In response, Packer's QC, Robert Alexander, put English cricket on trial. Day after day, he mocked its anachronism and its delusions. He berated the authorities for acting as if they had the legal authority of a sovereign state. He compared them to medieval landlords and the players to serfs. He accused them of failing to make the most of the game in the modern marketplace – and asked why the players should be asked to suffer for this failure. He reminded the court repeatedly that the cricket authorities issued no contracts to Test players, that they expected loyalty and service and offered nothing in return. Jack Bailey, giving evidence for the ICC, testily pointed out that barristers too worked without contracts.

At the end of the thirty-two-day hearing, Justice Slade ruled for the plaintiffs. The TCCB and ICC found themselves liable for £250,000 costs and damages. Slade accepted that the nature of sporting institutions placed limits on the normal rules of the market. The TCCB and ICC were indeed, as they claimed, 'custodians of public interest'. But their ban was retrospective and hence unfair. The players had not been under contract to the TCCB or ICC when they had signed with Packer.

> A professional cricketer needs to make his living as much as any other man. I think it is straining the concept of loyalty too far for the authorities ... to expect him to enter into a self-denying ordinance not to play cricket for a private promoter during the winter months, merely because the matches promoted could detract from the future profits made by the authorities, who are not themselves willing or in a position to offer him employment over the winter or to guarantee him employment for the future.

In Slade's opinion, the failure of the TCCB to offer Test players 'any real career structure' or realistic remuneration had left 'the path open to an aspiring commercial promoter of cricket'. Slade was only surprised Packer hadn't come along sooner.

He reminded the TCCB that the contracts signed by the players with

Packer were entitled to the protection of the law and the state. The ban had been a flagrant inducement to the players to break those contracts and was therefore illegal. He added that the TCCB had assumed rights and privileges belonging to an employers' association when it had failed to establish that status in law. This was the worst blow of all. For the first time, the powers of English cricket had been tested in a court of law. As a semi-feudal institution, it had always relied on customary rights. It had assumed the court would sanction these rights and was shocked by the rebuff.

Slade's decision cleared the way for Packer to engage the authorities in open competition, but that had never been his aim. Packer did not want to run world cricket. He wanted the right to exploit it through television. In World Series Cricket, broadcasting called the tune; the matches were staged entirely for its benefit. Spectators were admitted free to the early WSC matches in order to provide 'atmosphere' for the television cameras. Through promotion and commentary, the WSC machine manufactured cricket drama for instant sale over the airwaves. There were Lillee and Thommo bashing Amiss and Greig, Viv Richards pulling Max Walker, Holding and Roberts bouncing the Chappells. It had all happened before – in official cricket. This was an all-action replay with the colours heightened and the boring bits edited out. It was 'virtual cricket', a contrived experience.

Packer did draw new spectators to cricket, but, in the end, the *Economist* was proved right. Despite the hoopla and jingoism, World Series Cricket simply did not mean enough to attract the stable audience Packer needed to defray his expenses. Unable to establish a true alternative, Packer did however succeed in spoiling the ACB's monopoly. The 1978-79 'official' Australians, badly beaten by Mike Brearley's England, were poorly supported by a public which felt that the 'real' Australian team was otherwise engaged. For the first time, an Ashes series lost money.

This mutual failure was the basis of the 'historic compromise' between Packer and the cricket authorities. The ACB met with Packer in secret. Without informing the ICC, it agreed not only to give Packer the TV rights but also to restructure its schedule to suit his needs. There would now be more one-day internationals, including day-night matches under floodlights with coloured clothing. A planned tour by the Indian side was cancelled and replaced by a flying visit from the more popular English and West Indian teams. Packer's organization was given a ten-year exclusive contract to promote and merchandise cricket in Australia. All this was conceded in return for the disbandment of WSC.

The Australian Board's sudden capitulation shocked its allies in England. After all, the ACB had been positively Churchillian in its vows of defiance. In the early days of the conflict, Packer had offended the Australian authorities by asking, 'Come on, what's your price? We're all harlots.' In the end their price was not monetary. It was simply the preservation of their own authority, even if that meant tainting the game with Packer's vulgarity. Their hypocrisy mirrored Packer's. He came as a liberator, but in the end was content to prop up the old structures, as long as he was allowed his share of the spoils.

Although the English authorities grumbled over the Australian deal, they learned to live with it quickly enough. Already, the Packer threat had proved a boon. In 1977, the TCCB had sponsorship deals worth £476,000. By 1980, they were worth nearly £2 million. In 1989, Bob Alexander, recently ennobled by Margaret Thatcher as Lord Alexander of Weedon, became Chairman of NatWest. English cricket's courtroom nemesis had become one of its major patrons.

Methodist Central Hall, Westminster, 27 January 1993. A Special General Meeting of the MCC has been convened to debate a motion of no confidence in England's Test selectors. The omission of David Gower from the England party to tour India and Sri Lanka has enraged the traditionalists of the MCC, who have finally joined battle with the modernizers of the TCCB. Nothing less than the soul of English cricket is at stake.

At least, that was how it was presented in some quarters. Looking back at the origins and outcome of the Gower affair, however, it becomes clear that although it was indeed the climax of a long-running dispute, it was not so much a struggle for power between opposing camps as an adjustment within an old partnership.

Back in 1977, the former Surrey amateur, Raman Subba Row (Whitgift, Cambridge), had argued that the lesson of Packer's intervention was the need for the TCCB to adopt 'a modern management approach'. The next year, he headed a TCCB working party on cricket's structures, in which he was aided by Ossie Wheatley (King Edward's School, Cambridge), a former Glamorgan amateur who had made a career in advertising. Subba Row and Wheatley recommended winding up the Cricket Council and replacing it a with a 'UK Board of Cricket ... based mainly on the first-class counties and the NCA'. The TCCB, they argued, was too cumbersome. They proposed a streamlined committee structure and the appointment of a Chief Executive, as well as a purpose-built TCCB HQ 'at Lord's or elsewhere'. As for the MCC, 'it could not be considered democratic' and therefore had no role to play in the governance of English cricket.

The MCC responded: 'Cricket, like Government, benefits from the use of a second chamber which is to some extent detached.' Increasingly in the coming years, Britain's unwritten constitution would be called upon to justify MCC's anomalous role. The counties rejected the working party's recommendations, but within a few years the composition of the Cricket Council was changed, with the MCC's collaboration, to give the TCCB an automatic majority, which made the Council redundant. At the TCCB itself, a Chief Executive was soon appointed to work hand in hand with a small Executive Committee. In *Wisden*, John Woodcock issued a warning: 'Beware the small, executive sub committee of businessmen to whom the charm of cricket is little more than a technicality.'

The eighties were marked by a series of petty disputes over control of Test matches and cup finals at Lord's. Repeatedly the MCC threatened to make a stand, only to concede ground to the TCCB. Just as Thatcher had pushed aside the old Tory grandees, despatching Carrington, Pym, Gilmour and Soames to the political wilderness, so the ruthless money men of the TCCB seemed poised to occupy the Lord's turf traditionally belonging to the men of landed leisure. MCC Secretary Jack Bailey, who had started off, twenty years before, as a modernizer, found he could no longer stomach the arrogance of the TCCB's 'bureaucratic clique'. His departure from the club was acrimonious, and fuelled suspicions among some members that the old values were being sold out.

His successor as MCC Secretary, Lieutenant Colonel JR Stephenson (Sandhurst, Royal Sussex Regiment), the son of an Oxford cricket blue and Yorkshire amateur, reassured the members: 'Through these difficult and transitional times MCC has an important role. It is the upper house – the House of Lord's, if you like.'

Lord Bramall restated the theme when he became MCC President in 1989, proudly describing the old club as 'the guardian and conscience of the game'. Under Bramall's aegis, the MCC for the first time adopted a formal statement of 'Roles of the Club', which included 'the right to encourage, warn and advise' the official cricket authorities. According to Bramall, the MCC would act as the constitutional monarch of English cricket. After the disastrous season of 1988, when four England captains took turns losing to the West Indies, Bramall was full of hope for the coming series against Australia. 'With Ted and David Gower and with the Australians coming ... I think it's going to be played more chivalrously.'

Clearly, the ancient amateur prejudices were still alive, at least in the heart of Field Marshal Edwin Noel Westby Bramall, KG, GCB, OBE, JP, HM Lord Lieutenant of Greater London, Chief of General Staff (at the time of the Falklands War), a former Commander of British forces in Hong Kong and, long ago, the captain of the Eton XI. But the Field Marshal's hopes for the new England regime were to be bitterly disappointed.

In 1989, the panel of selectors which had chosen England Test sides since 1899 was replaced by a new 'England Committee', composed of a Chairman, Ted Dexter, the team manager, Micky Stewart, the Chairman of the TCCB Cricket Committee, Ossie Wheatley, all appointed by the TCCB, and the Test captain, appointed by the England Committee itself. The new Committee was the brainchild of Subba Row, the retiring TCCB Chair, who believed it would streamline and stabilize the English system. It was given a wide remit over the development of English cricket and the services of an ever-growing battery of scouts, coaches and fitness trainers. Dexter (Radley, Cambridge) was paid £40,000 a year, making him the first properly remunerated Chairman of Selectors. 'At home the selectors tend to become meat and drink to the media,' Dexter explained. 'our aim is to reduce this pressure.'

In the Ashes series that followed, the England Committee selected twenty-nine players, the largest and most fruitless trawl since the traumatic years after World War I. The Australians took the series, 4-0. Gower was stripped of the captaincy and left out of the following winter's tour to the West Indies.

Gower, it was said, simply did not fit into the brave, new world of Micky Stewart, who had opposed his appointment as captain. Stewart was a bookmaker's son who had attended a public school and played amateur football for Corinthian Casuals. But at Surrey, he played for eighteen years as a pugnacious professional, and as the first England team manager, he instituted a regime of intensive training and scientific preparation. His philosophy was in keeping with the unsparing competitive ethos of the eighties: 'They say, why should a young child experience failure before he's prepared for it? Well, I think you succeed and fail from the time you come out of the womb. And I believe that cricket is an important part of the character of the average Englishman.'

The appeal to nationalism was not quite the non-sequitur it appeared. The national heritage, Stewart was implying, was under threat from excessive egalitarianism. This was a common Thatcherite theme. Stewart's was the old masochistic public-school games ethos stripped of its veneer of gentlemanly disinterest. That was why so many of the gentlemen didn't like it. Many within the MCC wanted the club to take up a crusade against the England Committee and all its works. With its emphasis on defensive cricket, physical fitness and commercial sponsorship, it was Pycroft's nightmare of professionalism run rampant.

E.W. Swanton, the Pycroft of our times, believed that in the TCCB the MCC had created 'a monster'. He fulminated against Stewart's 'dreary tracksuit, work ethic' with its contempt for 'individuality and flashy brilliance'. His antidote was a reassertion of the influence of the MCC in the affairs of English cricket. Unlike the mercenary-minded TCCB, the MCC represented 'a thread of homogeneity among cricketers of all types from the village green to St John's Wood'. Tony Lewis, now on the MCC Committee, went so far as to accuse the TCCB of the 'subjugation of the counties to a police state'. A letter to *The Cricketer* summed up the feelings of many, inside and outside the MCC: 'The TCCB and ICC are not only ineffectual, but also seem to be stupid, and money is their god.'

Gower returned to the England side against India and New Zealand in 1990, and was taken to Australia in the winter of 1990-91, when England lost the series 3-0. After Gooch, Gower was the most consistent England batsman, averaging 42 with two hundreds, but in the course of the tour he made clear his disrespect for the current England regime, spurning the training sessions organized by Gooch and Stewart. Worse yet, along with John Morris, he took time off from a match against Queensland (the only first-class match England won in the course of the tour) to hire light aircraft which they then flew at low altitude over their colleagues still toiling in the field. Gooch and Stewart were not amused. The miscreants were fined £1,000 each. The next summer, Gower was left out of all five Tests against the West Indies. He was then omitted from the England squad for the World Cup in the spring of 1992.

Finally recalled to the England side for the third Test against Pakistan later that summer, Gower scored 73, in the course of which he overtook Boycott to become the highest run-scorer in English Test history. Outrage greeted the England Committee's decision to leave him out of the winter tour of India and Sri Lanka. Dexter failed to offer any explanation. Fletcher, who had just succeeded Micky Stewart, mumbled something about not wanting too many batsmen in their mid-thirties. In *Wisden* Matthew Engel observed: 'There was no sustainable cricketing case for the omission of Gower from a Test series against India. No one seriously made one.' Engel also noted the contrast between the England Committee's treatment of Gower's misdemeanours with the precipitate welcome it had offered the newly reprieved South African rebels, Emburey, Gatting and Jarvis.

For many critics of the TCCB, the omission of Gower and Jack Russell, the country's leading specialist wicket-keeper, was final proof that the England regime preferred automatons to artists. Two MCC members, Dennis Oliver, a Kent businessman, and Donald Trelford, then editor of the *Observer*, launched a campaign to get Gower reinstated, which was, in effect, a campaign against the TCCB and its England Committee.

Around the Gower affair, the old antinomies of English cricket were played out. Stroke-makers or accumulators, risk-takers or risk-reducers, style or utility? To Gower's MCC champions, all of these were reducible to the most basic dichotomy of all: 'amateur or professional'. Gower, however, was every inch a professional cricketer, down to his ghosted tabloid articles and sponsorship deals. Rejected by England, he turned up in India with Sky TV. This did not deter the MCC dissidents, who wanted a cavalier martyr to thrust in the face of the TCCB roundheads. Because of his voice, his bearing and, above all, his style of play, Gower fitted the mould. But his appeal extended far beyond the MCC traditionalists. His treatment by the England Committee offended all those who looked to cricket for joy, and were fed up with being offered only drudgery.

Encouraged by a sympathetic press (and extensive advertisements in the *Observer*), 286 MCC members signed the call for a Special General Meeting. The MCC Committee was aghast. EW Swanton had attacked the omission of Gower but deplored Oliver and Trelford for showing 'lack of respect for authority and tradition'. In *The Cricketer*, Richard Hutton expressed sympathy for the rebels' cause, but warned that 'should the principle of selectorial confidentiality be abandoned the road to anarchy is open'. JJ Warr, a former Cambridge captain, Middlesex amateur, MCC President and Chairman of the City-based Union Discount, described the no-confidence motion as 'a perfect example of abusing the umpire and showing palpable and obvious dissent'.

But Oliver, Trelford and their supporters, including Mark Bonham Carter, a Liberal peer, and Ian Gilmour, a Tory grandee, were only asking the MCC to live up to its rhetoric. As English cricket's constitutional monarch, the club had a duty to stand up to the mercenary time-servers of the TCCB. That year's MCC President, Dennis Silk (Christ's Hospital, Cambridge), a former housemaster at Marlborough and warden of

Radley, tried to talk the dissidents round at a private meeting in the Long Room. 'We were treated like recalcitrant fifth-formers,' complained Oliver. The Special General Meeting went ahead, at a cost of £20,000.

In Central Hall, there was no crime against cricket of which the England Committee was not accused. Ironically, the amateur traditionalists accused the pragmatists of the TCCB of 'double standards'. Gower had been judged for his nonchalant conduct off the field rather than his heroic performances on it. Stewart would not tolerate independent minds and Gooch distrusted all potential rivals. The MCC Committee responded with a robust attack on the logic and motives of the rebels. Lord Bramall defended Gooch: 'What commander worth his salt does not want to have some right to decide the men he wants to take with him into the fray?' The vote in the hall (where the average age was sixty) was 715 for the motion and 412 against. But thanks to the ever-loyal postal vote, the motion was defeated by 6,135 to 4,600. The MCC Committee had won the day. The Gower rebellion, an attempt to assert old MCC prerogatives and amateur values against the new-fangled TCCB, was quelled in the end, not by the TCCB, but by the MCC itself.

This should have surprised no one. The war between the MCC and the TCCB was always a phoney one. Their shadow boxing enabled all concerned to avoid facing the real causes of failure and decay. The TCCB was the creation of the MCC. Throughout the new body's evolution, its guiding figures came from the heart of 'the premier club'.

As MCC Assistant Secretary, the former Derbyshire 'shamateur', DB Carr (Repton, Oxford), had taken charge of both the TCCB and the Cricket Council. In 1974, he became TCCB Secretary, a position he held until 1986. DJ Insole (Ealing Grammar, Cambridge), a former amateur captain of Essex and marketing director, was Chairman of the TCCB Cricket Committee from 1968 until 1987, during which time he also served on the MCC Committee. He brought Cornhill into Test sponsorship with the aid of another MCC Committee man, one-time Cornhill Chairman JT Faber (Winchester, Cambridge), who was also a director of Morgan Grenfell, the merchant bankers, and Chairman of the tobacco giant, Willis Faber. The former England captain George Mann (Eton, Cambridge), a director of Watney Mann and the Extel Croup, was Chairman of the TCCB from 1978 to 1983, then President of MCC in 1984-85. CH Palmer, a 'shamateur' captain of Leicestershire in the fifties, was MCC President in 1978-79 and TCCB Chairman from 1983 to 1985.

Even in 1993, twenty-five years after the creation of the TCCB, fourteen of the eighteen county chairmen who made up the TCCB's ruling body were members of the MCC – which, it should be remembered, has a thirteen-year waiting list. Jack Bailey missed the point when he accused some members of the MCC Committee of 'wearing two hats'. There was no conflict of interest. The role of the TCCB was to preserve control of English cricket in the hands of the elite, the same elite which had governed the MCC for so long.

English cricket has been transformed not by new personnel from outside, but by the last generation of amateurs, notably Subba Row and Ossie Wheatley. Alan Smith (King Edward School, Oxford) was director of an advertising and marketing firm until he became Chief Executive of the TCCB under Subba Row. Peter May (Charterhouse, Cambridge) had been considered a classical amateur batsman, all grace and timing. After his early retirement from cricket, he became a Lloyd's broker and company director, serving on the board of Willis Faber, among others. He followed his stint as MCC President in 1980-81 with a seven-year term as the TCCB's Chairman of Selectors, which culminated in the inglorious summer of the four captains.

The best example of the old amateurism in transition is May's former England colleague, Colin Cowdrey (Tonbridge, Oxford), an establishment favourite throughout his career. He chaired the TCCB's County Pitches Committee in the mid-eighties before becoming MCC President in 1986-87. In time-honoured fashion he had been nominated for the honour by his predecessor, the former Kent amateur, JGW Davies (Tonbridge, Cambridge), executive director of the Bank of England and director of Barclays, which also happened to employ Cowdrey as a 'consultant'. Cowdrey had recently married Lady Herries of Terregles, a racecourse trainer, spaniel breeder, and daughter of the Duke of Norfolk, one of English cricket's major benefactors. Cowdrey thus completed a long social climb, from the lower echelons of the old imperial elite (his father managed a tea estate in southern India) to its landed pinnacle. As MCC President, he helped remove the troublesome Bailey and ensure MCC compliance with Subba Row's new order.

The cricket elite is still a faithful mirror of the country's ruling class, especially in its historic slant to City and overseas trade, a slant exacerbated by Thatcherite deregulation and the globalization of the economy. The barristers, military men, public-school masters and alcohol kingpins have been joined by accountants and public-relations experts, but landed wealth remains a powerful presence. Between 1990 and 1994, Frank Chamberlain served as Chairman of the TCCB. He had played first-class cricket for one season (as an amateur) and had later served as Chairman of Northamptonshire CCC. More to the point, he came from a family of merchant bankers, was a director of NatWest, had been a member of the CBI Council, and was High Sheriff and Deputy Lieutenant of Northamptonshire.

Another spiritual descendant of the Star and Garter gentlemen is Robin Leigh-Pemberton (Eton, Oxford), a former barrister, Chairman of NatWest and Governor of the Bank of England. As the scion of an old branch of the Kent country gentry, he has refurbished the cricket ground at his family estate and become a trustee of the county cricket club, not to mention Her Majesty's Lord Lieutenant. He lists his principal recreation as 'country life' and is a member of I Zingari, which plays an annual fixture on his private ground.

I Zingari withdrew from first-class cricket in 1904 but still play annual matches against the Guards, the Duchess of Norfolk's XI, the Earl of Carnarvon's XI, Eton, Harrow, Charterhouse, Winchester, Royal Armoured Corps, Royal Navy, Sandhurst Wanderers, JP Getty's XI, Leicester Gentlemen and South Wales Hunts XI, keeping alive the exclusive traditions of country-house cricket. Among its current members are Lord Bramall, Lord Home, George Mann, JP Getty, and eight former England captains, including David Gower. Between 1953 and 1993, its Honorary Secretary, successor to Ponsonby Fane, was the one-time Sussex amateur, Sir William Becher (Harrow, Cambridge), an Irish-born army officer, Lloyd's underwriter and landowner.

Clearly, continuity rules in English cricket, as in so many British institutions. Of course, new blood is admitted; these people are nothing if not flexible. But in Britain, new money always apes the old, not least by patronizing cricket. Thus the old culture endures, exclusive and undemocratic.

That was why, despite the occasional huffing and puffing, the grandees in both the Tory Party and the MCC (and to a remarkable extent they were the same people) were so feeble in their resistance to the free marketeers. They saw here a radical solution to long-standing quandaries, and guided by ruthless realism, they embraced it as the only means of sustaining old privileges.

Nowadays, the MCC Committee looks after the TCCB interest, answering complaints from its own members with the counsels of realpolitik and worldly reminders of the ineluctable dictates of the market. The MCC Committee, more than the naive rank and file, knows that in this society authority derives from money. It knows that the MCC coffers are full because of the TCCB's embrace of the market.

Sponsorship and television exposure have enhanced cricket's status, and ensured that MCC membership remains as desirable as ever. Walter Bagehot argued that under Britain's unwritten constitution, 'Money is kept down, and so to say, cowed by the predominant authority of a different power.' It would be more accurate to say that the power of money has been *disguised* by that authority. What upset the MCC rebels over the years was that the disguise had slipped.

This was the source of the rumpus over the TCCB decision to paint the sponsor's logos on Test match grounds. In 1992, MCC President Michael Melluish (Rossall, Cambridge) assured the club's AGM that the Committee had 'continued to resist all attempts to paint logos on the turf at Lord's'. Compromise, however, had proved inevitable. There would be no logo at the Pavilion End but there would be a portable one at the Nursery End (removed after the match to preserve Lord's from the curse of the 'unsightly fading logo'). The MCC members would be able to benefit from malodorous commercialism without having it thrust under their noses.

If final proof was needed of the real nature of the MCC v. TCCB squabble, it came with the report of the Griffiths Inquiry of 1993-94. After the Gower rebellion had been put down at Westminster Central Hall, MCC Secretary Stephenson had acknowledged that there was 'a message' for the TCCB about the need for better 'communication'. As a concession to the dissidents, the MCC Committee set up a broad inquiry into the administrative structure of cricket and, in particular, the 'public accountability' of the TCCB. Dennis Oliver was co-opted on to the inquiry, which was chaired by Lord Griffiths.

WH Griffiths (Charterhouse, Cambridge), a one-time Glamorgan amateur, had ascended the judicial ranks to become a Lord of Appeal in Ordinary. He had served on Heath's ill-fated National Industrial Relations Court and as Chairman of Thatcher's Security Commission between 1985 and 1990. A long-time member of the MCC Committee, and Club President in 1990-91, he possessed the proverbial safe pair of hands. His report to the MCC, published in early 1994, called for the abolition of the Cricket Council and its replacement by a single administrative body for all cricket in Britain, amateur and professional.

Not surprisingly, the TCCB welcomed the idea of a merger with the NCA. Their marketing and finance departments had already been integrated. If the Griffiths Report is implemented, as seems likely, its main effect will not be to reform professional cricket but to bring the welter of organizations in recreational cricket under direct TCCB control.

Griffiths's answer to the problems of English cricket – and how telling it is that it comes from the heart of the MCC – is more of the same. English cricket will become more centralized and less democratic than ever.* Supervising that process will be the new Chairman of the TCCB – Dennis Silk, the retiring MCC President.

When it was created back in 1968, the TCCB was supposed to be an accountable pubic-sector-style body. But a funny thing happened *en route* to democracy: the TCCB became a corporate, private-sector-style bureaucracy, which the punters found just as unaccountable as the feudal institution it supplanted. In the image of its progenitor, the MCC, the TCCB was a central authority placed over and above its constituent counties (not to mention the 20,000 cricket clubs in the country). English cricket remained a mirror of the British state, in which authority emanates from the Crown in Parliament and is disseminated downwards. The justification for this has been the overriding importance of the England Test side. According to the TCCB constitution, the body's 'essential object' was 'the achievement of the highest possible standards at international level'. With the TCCB controlling the purse-strings as never before, it has been able to subordinate the needs of counties and clubs, players and fans, to whatever it deems to be the national interest. Like the quangos set up by the Tories to run the NHS, public transport and higher education, the TCCB has imposed so-called business methods on a public service, and like those quangos it has become a byword for the misrule of invisible accountants.

Conventional economic models rarely apply to commercial sport. Even football club owners are frequently guided by considerations (vanity, politics, loyalty) other than the maximization of profit which is the ruling principle in their other activities. If this is true in football, how much more so in cricket, with its pre-industrial baggage. Despite cricket's recent embrace of the market, what might be called its political economy continues to function in a kind of parallel universe, not quite conforming to the norms that govern other commercial ventures.

In 1992, first-class cricket enjoyed a turnover of £40 million, half of which was centrally generated by Tests, one-day internationals and TCCB-organized sponsorship deals. More and more money has gone into the game, but county finances remain parlous. The difference between profit and loss may be a rainy festival week or a good run in the

* And so it has come to pass. See Chapter 8, pages 327-329.

NatWest. Not a single county would break even without the hand outs from the TCCB, which account for between 33 per cent and 44 per cent of county incomes. Sponsorship, hospitality boxes and merchandising account for another 25 to 45 per cent. Members' subscriptions (except in Lancashire and Yorkshire) yield a mere 10 to 12 per cent – and ordinary ground admissions an almost irrelevant 2 to 6 per cent.

When the Australians played Kent at the 152nd Canterbury Week in 1993 6,500 came through the gate. But altogether they put less in Kent's coffers than the thirty-seven firms offering corporate hospitality and the twenty-two private marquees that circled the ground. In 1991, Northamptonshire received £48,000 in gate receipts, of which £31,000 was from the Sunday League. Members' subscriptions amounted to £88,000, but hospitality facilities brought in £93,000. In 1992, total gate receipts for Sussex for all contests were £53,000, including £10,000 for car-parking fees. But various sponsorship and marketing activities brought in £315,000. Advertising boards alone accounted for £110,000.

Ironically, the very consumer capitalism which stripped cricket of a live audience and seemed to threaten its survival has proved the sport's salvation. But, of course, there has been a cost. The field is no longer full of 'ghostly shades' but, in Scyld Berry's words, 'diseased by the eczema of logos'. The Test team is sponsored by brewers, the Test matches by insurers, the umpires by a privatized electricity company. Even sight screens are now turned into prime-site hoardings. They could stage most county cricket in private these days and it would make little difference to the accountants. To supplement TCCB largesse, the counties recruited a plethora of local sponsors: privatized gas and electricity companies, law and insurance firms, chartered accountants, private health-care providers, banks, investment advisers, travel agencies and wine merchants. At Warwickshire the paint, floral displays and waterproof clothing are all provided by 'direct sponsorship'. At Essex cars and vans are sponsored by fourteen different local firms; match balls are sponsored by another thirty-three. At Yorkshire, a minibus, clothing, training and coaching schemes, the county magazine, players' cars, footwear, even the overseas signing are all sponsored. County sponsorship is a kind of barter, difficult for either party to quantify in cold cash and maintained through good will and incessant 'liaising' .

In the eighties, the cricket authorities, having lagged behind for decades, rushed to catch up and surpass other sports in the race for sponsorship. This was in keeping with government policy, which encouraged private sponsorship of sport (and just about everything else).

In Britain today, direct sponsorship of sport is worth £250 million, with £17.5 million going to cricket. The grace and favour of the sponsors have replaced the grace and favour of the landed elite. But there is a difference. When the sponsors sign a contract, they expect a return on their investment. The sponsors' names must be visible as often as possible, preferably on television.

As always, individual enterprise preceded the lumbering cartel. In the late seventies and early eighties, a number of leading players signed contracts with sponsors committing them to wear logos on the field. The TCCB stepped in to ban the practice, ostensibly because it was 'unsightly'. However, within a few years, the TCCB itself was plastering logos on everything in sight. When the TCCB accepted Tetley Bitter's multi million-pound offer to sponsor the England side in 1992, Brian Downing, chair of the TCCB Marketing Committee (and the man who put the Fosters into the Fosters' Oval) said the object of the sale was 'to preserve five-day Test cricket'. That was not quite true. The object was to preserve it *under TCCB control*, to keep it out of the hands of pirates.

Of the forty-odd companies involved in sponsorship of English cricket at any level in 1992, half were in finance or insurance; a quarter were brewers, distillers, or food and drink retailers. The retail and financial sectors dominate English cricket just as they dominate the British economy.

According to a NatWest official, English cricket's chief attraction to sponsors is 'its image'. The TCCB promotions manager explained: 'There is no doubt that it is primarily the image of the game and its track record of successful association with the business world which continue to attract corporate advertisers.' The man from NatWest added: 'Its appeal is right across the social spectrum.' In the words of a Cornhill official, 'Cricket is classy, popular, has a broad appeal and gets good media coverage.' It has more ABC1 followers than football, more C2s and DEs than golf or tennis. Trevelyan's vision of cricket as a national sport binding together the different classes has been turned into a marketing ploy.

Texaco chose cricket for its 'quintessentially British' image: a 'family sport with a diverse audience and one associated with fair play'. The US-based oil company is not the only sponsor for whom cricket's Englishness' is a prime asset. Cornhill Insurance plc is owned by Allianz AG Holdings in Germany. Fosters is a subsidiary of the Fosters Brewing Group, Australia, which also owns Courage, John Smiths, Websters and now even Watneys. Tetley Bitter is owned by Allied Lyons, a world-spanning food and drink conglomerate. Benson & Hedges is owned by BAT, an international retail giant. AXA Equity and Law is owned by a French-based multi-national. In 1992, keen to re-establish an 'English' image after merger and reorganization, it signed a £2.5 million deal with the TCCB to sponsor the latest version of the Sunday League. At relatively little expense, these trans-national enterprises lease an English national identity from the TCCB.

Cricket's sheer longevity is an added appeal for the insurance and finance companies. Their aim is to convince would-be customers that their money will be in safe hands. They want to be associated with prudence and permanence, and English cricket offers both. National Grid began sponsoring umpires in 1993. 'We're in a position to take the unbiased view,' their adverts claimed, reminding the public of the company's 'duty of seeing fair play in the electricity market and encouraging fair competition between powerful interests'.

However, the ordinary publicity-seeking rationale of sports sponsorship does not entirely explain its role in cricket. The counties' Second XI competition, rarely in the public eye, is sponsored by Bain Clarkson, insurance brokers, underwriters and asset managers. The company is wholly owned by Inchcape, a Far Eastern-based shipping, property and financial giant. It is hugely profitable, but hardly a household name. It doesn't need to be, as its business does not require it to deal directly with a large cross-section of the public. Rapid CricketLine, part of William Hill Leisure, also sponsors Second XI cricket, though it is a competition which draws few punters to the till. Similarly, Middlesex is sponsored by SmithKline Beecham plc, which manufactures Lucozade, Beechams Powders, and a host of cosmetic and pharmaceutical products, but markets nothing directly to the public under its own name.

In recent years, Whittingdale, a specialist in unit trusts and fixed interest securities, has poured millions into preparation for overseas Test tours and elite youth cricket. The company was established only in 1987. Its investment in cricket is a way of making itself known and respected, not to the public at large (who have no need of its services), but within the square mile of the City. Like other sponsors, it uses cricket to sell an exclusive product to a small but lucrative market.* In 1982, Hambros

---

*Whittingdale lost patience with English cricket in 1996, and withdrew its sponsorship. Other sponsors have come and gone, and new money has come from the communications industry. But the clubby interface between the game and its

Bank, for similar reasons, sponsored a history of I Zingari.

Cricket brings prestige in these circles because of its long association with the English ruling class. Sign up with the TCCB and you can take your place among the peers of the realm as a benefactor of the national game. In addition, cricket offers today, as it has always done, excellent contacts, of commercial, political and personal use. Hospitality facilities are more than just the trimmings in sponsorship deals. Sponsors' demands for tickets, boxes and other perks grow more voracious every year. The new Mound Stand at Lord's has twenty-seven boxes, each with bar and television, and each available for hire at £20,000 a year. In 1992, NatWest entertained 9,000 guests at cricket matches. Like the Eton v. Harrow matches of old, today's cup finals, one-day internationals and Test matches provide occasions for the intermingling of the 'top people'. Modern cricket sponsorship has inherited from traditional cricket patronage an ancient function: the binding together of an elite.

The insignificance of gate money has stripped spectators of what little power they ever had. Sponsors now take priority even over county members, who are asked to pay more for less. For annual rates of between £60 and £80, members are free to wander in and out of county championship matches which no one else wants to see, but must pay additional charges for cup and Test matches staged on their home grounds. Advertising hoardings drive fans from the boundaries. The great lie of Thatcherism has been the lie of the TCCB: that giving the market free rein would automatically benefit the consumer.

In its endless quest for sponsorship and advertising revenue, the TCCB is not seeking out a mass audience for its product. The corporate hospitality industry enjoys a minority market, as does satellite television, which now broadcasts more cricket than BBC TV. English cricket is being reshaped according to the needs of an increasingly stratified sports market. Its famously 'national' audience is being divided into niches. Brian Downing described his strategy for the future of cricket as 'new sponsorship and bolder pricing'. For the cricket authorities, most cricket fans are surplus to requirements, except as a stay-at-home television audience, to be used as a bargaining chip in procuring sponsorship deals.

sponsors endures. When Tetley dropped out in 1997, it was replaced by Vodaphone, which had become the thirteenth biggest company in the country after only a decade in business, thanks to the mobile phone boom. The sponsorship deal with Vodaphone was quickly and quietly arranged by Lord MacLaurin, who also happened to be a director of the company, and became its Chairman a year later.

While money pours into the game as never before, rewards for professional cricketers remain modest. Since the early eighties, players' wages as a proportion of the game's total expenditure have gone down, as administrative costs (including the costs of 'liaising' with sponsors) have gone up. Very few English players earn more than £30,000 a year directly from the game. A cricketer must spend two years on a county staff before qualifying for the minimum wage, which now rises to £20,000.* Prize money even for a highly successful club rarely exceeds an extra £5,000 a year per player. Professional cricketers work harder than ever for relatively meagre rewards. Bonus and prize money is now shared out systematically, undercutting the old powers of patronage, but the professionals still enjoy little mobility. The TCCB's list system restricts the county-to-county movement even of non-capped players. A player wishing to move must refuse the contract offered by his current club before even discussing possible alternatives with any others. Since Packer, the TCCB is wary of being caught in 'restraint of trade' but remains implacably opposed to a 'football-style transfer system'. It fears that deregulation, a free market for professional cricketers, would throw the rickety old county structure hopelessly out of balance as a few rich teams bought up all the best players.

The players remain chained to the clubs, which nonetheless fail to provide them with any long-term security. The ancient benefit system is still in force. The players have learned to exploit modern fund-raising expertise, but the benefit is still an award from the county committee, not a right belonging to the player. The Professional Cricketers' Association (PCA) has long argued for portable endowments to replace benefits, but the authorities know that the benefit system gives the authorities vital control over employees. The relation between professional cricketers and their employees is still anomalous in the modern labour market, even compared with other sports.

The PCA has too often seen itself as the junior partner to the TCCB and accepted the old argument that 'what's good for the game', as defined by the TCCB, must be good for the players. Cricket was a latecomer to trade unionism, and most of its commercial growth has taken place during a period of declining union power. Its administrative costs are paid by the TCCB, which keeps it off all key decision-making bodies. Most cricketers are politically conservative. Collective action remains confined to the playing field. The gains players made from the Packer

*As of 1998.

intervention have been undermined by the emergence of a 'star system' and with it ever-widening differentials in cricketers' pay. The handful of stars are the only ones with any real weight in cricket's labour market and they rarely use it on behalf of their fellow cricketers.

The co-option of former professional cricketers into the TCCB and even the MCC administrations, and especially their increasing presence in the media, might give the impression that the professionals have enjoyed a spectacular rise in status since 1963. But finding a decent job after a cricket career is as hard as ever. There are far more ex-pros than there are positions in coaching, administration or media. Cricketers remain, as ever, beholden to those with the power to dispense these sinecures. Despite Packer, the TCCB and their own delusions, they are not freelance mercenaries like William Clarke's All England XI. They remain an adjunct to the English cricket establishment, which may be why they seem unable to articulate any independent vision of English cricket renewal.

The English county championship is a relic, saturated with nostalgia, its contestants festooned with the traditional emblems of communities which often no longer exist. Followed closely by a small band of aficionados, it survives today only by virtue of a huge subsidy from international cricket. Its advocates insist it is 'real' cricket, and must be safeguarded like 'real' ale. 'Modernize or perish', the motto of the Thatcher years, is anathema to them, as they made clear in their response to the Murray Report of 1992.

The report, 'A Blueprint for the First Class Game', was produced by the TCCB's 'Structure Working Party', chaired by the former Middlesex amateur and county club chair, Michael Murray, a bank manager. Among the party's other members were: Brian Downing, the TCCB Marketing Committee Chairman and former marketing director of Mirror Group Newspapers; Sir Iain MacLaurin, an MCC Committee member, Chairman and former Managing Director of Tesco plc, and Deputy Lieutenant of Hertfordshire; the multi-millionaire, Lyn Wilson, one of the hundred richest individuals in Britain, according to *The Sunday Times*; TCCB Chairman Frank Chamberlain, Chief Executive Alan Smith, and Cricket Secretary Tim Lamb (Shrewsbury, Oxford), a former Middlesex and Northamptonshire medium-pacer.

The working party was asked to deal in one fell swoop with all the ills of English cricket, and was specifically charged with rationalizing its baroque schedule. It proposed that the county championship should consist entirely of four-day matches with each county playing all the other counties once and once only. The matches would start on Thursday and be completed on Monday. The intervening Sunday would be used for the new, fifty-over AXA Equity and Law League. All of this would leave England players with at least two full cricket-free days before starting any Test. Giving international players time to prepare for the big matches was also the reason for the elimination of the round-robin zonal matches of the Benson & Hedges Cup, which for twenty years had preceded the cup's knockout stages and provided the main spice of the early season.

In *The Times*, Alan Lee welcomed the report: 'the cluttered chaos of recent years will now give way to ordered symmetry'. But the counties were wary. Four-day cricket would mean fewer home fixtures and loss of revenue, as would the truncated B&H Cup. The new Sunday League was offered as compensation, though for most county members it was a dubious trade-off.

EW Swanton damned the report as 'dangerously plausible'. Because there were fewer matches, he argued, the new schedule would entail the loss of first-class cricket at peripheral county grounds, including some of the most attractive, if least financially viable. It would endanger festival weeks and would give batsmen fewer first class innings: 'A four-day diet encourages a workaday grimness, putting initiative and variety at a discount. It is all of a piece with the defensive philosophies of Messrs Stewart and Fletcher.'

In the end, Swanton's argument rested on an appeal to the past: 'The three-day game has been the focus of national interest and the training ground for the England XI for more than a century.'

The report was offered to the counties on an all-or-nothing basis. Murray wanted the new system given a five-year trial. In order to get it adopted, he had to accept a reduction to three years. Even so, it was agreed, in May 1992, only by an 11-8 vote.

The adoption of the Murray Report was the culmination of a long running campaign by top TCCB officials for four-day cricket. In 1984, in the wake of Test defeats at the hands of Pakistan and New Zealand, the TCCB had commissioned the Palmer Report. It concluded that England's Test performances reflected the poor quality of the domestic competition. It therefore proposed to revamp the county championship. The season of twenty-six three-day matches would be replaced by sixteen three-day and eight four-day games. The number of forty-over Sunday games would be reduced by splitting the Sunday League into two divisions, with promotion and relegation. After much debate, the counties agreed a championship schedule of six four-day and sixteen three-day matches in the championship. At the same time, they adopted a new format for the Sunday League, involving an increase in the number of forty-over Sunday games.

The first four-day matches were held in 1988. Though the results were inconclusive, the TCCB hierarchy remained convinced it was the answer to England's problems. In 1989, a championship of sixteen four-day games was proposed; the counties postponed a decision till 1990. By then, the idea had received well-publicized support from the TCCB's England, Cricket and Marketing Committees, the latter of which argued in favour of the apparently uneconomical four-day game on the grounds that poor England performances would lead to a decline in the Test revenues which subsidized county cricket. In May 1990, the counties rejected the proposal by 14-4, then voted by 12-6 to retain the existing format. Ossie Wheatley, Cricket Committee Chairman, offered his resignation, which was not accepted. Two months later, the TCCB bosses were back. An emergency meeting in Edgbaston was asked to approve an increase in the number of four day games from six to eight. The vote was tied and the proposal was declared defeated.

By insistently linking the question of the four-day game to the needs of the Test side, the TCCB persuaded the counties to commission the Murray Report in 1991. A year later, the battle cry of 'anything for England' ensured its adoption. The aim of the TCCB's various proposals for restructuring has not been to make the domestic game more attractive or accessible to spectators or even more competitive, but simply to breed cricketers for England. An experiment with Saturday starts was rejected by Murray because a mid-week finish would leave less time for selected players to prepare for Test matches. So the counties ended up staging the third day of a four-day match on a Saturday with the final day postponed until Monday so that a limited-over league could be played on Sunday. Only in cricket could such an arrangement be promoted as 'rationalization'.

Back in the seventies, it had been argued that sponsorship of Test cricket was necessary to keep the county game alive. But twenty years of financial dependence has reversed that equation. Now it seems the sole justification of county cricket is as a nursery for Test cricket. The success of the England team, it appeared, could be purchased only at the price of distinctively English traditions. Among these was the uncovered pitch, sire of the famously English 'sticky wicket' – a phrase I had heard long before I even knew it referred to cricket.

It might seem that, along with mowing and rolling, covering pitches would be a logical means of standardizing the playing surface and ensuring a fair contest. But in cricket what constitutes a fair contest is always in dispute. In 1990, John Arlott, gloomily reflecting on the English game after a spell in hospital, observed that cricket is 'at heart divided and divisive, probably more so than any other game'. Everyone is 'either a batsman or a bowler' and the administrators who runs the game are either 'batsman-minded or bowler-minded ... they behave with complete bias while invariably protesting – and believing that they are disinterested'. Arlott argued that while the covering of pitches for county matches had been a boon for batsmen, it had led to 'a major crisis for the technique of bowling in England'. Seam had replaced both spin and pace.

The pendulum swings endlessly between bat and ball. High scores after World War II led to grassier pitches, which led to lower scoring. In 1959, the counties tried a one-year experiment with covered pitches. In the sixties, slower and poorer pitches encouraged medium pace and cautious batting. Ken Barrington warned in 1968: 'The value of the first-class game as a spectacle has declined ... the game has become very professional ... which has resulted in a development of defensive skills.' He advocated the covering of wickets to produce 'fast, true pitches'.

In 1980, the TCCB decided to cover all county pitches. The idea was to give the England team a boost by making the surfaces for the domestic competition more like those encountered in Tests. The snag was that English pitches lacked the bounce of Australian or West Indian pitches or the turn so readily available on the Asian subcontinent. Covered pitches were not so much 'true' as dead. Derek Underwood observed that 'slip has become a luxury position'. He doubted whether he could have pursued a successful career had he started out under such conditions.

In the mid-eighties, the Palmer Report recommended a return to uncovered pitches, but this was rejected at the TCCB by nine votes to six, with four abstentions. In 1987, the TCCB conducted an experiment in which pitches, but not bowlers' run-ups, were left uncovered during the hours of play for half the domestic season. This was soon abandoned, as was a suggestion to award bonus points only to bowlers. In keeping with the old amateur ethos and the game's ancient division of labour, the TCCB seemed intent on creating a batsman's paradise.

In 1990, counties were instructed to prepare 'batting' wickets. Twenty-five points would be deducted from the county championship total of any county should one of their pitches be deemed sub-standard. Pitches should be 'white or straw-coloured', the TCCB ruled, with 'no trace of greenness'. It also lowered the seam of the ball, which resulted in ludicrously high scores and unfinished matches.

That winter, the TCCB rejected a proposal to uncover the pitches by 15-4. Instead, on the recommendation of the England and Cricket Committees, it ordered the laying of ten experimental pitches, combining various types of loam and grass seed. The aim was to discover a formula for the ideal pitch and then to use it to make playing conditions in England uniform. But the TCCB could not itself agree on what constituted an ideal pitch. It revised its earlier instructions to groundsmen. Colour, it accepted, was not the main issue. A good pitch should be 'dry, firm and true' at the beginning of a match, provide 'pace and even bounce throughout' but 'ideally wear sufficiently to give spinners some help later in the game'. Two years later, it offered further clarification: though colour was still not an issue, green and grassy pitches were definitely out.

Like so many would-be modernizers, the TCCB presumed it was possible to exercise total control over the natural environment. Groundsmen were understandably piqued at the TCCB's illusions. They were being asked to do the impossible. Even the TCCB admitted that a good pitch should change in the course of a game, but it wanted that change stereotyped, reduced to something predictable and marketable.

The Murray Report dismissed uncovered pitches as 'out of the question' for commercial reasons. For Swanton, this was the worst of Murray's sins. Uncovered pitches made for 'intriguing, sometimes heroic cricket', he argued. What's more, they were 'English'. However, Swanton was inconsistent. He had argued against the four-day game on the grounds that it reduced the total amount of first-class cricket. 'The more matches the less will be the influence of the weather.' And yet the argument for uncovered pitches was precisely that they increased the influence of the weather – and thereby enriched the game.

Those who claimed that uncovered pitches were the key to Test match renewal overstated their case. After all, English cricket had gone into decline long before 1980. But they were right to be suspicious of the TCCB's efforts to pummel the old English game into harmony with international conditions. The debate about covered pitches is ultimately unresolvable because the early origins of the game anchor it in the refractory earth. Its autochthony seems to frustrate all efforts to make the game fit into the space available for it in a modern society.

The one-day game is an attempt to do just that. No other sport had to mutate so radically to squeeze itself into a market niche. Modernity was accommodated by splitting the game in two – but keeping both versions under one command. One-day cricket was created as a junior, and avowedly vulgarized, appendage to a 'first-class' cricket in danger of imminent demise. Its evolution has been entirely market-driven and no attempt is made by the cricket authorities to justify it for its own sake. They simply repeated *ad nauseam* that one-day thrashes are essential for the economic survival of the traditional game.

Echoing Pycroft, detractors of the one day game have combined an aesthetic with a moral critique. In the 1993 *Wisden*, Matthew Engel declared it 'a mutant game ... essentially shallow'. This verdict is shared across a surprising spectrum of cricket opinion. Even Ian Chappell agrees: 'A Test match is like a painting. There's time for artistry and it requires a lot of hard work, thought and patience ... a limited-overs international is like a Rolf Harris painting.' Engel's predecessor at *Wisden*, Graeme Wright, compared the appeal of the one-day game to fast food. 'Most children will eat hamburgers and chips in preference to a healthy well-balanced meal when given a chance.'

So the one-day game is seen as the McDonalds of cricket: universally accessible, virtually pre-digested, quick and uniform. Compressed in time and unequivocal in result, it is an attempt to make a hyper-modern sport out of a proto-modern one. As in popular fiction, a clear separation of victory from defeat is required. There is no room for ambiguity. In ruling out the possibility of the draw, one-day cricket, many believe, sacrifices the civility of the old game. 'Those who can't win don't always have to be losers,' Graeme Wright pleaded. 'Many of us try to live honourably drawn lives and have to work hard to do so.' To its critics, one-day cricket is a symbol of a cut-throat age – an age eschewing subtlety and demanding instant gratification.

One-day cricket has become the great scapegoat. More even than covered pitches, its proliferation is blamed for the erosion of skills and the general decline in English cricket. It is also blamed for allegedly deteriorating standards of crowd behaviour. Along with the elimination of the draw, and the increased emphasis on the fortunes of the team as a whole, comes increased partisanship, which is always seen as alien to English cricket – something reserved for foreigners, women and working-class football supporters. The one-day crowd, it is reasoned, cannot really have come for the cricket – since the cricket is of such a low order – so it must have come for other reasons: the beer, the crack, the bother. Hence the boorish chanting, piercing the meditative calm required to watch cricket, portrayed as a high art.

As always the authorities want to have it both ways, reaping the profits of the modern while claiming the sanctity of the past. They want the new audience – but they want it to behave like the old one. They still believe that, within cricket, the brute struggle for dominance, like the power of money, ought to be discreetly veiled.

One-day cricket has virtues of its own which deserve greater recognition. It is satisfying to watch a game to its conclusion. And the game is a leveller: the underdog always has more chance than in a two innings match. Limited-overs cricket has made batsmen more powerful and faster between the wickets and has taught them how to score quickly under pressure. Fielding, always the weakest element in the English amateur tradition, has improved beyond recognition. The one-day game also encourages the all-round bits-and-pieces players – and thus gives the unsung county regulars a rare chance to shine in the public eye.

All these are genuine attractions and ought not to be dismissed as second-rate pleasures. Yet too much of the one-day game does pall. The Sunday League was thought to be the ultimate in modern-style cricket but attendances fell away in the eighties and early nineties. Everyone – players, spectators, television producers – was bored with it. Even the one-day game, it seems, does not quite fit into the modern market. Absurd calculations are required to set targets in rain-affected matches, leaving spectators bewildered. Major matches sometimes end in darkness. Authorities and sponsors tinker endlessly with the rules, which vary between competitions and countries. Without a close finish, the whole exercise becomes predictable and pointless. It is impossible to compile meaningful averages. The introduction of fielding circles (a Packer innovation) is an attempt to force the one-day game into the mould of first-class cricket and raise the premium on skill. It is an acknowledgement of the artificiality of the format.*

Cricket needs its two innings, its second chances. Without them, it becomes a mere run chase. The results become arbitrary, produced by spur-of-the-moment mistakes and accidents rather than the long maturation of a complex balance of collective strengths and weaknesses.

---

* Watching the World Cup held in south Asia in 1996 has forced me to revise my views on the limited overs format. England, once a leader in the one-day game, slipped back in the nineties; the insistence on the supreme importance of Test cricket, and the concomitant assumption that the one-day game was merely a commercial spin-off, led to complacency and routinism in the English approach to the junior form of the game. Elsewhere, experimentation and tactical adventure flourished. I think the one-day game is still in evolution, and could reveal greater variety and complexity than many of its critics suspect.

The unpredictability of one-day results is in inverse proportion to the predictability of the play. This makes the game more accessible to the neophyte - and that is not a virtue to be sneezed at - but it also reduces its depth of interest and feeling. Cricket runs according to its own pre-industrial clock. Force it into step with the modern metronome, and it loses that limitlessness of possibility which it carries with it from an earlier age.

The most fundamental and persistent dilemma about one-day cricket is how to integrate it with first-class cricket. Since the two types of game are played by the same personnel, cricketers must develop skills and styles suitable for both games – but it is not always easy to shift from one to the other. What's more, the proliferation of one-day competitions has played havoc with the traditional cricket calendar, giving new grounds to the age-old complaint about too much play dulling the professionals.

The Murray Report was supposed to address the problem of 'too much cricket'. It was predicated on the assumption that England's Test performances suffered because three-day cricket had been devalued. Yet it increased the ratio of one-day to first-class cricket – and stuck a Sunday limited-overs thrash in the middle of nearly every championship game. It tried to compensate for that by extending the Sunday competition from forty to fifty overs a side and removing restrictions on the bowlers' run-ups, thus making Sunday cricket more like the 'real thing'. But, to the horror of the traditionalists, it also recommended that the Sunday League be played in coloured clothing with a white ball.

No one doubted that the Sunday League needed a shot in the arm. In 1991, Ossie Wheatley's TCCB Cricket Committee had proposed a divisional structure, with promotion and relegation. The counties rejected it for the obvious reason – some of them would wind up in the second division. Instead they decided to jazz up the appearance of the competition, ignoring the results of a questionnaire sent out to county members, which showed a large majority against coloured clothing. AXA Equity and Law were delighted with the idea, but it originated with the TCCB, not the sponsor.

The TCCB argued that cricket had to move with the times: 'County cricket administrators have to attract the family back to cricket and we feel we are most likely to achieve this by gaining the interest and support of the "fashion-orientated" sporting youngster.' The new Sunday League was cricket's attempt to compete with Nintendo and MTV.

What was remarkable in the arguments that ensued was their sheer moral fervour. Once again, something delicate and irreplaceable seemed to be threatened by the remorseless tide of crass modernity. EW Swanton waged a fierce campaign against the new strips, which, he argued, sullied the 'dignity of the game'.

Whites are among English cricket's premier 'invented traditions'. As late as the 1880s cricketers took the field in a riot of colour. The Harlequins wore crimson-and-buff shirts and blue trousers. Oxford and Cambridge, of course, appeared in blue. Individuals elaborated as they pleased. I Zingari members, however, were asked to refrain from wearing coloured shirts or trousers, confining flamboyance to hats, ties and belts. In the 1870s, pill-box hats gave way to club caps. By 1890, colour was confined to caps and to county emblems on sweaters.

A bizarre but apt comparison is with the clothing of Hasidic Jews. There is nothing in the least biblical about their long coats and fur hats. This is the dress of the late-eighteenth-century Polish ghettoes, where Hasidism originated. Over the last two hundred years it has been sacralized, and to deviate from it now is to deviate from the faith. Similarly, the ritual of cricket, born out of an emergent modern society with a growing consciousness of the past, must be re-enacted always in the same traditional garb, the dress of its 'Golden Age'. Whites are the visible token of the past in the present.

But it was not only the crusty old traditionalists who found coloured clothing distressing. Whites were one of the first things that attracted me to cricket and I mourn their loss on Sunday as much as anyone. Coloured clothing, even with the names on the back, seems to make the game more anonymous. It imposes a rigid corporate identity on a game whose charm lies in the fluid and complex interaction of individual and collective. Precisely because whites are universal and uniform, they showcase individuality. The tilt of a sunhat, the roll of a sleeve, the flair of a collar can speak volumes. At the same time, whites give the game a visual purity, a classicism that is its own justification. The worst thing the advocates of whites could have done for their cause was to burden it with the argument of precedent, which is no argument at all.

Coloured clothing was introduced not because of any groundswell of demand but because it meshed with the TCCB's pre-conceived scheme for a modern, financially successful popular sport. The new strips were supposed to be aimed at members of the public as yet unconverted to traditional Sunday cricket, but they were part of a package which involved starting play at noon, instead of 1 pm, thus preventing large numbers of casual spectators from seeing the full course of the match. The main function of the lurid outfits was not to build a new audience but to increase revenue through the sale of replica kits.

The TCCB and the counties decided to milk the parents through the kids. The coloured strips have a built-in obsolescence; they can be altered every year, enabling the counties to exploit the same market again and again. Sponsors were keen. At no extra cost, their logos would now be worn by fans as well as players.

In the first year, 70,000 were sold at £25.99 each. With a 50 per cent mark-up on the production cost of each shirt, profits were handsome. But there was little evidence of any sizeable new following for cricket among young people. Along with sponsorship, hospitality boxes, and catering, coloured clothing is just another way to get more money into the old game without bringing more people into the grounds to watch it.

Curiously, the white ball, originally introduced for floodlit cricket in Australia, now became a totem of modernization in itself. Without any definitive evidence, it was assumed that it would be easier for spectators to follow. The funereal black sightscreens which accompanied it, however, appeared to be an afterthought, though they impinged on the spectators' consciousness far more than the colour of the ball.

Despite the mandatory three-year trial period agreed by the counties when they endorsed the Murray Report, the new structures were amended after their first season in operation. The Benson & Hedges zonal matches were reinstated and the Sunday League was reduced to forty overs. I am sure we will see many more revisions, even outright reversals, in the coming years. The same arguments will come round again and again – amateur or professional, one day, three days or four days, covered or uncovered pitches, coloured clothing or whites – and none of them will ever be resolved. Shaped by its peculiar historical origins, English cricket will continue to frustrate both those who would redesign it for the modern market and those who would preserve it in aspic. The attempts to modernize county cricket will fail – but they will be incessant nevertheless. Those who hope for a return to the stability which was the hallmark of English cricket for eighty years will be bitterly disappointed.*

To the war between modernizers and traditionalists, there is no end. Like the struggle between the TCCB and the MCC, it is an illusory one – and for that reason, perhaps, all the more potently symbolic. But a socialist

---

*The MacLaurin report of 1997 went further than previous attempts at reform, but encountered the same resistance and was tangled in the same contradictions as its predecessors. See Chapter 8.

would be foolish to take sides in it.

The real problem for English cricket is that its social base is too narrow. Cricket has always been a minority sport, but that minority is smaller now than ever. Twenty times more people attend football than cricket matches. Rugby League, though regionally based, attracts 50 per cent more. A crowd for an average county cricket match – all four days of it – would easily be outnumbered by an average crowd for a Third Division football game. Nowadays. in England, more bets are taken on the Super Bowl than on an entire Test series.

Only a minuscule proportion of the general population takes part in cricket. Among sixteen- to nineteen-year-old males, the group from which first-class English cricket recruits, a mere 7 per cent play cricket even once a month – the same number play basketball, that most American of sports, just as often.

The NCA claims that there are now between three and four hundred thousand regular club cricketers, a substantial base for the sport. But at the grass roots, cricket is poverty-stricken. It remains dependent on the collective voluntary effort of tens of thousands who go where sponsors cannot be bothered to tread. Decent cricket facilities are few and far between, especially in the cities, sacrificed to rising property values and cuts in public spending. The few inner-city public pitches that survive are often poorly maintained. Penurious local authorities cannot afford to subsidize cricket in state schools. The destruction of the mining communities and old industrial villages of the Midlands and the North has stripped English cricket of its major working-class base. The growth of ersatz village-green cricket in the spreading suburbs hardly compensates.

Cricket today is disproportionately upper-class. In a 1987 survey, 2 per cent of the upmarket ABC1 s had played in the four weeks before interview, compared with 1 per cent of the skilled C2s (7 per cent of whom had played football). So few of the unskilled and unwaged DEs had played cricket that no percentage was registered at all, but 4 per cent had played football.

The NCA, run by old amateurs, loyal ex-professionals and public school figures, has done little to rectify the class imbalance. Excessively influenced by the English Schools Cricket Association (ESCA), which brings together the private schools, it has concentrated on coaching, rather than grounds and equipment, thus ensuring that more shall be given to those who already have enough.

In 1991, a Cricket Council report on the NCA listed the organization's weaknesses: 'no facility provision', 'no direct contact with cricketers', 'limited communication activity', 'no activity to recruit members', 'affiliated bodies not fully supportive of the association', and, of course, 'reduced opportunities to play cricket in schools'. Women's cricket is mentioned nowhere in NCA reports.

In recent years, the NCA has concentrated on securing sponsorship for prestige youth events. Its partners in the 'Development of Excellence' project (now sponsored by NatWest) are the TCCB and the ESCA. Its 'Cricket in the Community' project has no sponsorship and no funding. The TCCB's commitment to cricket at the base is pathetic. In 1992, through the NCA, it spent £750,000 on recreational cricket; at the same time, it gave over £430,000 to each of the eighteen first-class counties.

The NCA has acted as the TCCB's junior partner. Its main role seems to be to plunder the base to prop up the apex. Dependent on largesse from the TCCB (which funds half its budget), it gives no voice to the game's grass roots. Under Micky Stewart's England Committee regime, it was harnessed to the prevailing elitist ethos. The proliferation of under-15, under-16, under-19 trials and 'tests' – underwritten by sponsors – means that English cricket now effectively runs an 11-plus system of early selection.

All of this has exacerbated English cricket's deepest ailment, identified by Rowland Bowen in the sixties. *Its dominant culture is still widely seen as belonging to an elite.* Even post-Packer, cricket seems more alien to inner-city youth than ever. If these youths ever met the people who run the English game, their worst prejudices would be confirmed.

The 1993 *Wisden* faithfully reflected the prevailing biases in English cricket. There are twenty pages on Oxford and Cambridge, fifty pages on 'schools cricket' (overwhelmingly public and grammar schools), seven pages on league cricket, and one page on women's cricket.* Of the 400 professional cricketers listed in the 1993 *Cricketers' Who's Who*, seventy-five (18 per cent) went to public schools, a slightly higher proportion than ten years ago. Another 20 per cent went to grammar or other selective schools. Seventy had been to university. Ninety had family connections with first-class or minor-counties cricket. This is not a fair refection of the population as a whole and makes nonsense of cricket's

---

*The 1998 Wisden at 1472 pages is 96 pages longer than the 1993 edition. There are twenty-three pages devoted to Oxford and Cambridge, 41 pages of 'schools cricket' with the same bias as five years ago, five pages on League cricket – of which two are on the Lancashire Leagues – and four pages on women's cricket.

claims to be a national sport.

Where then lies salvation for English cricket? What is needed is a living bond between the 'top' and 'bottom' of the game. A divisional structure with promotion and relegation has often been advocated, but as long as it maintains the gulf between the counties and the rest of cricket, it will be of limited use. The overriding need is to heal the Victorian rupture between first-class and all other cricket, both on and off the field.*

But tinkering with competitive structures will not be nearly enough. Ticket prices for all games should be slashed – or even done away with altogether. Cricket authorities worried about attendance at four-day county matches should grant free admission to the unemployed or under-employed. More important, the counties have to become democracies, and ways have to be found to enfranchise all club cricketers and committed spectators. And the counties themselves have to become part of a unitary, representative structure which elects – and removes when necessary – all the game's leading officials. At last cricket would have its parliament and at its disposal would be all the resources of the English game. The county grounds and Lord's would be nationalized – with no compensation for the MCC or others who have appropriated community property for so long.

Democracy and the market arose together and together they forged English cricket. But increasingly these two forces are pulling in opposite directions, in cricket as elsewhere. English cricket, like English society, can be renewed only by more democracy – but in today's world that means less market. The dictatorship of the marketing men and the sponsors has to be challenged and overthrown – but not to be replaced by the old amateurs. English cricket, like the British economy, has to be reconstructed from the bottom up.

*Bridging the first-class and recreational games was one of the aims of the MacLaurin Report of 1997, but its proposals implied not a partnership, but a crude take-over of the latter by the former. See Chapter 8, pages 326-327.

5

The Level Playing Field

The Tebbit test ● *Don't mention racism* ● *The trauma of West Indian supremacy* ● *Pakistan in England, 1992* ● *The embattled majority* ● *'Cheating'*

'Which side do they cheer for?' Norman Tebbit first proposed his cricket test in an American newspaper, the *Los Angeles Times*, in April 1990. He was being interviewed about his attempt to mount a backbench Tory rebellion against the government's Hong Kong Bill, which proposed to admit 50,000 heads of Hong Kong households to the UK after 1997, when the People's Republic was scheduled to take over the colony. For the government, this was an obligation of empire. For Tebbit, it was a threat to national integrity.

In the interview, he warned Americans that the 'special relationship' with Britain was under threat from the changing demography of the United States. Under the impact of a long wave of immigration from non-English-speaking Third World countries, American culture was becoming less 'Anglo-Saxon'. To illustrate his point, he cited England's post-war experience. Too many Asian immigrants, he said, failed what he dubbed 'the cricket test'. When England played India or Pakistan, whom did they cheer for? 'It's an interesting test,' he said. 'Are you still harking back to where you came from or where you are?'

Tebbit had chosen cricket to illustrate the importance of cultural continuity to an American audience. It was a canny choice: to Americans, cricket and Englishness are one and the same. But, as Tebbit knew, cricket no longer belonged to the English. Tebbit posed his test in order to exploit the fear that, perhaps, England, too, no longer belonged to the English.

'These islands of ours are already overcrowded,' he declared in the Commons. 'Great waves of immigration by people who do not share our culture, our language, our ways of social conduct' were threatening to become 'a destabilizing factor in our society'. The death threats made by some British Muslims against Salman Rushdie 'showed their contempt for our society and our laws'. The next morning, the *Sun's* front-page headline ran: 'Hong Kong migrants would ruin our nation says Tebbit'.

Tebbit's revolt collapsed, partly because the government made it clear that the purpose of its Bill was to *limit* Hong Kong immigration, and partly because, in the midst of the poll-tax fiasco, the government was just as keen to play the race card as Tebbit. Thatcher declared that protests would not deter her from visiting South Africa. Pressed by reporters, Angela Rumbold, the race-relations minister, refused to distance herself from what had quickly become known as 'the Tebbit test'. Within a week of the Commons vote, Education Secretary John MacGregor backed parents' rights to withdraw their children from mixed-race schools in which they were allegedly 'learning Pakistani'.

The media gave Tebbit ample opportunity to expound his thesis. He insisted he was not racist but 'integrationist'. Referring again to the Rushdie case, he claimed, 'There are a large number of them who sympathize with those who claim that British law is not satisfactory.' His remarks, he explained, were not aimed at 'all immigrants', but primarily at 'second-generation' British blacks whom he accused of having 'split loyalties'. He cited the Headingley Test of 1987, when Bradford-based Asians had cheered Pakistan:

> When people come to a new country they should be prepared to immerse themselves totally and utterly in that country ... If someone is looking back to the country from where their family came instead of to the country where they live and make their home, you say are they really integrated or are they just living here?

True to form, the *Guardian* missed the point. While regretting Tebbit's remarks, it endorsed his 'integrationism'. It talked about the need to understand the 'slow process' through which 'new loyalties' would replace 'old loyalties'. Oblivious to the implied menace of the Tebbit test, the *Guardian* accepted his assumption that there could or should be a unitary British culture – and that one of its components was supporting England in Test matches.

Tebbit's own confidence in the integrity of British culture was not as complete as he pretended. He could define it only by exclusion. But in insecure times, in a violently competitive world economy, exclusion is powerful stuff. This was the core of his message – which was aimed not at the black minority, but the white majority.

Tebbit's 'cricket test' was a perfect example of the new racism in which the old naked assertion of white superiority, discredited by the collapse of empire and the decline of England as a world power, is replaced by an emphasis on mutually exclusive cultural identities. The new racists say they do not want to dominate, merely to claim a space of their own. That is why it was so easy for Tebbit to attack Muslim fundamentalists for being out of step with 'British laws' while at the same time accusing their enemy, Salman Rushdie, of 'an assault on his own religion'. Tebbit was using cricket to build what Benedict Anderson calls 'an imagined community', that solidarity in anonymity which gives 'the nation' its extraordinary power of attraction. The message to the white majority in Britain was that they *belonged* because others did not. And what they belonged to was *the nation*, defined not as a territory or even a race, but as a culture.

Tebbit could not resist the well-worn tactic of divide and rule. 'Look at some of the West Indian-born bowlers who played for England in the last Test – Gladstone Small and Malcolm: it's clear where their hearts are.' The Test he referred to had been against the West Indies. Small and Malcolm had proven their loyalty by bowling fast against 'their own' people. Tebbit was telling British blacks that to be British meant to repudiate all other loyalties and traditions. This appears to give them a choice, but it is a spurious one. The real effect of the Tebbit test was to insinuate doubts about whether black people have a legitimate place in the national community.

Tara Mukherjee, President of the Confederation of Indian Organizations, pointed out that the black people were being judged by standards that the white English did not apply to themselves. 'I would suggest he ask the English settlers in Australia which side they support when a Test is played in Australia against Australians.' And what about Scottish, Welsh and Irish people living in London, Birmingham or Manchester? Were they expected to support 'England' against Scotland, Wales or Ireland in football or rugby? Were they considered disloyal for celebrating their roots in the sporting arena?

Days before the vote on the Hong Kong Bill, Home Office Minister Tim Sainsbury had revealed that between 500,000 and one million South African whites could be entitled to claim British citizenship. Earlier in the month, the government had extended voting rights to expatriates, principally South Africans, who had left the country up to twenty years previously. Tebbit did not accuse these ex-pats of 'harking back'. His cricket test was racist to the core because it was not and could not be applied universally and equally.

The reality is that we live in an age of unprecedented mass migration, a product of the global supremacy of the market system which Tebbit has always championed. The TCCB's argument for staging the 1996 World Cup in Britain was precisely that resident minority communities retaining old loyalties provided a market for it. Increasingly, the human norm is to have experience of and therefore attachments to more than one society, more than one 'homeland'. My peculiar bi-national experience is not as atypical as it might seem. The lie behind the Tebbit test is that human beings must be one thing and one thing only, that human cultures and societies are cast in concrete and are mutually exclusive. For Tebbit, the nation is a finished product, something pre-existing in which one takes an assigned place, not something which changes and is changed, from within and without. The 'second-generation' black British so resented by Tebbit are creating a *new* culture, a hybrid one, like all other cultures. Cricket is one of the elements of that evolving culture, which has just as much right to be called English as the old amateur culture of the public schools.

The irony is that no one had preached the gospel of the free market with greater fervour than Norman Tebbit. This was the man who had told the unemployed to 'get on your bike', which was exactly what the black immigrants to Britain had done. The man who vowed undying opposition to the European Community ('the British are not willing to be governed by foreigners') was the same man who encouraged the American-based General Motors to take over British Leyland Trucks and Rover and let the Egyptian Fayed brothers buy Harrods.

Tebbit wants an open economy but a closed society. This is not merely hypocrisy. The capitalism which Tebbit has served so well creates a world labour market, then exploits national and racial divisions in order to control it. The market as a world system is both unifier and divider. Apparently a levelling and liberating device in which nothing counts but the colour of your money, it actually intensifies long-established inequalities (of race, gender, nation) and generates new ones. That is why the much-hailed triumph of the free market has been accompanied by escalating appeals to race, nation or religion, all those things to which the market is allegedly indifferent.

The 'level playing field' to which the market is often compared is, of course, a metaphor from sport. But as a metaphor it is a grand deception. The market makes a promise – the promise of equal chances for all – that it cannot fulfil. Cricket's level playing field, arising out of the nascent

English market economy of the eighteenth century, offers democracy and inclusion, but again and again, as in the Tebbit test, it is used to restrict and exclude.

Of all the ugly facets of the Tebbit test, perhaps the most absurd was the most obvious: the idea that it should matter at all whom one supports in a cricket match. Tebbit was arguing, in effect, that if one did not support a certain country in cricket one could not claim the same rights as other citizens of that country. This is grotesque. A Test match is not a war. Cricket is fundamentally trivial, which is what makes it beautiful and delightful – and which is its best defence against those who, like Tebbit, would abuse it for their own ends.

While I was researching this book a copy of the synopsis found its way into the press room at Lord's. There it was glimpsed by a veteran broadsheet correspondent who spied the phrase 'racism in English cricket'. It made him very angry. 'Oh god,' he moaned, 'I hate all that.'

What he hated was not the ugly fact of racism, but the idea that someone should associate it with the sacred name of 'cricket'. In English cricket, if you mention racism you are seen as an intruder, someone with an ulterior motive, not someone fully and truly dedicated to the game. After all, we're all equal on the cricket field – that is the gentleman's code. Those who decry racism in the game are needlessly introducing conflict into a zone of camaraderie. The truth, of course, is that this conflict is introduced by racists and, more surreptitiously, by racist ideas and assumptions.

Because they are regarded as 'not cricket', racism's more obvious manifestations are disdained. But they are merely disdained, not challenged and eradicated. In the final analysis, racism is not only tolerated but sanctioned by the English cricket authorities, just as it is by the British government, courts and police.

The Tebbit test was virtually ignored by English cricket. *Wisden* made no comment and none of the major cricket periodicals even mentioned it. Here was a prime example of that heinous crime against cricket of which so many 'Third World politicians' had been accused: using the game to score political points, to 'whip up hatred'. But Tebbit was spared the opprobrium heaped on others.

The same commentators who boil with rage at the Mexican wave seem singularly unmoved by racist chanting. Usually, they fail even to acknowledge its existence. Yet surely racism in any guise is an affront to the common humanity which gives cricket its only legitimate meaning, and which is the real source of its beauty.

Sport has been a vehicle of personal advance for members of oppressed groups in societies all over the world – because the premise of sport is that everyone is subject to the same rules, everyone starts at the same line and is timed with the same stopwatch. Cricket, like the law and the market, is supposed to be colour-blind. But just as Britain's black communities have found that they do not enjoy an equal footing in either the courts or the job market, so they have also found that on English cricket's level playing field, some people are 'more equal' than others.

Cricket brought together all the classes on the village green, but it did so, as we have seen, in hierarchical fashion. That hierarchy was later extended to the empire. Playing cricket became a touchstone of Englishness, a measure of people's right to be included, either in nation or empire. At the same time, it became a means of ensuring that people knew their places, within both nation and empire. Inclusion was always conditional. That is why, as the Tebbit test showed, cricket could be used as an instrument of exclusion - exclusion from the level playing field and the league of gentlemen. Racism is not the negation but the paradoxical complement of English cricket's invented tradition of social inclusion.

The most notorious example of racial exclusion in English cricket is the long-standing failure of Yorkshire County Cricket Club to play any Yorkshire-born black cricketers in its first XI, despite the abundance of keen and talented local black cricketers (born in and therefore qualified for Yorkshire).

That may change soon.* The county is under scrutiny and its current President, Sir Lawrence Byford, a former Chief Inspector of Constabulary, Foreign Office adviser on 'internal disorder' in Turkey and 'security liaison' in Northern Ireland, Hong Kong and Egypt, knows a thing or two about the value of multi-racial window-dressing. He also knows that the Yorkshire-born policy is yet another of cricket's 'invented traditions'. Never formally agreed by the club membership, for years it was applied more strictly to professionals than amateurs. But after 1968, and the influx of overseas players into county cricket, this article of faith took on a new dimension. According to Richard Hutton, who played for the county between 1962 and 1974, the presence of overseas players in opposing sides 'guaranteed appropriate comment from Yorkshire sides, jealous of their racial and geographic integrity'. Playing a Warwickshire

---

*As of May 1998, it had not. Even Yorkshire's most dedicated apologists seem to be running out of excuses.

side which included Lance Gibbs and Rohan Kanhai, Fred Trueman observed, 'They only needed a green 'un to make a snooker set.'

The emphasis in both comments on race or colour gives the game away. Clearly, being a Yorkshireman is not just a matter of where you were born, as talented Asian cricketers, born in Yorkshire, have discovered. 'There is a "don't call us, we'll call you" mentality,' said one. Another recalled how, after he had hit a quick 30 in a one-day game, a watching Yorkshire official commented, 'Typical Paki. Never get their heads down.'

When asked in the late eighties why no black players had appeared for Yorkshire, Joe Lister, then County Secretary, explained: 'I'm told there is an Indian League, a Pakistan League and a West Indian League in Yorkshire and that they tend to keep to themselves.' Besides: 'The bulk of the West Indian supporters who come to a Leeds Test come from Birmingham and London. The local Indians or Pakistanis don't come at all.'

Lister's comments only proved how spectacularly ill-informed he was about the people he lived among. But his reasoning was not nearly so tortuous, or belligerent, as that offered by Brian Close, Chairman of Yorkshire's Cricket Committee since 1984:

> Did you know that over in Pakistan and India the poorer people didn't know cricket existed? There's a hundred years of bloody tradition in Yorkshire lads. As soon as a male's born, bloody hell, the fellow says, 'Good, I'm glad he's born in Yorkshire.' By the time he's toddling he's got a bat in his hand. Bloody Pakistanis didn't know the damn thing existed.

For Close, Asians, even Yorkshire-born ones, are ineradicably and irredeemably foreign. Cricket is not their game, so their exclusion from it by whites is in the natural order of things. Conversely, for Lister, the Asians exclude themselves because they like to play on their own. The spirit behind both rationalizations was the same that motivated the taunting of visiting black players by sections of the Headingley crowd. 'I was standing on the boundary line and there was a whole section calling me all the names under the sun,' recalled Gloucestershire bowler David Lawrence. 'They called me nigger, black bastard, sambo, monkey, gorilla; they threw bananas and I had to take these insults.' After a Somerset match at which Headingley spectators abused Viv Richards, Ian Botham called them 'racial idiots'. The Yorkshire Committee had the nerve to demand an apology.

The roots of racism in Yorkshire cricket are set deep in the county's peculiar regional chauvinism, a chauvinism warped by years of cricket failure. This is the county club with the largest and broadest popular base. It is also the most faction-ridden and the most anguished about its lack of success on the field. Decades ago, Wilf Rhodes explained the Yorkshire approach: 'We don't play cricket for fun.' This philosophy reached its apotheosis in Boycott, as he stripped his game to the hone, eschewing any shot that carried even a hint of risk. Cricket was played not to entertain, not even for money; cricket was played to win and for the greater glory of Yorkshire, the only county that speaks of itself with the awed reverence usually reserved for 'England'. Back in the late 1950s, the Yorkshire Chairman Brian Sellers dropped professional Johnny Wardle after Wardle had published criticisms of the authorities in the *Daily Mail*. Wardle was a member of the England squad, but that did not impress Sellers. 'Good enough for MCC,' he said, 'does not mean good enough for Yorkshire.'

'Yorkshireness' has become something to be valued in its own right, a cultural and even moral identity attached to a territorial unit no longer recognized in any form by the state. The powers that be at Yorkshire have for many decades preferred the spurious roots of racial and cultural identity to the living roots of the game as it is actually played in the locality. It stands proudly not for the mixed culture of contemporary Yorkshire – industrial and urban, black and white, immigrant and native – but for a reified, hollow culture of boastfulness and bigotry. It is, at its core, profoundly exclusive. As one Asian cricketer put it, 'Yorkshire just hate everybody. I've seen really good white lads frozen out, too, because they don't fit in.'

Of course, racism is not confined to Yorkshire. In 1981, there were twenty black county cricketers qualified for England. Ten were first team regulars, but none of these was British-born. In 1993, forty black county cricketers were qualified for England, of whom fifteen were first-team regulars and ten were British-born. The percentage of black professional cricketers is now about double the percentage of black people in Britain. But black people form a much higher percentage of cricket supporters and, even more important, of active cricketers, than they do of the general population.

There is a parallel world of black cricket in this country, including leagues and clubs scattered wherever there is a black population. The Quaid-i-Azam League in Yorkshire was founded in 1980. Matches were held on Sundays because players worked in shops and restaurants on

Saturdays. In London, the Inter-Island Amateur Cricket Cup brings together black cricketers, many born in Britain, under the banners of the various West Indian countries. There is the Clive Lloyd Cup (won in 1997 by an Asian side), the Sri Lankan League, and many others. This parallel world is reported in the black press but hardly acknowledged by the cricket media, except when its existence is cited as support for the thesis that 'they tend to keep to themselves'.

In fact, black and Asian clubs do compete in mixed competitions and have made it repeatedly clear that they would like to join the longer-established, white-dominated leagues. But they have not always been made to feel welcome. In 1993, the Muslim players of Kashmir Cricket Club visited an all-white team in Woolaston for a match in the Morganite Hereford and Worcester League. When they were served ham sandwiches for tea, they allegedly swore at the local caterers, for which offence their team was docked twenty-five points by league officials. In this context, it is understandable that people should seek refuge in the separate world of black cricket. But it is more than a refuge; it is a celebration of a common heritage and experience, of which cricket is a vital component. Because of that, it represents an immense potential resource for English cricket - provided that English cricket is prepared to redefine its notions about what constitutes 'Englishness'.*

The discourse of cricket is shot through with racism. Again and again, in the most casual fashion, race is used to explain developments on the field of play, and especially the ups and downs of Test cricket. The best example is the English response to the long trauma of West Indian Test supremacy.

In the good old days, before the West Indies started beating England regularly – and before there was a large West Indian population in this country – West Indian cricket was damned with faint praise. Cardus summed up the prevailing view: 'The erratic quality of West Indian cricket is surely true to racial type. At one moment these players are eager, confident and quite masterful; then as circumstances go against them you can see them losing heart.'

* In 1996 I met an opening batsman for a team called Khalsa in the Quaid-I-Azam League. His name was Everton and his parents were from the West Indies. I asked him if he thought it was strange that he was an Afro-Caribbean batsman playing for a Sikh side in a Muslim league. 'I never thought of it that way,' he said, 'We've got a couple of white lads as well. We just love our cricket, and none of us fits in with the old leagues.' See Chapter 8, pages 314-318.

Fallibility made the West Indies cricketers lovably unthreatening. Viscount Cobham lauded them as 'colourful', 'unorthodox', 'joyous and uninhibited', but Australia were his preferred opponents because 'the old enemies are the best enemies'. EW Swanton praised West Indian batsmanship for 'mocking the utilitarian and the humdrum'.*

But with the rise of Clive Lloyd's all-conquering side of the late seventies and eighties, the tune changed. Carefree amateurism had been replaced by a hardened professionalism, and the English, who gave that professionalism to the world, did not approve. At the start of the 1984 season, Robin Marlar belittled 'Lloyd's army of weary mercenaries'. He could have been Pycroft berating English professionals in the 1860s. Then came the 5-0 'blackwash', one of the most powerful displays ever by a touring Test side, featuring exceptional batting, bowling and fielding from a host of West Indian stars. Marlar, and many others, objected repeatedly to the 'slow play'. The TCCB had pressed for a higher minimum number of overs per day, but the West Indies Board demurred. Lloyd's rotation of four fast bowlers with long run-ups did mean that fewer overs were bowled. But where West Indies bowled on average 13.5 overs per hour throughout the series, England bowled 13.4. If runs weren't being scored, wickets were tumbling, and the West Indies won most of the Tests outright well within five days.

John Woodcock mounted his *Wisden* pulpit to denounce the 'chilling' West Indian pace bowling. Its 'viciousness', he warned, was 'changing the very nature of the game'. In *Wisden Cricket Monthly*, David Frith waged an angry campaign against the West Indies quicks: 'Their game is founded on vengeance and violence and fringed by arrogance.' He called for 'sanctions against the bullies', which presumably meant, ultimately, expelling West Indies from Test cricket.

Even Geoffrey Moorhouse, often a sensitive commentator on the game, declared himself 'sickened' by 'the downright thuggery of fast bowlers working in relays to remove batsmen by hurting and

---

*For West Indian cricketers in England during this period, racism was a grim reality, as Learie Constantine explained in his forward to the *Daily Worker's* 1950 cricket handbook: "West Indies cricketers come to England and find the most refrigerated cricket the world has to show ... The cricket officials were polite, impersonal, never saying two words where one would do or one if silence could serve ... Then there is the wretched colour problem which always affects West Indies touring teams ... off the pitch remarks are overheard that are remembered with hurt for years. I have had some of it and I know."

intimidating them': 'I shall not be watching the West Indies this summer, or ever again, unless another Worrell or Sobers can be found to captain them. These were upright men who believed in fair play.'

For many English commentators, West Indian 'exuberance' had been replaced by boorish aggression. In the 1990 Test in Barbados, captain Viv Richards, believing English batsman Rob Bailey had been caught behind, swooped noisily across the field from slip. After a moment's hesitation, the umpire gave Bailey out. On the radio, an outraged Christopher Martin-Jenkins accused Richards of 'cheating' and contrasted him unfavourably with Bailey, 'one of cricket's gentlemen'. In the Barbados *Sun*, columnist 'Adonijah' mocked Martin-Jenkins: 'The picture was clear. On the one side was the goodly English gentleman Bailey ... and on the other the screaming and gesticulating natives, led by Viv Richards. Waving the hands, of course, comes easy to the natives, who need long hands to pick the coconuts they drink all day.' The BBC was forced to pay damages to the West Indian umpire, who was affronted by the implication that he had made a decision in response to home-side pressure. Martin-Jenkins withdrew the word 'cheating', but resented the allegation of racism. He believes he is motivated by nothing but a concern for cricket, which transcends race, class or nationality. He seems utterly unaware that his commentary is often heavily inflected by these three concerns.

In *Wisden Cricket Monthly*, Frith saw fit to publish this letter in response to the Barbados Test: 'Until we can breed seven-foot monsters willing to break bones and shatter faces, we cannot compete against these threatening West Indians. Even the umpires seem to be scared that the devilish-looking Richards might put a voodoo sign on them.'

To describe such comment as racist is not to imply approval of Richards's behaviour. He was a mediocre captain (he had a tough act to follow) and sometimes seemed ruled by egomania. But that does not excuse the double standards of the English. As Imran Khan pointed out after the Bridgetown incident, English players touring India in the seventies tried to pry Gavaskar out by rushing to congratulate each other before the umpire had responded to their appeal. Canny gamesmanship or unfair play? It's all in the eye of the beholder.

For years, the TCCB lobbied the ICC to increase the over rate and limit bouncers. To Clive Lloyd, the aim was clear: 'The emphasis that is being placed on over rates amounts to nothing more than an attack on the West Indies. It is an attempt to reduce the effectiveness of our pace attack.'

The English had seemed happy enough with the old rules until someone else started to win under them. At least, that is how it was perceived in the West Indies. Michael Holding put complaints about West Indies' 'intimidating' fast bowling in perspective: 'All the fuss stems from the fact that one team has been very successful with a particular mode of attack, perfectly legal, that the other teams have been unable to combat. Opposing captains have admitted that if they had such bowlers, they would employ them similarly.'

It's an old story. Learie Constantine recalled West Indies' 1933 tour of England:

> When we played Nottinghamshire during that tour, Larwood sent ball after ball so near our men's faces that presently some of them kept away and their wickets began to fall. We did not complain. If we could not make fours off that sort, it was our fault, not Larwood's. But we did resent the blindness of some of our critics who professed to see danger in those balls when we put them down and none when English players bowled them.

The effect of the English commentary on the West Indians has been to assign their marvellous achievements to a sphere separate from past English successes, which, it is implied, owed nothing to cold-blooded professionalism, heavy-handed intimidation or 'unfair play'. The West Indies' mastery is begrudged. It does not belong to 'cricket' in the higher sense. All this is predicated on the delusion that violence and aggression are somehow alien to English cricket, that blind brute force had to be imported from abroad.

Despite the radical changes in tone, there is an underlying consistency in English perceptions of West Indian cricket. The West Indies clash with England is nature against art, the raw against the cooked, the savage against the civilized. In 1993, Ray Illingworth explained that English players needed more technical instruction than West Indians because the latter have 'looser shoulders and are bigger'.

The myth of West Indian natural ability and 'spontaneity' is a powerful one, on and off the cricket field, but it will not do as an explanation for West Indies' achievements in Test cricket. You cannot spontaneously invent something as complex as a square cut or a fast inswinger to the ribs; as CLR James would remind us, both are products of centuries of social and technical development. The West Indian fast bowlers in the eighties relentlessly *out-thought the England batsmen*. Pace alone would not have been enough. Each of the great West Indian quicks – Roberts, Holding, Garner, Croft, Marshall, Ambrose, Walsh – worked to create his own style, experimentally varying height and angle of delivery, line and length. They enjoyed success everywhere, proving themselves in the process among the most adaptable cricketers the world has ever seen.

How can a game as cussedly awkward as cricket, with its side-on axis defying the body's natural, two-eyed approach to the world, he played without premeditation? When people talk about spontaneity in West Indian cricket what they are really referring to is risk-taking, which demands complex calculation, speed of reaction and sophistication of technique. Cricket's appeal is its difficulty, its unnaturalness. If the West Indian cricketers sometimes manage to make it look natural, it is their greatest achievement: the art that disguises art.

Many of the English players who confronted the great West Indian sides of the eighties were well aware of that. And not all English commentators bought the Frith line. As a new generation of ex-England cricketers takes to the airwaves and the presses, West Indian cricket may begin at last to receive a fair shake. Of course, this has also coincided with an unsteady period in West Indian cricket, on and off the field, as it seeks a new place in a culture and commerce increasingly dominated by North America. If West Indies' Test supremacy endures, as seems likely, it will be because of the game's special place in West Indian society.

In the West Indies, by the beginning of this century, all social classes had taken up cricket. Its mixed population – former slaves from Africa, indentured servants from Asia, traders, farmers, soldiers – was united only by a superimposed English colonial culture, in which cricket played a major role. CLR James recalled how Trinidadian cricket was minutely stratified according to skin tone, from the whites of Queen's Park to the blacks of Stingo, each with its own stylists and heroes. Ironically, this stratification, which included everyone while maintaining social hierarchies, turned cricket into the truly national sport of a nation that does not formally exist.

For CLR James, the West Indies side which toured Australia in 1960-61 under the captaincy of Frank Worrell was 'something new, not only in West Indies cricket but in West Indies life'. He linked its achievements on the cricket field to the islands' new independence from colonial rule. Worrell, the first black man to captain West Indies, had instilled unity, integrity and mutual respect in a side previously notorious for inconsistency. 'Clearing the way with bat and ball,' James declared, 'West Indians at that moment made a public entry into the comity of nations.'

Even as James wrote these words, the nascent West Indian Federation was falling apart. As the islands pursued different political and economic directions over the following decades, the cricket team became the only living expression of West Indian unity. Clive Lloyd took over the captaincy in 1974, just as the oil-price rise and global inflation were sending many of the island economies into recession. Exploiting a rich seam of fast-bowling talent, Lloyd built one of the greatest Test sides in cricket's history, a side that embodied the independence and unity rarely apparent at home. That only made it more important in the lives of the people, and gave the players themselves greater power.

Lloyd led virtually his entire squad into World Series Cricket. He knew that none of them could afford to pass up Packer's offer. But he never surrendered either his own or his team's independence. With the help of Jamaican Prime Minister Michael Manley, he prevented Packer from playing Graeme Pollock in World Series matches, because he knew that Pollock's presence would raise suspicions that Packer was a stalking horse for South Africa, keen to find a way back into international cricket. When it appeared to Lloyd, in 1978, that some of his players were being victimized for their association with Packer, he led his team in a boycott of the Guyana Test, played at the Bourda, his home ground.

This generation of West Indies cricketers broke, much more radically than Frank Worrell's, with the traditional servility of professional cricketers. The eighties were a time of political reaction and growing impoverishment in the islands. But the cricketers' peripatetic existence gave them an independence from the bickering and backward home authorities. Distinctively and powerfully individualistic, they transcended insularity and division by organization and professionalism. Unfortunately, there was no corresponding process in Caribbean society as a whole, which is why West Indian cricket supremacy remains fragile.

A casual glance at the autobiographies and biographies written by or about leading West Indies cricketers of the eighties reveals a common thread among much diversity. All acknowledge that being West Indian and black – in a world dominated, for so many generations, by colonialism and racism – has been a powerful motivation for success in international cricket. They are also highly conscious that they play on behalf of the West Indian diaspora, not just the people in the islands, and that diaspora increasingly sees itself as West Indian, not Trinidadian, Jamaican, Antiguan or Guyanese.

England's nadir against West Indies came in Trinidad in March 1994. Mike Atherton's young English side, chasing a total of 194 to win a close match in the fourth innings, were bowled out for 46, England's lowest Test score since 1887. After taking 6 wickets for 22 runs in seven decisive overs, Curtly Ambrose explained: 'I understand how important it is to play my cricket hard. I do it for the people. They expect nothing less and we're very conscious of them whenever we go on to the field. Their love is very strong. It is demanding on you, but it also makes you strong.'

It is impossible to imagine any contemporary English cricketer speaking this language of solidarity. For Ambrose, as for many West Indies Test players, there is a living bond with a broader West Indian public. It may often be a fraught relationship, but it is felt by the players as an intimate and inescapable one. This is why the West Indians who toured South Africa, unlike their reprieved English counterparts, could not be reintegrated into the official side. Vengeful politicians had nothing to do with it. In the West Indies, the Test side had come to stand for solidarity, anti-colonialism, national self assertion. Mercenaries for apartheid simply did not fit in.

There is one thing West Indies and England, as nations, do have in common: they are the only units playing Test cricket which are not also nation-states. However, where one (West Indies) prefigures a greater unity yet to be built out of social diversity, the other preserves an ancient exclusivity (England) within an inchoate diversity (the 'United Kingdom').

This old England sees not only West Indian cricketers but also West Indian cricket crowds (especially when they appear at English Test grounds) as foreign to the mores of the game. The famous 'carnival spirit' of West Indian cricket, like the West Indian Carnival itself, is an adaptation of ancient folk tradition. At a West Indian Test ground you will see, and especially hear, local Lords of Misrule entertain the crowd with music and mockery. Some engage in cross-dressing, an ancient symbol of social inversion, mirroring what is happening on the field, where the historical hierarchy among nations is so often being turned upside down.

It is one of the many ironies of the game's history that cricket and carnival, those two survivors of pre-industrial society, should meet again in the West Indies. But the response of English commentators to this meeting tells us a great deal about what has happened to English cricket, and England, in the meantime. For all those who place their faith in hierarchy and authority, carnival is a deeply uncomfortable experience, especially when it is imported into one's home ground.

The first West Indian Test victory in England took place in 1950 (thanks to spinners Ramadhin and Valentine) at the same time as the first large-scale immigration from the islands to Britain. 'Calypso cricket', the papers dubbed it, noting the presence for the first time on English Test grounds of West Indian spectators, with their exotic ways of showing enthusiasm. But as the West Indian community here grew, and as West Indies established dominance in Test cricket, the pundits grew less amused. In the seventies and eighties, complaints about the 'endless din', 'mindless cacophony', 'inescapable racket' of the West Indian fans at Tests and one-day internationals became commonplace on 'Test Match Special' and in the columns of *The Times* and *Telegraph*.

In 1987, in reaction to disorder at the Edgbaston Test against Pakistan, the English cricket authorities banned flags, banners and 'excessive' amounts of alcohol (which forced spectators to purchase the over-priced beer sold on the ground). Soon, drums, whistles and klaxons were also taboo, and along with them, 'calypso cricket' and the spirit of carnival. Within two years, the open area in front of the Lord's Tavern, which had become the haunt of boozers and chanters, was covered with seats, as were the West Terraces at the Oval and the Rea Bank stand at Edgbaston. Since then, ticket prices have climbed steeply and virtually all seats for major fixtures are now booked in advance. All this has made English cricket less accessible to working-class people in general. It has also sent out a clear message to West Indian supporters in England: unless they behave like 'English' people, they are not welcome at English cricket grounds.

Not surprisingly, during both the 1988 and 1991 West Indian tours, black spectators were notable by their absence, especially at Edgbaston and the Oval, where they had previously turned up in large numbers. The result, in the words of Tony Cozier, the West Indies cricket broadcaster, was that 'members can once again sleep in the Long Room without being interrupted'.

Ironically, the musical theme used by BBC television to introduce its cricket coverage, Booker T's 'Soul Limbo', with its heavy syncopation and hint of steel drums, invokes the spirit of Caribbean carnival. Much loved by fans as a harbinger of cricket, this song of summer has become the anthem of the English national game. It is clear that in West Indies cricket many English people find a joy and confidence absent from the English scene. The angry old men ranting about bouncers, slow over rates and bad behaviour speak for a minority.

At a dinner on the eve of the 1992 World Cup final, an Australian drag artist entertained the assembled players and officials with an unflattering impression of the British sovereign, then in the midst of her *annus horribilis*. It was too much for Graham Gooch and Ian Botham, who walked out. 'I am very proud of our heritage,' declared Botham. 'Unlike the Australians, at least we have one!' The following day England were beaten in the final by Pakistan, a country with a heritage stretching back 4,000 years. 'When naked talent overcomes solid professionalism, who can complain?' asked Vic Marks. The answer was Ian Botham, who insisted Pakistan were 'lucky to have got to the finals' and that England were 'the best side overall'.

Botham's hostility to Pakistan was nothing new. Years before, he had told radio listeners that he wouldn't 'send his mother-in-law' to Pakistan. In the moment of World Cup victory, more than one Pakistani player could not resist taunting Botham: 'Who wants your mother-in-law anyway!' In a more reflective moment, they might have pointed out that they had more cause to be offended by his broadcast insult to their entire nation than he had by a send-up of the Queen at a private party.

All this was merely the prelude to the rancour which ripped through the Pakistan tour of England the following summer. Cricket relations between the two countries had been sour for some time. Repeated complaints about biased umpiring, both in England and Pakistan, had come to a head in Mike Gatting's face-to-face exchange of obscenities with umpire Shakoor Rana in Faisalabad. The attitude of the English tourists to their hosts was neatly expressed by Bill Athey, who had declared, shortly before the bust-up with Rana, 'The sooner we get out of this fucking country the better.' When the umpire turned down an English appeal for a bat-pad catch, Gatting muttered, 'One rule for one and one rule for another.' Tempers escalated. Rana was sure Gatting had called him a 'fucking cheat'. When asked to apologize, Gatting said, 'Does Maggie back down when she's given no choice?' But the Foreign Office made it clear to the TCCB that Britain enjoyed friendly relations with the Pakistani government and did not want these jeopardized. Gatting apologized. Pakistan offered to secure neutral umpires for the next Test, but the TCCB refused. When the England party then objected to one of the proposed Pakistani umpires, he was replaced by the Pakistan Board without demur. In the meantime, the TCCB dished out a £1,000 cash 'hardship' bonus to each of the English tourists in recognition of the torments they had endured in Pakistan. There were no Tests between the two countries for five years. At the ICC, the TCCB led resistance to Pakistan's demands for the appointment of neutral, third-country umpires for all Tests and one-day internationals.

Pakistan arrived in England in 1992 already labelled the awkward squad of world cricket. Even before the tour, ICC Chairman Colin Cowdrey had warned the visitors against 'hysterical appeals'. There was little English confidence in the Pakistan captain, Javed Miandad, a brilliant batsman whose temper had got him into trouble in cricket grounds in four continents. But there was hope that the team manager, Intikhab Alam, a popular Surrey cricketer for thirteen years, and the Harvard-educated tour manager, Khalid Mohammed, would keep everything cosy. And the performance of fast bowlers Wasim Akram and Waqar Younis, Imran's proteges, was anticipated with relish. Both, however, were carrying injuries. They did not appear together until mid-June, six weeks into the tour, against Allan Lamb's Northamptonshire, whom they beat by seven wickets.

The international season started with two one-day matches during which, *The Cricketer* reported, 'The lads in the tabloids were busy drumming up a nice little line in Christian/Muslim warfare which made the Crusades seem like a forty-over match.' The *Mirror* dubbed Miandad 'Cricket's Colonel Gadaffi'. Under the headline 'Looking for revenge', Botham cried, 'Let me at 'em.' According to the *Sun*, Wasim threatened, 'We'll pitch it in short for a real battering.' As it turned out, this was precisely what he and Waqar had decided not to do.

In the second one-day international at Lord's, umpire Merv Kitchen gave Miandad out LBW to Botham for 38. A triumphant Botham made a point of sending the irritated Pakistani captain 'on his way' with a manual flourish. Ken Lawrence, the newly-appointed TCCB media manager, gleefully informed the press, 'Miandad says Botham told him to fuck off.' The next day, the *Mirror's* back page announced: 'Beefy told me to *!@* off!' Asked about Botham's behaviour, Micky Stewart, the England team manager, dismissed it as 'a run-of-the-mill thing'.

In the run-up to the first Test of what the *Mirror* dubbed a 'potentially explosive' series, it was announced that 200 'specially trained' stewards (backed by the latest in surveillance technology) would be on hand at Edgbaston to prevent a repeat of the crowd violence that had attended the Pakistanis' last appearance there. According to the *Mirror*, the stewards would confiscate 'flags, whistles and bugles brought in by Pakistan supporters'.

In the week before the Test, the *Mirror* claimed the 'huge Asian community in Birmingham offered £500' to any Pakistan bowler who could dismiss Botham – and £100 for every six hit off Botham's bowling. Wasim, injured, did not play; Waqar took 1 for 96. There were seventy ejections and forty arrests during the rain-affected, high scoring draw. At close of play on Saturday, groups of English and Pakistani supporters clashed at the back of the Hollies stand. Throughout the day, England supporters chanted, 'There's only one Salman Rushdie.'

In the second Test, at Lord's, Waqar took 5 for 91 in the first innings ('England Waqared!' chortled the *Mirror*) and Wasim 4 for 66 in the second ('Wham! Bam! Thank you Akram!'). The two then came together for a match-winning ninth-wicket stand of 46. Chris Lander, the *Mirror's* chief cricket correspondent, praised the final day's play as an example of 'the wonderful appeal of Test cricket' and even lauded Miandad's 'undying love of playing for his country'.

In the third Test, at Old Trafford, umpire Roy Palmer made his international debut. His first decision was to give Rameez Raja caught out for 54 off an edge which, *Wisden* observed, was 'discernible' only to him, in response to 'an appeal too lukewarm to be called half-hearted'. All of the second and most of the third day's play were lost to rain. Then, towards the end of the England innings on the evening of the fourth day, the tabloids got what they had been waiting for.

Aqib Javed, previously referred to in *Wisden Cricket Monthly* as 'a quiet young man', greeted England bowler Devon Malcolm, one of the most inept number elevens in Test cricket, with a bouncer. During the Pakistani innings Malcolm himself had bowled bouncers at tail-ender Waqar Younis. Umpire Palmer indicated his unhappiness with Aqib's tactics. When Malcolm ducked into the next delivery, Palmer called a no-ball and issued a warning under Law 42.8 (which covers fast, short-pitched deliveries). Indignant, Aqib bowled yet another short one, but this time was neither no-balled nor warned. In the confusion, Palmer allowed Aqib to bowl an extra ball, which made this contentious over, including the no-ball, eight balls in total. At its end, Palmer handed Aqib his sweater in a manner that the bowler found insulting. Suddenly, Palmer was surrounded by a group of Pakistani players led by their captain. One aggrieved Pakistani supporter ran on to the ground waving a rolled-up newspaper. He was chased and removed by two security men.

Wisden later reported that Palmer returned Aqib's sweater 'with more emphasis than usual, probably because it was caught in his belt'. The *Mirror's* instant version was different: 'Palmer, clearly annoyed, then thrust the sweater at the bowler in a dismissive fashion.' According to Richard Hutton, editor of *The Cricketer*, Palmer was then 'besieged by another fuming horde'. Miandad, however, insisted he was only trying to ascertain why Palmer had issued the warning. He observed that people in England seemed to misunderstand his 'gesticulations'. However you apportion blame, one thing is clear, at least to anyone who has spent time in the subcontinent. This was a classic case of mutually misinterpreted body languages.

After the match, Intikhab criticized Palmer's warning to Aqib and insisted that the umpire had 'insulted' the Pakistan players by the way he returned the bowler's sweater. He also complained that both umpires had made great play of inspecting the ball when Pakistan were bowling, while doing nothing of the kind when England were in the field.

Over a big back-page photo of the newspaper-waving Pakistan supporter being bundled away by stewards, the *Mirror* ran the dual headlines: 'Pakistan Go to War' and 'Test of Shame'. Gower's feat in overtaking Boycott as England's top Test run-scorer was relegated to the inside pages.

After studying tapes of the Aqib Palmer confrontation, ICC match referee Conrad Hunte exonerated the umpire and fined the Pakistani bowler 50 per cent of his match fee. He also criticized members of the Pakistan side for crowding the umpires in a manner not 'within the spirit of the game'. He urged both Gooch and Miandad to ensure their players maintained this 'spirit' and reprimanded Intikhab for publicly criticizing Palmer.

'Pakistan Test Shame: GUILTY!' cried the *Mirror*. Hunte's adjudication was described as a 'desperate bid to stop the series bubbling into all-out war'. Inside there was a feature on 'Javed's Brat Pack', illustrated with an old photo of Gatting's facing off with Shakoor Rana in Faisalabad. Buried away in the text was a small note: 'Gooch seemed to draw the umpire's attention to the fact that one side of the ball had been scuffed – a factor that aids swing bowling.'

For the first time, Mike Langley, the *Mirror's* in-house sports moralist, got stuck in:

> Javed Miandad looks like a wild man with a face you might spot crouched behind rocks in ambush along the Khyber ... better suited to leading warriors than cricketers ... Ian Botham called Pakistan a good place to send your mother-in-law. This was so true. I thought they'd laugh their curly slippers off ... even hotter on apologies than they are on vindaloos.

He finished his diatribe with a warning: 'Miandad should also bear in mind England's ineradicable curiosity about how Pakistan's bowlers can swing a worn ball on days when new ones won't deviate.'

In a *Sunday Telegraph* article headed 'The pariahs of cricket', Simon

Heffer, a political correspondent, accused Pakistani players, officials, umpires and supporters of 'degrading' cricket. He urged the TCCB to bar all future tours by or to Pakistan. The Pakistani High Commissioner in London called the article 'odious and objectionable' and a writ was served in the names of Intikhab, Khalid Mohammed, Miandad and the Pakistan Board.

In *Wisden Cricket Monthly*, Frith described the Old Trafford incident as 'the most distasteful charade ever seen on an English first-class cricket field'. In *The Cricketer*, Richard Hutton went even further in condemning the 'monstrous behaviour' of 'these anarchists': 'Of all the eight clauses in the Code of Conduct the Pakistanis have failed to breach only one, that relating to the use or distribution of illegal drugs ... so far as we know.'

The cricket authorities, and especially Hunte, derided by Frith as a 'conciliator', were sharply criticized for letting off the Pakistanis with only a 'slap on the wrist'.

A week later, the *Mirror* exclaimed, 'The umpires strike back'. In an 'exclusive' report, Chris Lander claimed that Ken Palmer and Merv Kitchen would refuse to stand at Headingley unless Roy Palmer received 'a fulsome apology' (apparently the Pakistanis were not the only ones 'hotter on apologies than vindaloos'). The source of the story was Don Oslear, Chairman of the First Class Umpires Association, who had been dropped from the Test panel in the mid-eighties. In the 1993 *Cricketers' Who's Who*, he declared: 'One of the best things in recent years is the fact that South Africa will be playing again at the highest level. The worst thing will be the introduction of an independent panel of umpires.'

Under the headline 'Cricket sinners must go', the *Mirror* quoted retired umpire Bill Alley, just out of hospital, at length:

At least when a side like Australia tries to rattle you they do so in a language you can understand ... even though most of the players speak very good English they jabber at you in Urdu ... English umpires are acknowledged as the best in the world. Mistakes are occasionally made but they are always honest ones.

Brian Close also took to the tabloids to denounce the 'animated, arm-waving' Pakistanis as 'unsavoury ... unacceptable ... a shocking show of dissent ... dreadful scenes ... we had a different philosophy in my day ...' This from the cricketer who had been stripped of the England captaincy by the MCC after he had refused to apologize for alleged time-wasting in a county championship match.

At Headingley, flags, bugles and booze were once again banned. The Yorkshire CCC Chief Executive explicitly warned 'racists' to stay away. Cowdrey and Clyde Walcott, on behalf of the ICC, met with Intikhab, Miandad, Gooch and Stewart to appeal for calm. On the morning of the first day, the *Mirror* reported, 'Graham stirs up the war'. Apparently, Gooch had given Cowdrey a letter complaining about Aqib's 'dangerous' bowling to Malcolm and protesting that he and the England squad had been unfairly tainted by Hunte's even handed warning. Hunte then apologized to Gooch for 'the wording of the press release'.

Although Waqar took 5 for 117 in the first innings, England won the match, thanks to Pakistani paranoia about the seaming pitch, Neil Mallender's eight wickets (he was dropped after one more Test) and, it was said, some patriotic umpiring. England were to lose their next seven Tests (in three different countries) and were not to win again for over a year.

In the first innings, both Smith (on his way to 42) and Gooch (135) survived repeated appeals for LBW. In the second innings, Asif Mujtaba, given out caught for 11, claimed the ball had hit his boot, not his bat. The most controversial decision was Ken Palmer's refusal to give Gooch run out when he was going for his 14th run in the second innings, with England still a long way from the 99 they needed to win the match. The television replay showed Gooch out of his ground by two feet. He went on to make 37 before being third out with the England score at 61. An over later, it was 66 for 4. Waqar, Wasim and Mushtaq stepped up the volume and frequency of their appeals, much to the disgust of 'Test Match Special' commentators.

To many observers – at least non-English observers – it did seem as if umpires Kitchen and Palmer had come to regard it as a point of professional pride not to respond to a Pakistani appeal. Substitute fielder Rashid Latif threw his cap to the ground in frustration when an icy Gower was given not out to an appeal for caught behind. He was calmed by Miandad but fined by ICC referee Clyde Walcott. Despite apologizing, he became the latest addition to the rogues' gallery of 'petulant' Pakistanis.

For the *Mirror* the Headlingley story was simple: 'HERO AND VILLAINS', i.e. Gooch and the Pakistanis. However, since the only Pakistani villain to hand was Rashid, it attacked the Pakistani fans. 'One hundred excitable fans kept up a non-stop barrage of noise ... four supporters – three of them Pakistani – had to be tackled to the ground by stewards.' The *Mirror* did not report that a small group of English fans had thrown a mutilated pig's head into an enclave of Pakistani supporters.*

In Pakistan, within days of the Test, buses were bedecked with a large photo showing Gooch being run out and Ken Palmer giving him in. The Urdu caption read: 'English professional umpires – the best in the world.' Fareshteh Gati, one of the few women in any country to fill a top cricket correspondent's berth, and a critic of umpiring in Pakistan, wrote:

> The Pakistanis, who cannot stomach the lunches served by the clubs at cricket grounds and often have to send out for samosas, chicken tikkas and kebabs, will now have to send out for lemon lozenges to soothe their sore throats after the appeals turned down by Kitchen and Palmer. They appealed at least nineteen times for leg-before decisions and even if you minus some as being very optimistic, there were five shouts which would have changed the state of the scoreboard. So much for integrity and fair play.

The *Guardian's* Mike Selvey observed that few of the Pakistani appeals were 'frivolous, and most of them marginal'. The LBW decisions 'were of an apparently arbitrary nature'. Sunil Gavaskar, no apologist for Pakistani cricket, argued in an Indian newspaper that the English win at Headingley was 'sneaked' with 'assistance of the men in white coats'. In that context, Gavaskar thought, 'the Pakistanis' behaviour was very restrained at Leeds'.

In the week after Headingley three British competitors were sent home from the Barcelona Olympics after failing drug tests. A rising tide of racist violence took the life of Ruallah Aramesh, a refugee from Afghanistan His family's house in Croydon had been besieged by a white gang shouting racist abuse; after Ruallah left the house he was set on and beaten to death by sixteen thugs armed with metal bars and wooden sticks.

Meanwhile, the *Mirror* reported that the Pakistanis were glad to have

*In 1998, I received a letter from Martyn Stankler, who witnessed this incident. 'I was the steward on duty in the area where it happened (what you have written is 100% accurate, I have to say) ... I was interviewed at some length by the chief steward about what had happened and for longer periods by the ground manager [who told me] he would take a dim view of anything printed anywhere that was not to his liking ...' Understandably, Mr Stankler was astonished that 'one of the most remarkable things (in my view anyway) to have taken place off the field of play at a cricket match' went unreported in either the local, national or cricket press.

Dickie Bird and David Shepherd, two popular and respected umpires, standing in the fifth and final Test at the Oval. The next day, the same paper ran a story headlined 'Imran's verdict on our umpires: RUBBISH!' In the course of the story, Imran made scathing remarks about the role of the ICC match referees and advocated the use of TV playbacks for run-out decisions but, contrary to the headline, said nothing about English umpires. Two days later, under the headline 'Test match video probe', it was reported that a TCCB official 'acting on his own initiative' was looking at the BBC tape of the final day's play at Headingley, during which, it was alleged, keeper Moin Khan had scuffed up the wicket outside Gower's off stump in an attempt to help the leg-spinner, Mushtaq Ahmed. Ken Lawrence was quoted saying: 'I heard the whispers going round and want to clear it up.' The allegation had appeared in none of the match reports. It was never mentioned again, even by the *Mirror*.

Dickie Bird's measured statements about the need for calm in the fifth and final Test appeared under the headlines 'I'll stop the war' (*Mirror*) and 'I fear Test war' (*Sun*). Bird himself had not used the word 'war' nor indeed any military metaphor.

At the Oval, Wasim took 6 for 67 in the first innings. Chris Lander declared it 'the finest display of fast bowling at the Oval' since Michael Holding's 8 for 92 in 1976. But England manager Micky Stewart was more grudging. 'The ball suddenly started to swing,' he told the press. 'I know why,' he added, but declined to elaborate. An irritated Wasim responded, 'I have played now in England for five years and no one has complained about the way I swing the ball.'

On Friday, Miandad was booed by sections of the crowd on his way back to the pavilion after he had waited for Shepherd to ask Bird whether the catch to Chris Lewis had carried. Under the headline, 'Oval and out! Miandad's at it again', Lander reported that Javed was 'booed and jeered by 20,000 spectators for not walking promptly'. The next day, debutant wicket-keeper Rashid Latif; the bad boy of Headingley, displayed a phlegmatic temper in scoring a half-century in classical style (he was one of six Pakistani batsmen to pass 50 in the tourists' first-innings total of 380). When England batted again, Waqar took 5 for 52, leading Pakistan to a ten-wicket victory on the fourth day, and with it, a 2-1 victory in the series – their third consecutive series victory over England.

At the post-match press conference, Stewart was pressed to clarify his earlier insinuations. His response only added to the confusion:

Yes, I know the method Wasim Akram and Waqar Younis use to make the old ball swing so much but that is all I wish to say. It has been discussed in the dressing room and we know how they do it ... I am not being mysterious at all ... I have said a lot but nothing improper.

Asked repeatedly whether or not he was saying that the Pakistani bowling was 'unfair' under the Laws of Cricket, he refused to answer. He hinted, however, that England would themselves employ the 'secret' in future matches.

'Bitter to the end' and 'Champs or cheats' were the *Mirror* headlines. Lander claimed that 'all summer English cricket has been highly suspicious about how the Pakistanis made the ball swing about so violently'. Yet Lander himself had failed to report any of these suspicions until the middle of the final Test. The *Mirror* chose this moment to divulge Robin Smith's claim that Waqar had said to him, 'I'm going to xxx kill you, you xxx' – at a match in Southampton *earlier in the season*.

The *Sun's* back page read 'NAILED – Waqar caught in new ball tampering row'. Murky photos showing Waqar holding the ball at his side were captioned: 'Waqar Younis appears to pick at the seam with his finger and thumbnail'. Waqar responded: 'I might fiddle with the seam sometimes, but no more than that. My thumbnails are short. There's no way I could have damaged the ball with them. The umpires inspected the ball regularly and the match referee looked at it after each session. Nobody mentioned anything.'

This did not stop John Lever insisting, 'They dig in their nails to form a groove that runs like a spiral from the seam towards the centre of the ball.' His Essex colleague, Gooch, merely observed: 'I am sure the Pakistani bowlers will be keeping the method to themselves.'

In what the *Mirror* dubbed an 'amazing attack on Test moaners', Salim Malik pointed out that Waqar had removed the first four England batsman at the Oval with the *new* ball. While claiming that the England players had scuffed up the wicket when he was batting, he also insisted – as did most players quoted by name throughout the summer-that personal relations between the two teams were friendly. The *Sun* headlined a similar report 'England make me sick'. It also published pictures of a cricket ball in various states of decay under the headline: 'Revealed! Secrets of Waqar the wrecker'.

The *Sun*, unlike the *Mirror*, offered balance in the person of Geoff Boycott, who said it was 'bloody bad sportsmanship to denigrate' the Pakistanis, an 'exciting, attractive and talented' team. 'They were magicians, not cheats.'

In *The Cricketer*, Richard Hutton fulminated: 'Cheating in Test cricket is now endemic.' His editorial consisted of a lengthy disquisition on how unnamed contemporary players doctored the ball to make it swing. Their most ingenious ruse, it seemed, involved bowlers filling their mouths with orange squash during drinks intervals and then drenching the ball with the squash when they were out of the umpire's sight. Hutton then denounced Pakistani players, specifically Waqar, for taking drinks from plastic bottles placed just outside the boundary ropes, a common practice in county cricket. 'It is all very undignified,' he concluded; 'allowing bowlers to swig away at the edge of the field cannot be conducive to the public good.'

With the Test series over, there remained three one-day inter nationals. England won easily at Trent Bridge but Pakistan hit back at Lord's, where the match was spread over two days because of rain. Pakistan batted first, scoring 204. Miandad was cheered by the crowd for agreeing to bat on in poor light on Saturday evening. The next morning, Allan Lamb, batting for England again after missing the last three Tests, complained quietly to the umpires about the state of the ball.

The umpires met with the match referee, Deryck Murray, during the interval. Also present was Don Oslear, acting as support for umpires John Hampshire and Ken Palmer. Murray called for Intikhab, showed him the ball and told him, according to Oslear, 'Someone had altered the condition of the ball and it would have to be changed.' Intikhab asked who was interfering with the ball. The umpires said they did not know. Then Intikhab – not Gooch – selected a replacement ball from a box of worn spares. Intikhab did not accept the allegation but was happy to change the ball. He and Miandad then asked to inspect the old ball, which Oslear, on his own initiative, had already locked away. Miandad wanted the old ball taken out again and replaced after a single delivery; it was Murray and the umpires who insisted on doing the whole thing secretly. Oslear then informed Micky Stewart, who passed the news on to the England players. Afterwards, Alan Smith, Oslear, Murray and Lawrence drew up a press statement. Before it was released, they were joined by Intikhab, Khalid and Miandad. At their request, a phrase in the statement declaring that the 'the condition of the ball had been altered' was deleted.

At this stage the crowd remained, in the words of Christopher Martin-Jenkins, 'blissfully unaware' of any controversy. *After* the ball change, Wasim and Waqar took five wickets to win the match.

A phone call from the England dressing room alerted a tabloid reporter to the fact that the ball had been changed over lunch. That evening's press conference was attended by neither the umpires nor the match referee nor the ICC Secretary. However, an anonymous Lord's official informed the media that the ball had been changed under Law 42.5 – the section dealing with ball-tampering under the general heading of 'unfair play'.

'GOT 'EM BY THE BALL', declared the *Sun*, whose cricket correspondent stated confidently that Murray, Palmer and Hampshire 'were convinced the Pakistanis had illegally tampered with the ball'. The *Mirror* reprinted Law 42.5 in full in a special box. Like the *Sun*, it was confident that: 'Murray's report will confirm that the ball was changed under Law 42.5.' In the *Daily Telegraph* Martin-Jenkins claimed that 'questions to those present at the lunch-time inspection of the ball confirmed that the decision to change it was made under Law 42.5'. This was surely a reference to Oslear.

Intikhab, however, insisted the ball was changed under Law 5, because it was going soft, and that there was no imputation of 'unfair play' on Pakistan's part. He pointed out that the ball was replaced by one in similar condition, as it should have been under Law 5, whereas under Law 42.5 it would have had to be replaced by an inferior ball. Khalid said: 'We would welcome a statement from Murray to clarify the circumstances under which the ball was changed. And we would gladly welcome the Lord's match ball to be put on show for everyone to see we have nothing to hide.'

The *Sun* alleged that Khalid and Intikhab were trying to high pressure Murray into 'changing' his report. As ICC Chairman Cowdrey was abroad, Secretary John Stephenson was left to handle the controversy. On the day after the Lord's match, Stephenson observed that the ICC would have to look into 'the whole issue of ball tampering ... we might even have to change the Laws of Cricket'. He was still waiting for Murray's match report, however, and could not comment on any specific allegations nor confirm or deny under which Law the ball had been changed. When England won the final one-day international at Old Trafford (Micky Stewart's last match as team manager), the *Sun* printed this despatch from the front line: 'England's stormtroopers won the final battle of their summer war with Pakistan.'

Despite mounting pressure from the media, Murray refused to say under which Law he had changed the ball. Disclosure of his match report, he insisted, was a matter for the ICC. Stephenson refused to publish the report, then muddied the water by commenting: 'The matter is closed for the moment ... I stress I am not referring to this incident, but ball-tampering must never be allowed to happen again.'

Intikhab and Khalid were furious. Because of the ICC's stonewalling 'an impression has been created that the change of ball was due to tampering by the fielding side'. They demanded that the ICC publish both the umpires' and the referee's reports. Boycott backed them, pointing out that in 28.5 days of international cricket, throughout which the ball was regularly inspected during and between sessions of play, there had not been one complaint from a single umpire or referee. Was it possible that ball-doctoring was going on and all these august authorities had missed it? Or were they all engaged in an elaborate cover-up for the Pakistanis?

The hacks were convinced it was the latter. '*Indecisive Cowardly Clowns!*' said the *Sun*, dubbing the ICC the 'biggest bunch of bungling jokers in world sport'. It promised readers that the controversy would 'rage on and on till we get the truth'. The *Mirror's* headline comment was: 'What a load of old ...' followed by five cricket balls. It called on 'the International Cock-up Council' to sling Pakistan out of world cricket. 'Maybe they should be apart until they have earned the total respect of the rest of the cricketing world' – in which case, an Australian observed, England would certainly have to join them in purdah.

With the series over and the Pakistani players preparing to return home, the *Mirror* looked around for a way to keep this hot story on the boil. On 26 August, the paper ran a double-page spread headlined: 'Allan Lamb (England Test Ace) on the cheats of Pakistan'. Lamb revealed:

> They gouge the damaged ball with their nails then smear the surface to fool the umpire ... Wasim Akram and Waqar Younis have been getting away with murder all summer ... Telling the truth might hit my chances of going to India with England this winter. But the issue is so serious that I can keep quiet no longer.

Lamb's chances of going to India with the Test party were nil in any case, as he well knew, especially after a summer in which he had played in two Tests and scored 54 runs at an average of 18. Throughout the summer, in ten innings in all cricket against the Pakistani bowlers, he had averaged 25. Long before the *Mirror* article was published he had made arrangements to spend the English winter playing for Western Province in South Africa.

Lamb claimed that Wasim and Waqar were using 'an old trick first shown to me a dozen years ago by my old Northamptonshire team mate Sarfraz Nawaz'. Northamptonshire, fearful that Lamb's remarks would get him banned from the upcoming NatWest final, took pre-emptive action, suspending their captain for two county championship matches and fining him two weeks' wages.

In an editorial comment, the *Mirror* said that Lamb's 'revelation' demanded a 'full-scale investigation', but then prejudged the outcome by calling on the TCCB to demand that the Pakistanis forfeit the Cornhill prize money. The *Sun* cast aside its usual rivalry with the *Mirror* to announce, in a 'Sunsport' editorial, that 'Lamby's batting for us all' and to attack the 'hush-it-up attitude' of the ICC and TCCB. It reported that Lamb was 'going public' with the 'full knowledge' of Gooch and Micky Stewart. In the same issue, under the headline, 'Javed's Outcasts', Bob Willis explained: 'The way they go about their business on the field is not acceptable ... It's just the way they are brought up to play their cricket. It's the nature of the beast. Everything is confrontational. They don't say sorry willingly and don't often accept that they are in the wrong.'

In the *Sunday People*, Fred Trueman urged the cricket authorities to 'kick 'em all out'. What's more, he said, 'Allan Lamb deserves a medal'.

The next day the story finally hit the front page, at least the *Mirror's* front page: '"Cheat" bowlers start racism rumpus'. Wasim and Waqar had issued a statement:

It is very convenient to blame the failure of the English players' batting techniques on us ... At no time has any official ever confronted us with an allegation of illegality ... We are amazed that a fellow professional has stooped so low as to make such unfounded comments. We can only guess at Allan Lamb's motives ... but we hope they are nothing so base as money or, even worse, our nationality.

Just what were Lamb's motives? The £10,000 he was reportedly paid for the original story – augmented by undisclosed further sums for the 'exclusive interviews' that followed – must have been enticing. The *Mirror* at first denied it had paid Lamb any money for the story – only one of several flagrant whoppers it told during the course of what it dubbed 'Lambgate'.

The chief prosecutor for the *Mirror* in this artificially prolonged inquisition was Mike Langley. 'Gouging the ball is now a lesser crime than rocking the boat,' he pontificated. 'Lord's must know his accusation is anything but erroneous ... I am aware that a majority of the England team agree with Lamb ... many umpires tell us privately that something funny has been going on ...' Langley alleged that Lord's was trying to 'gag' not only Lamb, but the entire English Test side, the umpires, the match referees and presumably the caterers.

Under the headline 'PAK OFF THE CHEATS FOR FIVE YEARS' the *Sun* reported the results of a telephone poll of its readers: 89 per cent thought Pakistan were 'cheating', but 59 per cent wanted neutral umpires. On its front page of 29 August, the *Mirror* claimed it had 'FINGERED!' the Pakistanis. It reproduced a still from the BBC's television coverage ostensibly showing Aqib Javed picking at the seam of the ball (this would have violated Law 42.4 on 'lifting the seam', not the now infamous Law 42.5) and claimed that this 'evidence of Javed's cheating fully vindicates Allan Lamb'. Aqib himself made a point that many fans had already noted: 'I've shared the same ball as Wasim and Waqar all series so why haven't I had the same degree of success? I can't because I am not as good as they are.'

The Lambgate saga rolled on for another two months. The *Mirror* sent reporters to doorstep cricket officials. Stephenson, cornered outside his home, said, 'It's a touchy subject and a difficult one and I'm not prepared to say anything.' It was claimed that 'prominent England players' and 'senior umpires' were backing Lamb, but none was ever named. The *Mirror* also reported that Oslear, as chairman of the Umpires' Association, had helped Hampshire and Palmer send a 2,000-word fax to Cowdrey protesting over the alleged removal of a reference to Law 42.5 in their report. This story could only have come from Oslear himself.

Mike Selvey initially condemned Lamb for breaking 'every rule in the book' but two days later was insisting he had 'stuck his neck out for the good of the game'. Robin Marlar in *The Sunday Times* was less ambiguous, declaring that 'Lamb is a man of mental as well as physical courage'.

Thanks to co-operation between the TCCB and Northamptonshire, Lamb (who had already been reappointed county captain) was allowed to play in the NatWest final. The *Mirror* appealed to cricket fans to 'Stand by your Lamb', and later claimed he was given a hero's welcome by the Lord's crowd. In fact, Lamb had been confronted first thing that morning by Sarfraz Nawaz's solicitor, who served him with a writ for libel. Members in the pavilion did indeed clap the Northamptonshire captain on his way out to the wicket, but the fans as a whole were lukewarm.

In the end Lamb was fined £5,000 plus £1,000 costs by the TCCB for breach of contract (the *Mirror* article had not been cleared in advance, as required by the contracts Lamb had signed with both the TCCB and Northamptonshire). He appealed to the Cricket Council, usually nothing but a cypher for the TCCB. Months later, in light of alleged inconsistencies in TCCB fining policy and its failure to pay 'sufficient regard ... to Lamb's outstanding contribution to English cricket', it ordered the fine cut to £4,000, half of it suspended indefinitely. Costs were also halved. The *Mirror* picked up the remaining £2,500 tab.

Virtually forgotten in all of this was the extraordinary success of the Pakistani side. It had played nineteen first-class matches, won twelve (including nine of twelve matches against the counties), lost only two and drawn five. Throughout, the Pakistanis had played attacking, inventive, entertaining cricket exploiting all the game's varied skills. No match was used merely for batting or bowling practice or to rest senior players, as had been the practice of other recent touring sides. Between them, Wasim and Waqar had taken forty-three of the seventy-one English wickets to fall during the Test series – twenty-six of them LBW or bowled and another fourteen caught behind. In the course of the summer, Wasim alone had captured eighty-two first-class wickets at 16.21 each, as well as taking five wickets in an innings seven times.

'Reverse swing' became the talk of the summer. Wasim and Waqar seemed to have turned upside down the received wisdom about the behaviour of a cricket ball in flight. Jack Bannister, no friend to Third World cricket, described their achievement as the 'first genuine fast bowling innovation since over-arm bowling was legalized in 1864'. What was new, he said, was the combination of high pace, late swing and the old ball.

The secret, it seems, is letting one side of the ball get dry and rough while weighing the other side down with saliva and sweat. In addition, a slight decrease in speed as the ball approaches the batsman is required if the peculiar torque ('reverse swing') created by the imbalance in the ball is to take effect. All this is entirely within the Laws of the game. And it is far more than a gimmick which others can copy. To get the complex physics working to order requires extraordinary accuracy, strength, speed and the most intricate muscular co-ordination. It is a feat of high intelligence, not low cunning.

Cricket lovers were enthralled by the contrasting yet complementary styles of the two strike bowlers, the fluency of their actions and diversity of their deliveries, their inventive, attacking approach to the game. Both unleashed irresistibly destructive spells at crucial moments, like men possessed of a greater, transient power that cannot by its very nature be sustained. And added to Wasim and Waqar there was Mushtaq, who had delighted fans all summer with his varied and deceptive leg-spin, taking 66 wickets at 24 apiece. At the crease, Salim Malik averaged 81 in the

Tests, Javed Miandad 60 and Aamer Sohail 51. In every Test match, at least one Pakistani batsman had produced a major innings.

The series was a huge financial success with takings of over £7 million at the gate (£250,000 above original estimates, despite rain at Edgbaston and Old Trafford). Over half a million spectators ventured out to see the Pakistanis in the flesh and very few went home unsatisfied. Throughout the tour, the visiting players were well received by local cricket supporters. Queues of mostly white English boys and girls waiting for Wasim's and Waqar's autographs never shortened, even after Lamb's 'revelations'. The Pakistan Board, following the precedent set by the TCCB in 1987-88, awarded the Pakistan players a bonus for withstanding 'the pressure of the British tabloid press'.

Shortly after the conclusion of the 1992 season the TCCB announced that Surrey had been fined £1,000 for ball-tampering. The county had already been warned for the offence in 1990 and 1991. A shocked Surrey Committee launched an investigation which revealed that earlier warnings had been kept in confidence between the cricket staff and the TCCB. Alec Stewart was advised that any further incidents would result in his dismissal as Surrey captain. Ken Lawrence, announcing the fine, couldn't help but add, 'After all the controversy involving Wasim Akram and Waqar Younis this summer, Lancashire and Surrey are well aware that people are going to be looking at their performances.' The formal TCCB statement had said nothing about Lancashire or either of the Pakistani bowlers. Waqar had played in only one of the three Surrey matches in which complaints had been made.

In the autumn of 1992, Don Oslear was voted out as Chairman of the Umpires' Association. Early in the 1993 season, he found himself standing in the Somerset v. Gloucestershire match. Mushtaq, now leg spinning for Somerset, went off for treatment to a damaged limb. When he came back, Oslear demanded to know whether he had used any hair gel or muscle spray that could be applied illegally to the ball. An embarrassed Jack Russell, Gloucestershire's acting captain, made clear he had no suspicions or objections.

Later that year, the *Sunday Telegraph* was compelled to apologize to the BCCP, Intikhab, Khalid, Miandad and 'to all Pakistani cricket followers' for the Simon Heffer article. The newspaper accepted that the BCCP officials 'were not corrupt', that they 'administer cricket in accordance with the game's internationally accepted laws' and that Miandad 'sought to ensure that he and his team played by those laws'.

Sarfraz's libel action finally came to court in November 1993. Chris

Cowdrey, Wayne Larkins, Robin Smith, Ian Botham and Don Oslear all queued up to testify for Lamb. Much of the testimony dwelt on what had happened in 1992, which had nothing to do with Sarfraz, who had retired in 1984. Chris Cowdrey showed the jury BBC videotapes in which various Pakistan players appeared to be scratching or roughing up the ball. After four days, the dispute was settled out of court. It was agreed by Lamb that Sarfraz had never cheated in any cricket match. Lamb, backed by the *Mirror*, stood by his original story. The legal costs were divided.

Both sides claimed victory. 'I was not prepared to tolerate breaches of the Laws of Cricket,' said Lamb. 'I am glad to pay what it costs me to clear my name,' said Sarfraz. The *Mirror* was triumphant. 'Victory for the Daily Mirror – Now kick out the cheats!' Botham challenged the TCCB to 'tell the world officially what the Pakistanis were up to'. As far as he was concerned, England could no longer be considered the losers of the 1992 series.

Not everyone shared the *Mirror's* view of the trial. *Eastern Eye*, a newspaper for Asians in Britain, declared: 'Sarfraz wins fight to clear his name ... Secret report clears Wasim and Waqar of ball-tampering. It claimed (as did the *Sun*) that two leaked ICC reports – one by Deryck Murray on the Lord's one-day international and one by Clyde Walcott on the Test series – both exonerated the Pakistanis. Murray's report stated explicitly that the ball was changed under Law 5.5.

The *Mirror* hammered away at the fourteen-month-old story. 'Pakistan are ... CHEATS' ('official') it declared over a story by Don Oslear ('World's most fearless umpire'), who had just been removed from the first-class panel because of his age. Oslear alleged that Pakistan officials had 'bullied' Alan Smith, Cowdrey and Murray. Ken Lawrence, sacked the month before by the TCCB and now employed as a journalist at the *Mirror*, claimed that Murray had changed his report on the insistence of John Stephenson, who now told the press that the President of the Pakistan Board had pressured him to clear the Pakistanis.

For many, the case was closed.

Coda: At the conclusion of the Sarfraz-Lamb hearing, Justice Otton addressed a courtroom packed with cricketers and journalists. His first duty was to dispose of the cricket balls used in evidence. He kept one for himself, gave six to the jury and the remaining three to the Royal Courts of Justice cricket team. The sixty-year-old High Court judge then asked Robin Smith to rise. Speaking for the nation, Otton declared: 'I am sure the jury and all cricket lovers in this court would like me to congratulate you on your selection for the team to go to the West Indies. We wish you and the team every success for a good tour.'

As an American, I could only marvel at the 'Englishness' of it all.

Shortly after the Pakistan Test side had flown home, Darcus Howe, Channel 4's 'Devil's Advocate', cross-examined David Frith and Trevor Bailey. His charge was that their criticism of Pakistan was 'sour grapes', that England simply could not stomach losing to its former colonies. Frith, tense, hostile, unapologetic, insisted that he had 'conclusive evidence' that the Pakistanis 'cheated'. Bailey, embarrassingly at sea, said he had nothing against Pakistanis: 'I buy my newspapers from them'. There was a gasp from the mostly black audience, but Bailey seemed genuinely unaware that this was a racist stereotype and that many black people would find it offensive. He blushed – a rare reaction from the hard-bitten 'Boil' – but was clearly bewildered by the whole thing.

At times during the summer of 1992, it seemed that the word Pakistani could not appear in print without the adjectives 'volatile' or 'excitable' appended to it. Frith attributed 'the volatility of several Pakistan cricketers' to the fact that 'nature irresistibly asserts itself'. In a single 600-word editorial, he applied the following adjectives to the Pakistan cricketers: 'indisciplined', 'petulant', 'peeved', 'overheated', 'distracted', 'aggressive', and, inevitably, 'volatile'. Like many others, Frith seemed unaware how the language he applied to the Pakistani cricketers was charged with time-dishonoured white prejudices about black people.

Inevitably, media abuse embraced not only the players but their supporters as well. Frith denounced 'the ranting Pakistan supporters', 'the raucous, rabid partisans', 'the zealots' consumed by 'the fires of fanaticism'. He warned of a 'holy war in the streets of Bradford'. This was perhaps the most disturbing aspect of the media coverage: the ease with which it made the transition from the Pakistani Test side to 'Pakistanis'.

The Pakistani community in Britain suffers all the disadvantages of the rest of the black population, but it suffers them disproportionately. Unemployment among Pakistanis (as well as Bangladeshis, also referred to as 'Pakis') is higher than among other black groups. Many of those in work are confined to low-waged, unskilled jobs. As Muslims, they were victims of the media jihad that followed the Rushdie controversy of 1989 and peaked during the Gulf War of 1991. They enjoy the unwanted distinction of providing the nomenclature – 'Paki-bashing' – for Britain's own special strain of the worldwide plague of racist violence.

The Pakistanis and Bangladeshis are the most vulnerable of Asian immigrants. They have made their way from poor, agrarian, traditional areas of the former empire to settle in the North of England and the East End of London, where they live cheek by jowl with white working-class communities suffering long-term economic decline. These communities are highly parochial and it has become all too easy for demagogues to link the arrival of 'foreigners' to the onset of local decay.

The language, religion, dress and diet of Pakistanis all appear – or are made to appear – tokens of an irreconcilably alien way of life. Because Pakistanis are seen as even more culturally foreign to Britain than other black people, they make the perfect target for the 'new racism' of cultural exclusivity. They fan the Tebbit test quite spectacularly.

Too often, this community is seen, incorrectly, as passive under attack. But there is one arena where even the racists acknowledge that the Pakistanis have fought back: the cricket field. For Pakistanis in Britain, the solidarity shown by the Pakistan cricketers in the face of racism and media persecution, both of which the community here knew only too well, made their victory in the Test series especially heady. But for the racists, the aggressive partisanship of the Pakistanis in Britain was all the more resented because it came from a people thought to be weak and marginal.

In Mike Langley's words, Pakistanis, cricketers and non-cricketers alike, are 'too prickly and nationalistic. Always on edge because their status in world sports amounts to nothing beyond hockey, squash and one-day cricket.' Just what England's status in world sports amounted to, Langley did not say.

The vocabulary deployed by Langley and others echoed the themes of British fascism with uncanny fidelity: Pakistanis have a foreign culture that cannot be accommodated within the traditional English way of life, embodied in English notions of 'fair play'; therefore they must be sent 'home'. The tourists were told to 'PAK OFF'. Because of their alien behaviour, they had to be expelled from the level playing field.

During the preceding decade, Iran, Libya and Iraq had all been branded rogue nations for violations of international law and order. The 'Islamic' and 'anti-Western' rhetoric of these three very different regimes was used to reinforce the old imperial belief that the principles of 'fair play' and the rule of law were intrinsically alien to the Orient. The Rushdie affair had strengthened the popular notion that Muslims were a foreign element in British society, unwilling to adapt to British norms.

The clash between 'England' and 'Pakistan' became not only a battle between nations, but part of a larger war between 'the West' (embodied in fair play, honest umpires, and decorum on the field) and Islam (embodied in extravagant appealing, disrespect for the umpire, and cheating).

It seemed to me, during the summer of 1992, that English pride, as manifested in cricket (but not only in cricket), was a brittle, puny, miserably inadequate buttress against a host of phantasmic fears. The country had recently re-elected a Tory government, without apparent enthusiasm. Already, that government's popularity was tumbling. With recession deepening and the Tories split by the Maastricht Treaty, the elan of Thatcherism receded into the past. The country squirmed impotently in the grip of a global economic maelstrom.

In this setting, it is not surprising that nationalism took a racist turn. Black people in Britain were a visible reminder both of vanished empire and a global market that did not respect traditional national boundaries. They were an invading force. Their success in cricket hurt precisely because cricket summed up all that was precious and all that had been lost in the national heritage. The level playing field became a standing reminder to English people of their vanished pre-eminence. For the tabloids, all this made cricket a handy means of selling their product in a national market increasingly beset with insecurity and resentment.

In the summer of 1992, the *Mirror* was still trying to extricate itself from Robert Maxwell's legacy of disgrace. During the period in which it was abusing the Pakistani cricketers, the paper was also abasing itself before the pensioners Maxwell had ripped off. Early in the summer, the *Mirror* orchestrated a war of words between Botham (under contract to it) and the Pakistanis, but as Botham faded from the Test scene, it became apparent that the *Mirror's* investment was not paying off. A new mouthpiece was required. Allan Lamb filled the vacuum. Following Micky Stewart's innuendo at the Oval, the tabloids were looking for a 'smoking gun' to justify their attack on the Pakistanis. It has been suggested that Lamb queried the ball at the Lord's match at the *Mirror's* behest.

The *Mirror's* editorial policy was subordinate to its marketing strategy. In the summer of 1992, that strategy was to attract readers by adding the spice of racial conflict to the sports news. The tabloid press likes to claim that it does no more than reflect popular opinion, but anyone who followed the coverage day by day could be in no doubt that the paper's management had decided to demonize the Pakistanis and foster controversy at every juncture of the tour. Often the headlines were more inflammatory than the articles. Some cricket correspondents were filing copy in accordance with a line determined in advance by people who knew nothing about and cared little for the game. By persistently employing imagery and metaphors drawn from warfare, from something which is quintessentially a conflict of nations, not cricketers, they helped create a climate in which the actions of umpires, players, officials and sometimes crowds became charged with racial and national meanings.

The tabloids' 'England' was a fragile entity, threatened from within and without by exotic hordes, people whose alien culture debarred them from understanding the meaning of 'fair play'. In response to this perceived invasion, many in the cricket world emulated Norman Tebbit and the British National Party in attempting to rally what they depicted as an embattled white majority, under siege in its own land. Next to a picture of Pakistan supporters celebrating a victory, the *Sun* observed, 'England have had to endure scenes like this' – as if these scenes had taken place in a foreign country where the England cricketers were an isolated, misunderstood minority.

The new racists claimed they wanted nothing more than the right to assert the primacy of their own culture in their own country. Of course, the argument that the white majority in this country is in any way under threat from the black minority is a monstrous inversion of the truth. But it was only one of the big lies disseminated by the racists. The other was that perennial favourite of the would-be champions of the embattled majority: the betrayal of the establishment.

The venom sprayed by the tabloids and their fellow travellers in the cricket press on the Pakistanis was matched by the scorn they heaped on the cricket authorities. The TCCB and the ICC were charged with bending over backwards not to offend Pakistan, and thereby neglecting their duty to ensure 'fair play'. When the authorities failed to deal more harshly with Miandad after the Old Trafford Test, it was allegedly because they feared a walk-out by the tourists and consequent loss of revenue. When they failed to spill the beans on Wasim and Waqar after the Lord's one-day international, it was allegedly because they feared legal action. David Frith argued that Lamb's 'courage' was 'lacking in some of those in high office'. Mike Langley came up with the absurd thesis that the BBC was conspiring to cover up for the Pakistanis by hiding an incriminating videotape. The implication, not only in the tabloids but in the quality and cricket press, was that the umpires, players and officials were all secretly backing Lamb but were tongue-tied by fear: of libel writs, of loss of income, of being branded 'racist'.

At first sight, it might seem bizarre in the extreme that anyone should accuse the cricket establishment of being a slave to 'political correctness'. But it should be remembered that the tabloids were not only against the Pakistanis, they were also for neutral umpires. For a hundred years the popular press has derided the mandarins of cricket. If you wanted to sell papers to the embattled majority, there was no better way than to suggest that a foolish and incompetent establishment was pandering to a racial minority for commercial and diplomatic reasons.

The attacks on the TCCB and ICC made by Oslear and his friends echoed classic fascist rhetoric. The elite had sold out the nation's birthright. The guardians of national pride had betrayed their trust by giving way to the high-pressure tactics of foreigners and minorities. All this was a mirage bred by nationalist paranoia, but it was a powerful mirage, masking the real causes of both economic decline and cricket failure.

Much of what the press said about the authorities was true. Their secrecy and ineptitude were astounding. Certainly, after the Lord's one-day international, the media had a right to feel aggrieved. The authorities were unwilling to confirm in public what they were saying in private. But the truth is that, far from being in cahoots with Pakistan, the authorities collaborated with the English media's hatchet job on the tourists throughout the summer. Not all the anonymous quotes from leading players, umpires and administrators were fabricated. At this time Micky Stewart, Gooch and Dexter were not yet the discredited figures they appeared a year later following the Ashes defeat. All of them refused to accept, at least in public, the plain superiority of the Pakistani bowling. Their new model national cricket system – the England Committee, fitness training, 'A' tours, under-17s competitions, etc – was in place. How then could they admit, as they ought to have done, if only to cool tempers, that England was losing simply because Pakistan was a better side?

A Pakistani supporter from the East End wrote to *The Cricketer* to complain of English 'double standards and hypocrisy' which, more than anything else, he said, were the cause of Pakistani anger. What was the difference, he asked, between Gatting's behaviour on tour in 1987 and what Aqib and the others had done in 1992? Richard Hutton was spurred into appending an editor's note to the letter. There was no double standard, he insisted. 'The events of 1987 were regrettable' (not 'monstrous', which was the word he had used for Aqib's behaviour at Old Trafford), 'but there was no accepted machinery in place at that time to deal with offences.'

A similar letter appeared in *Wisden Cricket Monthly*. Like Hutton, Frith could not resist adding an editor's note. The umpiring in Pakistan in 1987, he argued, was 'quite appalling' and 'not comparable' to the standards maintained in England in 1992. It seemed, then, that the umpire's decision was final only if the umpire in question was English.

A year after the Aqib incident, at the Edgbaston Test against the Australians, England vice-captain Alec Stewart charged out from behind the stumps to claim the wicket of Merv Hughes (television showed no hint of an edge). His flagrant attempt to gain advantage by putting pressure on the umpire in front of a partisan English crowd was excused by the same people who had been enraged by Pakistani behaviour the year before (not to mention Viv Richards at Bridgetown in 1990). When the Australians sledged and bellowed and eyeballed the umpire in 1993 it was all part of their admirably 'competitive' approach to the game. When the Pakistanis did the same, it was 'unfair play'.

In 1991, Wasim had been fined £1,000 by Lancashire for muttering 'shit umpiring' under his breath during the course of a sparsely attended county match. Other Lancashire players, by no means all Wasim's chums, stumped up part of the fine because they felt it was so disproportionate to the crime. When Allan Lamb publicly accused the umpires, referees, and officials involved in the 1992 series of an attempt to cover up 'cheating', he was fined only twice that amount and treated as a hero by the most of the British media.

Double standards, the mismatch of words and deeds, have been seen abroad as characteristically English for two centuries, cricket's lifetime, and have always outraged the victims of colonialism. They expose the promise of empire, the promise of the level playing field, as a ruse for domination. The secrecy of the English cricket authorities was not designed to cover up for the Pakistanis, but to protect these double standards from scrutiny.

There is evidence that the bulk of the public simply did not buy the media notion that the Pakistanis were 'cheats'. I attended the Saturday of the Oval Test and watched Waqar remove Gooch, Stewart, Atherton and Gower. In the section of the crowd where I sat, no one thought this was anything other than a display of brilliant cricket, except, perhaps, the drunk accountant who railed at the English batsmen for playing like 'poofs'. On radio phone-in programmes, Lamb's allegations were a popular topic. Many of those who called felt Lamb had discredited England by making it seem a nation of bad sports. The public, I suspect, was more willing than either the media or the authorities to admit that the better side had won.

There were racists at the Test matches and one-day internationals, but the majority of spectators did not come to see a bust-up or to celebrate or deride anyone's nation or race. They came to see the high-quality, full-throttle, dramatic cricket played by the Pakistanis – the kind of cricket whose absence the pundits have bemoaned for decades. Most English cricket fans live in the real world, a world they are happy to share with people from different countries and different colours and religions. This is more than can be said for many commentators and journalists, whose year-round confinement to the cricket circuit breeds tunnel vision and confirms long-held prejudices.

Even during the tense summer of 1992, organized fascist groups rarely showed their faces at Test grounds. It would seem to make more sense for the BNP to turn up at cricket matches against West Indies, India or Pakistan than football matches against Sweden or Luxembourg, but the partisanship and parochialism which the fascists batten on in football is much weaker in cricket. The spectators are more relaxed. What is more, the presence of West Indian, Indian or Pakistan supporters is a deterrent to the fascists, who have never been keen on the level playing field. Their *modus operandi* is the mass gang attack on the isolated black individual. Fair play and fascism, as Hitchcock observed in *The Lady Vanishes*, are hard to square, though CB Fry certainly tried. But the notion that racism 'isn't cricket' has a double edge: it veils the polite racism of the authorities, embedded in their inveterate double standards.

For some years, English cricket's resentments had focused on the uppity, ungentlemanly Pakistanis. In 1992, this elite impatience with black self-assertion merged with a raving tabloid racism, which had singled out Pakistanis for its own reasons. The combination proved highly combustible.

During the summer of 1992, all kinds of people tried to use cricket to mobilize the embattled majority against its imaginary enemies. The real impact of their rhetoric was felt not by whites, but by blacks. According to the Home Office, there were 130,000 verbal or physical racial attacks in 1992, a 15 per cent increase on the previous year. In the wake of the Sarfraz-Lamb trial, fourteen months after the Pakistan cricketers had returned home, a cricketer from Keighley wrote to *Eastern Eye*: 'I am a big fan of the Pakistan team and play cricket for my local club. Since the whole affair of "doctoring" the ball began I have constantly been verbally assaulted by opposition teams.'

The campaign against the Pakistan cricketers in 1992 – a campaign for which the English cricket establishment was as much to blame as the tabloids – helped create the climate in which this was possible. The Pakistani community in Britain was paying the price for failing the Tebbit test.

But did the Pakistanis cheat? It all depends on what you mean by 'cheating'.

In *Jardine Justified*, a book published in the wake of the bodyline flare-up of 1932-33, the author, Bruce Harris, observed: 'So used are batsmen to being on top that when a form of attack is evolved to put bowlers on terms again up rises a wan of protest.'

He could have written the same sixty years later.

That primitive, pre-industrial object, the cricket ball, has always been subject to manipulation. Its complex properties are revealed only through the passage of time and changes in the prevailing conditions, including the physical condition of the ball itself. And it has always been recognized that part of the skill of bowling is to know how to exploit and enhance those changes.

At Lord's in 1806, Billy Beldham slapped a lump of wet dirt and sawdust on the ball and then swung it sharply to take the wicket of Lord Frederick Beauclerk, who was in those days the virtual dictator of Lord's. In 1921 in Australia JWHT Douglas, the England captain, threatened to report Arthur Mailey for illegally using resin to grip the ball. Mailey retorted by pointing out that Douglas's own thumbnail was worn to the flesh from lifting the seam.

Arguments about tampering with the ball have always been part of the broader argument between batsmen and bowlers about whom the Laws of the game should or should not favour. The pendulum is never still. In county cricket, polishing the ball was banned in 1966 – and relegalized in 1967. In 1980, Law 42.5 was amended to prohibit rubbing the ball on the ground. The intention was to push the pendulum back towards the batsmen (this was the same year that pitches were covered). But there seems little logic in allowing bowlers to smooth rough spots but not to roughen smooth ones.

In England, flat wickets, low seams and soft balls combined in the late eighties to create batsmen's paradises. Bowlers, who always believe the deck is stacked against them, tried to level the odds by doing things to the ball. Lifting the seam and scuffing the surface became commonplace. There was little secrecy about this and umpires took no action, though concerns that the practices was getting out of hand began to surface in

1990. That year, it was agreed that roughing up one side of the ball would be penalized in the same way as picking the seam.

During the furore of 1992, Mike Selvey reminded readers that 'lifting the seam is common practice and always has been. Ironically no one knows this better than Ken Palmer, a seam bowler for Somerset and England.' Christopher Martin-Jenkins added, 'Let him who has never lifted the seam of a cricket ball cast the first stone.' John Woodcock thought 'the wholesale pillorying of Pakistan ... a good deal too self-righteous'.

The Pakistanis were bitter because they felt they were being singled out for something others did as well. Earlier that year, South Africa's inaugural international cricket match at Eden Gardens in Calcutta was marred by complaints about ball-tampering. The Indians thought the South Africans were being 'naive'. In an effort to avoid further embarrassment on a tour of such political magnitude, Ali Bacher, Managing Director of the new South Africa Board, and Madhavrao Scindia, Chairman of the Indian Board, let the press know that they intended to 'set an example to the rest of world cricket' by instructing both teams to refrain from the 'accepted practice' of scuffing the ball. The statement was never issued in this form because it dawned on the authorities that it was tantamount to an admission of widespread misconduct.

When Colin Cowdrey finally decided to open his mouth on the Pakistani affair, his comment to the *Mirror* was: 'They're all tampering with the ball.' But they weren't all being subjected to the kind of attacks appearing in the English media.

What had happened in the summer of 1992 was a conjuncture of otherwise disparate Pakistani and English experiences. Grounds in Pakistan were dry and hard, wickets often dead, high scores and unfinished matches common. The new ball quickly lost its shine. As Wasim explained, unless you could 'do something' with the old ball, battered and scarred as it was, you would not succeed as a bowler in Pakistan. Dead pitches and low seams in English county cricket also favoured batsmen, but here grassy outfields meant that the ball kept its shine for much longer. To bowlers from Pakistan plying their trade on English wickets, as to many English bowlers, it was logical to scuff the ball. It was no more than an attempt to make the playing field level – which is why the Pakistanis were so annoyed to find themselves accused of violating that very principle.

If the gist of the complaint against Aqib and Miandad at Old Trafford was their failure to accept that the umpire's decision was final, then the problem with the ensuing controversy about ball-tampering was that *there was no umpire's decision*, or if there was, it was shrouded in ambiguity.

In 1992 the Pakistani tourists became victims of cricket's 'unwritten constitution'. The vagueness and subjectivity of many of cricket's Laws, above all the nebulous requirement of 'fair play', places inordinate power (and responsibility) in the hands of umpires. Take, for example, Law 42.8 under which Aqib was warned at Old Trafford. Under this statute, a 'fast, short-pitched' delivery is deemed 'unfair, if in the opinion of the umpire at the bowler's end it constitutes an attempt to intimidate the striker'. Since one of the aims of *all* bowling is to intimidate the striker, this is of little help to an umpire. Even the further clarification, specifying that the Law applies to deliveries which 'are intended or likely to inflict physical injury on the striker' sheds little light, especially given the further rider that 'the relative skill' of the striker must be 'taken into consideration'. The Law appears to require telepathic skills on the part of the umpire in order to determine the bowler's intention; it also requires that a number of factors be 'taken into consideration' without making clear what relative weight should be given to them.

Law 42.5, which for the *Mirror* became the eleventh commandment ('thou shalt not tamper with the ball'), is no easier to enforce. It makes clear that you can polish the ball (as long as you do not use an 'artificial substance') or dry it or remove mud from it, but you cannot 'take any other action to alter the condition of the ball'. Spit and sweat are deemed not to be 'artificial substances' but what mixture of hair gel, lip salve or orange squash is permitted remains unclear. And though you cannot 'rub the ball on the ground' you can allow the ball to roll along the ground or bang into boundary boards.

In cricket, the Laws charge the players themselves with maintaining the highest standards of conduct, but do not tell the umpires what to do if these standards are breached. In soccer or rugby, basketball or American football, officials police boundaries: territorial boundaries (in touch or out, offside or on) but, above all, the boundaries of permitted physical contact between players. Their main task is to prevent abuses - which is why at their best they keep the game flowing. In cricket and baseball, however, umpires are called upon to make an adjudication on nearly every ball. Just how subjective those adjudications can be was demonstrated by a BBC TV survey in 1993, which revealed that county captains, who mark umpires at the end of each match, are 17 per cent less likely to be given out LBW than other batsmen.

In baseball, dissent is commonplace; abusing the umpire is a cherished national tradition. If the umpire thinks a player has gone too far, he throws him out of the game, and that's the end of it. Not in cricket. Here the umpires' remit is wider – nothing less than the maintenance of the high moral standard attached to the game by its elite rulers – but their powers are less clearly defined, especially when it comes to punishing offences. In ice hockey, football, rugby, American football or basketball, unfair play is punished on the spot by penalties. In athletics, if you violate lanes or jump the gun twice in succession, you are out of the race. In baseball, if you throw a beamer and hit a batter's body, the batter goes automatically to first base; the pitcher may have hurt him, but a price has been extracted. In all these sports, the penalty for unfair play is designed to have an immediate and substantial impact on the contest in hand. In cricket, the penalties for unfair play are sometimes more severe than in other sports, but they are largely irrelevant to the course of the match.

This is a problem for umpires as much as for players. The sheer gravity of alleging unfair play makes umpires reluctant to take action on violations, especially in public. Because cricket is supposed to embody the spirit of fair play, infractions are either glossed over or blown up out of all proportion. It is impossible for cricket umpires to penalize players without calling into question their 'sportsmanship', their commitment to 'fair play' and therefore their right to take part in cricket's community. If the Laws provided a systematic and graded range of practical penalties, much ill-feeling would be obviated. If umpires had the power, say, to remove immediately from play any ball which they believed had been illegally doctored, or to suspend for one session anyone they caught scratching the surface of the ball, there would still be protests, decisions would still be disputed, but in the end most would be accepted as part of the course of the game, just as they are in other sports. In baseball, applying spit or in any way interfering with the surface of the ball is strictly prohibited. But great pitchers often become legendary for the cunning with which they break the rules. 'Cheating' is a recognized part of the culture of professional baseball. When caught, players are punished, but the real opprobrium is reserved for those caught gambling or taking bribes. In cricket, however, an alleged infraction of an ambiguous technical rule, like Law 42.5, can be used to strip you of your status as a cricketer and your right to enter the level playing field.

Although Law 42.1 specifies that 'the umpires are the sole judges of fair and unfair play', in practice it is more often than not journalists and commentators who set the parameters of 'fair and unfair play'. The Laws themselves are usually adapted either to accommodate or to banish a particular practice years after it has become common.

Umpires have always been hired professionals and therefore subordinate within the hierarchy of the game. In the 1880s, Lord Harris mounted a high-minded campaign (backed by *The Times*) against 'chucking' in county cricket. When Harris asked a leading umpire why he and his fellows persisted in not calling the 'chuckers', he was told: 'My Lord, the umpires are going to do nothing. It is you gentlemen who have got to do it.' Hence, the traditional method of dealing with 'unfair play' in English cricket: 'the word in the ear'. Throwers, both English and foreign, ball-greasers and seam-pickers, naughty wicket-keepers and over-clever captains, all have been dealt with over the years by discreet warnings, largely off the field of play.

Like the antiquated restrictions on language in the House of Commons, these 'gentlemen's rules' are designed to shore up the fiction that the country's elite is bound together by adherence to higher codes of behaviour.

The umpire's authority is shrouded in as much mystery as the British judiciary. No one knows precisely how you get on the Test panel or why you are removed. Captains make secret, written assessments and on that basis umpires are retained, promoted or dismissed, but there is never an explanation. All this helps reinforce the notion that it is a game governed by Laws, not individuals. The Pakistanis, coming as they do from a society where the mask of law is flimsier and the rule of individuals more blatant than in Britain, know otherwise. That is why they championed neutral umpires long before others.

The Pakistan Board first introduced neutral umpires for the Pakistan v. India series in 1989-90. This is the most fraught international confrontation on the cricket calendar, and it was simply too dangerous to proceed without neutral umpires. Pleased with the result, the Pakistan Board thereafter requested neutral umpires for every series home and abroad, but other countries, especially England, remained adamantly opposed to the idea. To the Pakistanis the demand for neutral umpires seemed a logical response to accusations that their own umpires were 'cheating'. To the English it was a declaration of war.

For outsiders, it was hard to see what all the fuss was about. After all, football had always had neutral referees for international matches. The Football League required two linesmen as well as a referee from 1898; cricket only brought in a third umpire for run-out decisions in 1993. But then, cricketers are not supposed to require outside assistance to settle disputes; they are supposed to be gentlemen and gentlemen regulate and discipline themselves. How can they be made subject to a higher authority, particularly one from another country?

Tony Lewis said Imran's campaign for neutral umpires was undermining the authority of existing 'home country' umpires. Most English cricket commentators agreed, and it was common to hear it argued that English umpires were not only more competent technically (because they stood in more domestic first-class games than foreign umpires), but also more imbued with 'the spirit of fair play' and less susceptible to pressure from crowds, players or officials.

As Frith, Hutton, Bailey, Lander and others made clear in the summer of 1992, showing dissent towards English umpires was not the same as showing dissent towards foreign ones. Behind their impassioned denial of 'double standards' was a deep-seated belief that 'fair play' belongs to 'us'. The English gave it to the world, particularly that part of the world which they brought into their empire, and to suggest that others might uphold its norms more rigorously than them was treason.

'If cricket has contributed anything to society as a whole it is the notion that the umpire's decision is final and that cricketers do not argue with it,' said Matthew Engel, but he added the crucial rider: 'This only works at professional level if umpiring is recognized as fair minded, competent and authoritative.'

The Pakistanis had good reason to be suspicious of English umpires. In 1982 at Headingley, David Constant (described by Sunil Gavaskar as 'Constant – in his support of England') gave Sikander Bakht out to a catch by Gatting; the TV replay showed daylight between Sikander's bat and the ball. Several observers, including *The Cricketer*, suggested that Constant's decision had been influenced by forceful English appealing, notably by Robin Jackman. Jackman's notoriously violent appealing was always regarded by the English media as an eccentricity to be indulged, a healthy sign of his 'wholehearted' approach to the game. The Pakistani cricketers and their supporters remembered this when their own appealing came under scrutiny ten years later.

One of the English umpires the Pakistanis recruited to stand as a 'neutral' in their series against India was the Barbados-born John Holder. Both Pakistan and India were highly satisfied with Holder's performance. In 1991, standing in England's final Test against West Indies at the Oval, Holder reprimanded the England captain, Gooch, about the condition of the ball. The England bowlers, it seems, had tampered with it in their pursuit of extra swing. Subsequently, Holder reported the matter to the TCCB. No action was taken and the story was downplayed by the media. The next year, Holder was dropped from the Test panel, even though the England authorities knew he was respected by the Pakistani tourists.

Shortly before the third Test of 1992, in a match between the tourists and Hampshire, Hampshire captain Mark Nicholas was given out caught at short leg by umpire Roger Tolchard. Nicholas lingered, queried the decision with the square-leg umpire, Ken Palmer, and was then reinstated, much to the disgust of the Pakistanis.

Non-English observers found much of the English umpiring during the 1992 series inconsistent. A former Anglophile Indian commented sadly, 'It seems your umpires are now no better than ours.'

Unlike the English, both Indian and Pakistani cricket fans know their umpires are flawed, sometimes incompetent, sometimes biased. Jokes and graffiti on this theme are common. In Pakistan, the idea of the umpire as the servant of the national elite was taken to extremes. Imran recalled how an umpire approached him in the dressing room before an international match to get his 'instructions'. Imran's passion for neutral umpires was driven by his vision of a modern, talent-based, profitable Pakistani cricket, freed from the greed and factionalism that gripped the Pakistani establishment. Because of his efforts, Pakistan will be seen, in years to come, as a pioneer in world cricket. Ironically, it was the country's backwardness which forced it to adopt the call for neutral umpires in the first place.

The history of cricket has left umpires, of whatever nationality, a daunting task. Charged with maintaining a level playing field in a world which is anything but 'level', they are also asked to adjudicate in the perennial dispute between bat and ball, in which, because everything in this dispute is relative, subjectivity is all. No wonder the summer of 1992 was an impossible one for English umpires. The confusion over which Law had been referred to when they changed the ball (quietly, they thought) at Lord's was the result of an attempt to square a circle. They were under tremendous pressure from the media. They wanted to keep the game going and avoid cause for complaint on either side. Allan Lamb did not like the ball, so it was changed, but in a way that did not disadvantage Pakistan. The fact that this seemed to fall outside all the known Laws simply indicated the inadequacy of those Laws.

For the Pakistanis, the summer of 1992 confirmed that fair play was not as straightforward as the English presumed. It is supposed to be a self-imposed and self-regulatory code, in which ruthlessness or connivance are spurned and generosity to an opponent is *de rigueur*. The supreme gesture is calling back a batsman who has walked. This is rarer in cricket than the game's romanticists would have us believe, but it is still something totally unheard of in other sports. In baseball, a player who disclaimed a catch given him by the umpire would be regarded by all and sundry as in immediate need of psychiatric treatment. After all, umpires are there to make these decisions. It's their job to worry about what's fair.

Fair play has always been more than just obedience to the Laws of the game. It is something to which the Laws refer and which supersedes them; it is a higher code but without a higher court. The ICC attempt to create such a court in the form of 'match referees' has only revealed that the code is not as clear-cut or universally agreed as some in English cricket like to think.

A new Law is introduced in cricket usually only when there is a conflict over interpretations of fair play, when the existing consensus over what constitutes fair play is broken. In other words, fair play is defined and redefined only by being violated. Traditionally, the commentators on the game have taken for granted that the ideal of fair play is consistent and self-evident. But the history of the game proves the contrary. From the day Shock White walked out with a bat wider than the wicket, through the introduction of over-arm bowling by the professionals, to rows about chucking and, of course, bodyline, there has been a contest over fair play – what it means and, above all, who decides whether it has been upheld.

Fair play, another one of cricket's inheritances from the eighteenth century, is both democratic and elitist. A universal code, applicable to all, it remains unwritten, a mystery into which cricketers are initiated. According to some of the game's high priests, this mystery belongs peculiarly to the English gentleman, who taught it to the world. For the Pakistanis, the summer of 1992 brought the old lie of empire to life: the same Laws apply to all – except when British interests are threatened.

The ball-tampering of 1992 was never as 'shocking' as the tabloids claimed. It was, in any case, an irrelevance to the outcome of the matches. No serious student of the game could put down Pakistan's supremacy to gouging bits out of the ball. Ball-tampering became an issue only because of its context: the TCCB's long-held resentment of the Pakistanis had fused with the media's racist campaign against Asians in Britain. Without the heated build-up, any concern about Law 42.5 would have been dealt with in the usual way, behind closed doors.

The following year, the ICC at last agreed to set up a panel of neutral umpires. The collapse of TCCB resistance was yet another sign of waning

English influence in the cricket world. Pioneered by the South Africans, the third umpire equipped with video replay had already become a feature of international matches, even those played in England. Along with the match referees, these innovations brought cricket more in line with the rest of modern sport. But they were all tantamount to admitting that, after all, the umpire's decision was not final. That's why they struck observers as so 'un-English'. *

*In 1994, television cameras showed England captain Mike Atherton removing dirt from his pocket and rubbing it on the ball during the Lord's Test against South Africa. *Eastern Eye* printed the freeze-frame on its front page under the headline, 'GOTCHA!' – hoisting the tabloids on their own petard. For the strange afterlife of the ball-tampering affair, see Chapter 8, pages 303-312.

6

Politics and the National Game

South Africa:England's cause • *The game's revenge*
• *The new order* • *Sharjah:global cricket* • *Argentina, Ireland,*
USA:apostate nations • *Market and nation in Indian cricket*
• *The supreme drama of Test cricket*

Throughout the twenty-year isolation of South Africa from world cricket, the battle cry of apartheid's apologists was 'Keep politics out of sport!' They appealed to a world transcending politics, a community of cricket, which was, in fact, the community of imperial white supremacy.

Of course, it was the English who brought cricket to South Africa. But, at first, they brought it mainly to black people. Fostered by missionary schools and military outposts, black South African cricket grew steadily in the second half of the nineteenth century. An educated, enfranchised, English-speaking black petty bourgeoisie emerged in the Cape, and it adopted cricket as part of the apparatus of civilization which, it hoped, would enable it to meet the white colonizers on their own terms. Cricket, with its level playing field, was a way of claiming a place in and protection under the British empire. For John Tengo Jabavu, a black politician, newspaper owner and chairman of two cricket clubs, the virtue of cricket was that it was 'calculated to make the Europeans and natives have more mutual trust and confidence than all the coercive and repressive legislation in the world'.

With the discovery of gold in the Transvaal in 1886, British interests in South Africa changed. Capital from the City of London facilitated rapid industrial development, which reduced the black population to cheap labour. Cricket was supplanted among the black proletariat of the Transvaal by football and boxing. The mining companies, including Lord Harris's Consolidated Goldfields, encouraged football in their company hostels as a cheap diversion for the workforce. At the same time, the British began to restrict the long-established black franchise in the Cape. English cricketers began regular tours of South Africa in 1888.

Standards were low, but the power of South African gold and the need to integrate the feisty Boers into the empire led the MCC, many of whose members had investments and family in South Africa, to establish close ties to the newly-founded all-white South African Cricket Association (SACA). In 1892, professional members of WW Read's England squad played a match against Cape Malays (the amateurs refused to take part). It was to be the last time a touring England side faced a black South African side until December, 1993. During the match, the bowling of Krom Hendrick, a 'Coloured' man, impressed the English players, who were surprised when he was left out of the South African side that toured England in 1894, on the instructions of Cecil Rhodes, the Cape Colony Prime Minister who financed the tour.

As British designs on the whole of South Africa became clearer, tensions with the Afrikaners mounted. When Lord Hawke's side visited South Africa in 1898-99, the captain refused to meet Kruger, the Afrikaner President of the Transvaal Republic, and announced that he had brought cricket to South Africa to 'comfort the English'. During the 'Boer War', imperial propagandists like John Buchan alleged the Afrikaners had no 'tradition of fair play'. Black Africans largely backed the British, hoping to secure the franchise, but they lost out profoundly under the political settlement which followed the war.

When Lord Harris took Plum Warner's England side to South Africa in 1905-06, he declared that cricket would bring together 'Briton and Boer'. In the interests of empire, cricket's level playing field was extended to the Afrikaners, but at the cost of excluding non-whites. The imperial integration of white South Africa was one of the reasons for the formation of the ICC in 1909. But it was always a selective integration. Between 1909 and the beginning of the boycott in 1970, South Africa played England, Australia and New Zealand regularly, but never played India, Pakistan or West Indies.

Ironically, there was more interest in cricket among the black majority than among the Afrikaners, who remained alienated from the 'English game' (though not from rugby) until the 1960s. Squeezed out of world cricket, African, Indian, and Coloured people continued to play the game under their own auspices. Gradually, separate cricket authorities for 'Bantu', 'Indian', 'Malay' and 'Coloured' cricket emerged, and found niches within the evolving structure of what came to be known as apartheid.

The MCC colluded with South African racism from the beginning. Ranji was omitted from a South African tour, apparently at the request of white South Africans. His nephew, Duleepsinhji, was left out of the England team which faced the visiting South Africans in 1929, after pressure from South African politicians, whom, Learie Constantine observed, 'could not face the risk of a century being scored against their team by a coloured man'.

An England side captained by FG Mann, and including Denis Compton, toured South Africa in 1948-49, when the new National Party government was passing the legislation which institutionalized apartheid – and ruled out the occasional inter-racial cricket that had previously been permitted. In those days and for decades to come, black South Africans supported the visiting side. When Neil Harvey scored a match-winning 151 not out for Australia at Durban in 1950, every stroke was cheered by the black spectators sitting in their reserved places, one of whom was the young lawyer Nelson Mandela.

The South African Cricket Board of Control (SACBOC) was formed in 1950 to unite the existing black federations. At first, SACBOC tournaments were run in accord with the dictates of apartheid: African, Indian and Coloured players were segregated not only from whites but from each other. However, black cricketers increasingly refused to compete along 'ethnic' lines. In 1956, a visit by a Kenyan Asian side led SACBOC to integrate 'non-white' cricket, inaugurating a golden age which produced, among others, the all-rounder Basil D'Oliveira.

Though SACBOC represented the numerical majority of cricketers, and was recognized by the South African regime as the black equivalent of SACA, it received no assistance from either the MCC or the ICC, despite their avowed mission to further the cause of cricket everywhere. SACBOC asked the MCC how it could take part in international cricket. The MCC said SACBOC would have to prove it could manage its own affairs, but offered no other guidance.

The South African Sports Association (SASA) was formed in 1958 with the aim of challenging apartheid in sport. It launched a successful campaign to stop a tour planned by Frank Worrell's West Indians, who had agreed to play against non-white teams entirely within the racial framework of apartheid. Dennis Brutus, the SASA secretary, wrote regularly to the MCC and ICC, but rarely received the courtesy of a reply. After Sharpeville, SASA officials' homes were raided and their correspondence seized. Brutus was 'banned' and later shot in the street. He survived, and in 1966 left South Africa for England.

The reality of repression rarely intruded upon the idyll enjoyed by the English cricketers and cricket writers who visited South Africa throughout this period. As Rowland Bowen observed, in South Africa 'an ideal kind of pre-1914 amateur cricket' still flourished. Only those few for whom the Golden Age was not the final word in cricket culture, like John Arlott, Jim Laker or Mike Brearley, saw anything amiss. Trevor Bailey recalled:

> From the social angle the most enjoyable of all cricket tours were those to South Africa. The hospitality was of a scale unequalled anywhere else in the world, the country varied and fascinating, the climate beautiful and the cricket excellent ... their basic approach was very reminiscent of public school sides ... it all stemmed from a life-style which, though materially rewarding, is at the same time rather narrow and isolated.

The cosy interchange between English cricket and its South African 'cousins' came to an end in the late sixties with the D'Oliveira affair. The selectors always insisted that their decision to leave D'Oliveira out of the England party scheduled to tour South Africa in the winter of 1968-69 was dictated entirely by the demands of cricket. Few believed them, especially as the day before the selection meeting D'Oliveira had scored 158 not out against the Australians at the Oval.

The attitude of white South Africa towards an appearance by D'Oliveira on its cricket grounds had long been unmistakable. In January 1967, the South African Minster of the Interior had announced: 'We will not allow mixed teams to play against our white teams here.' A year later, Billy Griffith, the MCC Secretary, wrote to SACA asking for confirmation that no conditions would be imposed on the selection of the England tour party. He received no reply.

In March, 1968, the MCC Committee received a report from Alec Douglas-Home, who had recently visited South Africa and met President Vorster. Douglas-Home advised the MCC not to press for an answer to Griffith's letter. The implication of his remarks was that the only way to save the tour would be to avoid selecting D'Oliveira. Meanwhile, Lord Cobham, a former MCC President and Treasurer, had also been talking with Vorster, who had told him point blank that D'Oliveira would not be welcome. Cobham passed on Vorster's views to the current MCC President, AER Gilligan, and Treasurer, Gubby Allen, but they kept the information to themselves.

The tenth Viscount Cobham, CJ Lyttelton (Eton, Cambridge) was a member of one of England's great cricketing dynasties. A former captain of Worcestershire and erstwhile Tory parliamentary candidate, he became Governor General of New Zealand and Lord Steward of Her Majesty's household. His mother was South African and he had extensive banking interests there.

The selection meeting that chose to leave D'Oliveira out of the South African tour was the last ever held under the auspices of the MCC. Every single one of the ten men present had played cricket in South Africa. None had ever uttered any public criticism of the apartheid system. The Chairman of Selectors, Alec Bedser, later became a founder member of the right-wing Freedom Association, which received funds from the South African government. The MCC President that year, the former Sussex amateur Arthur Gilligan (Dulwich, Cambridge), had visited South Africa many times. He was the amateur England captain at the centre of the row between Lord Hawke and the professionals in 1925, and for several years a member of the British Union of Fascists. He wrote an article for the BUF *Bulletin* entitled 'The Spirit of Fascism and Cricket Tours'. Gilligan argued that cricket tours (in which 'it is essential to work solely on the lines of fascism') strengthened 'the crimson ties of friendship ... and the crimson bonds of kinship'.

The selectors' decision was ratified by the MCC Committee as a whole before being released to the press. In South Africa, the Minister of the Interior interrupted a speech to the ultra-right Orange Free State Congress of the National Party to announce D'Oliveira's omission, which he welcomed as a triumph for apartheid. In England, the MCC's excuses for leaving out D'Oliveira came under scrutiny. One of the most bizarre was the assertion that a player of D'Oliveira's style would not perform well in South African conditions. Doug Insole insisted that overseas D'Oliveira had to be regarded primarily as a batsman, not an all-rounder. But when the medium-pacer Tom Cartwright withdrew from the tour because of injury, the MCC, fearful of public outrage, replaced him with D'Oliveira. Vorster then banned the tour. 'It's not the MCC team,' he said. 'It's the team of the anti-apartheid movement ... it is a team of political opponents of South Africa. It is a team of people who don't care about sports relations at all.'

At that year's annual general meeting, the MCC overwhelmingly rejected a proposal to end cricket contacts with South Africa pending 'progress by South Africa towards non-racial cricket'. Leading the attack on the proposal was Dennis Silk, who insisted, 'We do not stand as the social conscience of Great Britain.' He also noted that South Africa was Britain's third largest export customer. He was backed by Subba Row and LWT chairman Aidan Crawley (Harrow, Oxford), a former Labour

MP who had turned Tory in 1957 and served briefly on Douglas-Home's front bench. He was to become MCC President three years later.

This was the MCC's final act as the official voice of English cricket. The next year it was replaced by the Cricket Council and the TCCB, which proceeded with arrangements for the South African tour of England scheduled for 1970. But any lingering fantasy that cricket could live in balmy indifference to the evils of apartheid was rudely dispelled by the campaign to 'Stop the Seventy Tour', which broke over English cricket like a thunderstorm in late 1969.

For the English cricket authorities, the threat of mass action against the South African tour was an assault on the national heritage and the game itself. They were deeply shocked by this intrusion into the game of what they regarded as the most offensive facet of modern life, the protest politics of the late sixties. 'Suddenly we weren't outside the US embassy or standing in Trafalgar Square,' recalled Peter Hain, the campaign's principal spokesperson. 'We were at the gates of Lord's.'

Cricket was especially vulnerable to direct action, which had already proved highly disruptive at rugby matches. The day-long play, the leisurely pace and wide-open spaces, the sheer delicacy of the game, made it an easy target for even small groups of protesters, no less the army that the Stop the Seventy Tour people were planning to mobilize. An entire five-day Test match could be wrecked just by digging a hole in the pitch. Some of the anti-apartheid protesters had more imaginative plots. One threatened to unleash a horde of grass-eating locusts on Lord's the evening before the Test match.

The anti-authoritarian brio of the late-sixties youth rebellion was the polar opposite to the genteel nineteenth-century ethos of English cricket. For many in the cricket establishment, this was an apocalyptic clash, a battle to rescue the game from the forces of anarchy. The TCCB declared its intention 'to uphold the rights of individuals in this country to take part in lawful pursuits'. In *The Times*, John Woodcock proclaimed 'a moral obligation to see the thing through' and blamed the whole affair on the 'intractable attitude of the non-white authorities'. The county chairmen on the new TCCB vowed to defy Hain and the demonstrators. One county secretary told the *Observer*: 'This was their opportunity to apply all their dislike and loathing of permissiveness, demonstrators and long hair. Staging matches with South Africa is their chance to make a stand against these things.'

Hain, a South African exile and Young Liberal, became a hate figure for the cricket establishment, but the man they took for cricket's nemesis, was, in fact, a cricket fanatic. As a would-be leg-spinner at Pretoria Boys' High School, he had followed the game with passion, and like other young (and not so young) fans had drawn up a personal World XI (Sobers was captain, Graeme Pollock the only South African). In the course of a search of his family's home, local Special Branch agents came across young Hain's World XI and for a moment mistook it for a terrorist hit list. The officers, all Afrikaners, did not recognize any of the 'English' sport's great names.

The threat of mass action precipitated public debate on apartheid and sport on a scale never seen before. In response to that debate, the Labour Party, the Liberals, the trade unions, the churches, the Police Federation, most of the press and even some Tories came out against the tour. Black workers on London Transport threatened to stage a one-day strike to coincide with the Lord's Test. The television technicians' union called on members not to cover any matches involving the South Africans. John Arlott declined to commentate on them. The Archbishop of Wales urged his fellow Glamorgan County Cricket Club members to resign if the tour went ahead. And the Queen let it be known that, contrary to custom, she would not attend the Test at Lord's. The tour had become too unpredictable for all concerned; even the establishment wanted it cancelled.

But the MCC was by no means isolated. It enjoyed strong support from some (but certainly not all) cricket fans, and it had friends in the Tory Party, who tried to whip up a 'law and order' frenzy against the protesters. Sir Peter Rawlinson, a future Attorney General, and Lord Hailsham helped draft legal memoranda for the Cricket Council. A 'Save the Seventy Tour Committee' was set up by the right-wing Monday Club. The South African government promised money to defray security costs. From May 1970, the new MCC President (and *ex-officio* chair of the ICC) was Sir Frank Cyril Hawker (City of London, Cambridge), erstwhile Essex amateur and currently Chairman of Standard Bank, which was associated with Standard Bank of South Africa. He was also Executive Director of the Bank of England, Sheriff of the County of London, a Free Forester and long-standing acquaintance of Vorster.

A siege mentality gripped Lord's. The MCC invited its members to volunteer as stewards for the Test matches. And for the first time they were driven to employ a public-relations consultant: Subba Row was taken on to help Jack Bailey promote the cause of the South African tour. Together, Bailey and Subba Row, later bitter enemies in the mid-eighties battles between the MCC and the TCCB, leafleted the rugby crowd at

Twickenham urging support for the cricket tour.

Looking back, the lengths to which the authorities were prepared to go to save the tour defy comprehension. They ordered 300 reels of barbed wire and decked out Lord's like a concentration camp. Other grounds followed suit. By encircling cricket pitches with wire and security guards, the authorities made them look like what the protesters said they were: fortresses sheltering apartheid. Early in the season, several cricketers were injured when they got tangled in the wire while fielding in the deep.

Coupled with the threat of mass action at home was the threat of a wide-scale boycott of British sport by African and Asian nations. Had the tour gone ahead, Britain might have faced expulsion from the Commonwealth and Olympic Games. The joint Pakistan and India tour arranged, after much delicate negotiation, for the summer of 1971, would certainly have been cancelled. Kenya, Uganda and Zambia had already called off an MCC tour planned for January 1970. The authorities were prepared to sacrifice a great deal of cricket, not to mention money, to save a tour that they had already been forced to cut back, for security reasons, to a mere twelve matches at eight grounds. Britain might face expulsion from the Commonwealth and Olympic Games, but the cricket authorities seemed to believe this was a price worth paying for their 'principles'. To them, the threat of a boycott, an example of international solidarity in action, was and remained 'blackmail'.

The Cricket Council wanted the Labour government, to which it was deeply hostile, to take responsibility for cancelling the tour. Contrary to all the claims made by Pycroft, Harris, Hawke, Plum Warner, Gubby Allen, EW Swanton and so many others over the years, English cricket's spokespersons now insisted that political and moral issues were outside their ken. Disgusted by the government's failure to stand up for 'law and order', they demanded government intervention – in order to protect cricket's autonomy! Years later, Jack Bailey revealed that during the controversy he met several times with Special Branch officers, one of whom had infiltrated the Stop the Seventy Tour committee.

The Labour government was as loath to act as the cricket authorities. It could not be seen to defend the South African tour, but it also did not want to be identified with the protesters, especially as the general election was planned for the first day of the Lord's Test. Home Secretary James Callaghan was forced in the end to make a direct request to the Cricket Council on behalf of the government. In response, the authorities at last climbed down. The invitation to SACA was withdrawn 'with regret'. The

Daily Telegraph likened it to the fall of the Bastille.

The success of the Stop the Seventy Tour took both the authorities and the Anti-Apartheid Movement by surprise. Because Hain, along with Dennis Brutus (a key organizer in the campaign), was a cricket nut as well as a radical, he was able to see the critical role that sport played in South Africa. 'We fused the back pages with the front pages,' he later explained. 'We brought radical politics into an intimate aspect of everyday life.' In so doing, the campaign revealed to many, for the first time, the latent political power of sport.

The cancellation of the 1970 tour proved to be a more important turning point for English cricket than the foundation of the TCCB in 1968 or the John Player League in 1969. From now on, the elite had to accept that it was helpless against both mass opposition at home and the new balance of forces abroad. Under coercion, English cricket was compelled to live with the exclusion of South Africa. But it did so grudgingly. Over the next twenty years, its leading figures sought repeatedly to weaken or sabotage the boycott.

In the early seventies, the cricket Maecenas and one-time Warwickshire amateur Derrick Robins organized tours of English professionals to South Africa and Rhodesia. These tours were blessed both by the South African government, which gave them special dispensation to play against non-white sides, and by English cricket officialdom, which recognized as first-class the matches played by the English tourists against whites-only teams. Among the young, white English cricketers Robins took to South Africa in 1972-73 were Peter Willey, John Lever and Robin Jackman, all of whom were to return to South Africa in the future. The tour was managed by Jack Bannister, a long-serving Warwickshire professional turned journalist.

Bannister was also at this time, and for many years after, a paid official of the Professional Cricketers' Association. On his instigation, the Transvaal Cricket Union offered £2,000 from the profits made by the Robins to the PCA. A majority of PCA members voted in favour of accepting the money, but Mike Edwards, the current chair and one of the body's founders, resigned in protest and soon after left the first-class game. 'I felt that to accept the money would prejudice the Association's ability to represent all its members,' Edwards recalled. 'We had about twenty-five black members at that time.'

Under pressure, South African cricket twisted and turned. In the sixties, it had breathed defiance: under no conditions would blacks be allowed to play with or against whites. But the international boycott hit hard and concessions were made. SACA announced that, in keeping with the government's new policy of promoting 'multi-national' (but definitely not inter-racial) sport, trials for the national side would be conducted between sides based on ethnic groups, thus 'keeping the races apart until representation at the highest level'.

In the mid-seventies, a new group of businessmen and professionals took over the reins at SACA. These 'liberals', headed by Joe Pamensky and Ali Bacher, were more sensitive than their predecessors to the need to placate international sentiment. At the same time, the National Party made overtures to Brutus and Hain. The mounting desperation to recommence international tours led, in 1977, to the formation of the allegedly multi-racial South African Cricket Union to replace the all-white SACA. A faction within SACBOC, led by its President, Rashid Varacchia, was co-opted into the new body, which recognized the right of all clubs to play with or against anyone they liked, regardless of colour. Varacchia believed that under SACU cricketers would be able to play what he dubbed 'normal' sport, i.e. sport without interference by the apartheid laws or the government.

Shortly afterwards, the National Party sanctioned multi-racial sport from club level upwards (crucially, school sport was to remain segregated). At a match at the Wanderers between a white side and an Indian side, the Minister of Sport said that from now on 'dirty, bloody politics' would be left out of cricket. But only a few white players were prepared to sacrifice white privileges by playing for black clubs. And there were even fewer blacks in white clubs. The liquor laws meant that while it was legal, at last, to play together on the field, it was still illegal to drink together in the pavilion.

Despite Varacchia, and despite the many blandishments on offer from Pamensky and Bacher, most black cricketers refused to enter the SACU fold. At the final SACBOC meeting of 1977, the majority of players and officials declared their opposition to the actions of the SACBOC officials. In Johannesburg the following year, the South African Cricket Board (SACB) was founded. Its constitution committed it to non-racialism in sport and solidarity with the broader liberation movement. The new SACB secretary, Hassan Howa, a Cape Town 'Coloured' of mixed Indian, Turkish and Scottish descent, repudiated Varacchia's championship of 'normal sport' with the slogan, 'no normal sport in an abnormal society', which became the watchword of the anti-apartheid movement.

With SACBOC disbanded, the SACB undertook supervision of a host of black cricket competitions. For the next fourteen years, deprived of finance and harassed by the authorities, it sustained black cricket at the grass roots. In comparison, the impact of SACU's much trumpeted 'development programme', with all the advantages of money, publicity and government co-operation, was minute. Playing on matting wickets spread over soccer or rugby pitches, the SACB cricketers were building a new sports culture as an integral part of the liberation movement.

In England, it was argued that SACU had gone as far as it could. The rest depended on the government. Richard Hutton, who had played for Transvaal after leaving Yorkshire in 1974, returned from South Africa to announce that ICC members would now have 'to stand and be counted. Then we shall know who wants to play cricket and who wants to play politics.' The SACB was accused of 'looking on cricket as a political lever and not for the sake of cricket itself'.

Before SACU, South African cricket had been a full and fair reflection of the mundane ugliness of apartheid. Now, it became a mask for that ugliness. The formation of SACU and its 'development programme' for black cricketers was of a piece with the National Party's efforts to convince the world that the South African establishment could put its own house in order. That was why Howa had declined to act as what he called a 'black front' for apartheid.

It was true, as Hutton and his colleagues kept saying, that the anti-apartheid movement had moved the goalposts. The Stop the Seventy Tour Campaign's original demand had been for an end to apartheid within cricket. That was no longer seen as sufficient. As the liberation movement gathered strength, both within South Africa and abroad, there was not only a growing unwillingness to compromise with the apartheid system, but also a deepening insight into sport's place within society. The level playing field could not be achieved in cricket as long as it did not exist in society as a whole. 'What is normal about an all white school playing cricket against an all-black school?' asked one SACB supporter:

> This is the very multi-national trap which South African propaganda tries to sell to the outside world as normality. Non-racial cricketers, unlike those playing under SACU's auspices, are not prepared to accept a compartmentalization of their lives which permits (literally) free association on the cricket held but rigid segregation elsewhere.

In 1979, over the opposition of Pakistan, West Indies and India, the ICC agreed a TCCB proposal (itself the result of SACU lobbying) to send a delegation to South Africa to report on progress towards multi-racial cricket. The delegation was headed by Charles Palmer, that year's MCC and ICC Chairman, and included representatives from Australia, New Zealand and England, all of whom had records as friends of South Africa.

Not surprisingly, their report commended the progress SACU had made in meeting the ICC's requirements. It proposed that a multi-racial ICC side be despatched to play against a representative South African side (by which they meant a SACU side); the proceeds would be used for the benefit of non-racial cricket (by which they meant the SACU 'development programme'). Nowhere did the report mention that, like other opponents of apartheid, members of the SACB were denied freedom of speech and association. Nor did it mention that it was illegal in South Africa to support sanctions, and that anyone who advocated the sports boycott was liable to imprisonment. It said nothing of the black cricketers arrested for playing on a white ground in Cape Town in 1978, nor anything about the harassment of SACB by security police, who took down the names of players appearing in SACB matches or even at non-racial nets. The ICC rejected the Palmer delegation's recommendations.

When the ICC met at Lord's in August 1980, a TCCB proposal that there be 'no recriminations' against any Test country choosing to play against South Africa was rejected. Outside the meeting room, TCCB delegates urged SACU representatives to make a written submission to ICC members, who would consider it in 1981.

SACU officials lobbied heavily in preparation for the next year's ICC summit. They assured delegates that the South African regime would soon exclude sporting bodies from the apartheid laws. But in the face of hostility from the black countries, neither England nor Australia was prepared to propose South Africa's readmission. New Zealand had its own troubles. The country was in the midst of tearing itself apart over a South African rugby tour.

As a result of that tour, the West Indies cricket board cancelled a planned visit by the New Zealand Test side. The ICC condemned the West Indian move, deploring 'sanctions on cricket as a result of actions by other autonomous sporting bodies'. But it made no move to readmit South Africa. At the same time, it voted to grant Test status to Sri Lanka.

John Woodcock complained that South African 'hopes had been falsely raised'. Peter Kirsten, considered one of the more enlightened South African cricketers, told readers of *The Cricketer* that South Africa's 'cause' had been set back by 'the infiltration of the ICC by Sri Lanka (a very minor cricketing body). Now the four non-white member countries can vote against the three white member countries.' He complained that he and his fellow cricketers were being frustrated in their 'ardent wish merely to take part in the contest of country versus country to show where one's identity lies'.

This was precisely the problem. The 'identity' of South Africa was not a settled thing. It was above all a political question and would remain so as long as the majority were disfranchised.

SACU's failure to secure readmission to the ICC led to a change in South African strategy. In order to prove its credentials to the English cricket establishment, SACU had opposed Packer, but it had also learned from his example. Official cricket could be made to bow before the power of the market. The English 'rebel tour' of 1982, and the West Indian and Sri Lankan tours which followed it, were testimonies to that power. But as with the Packer affair, the authorities themselves had laid the basis for it in preceding years.

In February 1981, the Forbes Burnham government in Guyana had revoked Robin Jackman's permit to enter the country because of his involvement with apartheid cricket (he had played for Western Province in 1971-72 and for Rhodesia, after UDI, in 1972-73, 1976-77 and 1979-80). Alan Smith, the TCCB tour manager, withdrew the rest of the England squad from the Test 'as it is no longer possible for the Test team to be chosen without restrictions being imposed'. The message from the English authorities, backed by the Tory government, was clear: English cricketers had every right to play in South Africa. The Burnham government's stance was widely seen in the Caribbean as an attempt to cloak one of the region's most repressive regimes in the robes of anti-imperialism. The rest of the tour proceeded in the islands without incident, but a warning note had been sounded.

When the English party to tour India was announced the following autumn, Indira Gandhi declared that Geoff Boycott and Geoff Cook, who had played in South Africa, would not be let into the country unless they publicly repudiated apartheid. George Mann, the TCCB chair, insisted: 'We will not alter our principles of selecting our side on merit. South Africans found that out thirteen years ago. Guyana discovered it last winter and now India's government know where we stand.' Nevertheless, Boycott and Cook issued the required statements, and the Indian visas followed. The TCCB then sent a letter to all county players warning them against playing in South Africa. The next month, Jackman, Hendrick, Larkins, Willey, Woolmer, Miller and Old went there to take part in a double-wicket tournament. The TCCB said nothing.

The rebel tour had its genesis when a South African businessman, travelling on a British passport, approached Boycott in the West Indies in 1981. In the midst of the Jackman affair, Boycott divulged the plans to Gooch and others (including Gower, Botham, Emburey and Dilley). All were happy to sign a handwritten letter confirming their interest in the venture. During the following summer, press reports implied that John Edrich, an England selector, was recruiting for SACU. On the arrival of the England squad in India, Christopher Martin-Jenkins revealed that if the official tour had been cancelled 'some of England's players might have joined a tour to South Africa'. Over the next few weeks in India, the final plans for the tour were agreed. Five of the sixteen England tourists were involved.

The rebel tour of 1989 was hardly, then, the well-kept secret both the rebels and the cricket authorities later claimed. Lord's' first communication with the rebels was in March 1982, after their tour had begun, and was delivered to their South African hotel in a British embassy diplomatic bag. On behalf of the TCCB, DB Carr and FG Mann warned that the 'strong reaction in England and other countries' might endanger the visits of India and Pakistan planned for the following summer 'thus seriously affecting the county finances and the possible future livelihood of fellow cricketers'. The TCCB advised the rebels that 'if it is thought practicable', they should 'refrain' from playing in 'international calibre matches'.

Gooch and Boycott claimed that the tour, sponsored by South African Breweries, was neither 'international' nor 'representative' and was therefore not banned under the Gleneagles declaration. Yet the rebels played what were billed as 'Test matches' as the 'SAB England XI' against a SACU-selected 'South Africa' decked in Springbok emblems.

If the purpose of the tour was genuinely to promote non-racial cricket, as its apologists claimed, the English players could have confined their activities to assisting the development programme. Even John Woodcock, a defender of the tour, was forced to admit: 'I wish I could say that the tourists found time to go to the townships and help them too. That they didn't was only partly because time was so short.' In fact, in the black communities the rebel tourists were seen as sanctions-busters. The whole enterprise profoundly alienated the black majority because it confirmed suspicions that SACU's one and only priority was getting back into the Test arena. The development programme was purely cosmetic. The white cricket authorities remained devoted to white cricket.

India and Pakistan made it clear they would refuse to visit England unless Gooch's rebels were banned from international cricket. The TCCB proposed a two-year ban; at the West Indies' insistence, this was raised to three years, and approved by the ICC in July 1982. The TCCB explained that it had been forced to agree to the ban 'to preserve international multi-racial cricket'. George Mann, the TCCB chair, virtually apologized for it: 'The players have broken no law, none of our rules. We are not trying to penalize them, merely taking the minimum steps needed to protect cricket.'

In the Commons, Thatcher struck a similar note. She said she did not approve of the tour but claimed: 'We do not have the power to prevent any sportsmen or women from visiting South Africa or anywhere else. If we did we would no longer be a free country.' This tallied with Gooch's own view of his cause: 'We had taken up the right of an Englishman to earn a living where and in whatever legal way he chooses, which is normally one very good reason for being English.'

Two higher loyalties were being invoked in defence of the rebels: the free market and the English nation. Only a few years before, however, in the Packer affair, these two had been portrayed as mutually exclusive. John Woodcock, who had denounced Greig as a national traitor for taking Packer's shilling, now damned the TCCB for 'bowing to political pressures to the consternation not only of the players concerned but also of the average cricket follower'. The ban, he said, made him 'sick with despair'.

The South African government placed full-page advertisements in the English cricket press protesting about the 'hypocrisy' of the ban. Support for the rebels was organized by the newly-founded, South African-funded Freedom in Sport, whose chairman was Lord Chalfont, an MCC member and Lord's Taverner, as well as a former director of IBM in South Africa and current Thatcher favourite. Chalfont told cricket fans: 'The TCCB has given in, without even a protest, to a straightforward and impudent piece of political blackmail.' If India, Pakistan or West Indies were not prepared to play an England team selected solely on merit, they should 'stay away'. According to Chalfont, it was the TCCB's patriotic duty to stand up for cricket against 'bully boys' and 'intimidating pressure groups'.

Like Woodcock, Chalfont claimed to be speaking for 'the average cricket follower'. He warned that English crowds would boycott Tests in which England was 'not represented by the best available players'. Nothing of the kind happened. Throughout the South African saga, commentators and authorities alike seemed unaware – or unable to admit

– that the sports boycott of South Africa enjoyed wide public support.*

The right-wing attacks on the TCCB for selling out to the Third World were expedient demagogy. It was easy for the likes of Chalfont and Denis Compton to call for actions that would have led to a black-white split in world cricket – there was no danger of the TCCB heeding their advice. The English cricket authorities worked hard to bring South Africa back into the fold and to ease the pain of isolation whenever they could. But they would do so only up to the point at which this activity jeopardized England's own place in world cricket. The ICC tried to maintain the fiction that each country was free to select its own team without interference, but everyone knew that Test cricket was now in the hands of much greater powers. The TCCB had no choice but to bow to that reality, much as it disliked it. Cricket commentators and right-wing politicians were free to indulge their fantasies.

In July 1983, the MCC held a special meeting to debate a proposal to send an 'England' tour party to South Africa. The proposal emanated from Freedom in Sport, which had formed a committee of MCC members, fronted by Denis Compton and Bill Edrich, to secure the fifty signatures necessary to force Lord's to call the meeting. Joe Pamensky announced that SACU would welcome an MCC party. One thousand members packed Westminster Central Hall for the club's first discussion on South Africa since the D'Oliveira affair. Across Parliament Square, the Commons was debating the return of capital punishment.

John Carlisle, the Tory MP for Luton North, managed that evening both to cast his vote for the death penalty and to move the Freedom in Sport motion at the MCC meeting. A strong supporter of tobacco sponsorship of sport, this former commodities dealer had already declared his belief that 'the system of apartheid in South Africa has worked in terms of government'. In his speech he denounced the 'hypocrisy' and 'double standards' of the TCCB and the ICC. The themes were then taken up by Denis Compton, Brian Johnston and the Tory MP for Basingstoke, Andrew Hunter, who had business interests in South Africa. Hunter too cast his vote for the rope that night.

The MCC Committee, represented by Colin Cowdrey and Hubert Doggart, opposed the motion, but accepted all the arguments about 'hypocrisy' and 'double standards'. The sad reality, they explained, was that passing the motion would have only one effect: to jeopardize MCC's

---

*By the mid-eighties, sanctions against South Africa were consistently endorsed by at least 70% of the population, according to opinion polls.

remaining influence and with it, Lord's future as a Test venue. The final vote, including postal ballots, was 4,344 for the motion and 6,604 against. Twenty-five per cent of MCC's traditionally docile membership had defied the Committee.

The ICC meeting in June 1983 refused delegations from both SACU and the SACB, though TCCB people met informally with SACU representatives, as they did throughout the eighties. Every winter, some seventy English cricketers played and coached in South Africa. The Cricketers' Association supported the right of cricketers to work and play where they liked – a principle which was abrogated in English county cricket by the TCCB's hostility to a transfer system. South Africa was, in effect, subsidizing county cricket, providing the winter employment which the counties refused to provide.

But the intercourse between English and South African cricket was increasingly unacceptable to the rest of the cricket world. In response to the rebel tours, the West Indies Board pushed for a clear ICC statement banning cricketers who went to South Africa in the future from playing in Test matches. They also proposed an amnesty for those who had gone in the past. This would have benefited the England side more than anyone else, but the TCCB persistently opposed the West Indies Board. In 1986, Bangladesh and Zimbabwe, both at that time merely associate members of the ICC, refused to receive English B teams which included cricketers who had played in South Africa. In *Wisden Cricket Monthly* David Frith accused the two countries of 'creating a new form of apartheid' which denied to 'the teeming thousands' of their lands 'the understanding which is bred through international cricket'.

At the 1987 ICC meeting at Lord's, West Indies and India proposed to ban from international cricket any player who thereafter engaged in 'sporting contact' with South Africa. The TCCB had been given a year's notice of the motion and had consulted with Sports Minister Colin Moynihan. With Australian support, it succeeded in deferring the matter to a select committee to be chaired by Colin Cowdrey, the new MCC President and *ex-officio* ICC chairman. Cowdrey's committee dithered and delayed and in the end came back with no suggestions to resolve the dispute.

During the summer of 1988 it was widely rumoured that moves were afoot to organize a new rebel tour. Thanks to Cowdrey and the TCCB, the ICC meeting at the Oval decided to postpone a decision on the West Indies/India motion yet again. The TCCB argued that British law and opposition by the Cricketers' Association (whose protests it usually ignored) made imposing a ban difficult.

Two months later, the Rajiv Gandhi government objected to eight members of the England side chosen for the winter tour of India. All of them had played in South Africa and appeared on the United Nations 'blacklist'. One of them, the putative captain Graham Gooch, disclosed that he had a contract to play in South Africa that winter but would forgo it for the sake of the England captaincy, which had just been offered him.

Long before the selectors met, the Indian Cricket Board had notified the TCCB that India's immigration laws prohibited entry to sportspeople on the UN blacklist. Nevertheless, Alan Smith, announcing the squad, said he would be 'surprised and disappointed' if the Indians raised objections. Peter May, the Chairman of Selectors, insisted, 'We don't pick the team for political reasons.' Earlier that summer he had removed Mike Gatting from the captaincy after it was revealed that Gatting had entertained a woman who was not his wife in a hotel bedroom. The selectors appeared quite prepared to take a moral stand, but not on South Africa. In the end the Indians maintained their objections to Gooch, Lamb, Barnett, Radford and Thomas and the tour was cancelled.

Jack Bailey, who had left the MCC the year before, was one of many within English cricket to accuse the Indian government of double standards. He lamented 'the remarkable gift of inconsistency possessed by politicians in that part of the world'. But other ICC members had little sympathy for England. The TCCB had dragged its feet at the ICC, where the matter could have been resolved without government interference. In the end, it was the unilateral Indian action which broke through the stonewalling defence of the TCCB and led to the ICC agreement of January 1989.

On behalf of the TCCB, Subba Row and JJ Warr had been engaged in negotiations with other ICC members for months. It was widely known that the ban and amnesty, as proposed three years before by the West Indies, would soon be agreed. At the TCCB meeting on 19 January, four days before the ICC meeting, Pamensky and Bacher were allowed to address the assembled county officials. Bacher made it clear that SACU was contemplating a new rebel tour. The South Africans were applauded, but after they left, the TCCB gave its ICC delegates, Subba Row and Doug Insole, a mandate to 'exercise the UK vote as appropriate', which everyone knew meant a ban.

Pamensky and Bacher also met with Carlisle and Norris McWhirter, chair of the Freedom Association, which applied to the court to stop the ICC meeting on the grounds that the proposed ban was an illegal act of 'blackmail'. This time the ICC was advised by its former adversary, Lord Alexander of Weedon. Justice Taylor ruled against the Freedom Association, describing its action as 'an abuse of the process of the courts'.

At the ICC meeting, the TCCB suggested that another 'fact-finding' mission be despatched to South Africa. This time no other country was prepared to support the idea. The long-standing West Indies proposal was seconded by Sri Lanka. In the interests of the 'unity and continuity of international cricket', it was agreed that from April 1989, no one would be selected for international matches who was in 'sporting contact' with South Africa. There was to be a clean slate – freeing Gooch and scores of other English players from future taint, as long as they desisted from going to South Africa.

As that year's MCC President, Lord Bramall had acted as chair of the ICC meeting and announced the historic decision to the press. 'It isn't in itself an action against South Africa,' he insisted. Subba Row admitted, 'These are the realities of international cricket. We have had to put a curb on our own players, something we had always resisted and we would still rather not do.'

The obvious reluctance with which the TCCB had submitted to the ICC majority made it vulnerable to the familiar charge of expediency. The authorities were accused of betraying England and all it stood for. 'Foreign governments must be taught that whatever restrictions they place on their citizens, we still live in a free country,' McWhirter railed. South African all-rounder Clive Rice lectured the TCCB on its national responsibilities: 'England have backed down on those principles of freedom of choice which they hold dear.' Here the English nation was harnessed to the free market, and both were placed at the service of the apartheid cause.

For David Frith, the betrayal of the nation was one and the same with the betrayal of cricket itself. 'Cricket, the sacrificial lamb, has had its throat cut at the altar of political expediency ... England has caved in against the forces of blackmail. And on the twenty-fourth anniversary of Churchill's death too ...' Frith's remedy to this national disgrace was a reassertion of the prerogatives of empire: 'The "Children" have been feeding off the Mother Country ever since the game was born in these various far-flung lands. What sort of "Mother" is she? Might she not have got tough with her offspring, especially the noisier ones?'

Frith's contempt for the autonomy of other lands was shared by EM Wellings, who used his *Wisden Cricket Monthly* column to declare 'a Hundred Years War' against the unbearable arrogance of the 'coloured countries'. Accusing the TCCB of a 'failure of leadership', 'continual retreat and surrender' and 'weakness', not to mention the heinous crime of having 'accepted dictation from West Indies', he called on the English authorities to 'retaliate' by expelling West Indian cricketers from the county championship.

Curiously, the ICC decision was seen as freeing SACU to play the market. Now that everyone knew exactly the price of busting the boycott, negotiations could begin. Mike Gatting observed, 'This will mean that there will be even more money knocking around to play in South Africa.' Jack Bannister reported that eight senior England players would prefer to join a rebel tour to South Africa, if the money was right, instead of the official winter tour to the West Indies.

That spring, SACU staged an expensive 'centenary' bash to mark the one hundredth anniversary of South Africa's entry into Test cricket. What was being celebrated here was the continuity of white South African cricket, making a nonsense of SACU's claims to represent a radical break with the racist past. Cricket administrators, journalists and former Test cricketers from across the cricket world were invited to the extravaganza. SACU wined and dined them, showed them the development programme, a game reserve, lashings of first-class cricket and specially-staged 'old-timers' matches.

Though the TCCB declined the SACU invitation, the English cricket establishment was well represented. MCC sent two official representatives, George Mann (a former TCCB chair) and JJ Warr (who had been acting on behalf of the TCCB only months before).

They were joined by former England players Peter May, MJK Smith, Norman Gifford, Keith Fletcher, Dennis Amiss and, Denis Compton. BBC commentators Trevor Bailey, Tony Lewis, Fred Trueman, Christopher Martin-Jenkins and Jack Bannister were also on hand. Bailey and Trueman had already appeared in a SACU promotional video. Martin-Jenkins acted as Master of Ceremonies at one of the SACU banquets. Bannister and Lewis had commentated for the South African Broadcasting Company, and Lewis had smoothed the way for Matthew Maynard and other Glamorgan players to spend winters in South Africa. Ali Bacher explained that Colin Cowdrey, 'an old ally of South African cricket' would have liked to attend the festivities but dared not for fear of compromising his chairmanship of the ICC.

The purpose of the whole affair was to encourage the foreign guests to tell the world that South Africa should be readmitted to the cricket community. David Frith was one of many only too happy to oblige. In a seven-page feature in *Wisden Cricket Monthly* he set out to make up for 'the outside world's crass refusal to listen, let alone give credit where it is abundantly due'. South Africa, he reminded his readers, was not the only country with 'shanties and slums'. Anyway, in Alexandra township, 'the shanties are being bulldozed away and replaced with blocks of flats' (which was not what the England A cricketers found when they visited the township four years later). Frith believed that apartheid was already largely dismantled 'apart from the universal suffrage claimed to be so simple and beneficial an achievement only by those who lack an understanding of South Africa's complex history'. Frith enjoyed the SACU-organized visits to Sun City in the 'independent homeland of Bophuthatswana' and to a 'Zulu compound' where 'villagers frenziedly danced themselves to exhaustion'.

At that year's MCC annual meeting there was strong support for sending coaches, kit and an under-15 side to South Africa. Compton and Colin Ingleby-Mackenzie, the former amateur captain of Hampshire, backed the proposal, but Lord Bramall and the Committee pointed out that if MCC was seen to defy the ICC it would be blamed for 'wrecking international cricket' and lose its last shreds of influence. John Stephenson, the MCC Secretary, later reflected:

> Is there a conflict in the role of Secretary of MCC and ICC? Well, a lot of MCC members would like to see the MCC helping in South Africa ... But at the same time we administer the ICC, and when we had a meeting in January 1989 there was a unanimous vote against those who play in South Africa. It's a bit of a tricky one, that.

In April, Ali Bacher was the special guest at the annual *Wisden* dinner, one of the premier events in the English cricket calendar. He boasted of 'the revolution taking place in South African cricket' and portrayed SACU as in the van of the 'progressive forces ... who want to destroy apartheid', which was certainly news to the ANC, the trade unions, and the civic associations. We have had a moratorium on international tours,' he explained, in order 'to concentrate on the development programme'. That moratorium had lasted all of two years. But SACU's patience, it seemed, like its commitment to township cricket, was meagre. Because the programme was 'costly', Bacher explained, international tours were necessary to fund it (though the previous ones had been loss-makers). 'We do not want to hurt world cricket with unofficial tours,' Bacher insisted, 'but it must be understood that we need outside contact.'

The warning could not have been clearer. News broke in mid summer that sixteen English players (including nine who appeared in that summer's Ashes series, among them former captain Mike Gatting) would tour South Africa during the coming winter. The TCCB found it 'particularly distasteful' that SACU had run 'a covert recruitment campaign ... even while their officials were enjoying consideration and hospitality from Board representatives'. True, SACU officials had been guests of the TCCB at the Edgbaston Test and the Benson & Hedges Cup Final. But their recruitment campaign was an open secret. Jack Bannister was spreading the word in the counties and dropping heavy hints in the press. Gatting told Micky Stewart about Bacher's offer. Before turning it down, he wanted assurances about his Test future. Apparently, Stewart failed to offer them. Certainly, Lord's did nothing to halt the tour.

The tour was announced on BBC TV by Jack Bannister, one of seven BBC commentators on duty that day who had attended the SACU centenary jamboree earlier in the year. As Cricketers' Association Secretary, Bannister had worked closely with its treasurer, David Graveney, who was to be the tour manager. His uncle, Tom Graveney, was also on BBC duty that day. Like the other commentators, he welcomed the tour. Ray Illingworth summed up the mood: 'we've been dictated to by these countries overseas for too long'. The bias was too much even for the *Mail on Sunday*, which reported: 'Christopher Martin-Jenkins announced the news with the air of a head prefect announcing a half holiday. Brian Johnston, his headmaster, smugly observed that, "They are in no way rebels. They are merely following their profession." "Absolutely," gushed Martin-Jenkins.'

In this instance, the BBC crew were out of step with the press, which was mostly hostile to the tour. To the *Mirror* and the *Sun*, the Gatting men were 'traitors'. Both papers opposed the sports boycott, but both were keen on 'national loyalty'. Unlike the 1982 tour, this one was in direct conflict with an official English tour, and one to the West Indies at that. But the main reason for the absence of public sympathy for Gatting's tourists was the deepening popular contempt for apartheid. Phillip DeFreitas and Roland Butcher, the only black cricketers in Gatting's sixteen, withdrew from the tour after pressure from the black community in Britain. Among cricket fans, black and white, there was widespread recognition that, in Imran Khan's words, 'The central issue raised by the rebel tour is a moral one.'

Earlier in the summer, a delegation from the Mass Democratic Movement, the umbrella group organizing internal opposition to apartheid, visited England to warn cricketers that any rebel tour would be met by mass protests. Krish Mackerdhuj of the SACB (later President of United Cricket Board of South Africa), told the press: 'Our message is simple. These tours will set back our efforts to develop non-racial sports. They will give comfort to the apartheid regime and its supporters. They will undermine the struggle to create a non-racial and democratic South Africa.' According to Matthew Engel, the MDM delegation were 'treated with the contempt to which black South Africans are no doubt accustomed'.

Announcing the tour, Gatting insisted, 'I know very little about apartheid. I do believe there shouldn't be any politics in sport.' On his squad's arrival at Johannesburg airport, police used dogs, whips and teargas to clear away demonstrators. 'As far as I'm concerned,' Gatting said of the protest, 'there were a few people singing and dancing and that was it.'

That evening, black workers in the English players' hotel marched through the lobby in opposition to the tour. Chefs, chambermaids, porters and other staff refused to serve Gatting's men, who were forced to help themselves and dine in an enclave cordoned off from other customers.

The Alexandra Civic Association mobilized thousands of township youth in a demonstration calling for an end to the SACU development programme, now hopelessly compromised by the tour. Police used dogs and bullets to disperse the crowd. Rebel tourist Chris Cowdrey was contemptuous. 'The demonstration was a mile and half from the ground. That wasn't much use to anyone, was it?'

Marches and vigils greeted the English cricketers wherever they went, despite SACU's decision to switch the first five matches to areas considered more 'moderate'. Five thousand gathered behind a banner proclaiming: 'Mike Gatting: we are the masses of Pietermaritzburg and we have arrived. We do not want you in our country.' Gatting was handed a petition detailing the racist bias of South African sport. Among other facts, it noted that despite what Bacher called SACU's 'revolution', whites, 16 per cent of the population, had exclusive use of 84 per cent of the country's cricket pitches.

Outside the cricket grounds, demonstrators, organized by the ANC sponsored National Sports Congress, chanted non-stop. A young black man showed Gatting buckshot wounds received on a demonstration outside a cricket ground. 'It's nothing to do with us,' Gatting told the man. Then he confided to reporters, 'He said he was shot on the way from a peaceful demonstration. That's bollocks.'

Bacher dished out free tickets in a desperate attempt to get black people into the cricket grounds. Freedom in Sport hired vans to transport them from the townships. But at the Wanderers, half the spectators were said to be police. The Gatting tour cost SACU 14 million rand, five times what it spent annually on the development programme.

Bacher realized he had miscalculated even before de Klerk announced, in the middle of the tour, the unbanning of the ANC, PAC and Communist Party and the release of Mandela and other political prisoners. Bacher was facing direct opposition on his home ground, the like of which he had never expected. It was an expression of the confidence and power of the mass movement for democracy which had matured through bitter struggles during the seventies and eighties. If even the National Party had to bend to this force, how could SACU hope to resist it?

Prodded by the ANC, Bacher and SACU entered negotiations with the National Sports Council. Declaring the moment 'a time for compromise', Bacher curtailed the tour. The *Mirror* gloated: 'Mike Gatting and his jackals of cricket are coming home early with their bats between their legs.' Like the barbed wire at Lord's twenty years before, the police cordon around Gatting's team in South Africa made all too naked the coercive reality of apartheid which the SACU promoters were hoping to disguise. In the fiasco of the Gatting tour, all the myths propagated by the South Africa lobby in English cricket for twenty years were stripped bare. The tours had nothing to do with township development or the advance of non-racial cricket. SACU did not enjoy large scale black support, was not independent of the government, and had not gone as far as it could. In fact, it had not gone nearly far enough – any more than the government had. All the high-toned rhetoric about a cricketer's right to work, about bridge-building, about keeping politics out of sport was shown to be nothing but an apology for apartheid.

Those who aided and abetted the cause of white South Africa during the years of isolation were by no means all out-and-out racists, unreconstructed Blimps, or cynical apparatchiks. The roots of English collusion with white South African cricket ran deeper, into the soil of empire, from which the real 'hypocrisy' in this long-running saga sprang.

Colin Cowdrey once said that cricket's motto was 'friends for life'. This apparently benign notion became, in the mouths of the English cricket establishment, a justification for white solidarity against black demands for equality. Jack Bailey explained their thinking: 'Those who played and administered cricket' [in South Africa] 'had fought side by side with England during the war. Now they needed our help and support ... We were fighting for the world of cricket as we knew it.'

Cricket was identified with empire and both were identified with the free market. In their way stood 'politics', portrayed with astonishing disregard for history as an antonym for cricket. In *Wisden*, John Woodcock warned: 'Administrators will always do well to remember that they hold the positions they do, not to act as politicians but as guardians of the game of cricket – in South Africa not least.' Jack Bailey claimed that the ICC ban 'made political considerations part of the process of qualification' for 'the first time'. That the ICC and English cricket had sanctioned the denial of black rights in South African cricket for generations did not seem to Bailey or Woodcock a 'political' consideration. It was simply the natural order of things.

Supporters of the boycott were always accused of being 'anti-cricket'. David Frith ranted regularly against 'their eager propensity for assaulting the game of cricket, which presents the most defenceless of targets'. 'These dabblers in inverted racism' and 'masters of the hatred game' were, to Frith and others, enemies of cricket because they wished to exclude white South Africa (and those who aided and abetted it) from the game. They could not accept that it was the exclusivity of apartheid that was inimical to cricket and that the exclusion of South Africa from world cricket was the only way to bring about a broader inclusion, in cricket and well beyond.

The new watchword for South Africa's friends was 'bridge-building', a variant on Lord Harris's imperial ideology. 'Cricket is just one way to bridge the gap between the old-fashioned white ruling class and the still largely primitive black tribes,' explained Martin-Jenkins. It was as if apartheid was based on a misunderstanding, a gap between cultures which cricket could breach.

For many in English cricket, there was something right and just about the world of white South Africa, a world where people knew their places, where white skin brought comforts and privileges which only considerable wealth could purchase in England's dog-eat-dog world. Here was a hierarchical, leisured society like the long-vanished England embodied in cricket's traditions. No wonder that for them the defence of white South Africa merged so easily with a defence of 'England'. No wonder they were unable to understand that by playing in South Africa they were rejecting the multi-racial reality not only of South Africa but of contemporary Britain itself. White supremacy was identified with the

Anyone But England

stability and orderliness which England had forfeited some time after the Second World War. The fact that in reality South Africa was one of the world's most unstable and disorderly societies did not stop some cricket writers from turning it into one of the many 'lost paradises' which resonate in the literature of the game.

Gooch, Boycott, Gatting and others openly admired the white lifestyle in South Africa. Gooch was impressed by the standard of cricket in white South African schools, which 'makes the English schools system look a sorry mess'. Boycott, according to Gooch, was 'in his element in South Africa, where he had plenty of friends, a great deal of contacts and – important to him – a true liking for the country'.

The English rebels and their supporters inevitably absorbed the logic of white privilege. They took refuge in the cultural exclusivism promoted by the 'new racism' in Britain and consonant with the 'multi-national' strategy adopted by apartheid itself in the seventies and eighties. 'South Africa's non-white races are anything but harmonious,' Gooch informed English cricket fans. 'The Indians, Africans and coloureds are invariably at odds with each other.' He had no doubt that 'to suddenly hand over control to the blacks would create a situation of pure farce'. Gatting, too, believed that 'the Zulus are more moderate', and that therefore the abolition of apartheid was 'more complicated' than people in England appreciated. Walter Hadlee, doyen of New Zealand cricket, insisted that 'the matter of separate development is for the determination of those who reside in southern Africa. There is evidence that some ethnic groups prefer separate development.'

If the cultures of southern Africa were thus mutually exclusive, it followed that cricket, the embodiment of the (English and white) culture of empire and the market, must be foreign to Africans. Richard Hutton informed readers of *The Cricketer* that 'among the African communities the natural inclination is still towards Association football'. Gooch picked up the theme, one of apartheid's hoariest myths: 'the blacks and the coloureds have no historical background in the game'. Accusing the SACB of practising a 'reversal of apartheid', he complained that 'coloured cricketers who choose to play in the predominantly white leagues have been persecuted by their own kind in an unpleasant situation which reminds me of striking miners attacking their working colleagues'.

Gooch was only repeating what he had been told by SACU and its defenders in the English media. Like the scabbing miners, those who played for SACU did indeed face ostracism within their own communities – but they were handsomely rewarded by the establishment. The real sacrifices were being made by those (mainly black) South African cricketers who resisted SACU's bribes. The career choices confronting these people were infinitely more difficult, more crucial to their standard of living and even physical survival, than 'the difficult choices' faced by Gooch and other English cricketers tempted by the rand.

Wisden, along with most of the cricket media, never acknowledged the existence of any non-SACU cricket. Until 1991, it refused to include the SACB in its international directory of cricket bodies, which listed the Argentine Cricket Association, the Israel Cricket Association, the Japan Cricket Association, the Scarborough Festival and the Sports Turf Researching Association. By blotting out the existence of SACB and the long tradition of independent black cricket it represented, the South Africa lobby was able to promote the township development programme as a benign missionary venture. Apartheid would be mitigated by white paternalism from above, not black struggle from below. Lurking behind the argument was the old imperial assumption that blacks were not capable of governing themselves. This was the subtext of the clamour against 'Third World hypocrisy'. Martin-Jenkins argued that the boycott was illogical because 'South Africa has no monopoly on racial prejudice. India, Pakistan and Guyana exercise some repression on ethnic and religious grounds.' He might have added Britain, Australia and New Zealand to his list. All differed from South Africa in that none openly disfranchised the majority of the population on the basis of skin colour.

However, the charge that cricket and sport in general were being asked to bear the brunt of the global crusade against apartheid, while commerce proceeded largely unfettered, was true. The rebels and their champions laid claim to nothing more than the freedom that British capital enjoyed in the South African market. It seemed to them grotesquely unjust that cricket should be 'singled out'. Gooch and Gatting, apparently oblivious to the student-initiated boycott of Barclays (which ultimately forced the bank out of South Africa) and the anti-apartheid pickets outside British supermarkets, protested that 'no one complained' about businessmen pursuing trade in South Africa.

The sports boycott was only part of the anti-apartheid movement's general call for sanctions, a strategy of isolating apartheid on every front. The strategy was more effective in sport than in other areas for one simple reason: *black nations have power in sport which they do not have in the market*. The boycott was always more tenuous in rugby and golf, where black players were rare, and more stringent in athletics and cricket, which depended commercially on black participation. The West Indies, India,

Pakistan and Sri Lanka could hold international cricket 'to ransom' because, within international cricket, they enjoyed an equality denied them in other spheres.

The friends of South Africa in English cricket believed they were upholding both cricket and the market (and the white race) against arrogant 'Third World politicians'. They could not understand that these politicians derived their power from cricket's level playing field, which upended the market that had drawn English cricket to South Africa in the first place.

The game itself had taken revenge. It was not an accident that sport led the way in forging international opposition to apartheid. Because it was familiar to millions, sport offered a powerful public focus to the anti-apartheid movement. Many found this objectionable. Jack Bannister whined: 'Sportsmen are again being asked to forgo huge sums of money to appease the consciences of others.' He assumed, it seems, that they had no consciences of their own. Asif Iqbal, in contrast, was 'proud of the fact that my sport should be serving as an instrument for a cause the morality of which is far above any banal platitude about politics and sport'.

The South Africa lobby's claim that it spoke for the cricket public in England was predicated on the assumption that this public shared its conception of 'what England stood for'. The rebels and their friends could not understand that their tolerance of apartheid in South Africa seemed to many a rejection of the multi-racial reality of Britain today, including British cricket crowds. One of the reasons the TCCB had to give way on the ICC was that it knew the public would not forgive it for getting England excluded from international cricket, no longer seen as whites-only cricket, for the sake of South Africa.

Throughout English cricket's long collaboration with apartheid, nation, market and cricket were invoked as avatars of each other. Yet it was the fractures between them that dictated the real course of events. Apartheid was sustained by the international market which had created it. English professionals claimed the right to play cricket in South Africa as part of their right to work and, above all, move freely in search of work – precisely the right that was denied the black majority under the Group Areas Act. The irony was that apartheid was itself an abrogation of the market: it kept blacks off the level playing field.

To assert the right to play cricket in South Africa was to assert ancient English prerogatives. But here the rights of the 'English nation' as asserted by the South Africa lobby came increasingly into conflict with other peoples' assertions of their own national rights, in the Caribbean, the

Asian subcontinent, Britain and, of course, South Africa. What tilted the balance in favour of the latter was cricket itself, which gave new and non-imperial nations a leverage that they did not enjoy elsewhere. Cricket became a democratic counter-force to the amorality of the market. It became a vehicle for anti-racist solidarity, just as it had served for so many years as a vehicle for the solidarity of the white rulers.

The reconciliation process which unfolded in South Africa after the collapse of the Gatting tour was applauded everywhere, especially in the cricket world. It did not, however, proceed without dissent, hesitations, ironies and strange reversals. Its ultimate outcome remains in doubt, as does the outcome of the larger, national reconciliation process which it so uncannily mirrors.

The first, tense meeting between the SACB and SACU was held in Durban in September 1990. The negotiations, under the supervision of Steve Tshwete, the former Robben Island prisoner and ANC sports spokesperson, took eight months. Eventually, a 'Declaration of Intent' was agreed. All parties pledged themselves to rectify the gross racial imbalance in South African cricket. Priority would be given to development, not international tours.

On 29 June 1991, the United Cricket Board of South Africa was born, with ten members from SACU and ten from SACB on its Executive. The event was celebrated with a banquet in Johannesburg attended by Walter Sisulu and E.W. Swanton, Sam Ramsamy and Ali Bacher, Sunil Gavaskar, Gary Sobers, Richie Benaud and the Pollock brothers. A few days later the UCBSA delegation flew to London for the annual ICC meeting.

Tshwete and Bacher lobbied the High Commissions of all the ICC members. It was agreed that India would propose the UCBSA's admission to international cricket. It would be too compromising for all concerned to have the TCCB propose it. West Indies and Pakistan abstained on the vote, but the rest supported the UCBSA application. Welcoming the decision, an emotional Ali Bacher at last acknowledged the role of the black SACB cricketers 'who deserve even more credit than we for keeping the game alive with very poor facilities'.

Not everyone was pleased at the speed of unification. For Hassan Howa, the whole business smacked of 'indecent haste'. He refused to visit the Newlands ground at Cape Town to his dying day in 1992. Nelson Mandela dismissed accusations that the ANC had given ground too quickly on the resumption of international cricket tours. 'We have extremists who say that there can be no normal sport in a racial society,' he pronounced, without intended irony, 'but it seems to me that sport is sport and quite different from politics. If sportsmen here take steps to remove the colour bar, then we must take that into account.' Only a year before, he had attacked Thatcher before the Wembley crowd with these words: 'It is only those who support apartheid who say that the Pretoria government should be rewarded for the small steps it has taken.'

The debate over the pace of change will only intensify in the years to come. How long before we see black players in the Test side? Will development or international tours take priority? Will affirmative action really change the SACU ethos of paternalism? Can the entrenched resistance of the old white guard, still ruling the roost in cricket clubs across the land, be overcome? Will development be aimed at producing showpiece players for the national squad, or will it tend the grass roots? Will it, as Khaya Majola, now the UCBSA director of development, promises, 'teach people that cricket is not just about survival, but joy'?

All these questions are echoed in the complex process under way today in South Africa. With the end of apartheid and the coming of democracy, will white and black in South Africa at long last share a level playing field? How will the legacy of apartheid be redressed? Are electoral democracy and legal equality enough? Or will more radical solutions have to be found?

The lesson of the years of isolation is that cricket cannot be an island. The tensions between the dictates of the market and the promise of democracy which will course through South African society in the years to come will also run through South African cricket.

English commentators have persisted in speaking of South Africa's 'return' to international cricket, but in South Africa itself there is greater awareness that this is not a return, but a new departure. Too many in the English cricket world have celebrated the resumption of a 'normal' cricket that never existed. The South Africa admitted to Test status by the ICC is not the South Africa of old and is far from fully fledged, either on the cricket field, or in the wider world. It is a nation still in the making, threatened by reaction and division, but full of a promise that England can only envy.*

---

*In an article in the South African journal *Transformation* (Issue 33, 1997), Vishnu Padayachee, a professor at the University of Natal, sketched some of the problems encountered by South African cricket since 1992:

'Despite the enormous changes that have occurred in this country in the last seven years, there are many areas of ordinary life which remain delicately poised between the practise of the past and the promise of the future, where tensions and suspicions still exist, and where therefore a great deal of care and sensitivity needs to be exercised by those who participate in them, in part because their actions do serve as role models for the present and future generations of South Africans. Sport is one such area. But is this sensitivity to issues of race really being displayed?

'Stereotypes about sports and racial 'identities' still persist among many South Africans. Like the *Daily News* reader who made the following comment in a letter attacking someone who had suggested that cricket has not made significant strides towards non-racialism: 'The realism of the situation is that generally, blacks in this country do not particularly want to play cricket. The fact that soccer is a giant sport in this country is because blacks want it' (April 15, 1997). Such examples of racist stereotyping , based on a complete ignorance of the long histories of 'other-than-white' sports in this country, are still widespread. Neither are they confined to the more yobbish elements of our society. They will continue to be a barrier to fuller racial integration both in sport and society.

'No clear programme for sports transformation, development and monitoring was agreed to in the early 1990s as a pre-condition for the ANC's 'blessing' of white-dominated sports. And it has been suggested repeatedly that the ANC's hasty decision has enabled some of these sports codes to re-establish international links without a concurrent commitment to sports transformation and development. The recent furore over rugby administration and its development programme demonstrates how premature the ANC decision may have been.

'In cricket noticeably more progress has been made, both in terms of changes in the game's administration and in cricket development programmes, but many questions still remain over cricket. Why have there not been more black players (Indian, Coloured, African) in cricket teams, at national, provincial and even club levels five years after unification, and despite the fact that South Africans previously classified as Coloured and Indian have played cricket in this country for over 100 years? Are the changes at top of cricket administration really significant, or are people like Ali Bacher and others (who pioneered rebel tours in the isolation era) still in reality calling the shots?

'In KwaZulu-Natal and elsewhere, a group of (black) cricketers and administrators have constituted themselves into a pressure group (Cogoc) to challenge the cricket authority's transformation and development programme, and have even spoken (unfortunately in my view) of establishing racial quotas for teams at all levels of the game in order to speed up change.

'Many South African blacks, including prominent ANC politicians like Finance Minister Trevor Manuel have come out in support of touring sports teams, because of their inability to identify with South African teams. This is of course most clear in rugby, but also increasingly emerging in cricket as well. Thousands of South Africans of Indian origin, for example, but perhaps excluding the young, would fail the Tebbit test if it was applied here. For they enthusiastically support India or

Pakistan against South Africa. These people love cricket passionately and many were eager to throw their weight behind the South African cricket team in the early 1990s, and especially during the 1992 world cup. Now many have had a change of heart.

'When one looks back at recent racial incidents, such as Steve Palframan's racial abuse of West Indian Franklyn Stephenson, and notices how lightly he got off, one must question the seriousness with which the new cricket authorities are committed to stamping out racial abuse on the field of pay. Incidents such as Allan Donald's verbal abuse of Indian batsman Rahul Dravid and Shaun Pollock's 'overzealous' send-off of Mohammad Azharuddin in the recent Test series between these countries may be qualitatively different from the Palframan incident but they are nevertheless symptomatic of a deeper ingrained racial socialisation, which is the product of an apartheid upbringing. These incidents sparked in KwaZulu-Natal a huge outcry, as is evident form the letters pages of local newspapers in the following months ...

'There is a lot that sport, including cricket, still has to do before it can be said to reflect the realities of the new South Africa, and to command the unqualified support of sports-loving South Africans ... If through its cricket, the English establishment still imagines and plays out the rules and values of a long-lost colonial past, is it not the case that through sports like cricket, tennis, bowls and especially rugby, many white South Africans continue to live out the rules and values of their recently-lost apartheid past?'

Padayachee is by no means alone in raising these concerns. In 1997-98, Ali Bacher's regime, once the envy of the South African sports world (and fellow members of the ICC), came under mounting criticism. At school and club level cricket remains largely segregated. Provincial sides seem reluctant to select players from the old SACB, or from the UCB's own development programme, and coloured and black players remain confined to the fringe of the national team. Mluleki George, the National Sports Council president, and former Robben Island inmate, commented: 'The UCB can talk a lot about development, but right now it looks more like a PR exercise than anything else and we're not seeing results.'

In March 1998, protesters in Port Elizabeth confronted Ali Bacher with a petition, signed by 1,000 local residents, complaining about the absence of blacks in Test and provincial teams. Bacher agreed that 'in 1998 it cannot be right that South Africa field a team of whites only' and hinted that more blacks would be selected in future. Soon after, twenty-year old Makhaya Ntini became the first black and the first graduate of the development programme to play Test cricket for South Africa. He had been preceded by Paul Adams, Roger Telemachus, and Herschelle Gibbs, but all these hailed from 'Cape Coloured' communities and had learned their cricket at exclusive schools. Ntini, from a Xhosa village on the Eastern Cape, never touched a cricket ball until he was fifteen. His selection was decried by some as a case of 'reverse racism'. Their ire was unlikely to be assuaged by Bacher's statement after the selection was announced: 'At the moment, particularly for matches in South Africa, we simply cannot afford to field a national team without representation from black communities.' It's hard enough making a Test debut without also having to shoulder the burden of historic resentments and expectations, but Ntini performed respectably on debut, taking the wicket of Aravinda de Silva, and was selected for the 1998 tour of England.

One of the ironies of the new South Africa is that many of those now clamouring for 'colour blind' selection were beneficiaries of the old apartheid order, which was anything but colour blind. Is it surprising that in these conditions, there are calls for 'affirmative action' to redress generations of racial discrimination? Many in the black communities simply do not trust whites to select on merit, and the slow and cautious introduction of non-whites into the provincial and Test teams confirms their worst suspicions.

The development programme does seem to have ignited an enthusiasm for cricket in many townships, but movement into high-level club and ultimately representative cricket has remained restricted. The best facilities are still monopolised by private white-dominated clubs and schools. In that context, critics of Bacher have demanded that the UCBSA superintend a much more radical redistribution of resources.

For all its shortcomings, the UCBSA still has lots to teach the ECB when it comes to putting its money where its mouth is. In 1996-97, takings at the gate for the Test and one day series played against India and Australia amounted to R24.5 million (about three million pounds), R4 million of which the UCB placed at the disposal of the development programme and other initiatives to promote cricket among disadvantaged populations. It is inconceivable that the ECB would ever contemplate donating one sixth of its Ashes series revenues, say, to inner-city, state school and black and Asian cricket. But then they've never come under the kind of mass political pressure which forged the UCB and still shapes its policies.

The ICC meeting which agreed to admit South Africa to the 1992 World Cup was held in Sharjah, twenty-five kilometres up the Persian Gulf coast from Dubai. This bright and arid desert city seems a long way from the misty village greens of England, but it is today one of the world's major cricket venues, and a fitting meeting place for the new world cricket order.

The game was first brought to the United Arab Emirates by British oil companies, but it was migrant workers from the subcontinent who put Sharjah on the international cricket map. The oil sheikhs had imported a proletariat. As elsewhere, this proletariat sought self-expression through sport, notably cricket.

Big cricket in the Gulf began in 1980, when Miandad's XI played Gavaskar's XI to raise money for the newly-established Cricketers' Benefit Fund. According to Asif Iqbal, who organizes the matches in

Sharjah for the CBF: 'We hoped to provide a much-needed service primarily for cricketers in the Third World and to do so in a more dignified manner than is done in England where he is virtually made to go around with a begging bowl.' It was a return to the old days of Clarke's XI, when professionals organized their own benefit matches. And like Clarke's XI, the CBF series opened up a new market for cricket, a market hitherto ignored by the authorities.

Between 1983 and 1993, twelve one-day international series were staged in Sharjah, which acquired a pavilion, floodlights and luxury boxes. The CBF organizers pay substantial sums to the official boards to send top-class teams. Prize money is handsome ($30,000 for the winner and $20,000 for the runner-up in the 1990 Australasia Cup, which cost over $1 million to stage). The participating boards now nominate the series' beneficiaries, who have included Gordon Greenidge, Wasim Raja, Salim Malik, Madan Lal, Allan Border and a host of lesser-known veterans. In 1993, in the Wills International Trophy (contested by Pakistan, Sri Lanka and Zimbabwe), the two beneficiaries, Sikander Bakht and Rameez Raja, received $35,000 each. The prize money is supplemented by donations and gifts from local supporters. In 1991, Javed Miandad received a new Mercedes and $150,000 from an expatriate Pakistani businessman.

Cricket at Sharjah is broadcast by the Hong Kong-based Star TV to hundreds of millions across Asia. Television, music and film stars from the subcontinent turn up at the matches to enhance their celebrity status. As the world's first 'neutral' cricket capital, Sharjah was recruiting neutral umpires five years before the ICC began appointing them for Test matches.

Between 1983 and 1993, Pakistan played thirty-five one-day internationals in Sharjah. India played thirty, Sri Lanka twenty-one, the West Indies fourteen, Australia ten, New Zealand six and England three. Australia have visited the Gulf three times; England only once, in 1986-87. Clearly, Star TV and its vast market mean little to the TCCB. But England have been reluctant to play in Sharjah for other reasons as well.

Ever since the flop of the Triangular Test series of 1912, it has been the received wisdom in England that punters will not pay to watch two foreign teams play on neutral ground. But the success of the World Cup tournaments, of the Nehru and Hero Cups in India, of the World Series Championship in Australia, not to mention the Sharjah series, suggests otherwise. Along with much else, England will have to abandon its old bilateral approach to international cricket if it is to assume a place as an equal among equals, not a former master, in world cricket.*

In the years after World War II, British officials held commanding positions in numerous world sporting bodies, both amateur and professional (the Olympics, athletics, tennis, soccer, hockey, boxing and, of course, cricket). Back in 1968, no one thought it necessary to specify that the new TCCB was the 'UK' or 'British' or 'English' TCCB, unlike its foreign counterparts, which all incorporated their countries' name. Similarly, Britain is the only country which does not print its name on its postage stamps. Back in 1968, the qualifying adjective 'British' or 'English' was also omitted from the names of the Football Association, the Rugby Football Union, the Lawn Tennis Association and the Amateur Athletics Federation. This nomenclature was a legacy of the origins of these sports in Britain, and an indication that British sporting bodies had yet to escape from old imperial presumptions. Like Britain's place on the UN Security Council, its continuing clout in the administration of world sport, particularly cricket, was an inheritance of the Industrial Revolution and empire. But it was no longer commensurate with the country's economic status nor with its performances on the sporting field.

Over the past decade, England has been gradually pushed aside within the ICC, which changed from a 'Conference' to a 'Council' in 1989. That year, it decided to elect its own chairman, rather than allow the MCC President to occupy the post ex-officio. Thus, Colin Cowdrey became the unlikely superintendent of England's loss of administrative supremacy within cricket, its last imperial sinecure. The veto enjoyed by the 'founder members', England and Australia, was surrendered. In January 1993, the ICC voted to appoint David Richards of the Australian Cricket Board as international cricket's first Chief Executive, replacing the MCC Secretary who had administered the ICC since its founding in 1909.

In July 1993 Clyde Walcott, the former West Indian batsman wicket-keeper, became the first non-English and non-MCC chair of the ICC. His only rival, the TCCB nominee, Raman Subba Row, was easily defeated. Walcott was backed by Ali Bacher, who seemed to have metamorphosed into one of those manoeuvring Third World cricket politicians his old supporters so despised.

Walcott and Richards share a belief that cricket, in Richards's phrase,

---

*This bilateralism remains the major obstacle to the construction of a coherent world Test league. However, England are at last embracing the realities of the global one-day circus. In December 1997, it sent a specialist one-day squad to Sharjah – and won the tournament.

'must be expansive'. Richards sees Sharjah as a model for what he calls 'off-shore cricket'. He wants the ICC to catch up with the new global media market. 'With the way the world is shrinking, what is absolutely essential now is to have a global attitude and to have people thinking internationally at all levels.' He sees satellite and cable TV bringing cricket to Europe, North America, South East Asia, even China and Japan, assuming the missionary role once played by imperial schoolmasters, civil servants, soldiers and vicars.

Recent years in Sharjah have shown that 'off-shore cricket' is not immune from international tensions. In the 1991-92 Wills Trophy final, the heart of the Indian batting order– Shastri, Azharuddin, Tendulkar – was wiped out by a hat-trick of LBWs from Pakistan's Aqib Javed. The Sri Lankan umpires were accused of bias, as were the Muslim officials organizing the event. For over two years India boycotted Sharjah. The oil sheikhs talking about fair play and the traditions of cricket could not gloss over the realpolitik of the subcontinent. Sharjah became the site for a proxy war between India and Pakistan.

In 1994, the United Arab Emirates, which had been admitted as an associate member of the ICC only three years before, won the ICC Trophy in Kenya and thus qualified for the next World Cup. Other competitors complained that the UAE team was in reality a 'Pakistan second eleven'. The global market that created cricket in Sharjah blurs national boundaries, but it does not necessarily reconcile nations. Indeed, by making the question of nationality so problematic, it intensifies disputes about who belongs to which nation, not least in England itself.

Richards's vision of the global spread of cricket is likely to prove as wide of the mark as Bowen's prophecy of terminal decline. The audience for cricket no longer inhabits a single, unifying economic market, as it did in the days of empire. And England is no longer the metropolis, the centre of gravity around which satellite countries revolve. The world may he shrinking, but it is also fragmenting.

The new democracy in the ICC is bound to be less stable than the old paternalism. The founder members' veto has been replaced by an understanding that major decisions must pass by a two-thirds majority. The nine full members, with two votes each, will have to look for support from the nineteen associate members, with one vote each. Will a stable alliance emerge to take the place of the old Australia/England axis? As the world divides into giant trading blocs, the Test countries are being pulled into conflicting economic and political orbits: the West Indies towards North America; England towards the European Community;

Australia and New Zealand into the eastern Pacific rim. India, Pakistan and Sri Lanka form a massive economic bloc in themselves with aspirations to compete with the big three. South Africa and Zimbabwe have links with all the blocs. Increasingly, only cricket unites these cultures – cricket and capitalism. As new alliances are forged and broken, new interests will come into the game, and with them new priorities and values.

Sport, like the market and the rule of law, is portable because its rules are impersonal and universal. Like the market and the rule of law, sport brings changes wherever it goes. All three integrate people into an international system, putting an end to self-contained cultures. But the portability of cricket, compared with other sports, is limited. Everywhere, it has to struggle before taking root in new soil - and that soil always changes it. It is adopted and adapted.

Cricket followed the English, but not systematically, not everywhere. Only where England wielded state power – where the British military and civil service supervised imperial interests – did cricket thrive. Where the public-school elite did not govern, it failed. With its roots in the landed gentry, the game was well suited to the needs of a colonial caste which allowed middle-class people to acquire land and servants and re-create themselves as landed gentry. Playing cricket, for them, was an assertion of Englishness in a foreign land. At the same time, its inclusive premises allowed it to become a means of bonding local elites to British rule. As a rule, little effort was made to inculcate Christianity or British dietary habits in the governed populations, but cricket was promoted relentlessly.

The cultural baggage cricket carries weighs heavily on the game wherever it goes. As the visible token of English presence, it flourished only where Englishness was identified with a wider, imperial community. Elsewhere, it floundered.

In Argentina, Portugal and other independent countries under British commercial dominance, cricket was played from the early nineteenth century. Clubs and competitions were set up, some of which still exist, but the game did not spread to the locals beyond the small minority who attended English-style public schools. In 1948, the nationalist demagogue Eva Peron demanded that the English-run Buenos Aires Cricket Club give up its historic ground, built in 1864, for a welfare scheme. When the gentlemen of Buenos Aires CC refused, she incited a mob to burn their clubhouse to the ground.

The Irish rejection of cricket was explicitly political. In the seventeenth century Cromwell issued a ban on cricket in Ireland and his troops confiscated cricket bats – an indication that cricket of some sort was popular among the Irish peasantry and not regarded yet as especially 'English'. In the nineteenth century it was played every where in the island, except, ironically, by the Scots Presbyterians in Ulster. An Irish cricket annual was published from 1865 (only a year after *Wisden*) until 1881, the year the land agitation began. In 1879 an Irish XI toured North America. Parnell was himself a keen cricketer, but under the impact of the national movement with which he was associated, Irish cricket crumbled.

This movement defined itself as anti-English and, increasingly, republican. As it became a mass movement in the late nineteenth century it embraced organized sport as a weapon. The Gaelic Athletic Association was founded in 1884 on the model of the Amateur Athletic Association in England, but soon rejected English sports and instead revised and codified traditional Irish games. It demanded that all participants in Gaelic sports boycott British games. While football survived, cricket was driven into a redoubt among the Ulster middle classes and the public schools in the south. It became a victim of the world's first organized sports boycott.

Billy Power, one of the Birmingham Six, acquired a taste for Test cricket during his seventeen years in British prisons. 'It kills a lot of time,' he explained. He described a triangular cricket tournament he had seen in Albany prison: the three sides were Irish, Black and 'English'. In an English gaol, playing cricket seems a perfectly good way to get back at the English. But in Ireland itself, not playing it is even better.

The greatest single national defection from cricket's cause was the United States. The traditional American explanation for baseball's triumph over cricket is tautologous. America embraced baseball because baseball was intrinsically American. Compared with cricket, it was faster, less time-consuming, more clear-cut, and thus in tune with an emergent national culture. Baseball simply grew, like corn and tobacco, out of the American landscape. What is missing from this argument is the element of struggle, the competition for cultural space which baseball entered in the late 1840s and from which it emerged, fifty years later, triumphant.

Although English immigrants and visitors had been playing cricket in America since the seventeenth century, it was not until 1850 that American-born youth in Philadelphia took it up. They were inspired by the English textile workers and potters in Germantown and nearby New Jersey, artisanal expatriates driven from England by poverty and political suppression, and carrying the same Chartist heritage which shaped William Clarke's itinerant XI. To the young Philadelphians, sons of professionals and stockbrokers, cricket seemed more sophisticated than the rudimentary stick-and-ball games then played across North America. It was worthy of regular practice and play, and investment in facilities. Clubs were founded and the game soon spread to New York.

Within a few years cricket had grown sufficiently to warrant the first-ever English overseas tour, a commercial venture organized by George Parr, Clarke's successor as captain of the All-England XI, and RA Fitzgerald, the future MCC Secretary. 'Cricket in Philadelphia,' Fred Lillywhite observed, 'has every prospect of becoming a national game.'

Baseball borrowed the terms umpire and inning (reduced to the singular) from cricket, but little else, though batters were initially called strikers. It was an urban phenomenon, played by New York clerks and artisans, who formed baseball fraternities which quickly donned colourful uniforms. In 1845, the New York Knickerbocker Base Ball Club drafted the sport's first set of rules. Foul lines were introduced, giving spectators a closer view of play. Each inning was limited to three outs, thus compressing it in time. Over the next decade, nine innings became the standard length of a game, which could now be completed in three hours.

In the mid-1850s, Henry Chadwick, an English expatriate, began writing about baseball for the *Brooklyn Eagle* and other papers. He gave it the box score and batting averages, both derived from cricket, and for over forty years pressed its claim to be the supreme American sport. In 1857, Porter's *Spirit of the Times*, a sporting weekly, argued that just as the English had cricket, so Americans should have 'a game that could be termed a "Native American Sport"', by which the paper meant baseball.

When Walt Whitman, Chadwick's fellow journalist at the *Brooklyn Eagle*, anointed himself the prophet of American democracy, he also took up the cause of baseball. 'It's our game, that's the chief fact in connection with it: America's game.' For Whitman (bizarrely echoing Thomas Hughes) baseball had 'the snap, go, fling of the American atmosphere – belongs as much to our institutions, fits into them as significantly, as our constitutions, laws: is just as important in the sum total of our historic life'. Baseball promised to unify the American diversity, something which cricket could not offer.

It has to be remembered that the 'special relationship' and popular American Anglophilia is a creation of the Second World War. Except among a narrow eastern white Protestant elite, Anglophobia was the rule, especially among the Irish immigrants who formed such a large proportion of the nascent urban working class.

Baseball and cricket grew side by side in the 1850s. Clearly, baseball enjoyed advantages in a mobile, expanding society. You didn't need to dig or mow a pitch. You didn't need stumps. You just needed a bat, a ball and 'bases', for which almost anything would serve. Just prior to the Civil War, the Brooklyn Excelsiors, one of the first professional baseball sides, toured the country, and like Clarke's XI introduced the joys of their game to new regions, including Philadelphia.

During the war, the British government was on the losing side, blockade-running for the Confederates whose slave-based cotton economy fed the mill industries of Lancashire. That could not have aided cricket's cause. More importantly, the Civil War brought together young American males from all over the country. Because it was already systematized and widely reported, baseball as codified in New York was adopted in preference to other local variants.

The Civil War created, for the first time in US history, a strong central state with a large standing army. It also unleashed American capitalism, and in so doing created a new American market, in which commercial baseball flourished. Mark Twain called the game 'the very symbol, the outward and visible expression of the drive and push and rush and struggle of the raging, tearing, booming nineteenth century!'

Baseball took to commercialism with much less fuss than cricket. The objections of the old co-operative fraternities, for whom amateurism meant not social exclusion, as it did in England, but independence from employers, were brushed aside by a booming market. In the 1870s, the leading clubs became joint-stock ventures. The first all professional club was the Cincinnati Red Stockings, sponsored by local businessmen and politicians and managed by the Englishman Harry Wright, a former cricketer. The National League was founded in 1876 by another former cricketer, Albert Spalding, who had become a professional baseball pitcher and later a team owner. Baseball had its first cartel.

In 1890 the Brotherhood of Professional Baseball Players rebelled against the owners' 'reserve clause' (which denied them freedom of movement), denounced the National League as 'stronger than the strongest trust' and set up an alternative Players' League. Harry Wright was one of the few scabs. Spalding warned of 'anarchy'. He suborned the Players' League's financial backers and forced the professionals back under the National League umbrella, which, he promised, would restore 'to all its purity our national game'.

As baseball became an American institution (William Howard Taft threw out the first ball of the season in 1910, thus linking the cult of the Presidency to the national pastime), it sought an exclusively American history. According to Spalding, saying that baseball had been invented in America was like saying 'two plus two equals four'. Chadwick pointed out the game's probable origin in English rounders, but this offended the baseball establishment. Spalding set up a special commission of seven men, including two US Senators, to investigate the game's origins. After due deliberation, the commission declared that baseball had been created in the year 1839 in Cooperstown, New York, by Abner Doubleday, later a Civil War general. Accordingly, in 1939, the sport celebrated its official centennial and opened its Hall of Fame in rural Cooperstown. Baseball, like cricket, had become a pastoral. Its roots in urban America were disguised.

It was cricket's associations, both national and social, more than its Laws of play, that left it vulnerable to the rise of baseball. After the Civil War, cricket, though still widely understood and played, became increasingly the pastime of a plutocratic Philadelphia elite. It became the property of men of property, men who wanted to differentiate themselves from the polyglot, multi-racial, multi-religious hordes busily creating a new type of 'American', not least on and around the baseball diamond.

Even as its appeal contracted, Philadelphia cricket, spurred by visits from England, reached a high plateau of excellence in the 1890s, producing several world-class cricketers, notably the fast bowler Bart King, who headed the English first-class averages in 1908, taking 87 wickets at 11.01. But English immigrants no longer proselytized for cricket. They wanted to become Americans, as did other immigrants, and baseball was (and remains) a way of doing that. Competitive US cricket lingered on until the 1920s when a new mass culture took shape under the impact of radio, movies and newspapers. Baseball boomed as never before. Cricket was swept away.

The characteristic illusion of US sport is its universality. Baseball has its World Series, American football its Super Bowl, and in basketball the NBA Champions are definitely the world champions. Bobby Thompson's pennant-winning home run in 1951 was 'the shot heard round the world'. There is an unself-conscious assumption here that America is in itself a world, maybe even that it is the world. The size of the American market and America's global military dominance have enabled the country to persist in this delusion, but it cannot last for ever. With the growth of the game in Latin America and the Far East, the majority of baseball players and fans are now non-English speaking. It may not be long before the US has to face the kind of historical humiliation which has been England's lot on the cricket field for decades.

Meanwhile, immigrants from the West Indies and South Asia have reintroduced cricket to North America, which David Richards sees as a new market for the ex-imperial game. But cricket is unlikely to carve out a niche in American culture the way reggae has. It faces too much cultural competition, not least from baseball.

Wherever cricket prospered, there was a contest, as there was in England, for control of the game. In Australia the battle was between Anglophile officials and the more 'Australian' working-class players and spectators. In the West Indies, the white plantocracy and merchants gave way to a black petty bourgeoisie. Again and again the same questions were raised: who owns the nation? To whom does the cricket side rightly belong?

In India, cricket was initially organized along communal lines. There were Parsi, Hindu, Muslim and Sikh sides. This was in keeping with the method used by the British for ruling India, predicated on the ahistorical notion that Indian society was made up of mutually exclusive religious communities. Gandhi, who knew that unity was the key to independence, condemned cricket matches played between religious communities.

Under the government of the secular Nehru, independent India did away with the communal competitions. Interestingly, this Old Harrovian barrister, who had turned the ideology of fair play and the promises of empire against the British, only really showed an interest in cricket *after* independence, when he would occasionally appear in matches with parliamentary colleagues. India had inherited cricket, along with its army, civil service, capital city, and the Ambassador motor car, from its former masters. But it is a common English misconception that the popularity of cricket in modern India is some kind of fond tribute to the Raj. It is not. Indian cricket today is something new and different.

The Congress governments of the fifties, sixties, and seventies used the state to build up indigenous Indian capital (including a major industrial base). A wall of protection shielded the country's economy from penetration by multi-nationals, just as its non-alignment kept it out of the Cold War. At the same time, Indian cricket acquired, for the first time, a mass base, putting down roots far beyond the old English speaking enclaves. Clubs were established in schools, colleges, factories and offices; a plethora of competitions grew up and, of course, a bureaucracy to supervise them.

Cricket in India unites the purchasing classes. As it did in Victorian England, it binds together middle and upper strata – only in India today it does so through a common consumer culture. Revealingly, cricket in India is sponsored by a much wider range of industries than in England. The Tatas, Mafatlal and other industrial and commercial giants are heavily involved, as are the civil service, where the Indian private and public sectors mesh, and the banks. International cricket matches are major social occasions. As Mihir Bose put it, cricket, like the film industry, 'mixes glamour with money'. Cricket is fashionable, as it was in late-eighteenth-century England.

The long era of Congress rule produced a new middle class whose aspirations the protected economy could not meet. Many turned away from Congress, whose electoral hegemony was maintained only by the muddle of its opponents on left and right. The Congress itself then turned to the free-market miracle cure. Since the late eighties, and especially since the end of the Cold War (and with it 'non-alignment'), 'liberalization' has become the new consensus.

Today, India, with the twelfth-largest GDP in the world, is trying to sell itself as the mega-market of the nineties. Indian companies now sponsor cricket to 'emphasize their global ambitions'. Reliance, Hero, Honda are all aiming at the jean-buying generation. Sachin Tendulkar advertises the Sunny 50cc motorcycle produced by Bajaj. The Indian middle classes, which have largely abandoned hockey, love cricket, the world game, just as they seek a place in, and access to, the world market.

When college youth, the consumers of the future, were asked by the magazine *India Today*, 'Who is your role model?' 25 per cent cited Rajiv Gandhi (a dead man). The most-often-cited living person was the Indian cricket captain, Mohammad Azharuddin (a Muslim), with 14 per cent. The Prime Minister, Narasimha Rao, was back in the pack with 4 per cent. Besides its own, vast internal audience, Indian cricket enjoys an audience throughout the Indian diaspora – in North America, Europe, South East Asia, South Africa and Australia. Liberalization has meant a new emphasis on the role of Non-Resident Indians (NRIs) in the economy, and cricket, through satellite and cable broadcasts, is a means of linking up with them. Indian cricket is thus becoming not merely a fusion of English and Indian experience but a meeting place for India and the new global media market.

That has disturbed the Hindu nationalists of the right-wing Bharatiya Janata Party, India's official opposition. They fear that Star TV may act as a conduit into India for alien cultures. Shortly after Rupert Murdoch bought Star in late 1993, he flew to India, where he met with the Prime Minister. The BJP denounced him as a pornographer and a threat to national integrity. Murdoch tried to assuage them by disavowing the *Sun's* page-three photos.

Meanwhile, Hindu nationalist sentiments have been growing among the cricket consuming classes. Chetan Chauhan, the former Indian Test opener, has been a BJP Member of Parliament. Like its right-wing counterparts in Europe, the BJP seeks to exploit popular cynicism towards politicians and bureaucrats by promoting an exclusivist national identity. The BJP claims that successive governments have 'pandered' to the 100-million-strong Muslim minority. Like Norman Tebbit, the BJP is trying to rally an embattled majority, and invoking the twin phantom enemies of that majority: the establishment and the minorities. They have even applied their own version of the Tebbit test to Indian cricket.

For ten years a Muslim aristocrat, Mansur Ali Khan, the Nawab of Pataudi (Winchester, Oxford), captained the Indian Test side. During his captaincy, India did not play against Pakistan. Another Indian Muslim, Abbas Ali Baig (Oxford) was not so lucky. After making a century on his Test debut against England, he continued to play well in 1959-60 against Benaud's Australians. But he failed in the 1961 series against Pakistan. His loyalty to the Indian cause was questioned by politicians and journalists. He was dropped for six years.

The same themes were sounded when India resumed playing Pakistan in 1978, after a gap of seventeen years. Hindu nationalist politicians suggested that Indian Muslims secretly supported Pakistan in cricket: proving that because they were loyal Muslims they had to be disloyal Indians. When Pakistan lost to Australia in Lahore in the 1987 World Cup, BJP activists distributed sweets in Gujerat, one of India's communal flashpoints. The ploy led, as the BJP intended, to the taunting of Muslims in the streets and outbreaks of violence.

In 1991, a Pakistani visit to India was cancelled for the second successive year following threats of disruption by Hindu communalists. Bal Thackeray, leader of the Shiv Sena, a semi-fascist party based in Maharashtra, declared that it was 'anti-national' to play against Pakistan. His supporters dug up the pitch at Bombay's Wankhede stadium and threatened to burn it to the ground.

The imperial game has become a national game. In India, this has made it a barometer for the tensions of liberalization: the contrary pulls of market and nation.

Nationalism explains why some peoples take up cricket and why others put it down. In India, Australia and the West Indies, it was disseminated by the elite, and there taken up by the masses. In Ireland and North America, it was disseminated by the elite, but there rejected by the masses. What seems to determine the success or failure of cricket in each case is the relation of the elite to the masses, and how race and nation enter into the struggle between them. The fate of cricket in South Africa, the United States, Ireland, the West Indies, India or Australia was shaped by the interplay between the inclusive and exclusive identities associated with the game.

If you see nations, including England, as monoliths, you can never understand why or how cricket survived or perished. Test sides do not display durable national characteristics, no less racial characteristics. But on the cricket field, in the course of pitting themselves against the representatives of other nations, they do display the highly contested process of national self-definition. Test cricket is a struggle between nations in which nations are forged.

Surveying global cricket, John Arlott observed: 'English cricket is a game apart. So is Australian, Indian, West Indian. Even Pakistani cricket is different from Indian.' The reason for this national differentiation, Arlott believed, was that cricket was 'the deepest game, the profoundest, requiring the deepest and profoundest thought'.

It is an old cliche that 'temperament' is the key to success at the highest level of sport. In contests in which high degrees of skill and physical prowess are often evenly matched, the subjective factors sway the result. Cricket's complexity, its open-endedness in time and space, gives even more scope for 'temperament' than other sports. It is often said that Test cricket is played in the mind. The mind of a Test player, as much as anyone else's, is informed by his sense of who he is in the wider world and what he has in common with the people he works or plays with. Because of that, the performances of Test cricketers are inflected by their understanding of what the people they 'represent' on the cricket field expect and believe.* This is what makes Test cricket such supreme drama.

---

*But this is an immensely complex and contradictory process, and only one among many which ultimately determine a team's fortunes on the field of play. The passage above has been cited by some critics in support of proposals (like Robert Henderson's) to enhance the 'Englishness' of the England side. But the phenomenon to which I was referring had nothing to do with individual players' 'commitment' to the national cause. On the contrary, it is an argument against any attempt to

It is also why politics is bred into cricket. It is not an optional ingredient, offensive to some and intriguing to others. It is the yeast that makes the dough rise. As Asif Iqbal put it: 'Sport is politicized the moment nation-states take the decision to enter the sporting arena under their national banners. England, Australia, India, Pakistan – these are nation-states, not sporting clubs.'

measure or judge national 'commitment', a simple word for what is always a most complex phenomenon. It is also an argument against any attempt to force-feed patriotism to national sides (or spectators). See Chapter 8, pages 287-303.

7

English Cricket in a Shrinking World

The 1983 World Cup final was hardly a feast of cricket genius, but, like all great cricket occasions, it was given spice by events and alignments off the field.

It was held, like the previous two finals, at Lord's. The West Indies, twice World Cup champions and for seven years the undisputed masters of international cricket, were 4-1 favourites over India, a bits-and-pieces side captained by the twenty-four-year-old Kapil Dev. India were considered lucky to have made the final at all. They were relative newcomers to the one-day game and their spin bowling skills were thought to be more suited to Test conditions.

I left home early that bright morning. My first stop was the local council's transport depot, where I had to pick up a mini-van before collecting a group from the youth club where I worked. We could have taken the tube to St John's Wood but the young men in my charge insisted that an occasion of this importance merited luxury transport. In the end they got their way and I booked the van. At the youth club I picked up Alex, a fellow youth worker with dreadlocks, and five local youth, Jeffery, George, Herbie, Frank and Theo. They were loaded down with holdalls bearing beer and beef-flavoured crisps. I was the only white person.

The youths had been badgering me for months to get tickets to the final. When I pointed out that their West Indian favourites might not progress that far in the competition, they laughed. Their confidence in their team was complete. We got the tickets from a member of our youth-club management committee, who happened also to be a member of the MCC.

As we drove to Lord's, our party was in good humour. You could see the sure anticipation of a West Indian victory on the young men's faces and hear it in their jokes and laughter. This was a day to celebrate the black kings of cricket and they intended to savour every moment. After we parked, we walked through the leafy streets past posh houses to the ground, mingling with little bands of West Indian and Indian supporters. Passing a group of turbaned Sikhs in suits and ties, my overgrown charges (they were all bigger than me) swaggered as if each one was Viv Richards strolling to the crease, as if each one partook of the power and majesty of the West Indian side.

All of us would have disgracefully failed Norman Tebbit's cricket test. Alex had been born in Jamaica, so I suppose he had an excuse, but all five of the boys had spent their entire lives in north London. They did not follow cricket with any zeal, but they had made the West Indian side their own. For them, the West Indies' combination of raw power and refined skills served as a magisterial reply to a racist society. Whatever they may have liked to think, they were not West Indians. They were not like their parents. Their loyalty to and pride in the West Indian Test side was a political choice.

All of this I admired. As an expatriate American, I enjoyed the luxury of picking favourites from one Test series to another. I dare say Tebbit would disapprove of this whimsical approach even more than of the 'disloyalty' of the black youth. However, in the Lord's cup final, I faced a dilemma.

I had first fallen in love with cricket during the hot summer of 1976, when the West Indies made the South African-born Tony Greig grovel. In 1983, Lloyd was still in charge of the side; Greenidge, Richards, Roberts and Holding were still its backbone. I felt attached to these players. I wanted to see them confirm their superiority today in a blaze of fast bowling and strokeplay. And solidarity with my young companions seemed to demand that I support the reigning World Champions.

But I was enmeshed in a peculiar conflict of loyalties. Repeated visits to India had instilled in me an affection for and unquenchable curiosity about the country. Besides, India were the underdogs. It would be a pity if they failed to put up a fight. And though I found it easy to sympathize with the proud commitment of my charges to their West Indian favourites, I was less keen on their contempt for the Indians, whom they usually referred to as 'Pakis' and whom they regarded as 'soft' because, they claimed, Asian kids would not stand up for themselves. 'Paki' shop-owners hassled them, they said, and accused them of stealing things.

In the van on the way to the ground I had tried to dispel some of their prejudices. I reminded them that there were Asian people who had lived for generations in the West Indies and that Alvin Kallicharran was as West Indian as Viv Richards. The only effect of this was to stimulate a discussion on whether or not Theo, who was what his friends called 'half-caste', would be mistaken for a 'Paki' at Lord's. Theo didn't like this at all.

We sat in the lower tier of the grandstand (under the Father Time weather vane). The overhanging upper tier permitted us only a long horizontal sliver of a view, which none the less took in the whole playing area as well as the scoreboard. Mine was one of very few white faces in this section of the ground. In the banter and boasting surrounding me there was a relaxed camaraderie and no hint of tension between rival supporters. The West Indian fans confidently awaited yet another triumph and looked forward to star performances from their favourites. The Indian fans, proud to have made it to the final, hoped their side would put up a good show but expected little. This made for good relations all around. Steel drums, klaxons, the smell of ganja mingled with Indian flags, chants of 'Jai Hind' and steaming pooris.

In front of us sat a middle-aged Indian factory worker from Wolverhampton. Round and short with a grey moustache and a heavy accent, he struck up a lively conversation with the black youth from Highbury, winning them over by referring to Holding and Garner as 'your great fast bowlers' and admitting he was worried about what 'your great Viv Richards' would do to India's modest attack. The kids were so pleased with this that they reciprocated by praising Kapil Dev, who was their kind of player.

The West Indies won the toss and Clive Lloyd confidently inserted the Indians. His decision appeared vindicated when Gavaskar was caught off Roberts for two in the second over. My gang was convulsed with rapture. Our Indian friend smiled and wagged his head in sad acknowledgement of the inevitable. He would certainly not begrudge the youth their moment. But a few overs later, when Mohinder Amarnath lifted Larry Gomes's slow bowling twice to the boundary for four, he glanced round with a twinkle of satisfaction.

Amarnath had enjoyed a roller-coaster of an international career, having been dropped and reinstated to the Indian Test side five times already. Early on, he had been humiliated by fast bowlers in various parts of the world. Insult was added to injury when his famous Test playing father, Lala, let it be known he would not allow his son to don the protective helmet which was then coming into fashion. At Lord's in 1983, his head ensconced in helmeted safety, Armanath displayed little in the way of stylish strokeplay but kept his nerve and stayed around longer than anyone besides Tamil opener Krishnamachari Srikkanth, whose 38 (which included a hook for six off a Roberts bouncer) ended up being the highest score in the match.

When Kapil Dev was out for a disappointing 9, the Indian gentleman in front uttered a sigh of resignation and consoled himself with snacks from one of those cylindrical steel tiffin carriers one sees everywhere in India. He offered us creamy Indian sweets which the black youth devoured gratefully. Normally they turned their noses up at anything besides Jamaica patties or Big Macs.

When the Indians were all out for 183, the only question seemed how long it would take the West Indies to knock off the runs and which of their star batsmen would shine. In the morning I had been discreetly pulling for the Indians. I wanted them to compile a decent score and make a match of it. Now I found myself filled with passion for the West Indies. I wanted to see a blistering batting display and the completion in some style of what seemed a one-sided contest. Though Greenidge was out early, the confidence of the West Indies supporters remained high. They had great batsmen still to come and they were facing a bowling attack made up of utility players like the worthy veteran Madan Lal, who normally spent his summers in the Lancashire League.

Their faith seemed more than justified when Richards struck Lal for three fours in his first over. There was something about Richards's strokes as they sent the ball sizzling across the outfield that was different from anything else we had seen that day. Greatness was at the wicket and promised to transform what had until now been a desultory competition. This was what my youthful party had been waiting for. As Richards's shots flew to all corners of the ground, they exchanged broad grins and nodded knowingly to one another. Our Indian friend turned around to congratulate the young men, as if the achievement were theirs. On 50 for 1, the West Indies, it seemed, were coasting to victory.

Then, out of nowhere, the mild-looking Madan Lal took his revenge. Richards mistimed a hook. The ball sailed high out of our field of vision. We all peered ahead, wondering where it would come down. Then we saw Kapil running back, nearly stumbling, and at the last moment grabbing a brilliant catch over his shoulder. Greatness was out for 33.

Among my party, stunned disbelief was followed by silent grief. Around us, the Indian spectators went wild. All were on their feet, cheering and chanting and embracing. The affable factory worker from Wolverhampton was suddenly a raving red-eyed patriot, dancing ecstatically on his toes, his fists held aloft as if he had just personally KO'd the world heavyweight champion.

I couldn't stop giggling. It was such a marvellous reversal of fortune. Infatuated with the moment, hopelessly opportunistic in my cricket attachments, I became then and there a wholehearted Indian supporter. I slapped the man from Wolverhampton on the back.

The remainder of the match went India's way, despite flickers of resistance from Dujon and Marshall. As so often in cricket, there was no single moment when all hope for the West Indies was lost or all anxiety for the Indians allayed. Imperceptibly, the West Indies slipped to defeat and India edged towards victory, helped by skilful, if unspectacular bowling by Lal and Amarnath (an unlikely but worthy Man of the Match). When the West Indies lost their last wicket for a meagre 140, Indian spectators swarmed on to the field. In the commentary box, I later learned, Farokh Engineer shouted: 'Give 'em a holiday, Mrs Gandhi.'

I wanted to share in the Indian celebration, but had to return home with the council van and some rather morose young men. I didn't let their sourness spoil my elation at having witnessed something so completely extraordinary. There is a near-universal delight in the victory of the rank outsider over the heavy favourite, especially as with that victory comes the confounding of pundits and bookmakers. It was the underdog's triumph that made the World Cup final of 1983 memorable and gave it a special significance to millions.

In the van, Alex, my fellow youth worker, was as down in the mouth as the rest. Surly and sulky, they acted as if they had been swindled. They could not bring themselves to speak well of any of the Indian players or poorly of any of the West Indians. For them, this was a calamity that had nothing to do with cricketing skill and everything to do with the malice of fate. Fortune had frowned on them today as it had so many other times in their lives, and they resented it. I felt for them and yet I had to laugh. These big, hard, nearly-grown young men who made a show of scorning sentimentality of any kind were pictures of child-like self-pity. It was understandable, but seemed so disproportionate. After all, this was only cricket.

Except, of course, there is no such thing as 'only cricket'. Especially not in a World Cup final played between India and West Indies. Especially not when it is played in the heartland of the old empire, England, and at the headquarters of world cricket, Lord's. Especially not when it unfolds before a crowd made up of black and Asian workers seeking, through solidarity with a 'foreign' Test side, a fleeting triumph over a hostile society. The World Cup final of 1983 was not a great day's play. Too much that happened on the field depended on error or accident. But no one could deny its global resonance.

That was clear enough from the street parties in Southall that night, when the Indian population (Hindus, Sikhs and Muslims) celebrated their unexpected moment at the top of world cricket with sweets and fireworks. On their return home, the Indian cricketers were feted for months on end. 'It shows we can do it,' Mrs Gandhi said, as if she were opening a new high-tech computer factory. Kapil's praises were sung in all quarters. He was a modern, inspirational captain who had forged a professional team. Even Jimmy Amarnath became, briefly, a national institution .

But India's joy and Kapil's glory were short-lived. Within a few months the West Indies exacted a humiliating revenge in a series of Tests and one-day internationals in India. The renaissance of Indian cricket predicted in the wake of the World Cup triumph never transpired. Amarnath was dropped, selected, dropped and selected again. Kapil, less than two years after his World Cup apotheosis, was stripped of the Indian captaincy and even, at one stage in 1985, dropped from the Test side. It was said that the financial rewards which flooded the Indian game after the World Cup victory had corrupted the players. Nowadays, wise old heads agreed, the young men 'thought only of money'.

The West Indies cricketers were shocked by the defeat (Malcolm Marshall wept that night as sounds of celebratory Indian drumming filled the hotel corridors), but shocked even more by the material rewards heaped on their victorious opponents: flats, cars, jobs and cash. West Indies had won the World Cup twice, had dominated international cricket for the best part of a decade, but had never received compensation on that scale.

A year later, I returned to Lord's with Alex and Herbie to watch England play West Indies in a one-day international, a prelude to the famous 'blackwash'. After lunch, Botham was out to a miracle catch by Roger Harper on the square-leg boundary. For years, a clip of it was shown during the title sequence of BBC TV's cricket coverage, to the accompaniment of its Caribbean-style cricket anthem. Later, when Viv Richards came in to bat, a gang of white kids sitting about ten rows behind us shouted, 'Get the black bastard!' Every half-hour or so, the white kids would punctuate the general din with another racist idiocy.

They threw paper missiles at a black woman sitting in front of them. At stumps, Richards was 84 not out and West Indies had won by 7 wickets. Alex and Herbie rose calmly and, without exchanging a word, strode up the steps towards the offending white gang, most of them groggy with drink. They singled out the loudest-mouthed of the lot and punched him in the nose. Together the three of us legged it for the turnstiles.

Alex became a senior officer at a local authority. Herbie is a firefighter and union shop steward. Theo became a youth worker. George went to gaol on a burglary charge. Frank was shot dead in the street by some drug-dealers who mistook him for his brother.*

In February 1993, one week after the climax of the Gower affair at the MCC's Special General Meeting, ICC delegates gathered in London to determine the locale of the next World Cup. After the Lord's final of 1983, the 1987 cup had been staged in India and Pakistan and the 1992 cup in Australia and New Zealand. The TCCB believed it was once again England's turn and that the matter had been settled the year before, when the ICC had agreed to rotate the venue for the cup. But the admission of South Africa, pursued for so long with such determination by the English, turned everything upside down.

Nothing if not ambitious, the new United Cricket Board wanted to table its own bid to host the cup. Ali Bacher argued that, in the interests of democracy, South Africa should at least be allowed to take part in a new vote on the venue for the cup. This was a democratic demand, but also a clever one. Bacher pleased the Indians, who wanted their own bid considered on equal terms with the TCCB's, and at the same time left himself free to back the TCCB bid, and thus repay old favours.

South Africa withdrew its bid, leaving the ICC members to choose between England and a joint proposal from India, Pakistan and Sri Lanka. The subcontinent offered £200,000 in total prize money, plus £250,000 to each full Test member, £125,000 to each of the three qualifying associate members, and £100,000 to each of the other sixteen associates. England offered more or less the same total amount, but proposed to distribute it differently: £250,000 in prize money, £300,000 to full members, £150,000 to the three qualifying associate members and

*Reviewing *Anyone but England* in the 1995 *Wisden*, Christopher Booker summed up the foregoing narrative (the only part of the book he liked) as follows: 'Marqusee's description of taking a group of cocky, Asian despising London/West Indian layabouts to the final of the 1983 World Cup...'

£65,000 to the other associates.

In the run-up to the meeting, the bids were well publicized and hotly debated. In the *Daily Telegraph*, Christopher Martin-Jenkins spoke for England: 'There was a time, before money and politics entered the equation, when the community of cricket nations looked no further than the United Kingdom to stage the World Cup.'

In his eagerness to assert England's traditional pre-eminence, Martin-Jenkins had forgotten that the World Cup was itself a relatively new institution, not an ancient tradition. As for 'money and politics', they had always been in the fray. They were the reasons why the first three World Cups, in 1975, 1979 and 1983, had been held in England.

'England's simple contention is that it is their turn again,' said Martin-Jenkins. He regarded it as self-evident that England's 'advantages cannot be matched by the rival bidders from a vast and frequently unruly subcontinent'. For a start, England would be 'more pleasant' for 'the indispensable media'. It was also unencumbered (at least in Martin-Jenkins's view) by the threats of 'terrorism' and 'widespread murders and rioting'. He condemned the 'blatantly self interested support of a majority of the nineteen associate member countries for the India triumvirate', but also blamed the TCCB, whose commercial approach to the game had undermined the missionary credentials of the old MCC.

Imran Khan answered Martin-Jenkins. He noted that the combined population of India, Pakistan and Sri Lanka totalled over one billion, and that a World Cup staged on the subcontinent would give cricket a chance to reach a massive new audience. Money from the gate, from television and sponsorship would help expand facilities and improve domestic competitions, all of which were in a state of rapid evolution. Staging the cup in Britain would 'only make the TCCB richer'.

For the representatives of Indian cricket, many of them linked to the Congress government, winning the bid for the World Cup was vital. In December, massed ranks of Hindu nationalists had torn down the historic Babri mosque in Ayodhya in north India. This was one of the most traumatic events in the nation's forty-five-year history. It precipitated a wave of violence, primarily against Muslims, and unprecedented soul-searching among the Indian intelligentsia. The secular order on which independent India had been built was under stress as never before.

At the ICC meeting, India was represented by Madhav Rao Scindia, its Board President (and a member of the Indian Cabinet), and Jagmohan Dalmiya, supremo of Bengali cricket and BCCI Secretary. Imran Khan represented the Pakistanis. Alan Smith, Doug Insole and Frank

Chamberlain spoke for the TCCB. The meeting was chaired by Colin Cowdrey, with John Stephenson acting as secretary. It was to be the last ICC conclave held under the old MCC aegis.

Under the ICC rules, the winning bid had to receive the votes of two thirds of the full members (including at least one of the two founding members) as well as a majority of all votes cast. Ironically, the old requirement for a simple majority had been abandoned, after the awarding of the previous World Cup to Australia and New Zealand, at the TCCB's request. Its aim had been to prevent the associates determining the venue *en bloc*.

England's bid was backed by five full members (the 'white' nations, plus West Indies and South Africa); the subcontinental bid had the support of four (the bidding three plus Zimbabwe). The TCCB exerted pressure on Zimbabwe to shift its vote, but this failed, not least because the TCCB, in contrast to the subcontinental boards, had given Zimbabwean cricket little support, either before or after it achieved Test status.

The Indians tried to get the meeting to revert to a simple majority vote. The TCCB warned that it would not consider any such vote to be binding. Seeking advice on the matter, Scindia set up a conference call to a High Court justice in Delhi. Cowdrey, advised by Stephenson, insisted on sticking to the previously-agreed formula.

Deadlocked, the meeting went on for thirteen rancorous hours. It ended after midnight only when England, pressed by Bacher and Clyde Walcott, agreed to withdraw its bid on condition that open bidding would be eliminated and future World Cups would be rotated, with England first on the list. The whole affair revealed England's fear of global competition and belief that it could maintain its status by protocol.

Stephenson described England's withdrawal as 'the most magnanimous, decent and wonderful gesture'. But in an extraordinary press conference, bitter TCCB officials seemed somewhat short on magnanimity. Alan Smith, normally a conscientious devotee of cricket's cult of official secrecy, let rip:

> We endured a fractious and unpleasant meeting. It was beset by procedural wrangling and there was no talk of anything like cricket. It was by a long way the worst meeting I have ever attended ... There seemed a grave danger of the ICC disintegrating. Therefore, in the best interests of the game, England ultimately agreed to withdraw their submission, but only under specific conditions which were felt crucial to the future well-being of international cricket.

Cowdrey declined to comment, as usual, but Scindia made his contempt for the former England amateur clear to the Indian media, in which he accused Cowdrey of abusing his position as chair to England's advantage. Imran agreed that it had been 'an unpleasant meeting' but insisted that this was 'because there was complete inconsistency'. The last two World Cups, he reminded English readers, had been awarded by simple majority votes. 'It ceased to be a democratic process,' said Imran, 'and that is where the problems lay.' He also recalled that, in the bidding for the 1992 cup, India and Pakistan had lost out to Australia and New Zealand because the latter had offered the associates more money. No one had complained then.

Martin-Jenkins divided his anger between the TCCB (which had 'appeased the Oriental lobby') and India, which he accused (as did Mike Selvey in the *Guardian*) of 'buying' the votes of Zimbabwe and the associate members. Casting aside two hundred years of cricket history, he asserted: 'Whatever else may have been true about world cricket when it was in the hands of England and Australia, greed and political point-scoring never entered anyone's heads.'

England ought to have staged the next World Cup, Martin-Jenkins repeated, 'because it was their turn ... and it is, anyway, the ideal place'. Tony Lewis, reporting from the England tour of India, denounced Indian 'slipperiness'. He predicted: 'The ICC is likely to become a commercial mess and a bazaar for backhanders.' Other critics of the deal, like Selvey, thought 'the ICC should know where its money is going to' and implied that it was irresponsible to give the likes of Fiji and Gibraltar £100,000. In *The Cricketer*, Richard Hutton seethed: 'Cricket is increasingly the province of Third World politicians whose concern for the good of the game is subservient to their lust for power and influence.'

Hutton noted with suspicion that many of the administrators in the associate countries were of Indian origin. This was, of course, a legacy of empire, in which Indians were often used by the British as middle men and law-enforcers. It was also the result of a new unity forged by the global cable and satellite revolution. What Hutton and the TCCB failed to realize was that Scindia's power rested on his access to this market: those newspaper-buying, TV-owning, Star-subscribing Indian middle classes and their NRI cousins.

In their rage at England's eclipse, the English media conveniently forgot that England had ceded its automatic right to host the World Cup after 1983, when Prudential had withdrawn as a sponsor. Back then, the TCCB calculated that a summer featuring a single-nation tour (in keeping with old bilateral tradition of MCC relations with overseas boards) would be more profitable than a World Cup because it would not have to share the revenues among so many parties.

Commercial exploitation of the 1996 World Cup promises to be more intensive than anything seen in cricket up till now. Through satellite television, it will be broadcast to the biggest audience the game has ever known, of which English people will make up only a tiny fraction.*

In November, 1993, the well-laid plans for the World Cup suddenly looked precarious when Pakistan, fearing attacks by anti-Muslim Hindu nationalists, pulled out of the Cricket Association of Bengal's diamond jubilee tournament at the last minute. That left West Indies, South Africa, Sri Lanka, Zimbabwe and India competing for the 'Hero Cup' (named after the Indian sponsors). Australia and New Zealand were mutually engaged in a Test series down under. The TCCB had declined the invitation (and the money) on the grounds that it did not want its international cricketers playing 'too much one-day cricket'. Alone among the national boards, it could afford not to play.

The Indian authorities had sold the television rights for the tournament to TWI, an independent production company (based in Britain and headed by an American) in preference to Doordarshan, the state-run television service. Doordarshan and its friends in the government were not happy. TWI's equipment was impounded by customs officers and it was denied access to the government-controlled satellite uplink, leaving the first three rounds of the Hero Cup untelevised, with a consequent loss of revenue from ground advertising. TWl, backed by the Indian cricket board, went to court. After some delay, the Supreme Court ruled that Doordarshan be paid a fee of £13,500 a match to provide domestic coverage while TWI supplied the world via the satellite uplink.

The *Guardian* claimed the affair proved that 'the volatile politics' of the subcontinent made the ICC decision to hold the World Cup there 'bizarre'. David Richards remained confident that the cup would go ahead as planned, but warned: 'There can be no cricket without television.' I.S. Bindra, the new Chairman of the Indian Board, explained to Indian cricket lovers: 'No one can take the World Cup away from us,

---

*The 1996 World Cup in south Asia proved even more profitable than predicted, and just as tumultuous and controversy-riddled as English critics feared. As a cricket tournament, it was a smashing success. I was lucky enough to attend. My account of this extraordinary event, *War Minus the Shooting*, was published by Mandarin in 1997.

but if the government does not change its stand, we might have to give it away to Pakistan and Sri Lanka.' This was a nightmare scenario for the Indian cricket public, and one for which, Bindra knew, no Indian politician would want to be blamed.

In the past, England had held sway because the hierarchy of empire was bolstered by English domination of the world market. Now, with empire gone and England pushed to the margins of that market, the peremptory assertions of Lord's were no match for the subcontinental political alliance, and it was no use complaining. The only surprising thing in the whole story was that the ICC meeting should have come as such a shock to the English. After all, it was only another sign of the changing balance of forces in world cricket, a balance in which England carries less and less weight, just as it does in spheres far removed from the cricket field.

Winning the World Cup bid was a much-needed fillip for Indian unity, especially as it was a joint bid with Pakistan and Sri Lanka. It enabled the Congress government to depict India as a go-ahead capitalist power, making its weight felt in the world market. For the cricket authorities, it was also a welcome distraction from the recent poor form of the Indian Test side, which had won only one of its last twenty five matches.

The Indians' historic tour of South Africa, coinciding with the demolition of the Ayodhya mosque, had been bitterly disappointing. It was alleged that the Indian cricketers had spent too much time boozing with NRIs. More to the point, the administrators' obsession with the one-day game (a product of that evanescent 1983 World Cup success) had become absurd: India had not played a home Test series for five years. There were calls for Azharuddin's removal as captain. His only victory in seventeen Tests in charge had been against Sri Lanka. In the end, the selectors reappointed him for the first Test only. At the same time, they dropped five other stars, including Ravi Shastri, a mainstay of the side throughout the eighties.

The England party which arrived in India in mid-January of 1993 was widely touted as the best-prepared touring side in English cricket history. Keith Fletcher had succeeded Micky Stewart as team manager. Whittingdale sponsored training sessions for the tourists at the National Sports Centre at Lilleshall to the tune of £750,000. It even paid for Fletcher to fly to South Africa to watch the Indians in action. On his return, he reported that he had seen 'nothing, apart from Tendulkar and Prabhakar, to make me feel concerned'.

Tony Lewis believed that English cohesion and professionalism would give them the edge:

> India, I guess, will be confident as long as things go their way, otherwise the captain will blame his team, the team disown the captain and the press scarify the lot, while calling for the head of Ajit Wadekar, the cricket manager and the resignation of the whole selection panel ... England must be seen as the better side. Graham Gooch is more assertive and positive than ever before.

The *Mirror* also had high hopes for the tour. 'Team manager Keith Fletcher is not the sort of man to whinge or look for excuses,' Chris Lander told his readers. He reported an early England success this way: 'England hit-man Chris Lewis sent two Indian batsmen to hospital with successive balls here yesterday – and then warned that there was more to come.' This was not the tone adopted when West Indians meted out the same treatment to the English.

The preparatory matches against Delhi and a Board President's XI hinted that the English might be vulnerable to spin. Salisbury, the leg spinner, was called into the squad at the last minute after impressing as a net bowler, an acknowledgement that the best-prepared English team ever might not be the best-balanced. At the same time, news of Gooch's separation from his wife broke in the British press.

Because of communal violence in Ahmedabad, the first one-day international was transferred to Jaipur. Lander was convinced that the hasty rescheduling was part of an Indian conspiracy to undermine the visitors: 'England's cricketers became innocent victims of the Indian rope trick.' England won, but had their first glimpse of the left-hander Vinod Kambli (who made 100 not out on his twenty-first birthday) in harness with his school friend, Sachin Tendulkar. Together they had put on 164 in twenty-eight overs.

Gooch failed in Jaipur and at the second one day international at Chandigarh, which England lost, then struck a century in a three-day match against an Indian Under-25 XI at Cuttack. This was supposed to be his hundredth hundred, but shortly afterwards the ICC confirmed that matches played by rebel tourists in South Africa would no longer be counted as first-class. Commentators and statisticians were outraged. Gooch struck his familiar posture of world-weary, wounded innocence. Once again, he had become a martyr at the hands of scheming Third World politicians.

According to Lander, India had become the new 'killing fields'. He warned that the English cricketers might get caught up in 'an escalating war between extreme Hindu and Muslim groups'. Robin Smith said his wife was worried. 'If the trouble gets any worse the authorities must put the safety of the players first,' he said, 'even if it means calling off the tour.'

A strike by Indian Airlines pilots (which led to Scindia's resignation as Civil Aviation Minister) compelled the English squad, and accompanying journalists, to undertake the journey to Calcutta by rail. It was a nine-hour haul. No press report was now complete without tales of rat-catching in the railway carriages and the discomforts of Indian train travel. 'It's a bloody nuisance,' Fletcher complained, 'India is too big a country for us to have to keep getting about by train.'

On arriving in Calcutta, England found its ranks depleted. DeFreitas was out with a groin injury. Atherton was struck by a 'mystery virus'. Gooch was ill but decided to play anyway. The day before the first Test, the Indian selectors named their squad, which included three spinners: Kumble, Raju and Chauhan. It was clear what they expected of the pitch. Bishan Bedi urged: 'Gooch must have faith in his spin specialists.' Instead, England chose four seamers plus Salisbury. Fletcher justified the selection: 'Remember how well the Indians play spin bowling.' Alec Stewart kept wicket and opened the batting. The defensive approach showed that, already, the English tourists lacked confidence in their own resources.

Azharuddin won the toss. India batted and were at one point 93 for 3. Then Tendulkar and Azharuddin added 123 at a run a minute. Azharuddin went on to make 182 off 197 balls. After the Indians were all out for 371 (Hick, the part-time off-spinner, was the most successful England bowler with 3 for 19), Stewart, having kept wicket for nine hours, was bowled by Prabhakar for a duck. Gooch, in his one hundredth Test appearance, was out cheaply to Raju. Gatting top scored with 33 (off 143 deliveries) and England were all out for 163. Each of the Indian spinners took three wickets (and not one fell to an LBW decision).

Following on, Gooch was soon stumped off the leg-spinner Kumble. Smith was hopelessly at sea against the spinners and was caught behind off Chauhan for 8. Gatting top-scored again with 81, but England were all out for 286. The Indian spinners took eight wickets between them and sent down 90 per cent of the overs. The Indian batsmen then scored the 79 runs needed to win for the loss of two wickets, both of which fell to Hick's off-spin.

'England have only themselves to blame for their defeat in the first

Test,' Gavaskar observed, 'for they went into the match with a defeatist attitude.' The India team manager, Ajit Wadekar, agreed: 'You are so predictable, you guys. We told you the pitch at Eden Gardens will turn ... and still we knew you would come up with the same old fast medium stuff. And we knew you would all be lunging at the spinners with the good old British forward defensive stroke.'

Dexter blamed Calcutta's air pollution. He announced that he would be commissioning a study into smog levels in Indian cities, thus earning a rebuke from the Indian government. Fletcher tried to explain the omission of Tufnell, England's most aggressive slow bowler, on a spinner's pitch: 'The lad has struggled a bit. He hasn't bowled well. Cricket is 60 per cent mental. It's not an easy tour. He hasn't looked happy in India but if you are in a country you have to go out and make the most of it.' According to Geoff Arnold, the England bowling coach, Tufnell's difficulties were 'more a problem with India than anything else'.

In the three-day match against the Rest of India at Vishakhapatnam, Tufnell was no-balled twice in one over. When, in the same over, wicket-keeper Richard Blakey missed a chance to stump Tendulkar, the left-armer went berserk, kicking his cap and abusing the umpire. He was fined £500 by Bob Bennett, the England Tour Manager. Tufnell then took four wickets for three runs in a brilliant spell on the final day of the match and was included in the side for the Madras Test.

The evening before the match, eight of the England side shared a dish of prawns in their hotel's Chinese restaurant. The next morning, three of them, Gatting, Smith and Gooch, were ill. The tourists blamed the prawns, but the hotel management accused the England players of 'greed' and 'over-indulgence'. Though Atherton was now fit, and was the only regular opener in the side apart from the stricken Gooch, he was not selected. A queasy Robin Smith was deputed to open with Stewart, who would act as captain. Blakey was brought in as a wicket keeper and batted at six.

India won the toss again. After the first Test, the British media had predicted that the home side would sit on its lead and play defensive cricket on flat surfaces. Instead, they were on the attack throughout. In the first innings, opener Navjot Sidhu hit a century, Kambli 59 and Tendulkar a stroke-filled 165. Amre, batting at six, made 78 and Kapil at seven added 66. During the course of a long first day in the field, England used four substitutes, one of whom, Emburey, dropped Amre fourth ball. India declared at 560 for 6. Tufnell had bowled forty-one overs for 132 runs and failed to take a wicket. Salisbury had taken 2 for 142.

The stark poverty of English spin became apparent when India took the field. Despite decent scores from Stewart (74 in 312 minutes), Hick (64) and Fairbrother (83), England were all out for 286. The spinners took all the wickets and bowled all but seven of the overs. England followed on, for the second successive Test. Kapil soon removed Stewart and Hick, opening the way for the spinners. At one point, England were 99 for 6. Then Lewis smashed 117 off 112 balls, one of the few displays of aggressive cricket from an England player throughout the tour. England were eventually bowled out for 252, and India had clinched the series.

Fletcher blamed losing the toss for the defeat. Others complained about Professor RS Rathore's inept umpiring, but his only real victim was Salisbury in the first innings. The *Mirror* decided to replay the previous summer's attack on the Pakistanis. After India's huge first innings total, it screamed: 'CHEATS! Indian Test cricketers scuffed up wicket.' Lander warned, 'a massive new international storm was brewing' and reported that 'four Indian cricketers were warned for pitch scuffing'. Stewart and Blakey, it was reported, were furious. Their protests were linked with Allan Lamb's 'brave' stand against ball tampering. The four offenders were named as Tendulkar, Kapil, More and Amre. Umpire VK Ramaswamy admitted he had asked some Indian players to be careful about running on the pitch, but insisted he had issued no warning. Cammie Smith, the ICC match referee, dismissed the incident.

'CHICKEN MADRAS' was the *Mirror's* comment on the Indian victory. Its sub-headline, 'Test shame', was ambiguous: did it refer to Indian 'cheating' or the England performance? Lander now laid into the 'the disgraceful shambles of a Test team which Graham Gooch's men have become in barely a fortnight'. The *Sun* blamed the 'poisoned prawns'. Boycott lambasted the TCCB's policy of producing flat pitches; he insisted the Indian bowlers were 'quite ordinary' and that the problem was that the English batsmen had 'neither technique nor temperament to cope'. Botham blamed Gooch for keeping out Gower. Gooch told reporters he had only one message for his beaten side: 'You are now playing for your pride.' But there was little of that in evidence.

Food and drink were flown in from Britain. The England cricketers feasted on tinned tuna, corned beef, boiled ham and baked beans. Bennett was photographed cooking a meal of spam and eggs for the players over a portable stove. The *Daily Star* sent out food parcels. According to the *Mirror*, the England dressing room resembled 'an army field tent'. When

Indian customs officials held up an emergency delivery from the England sponsors, Tetley Bitter, the *Sun's* headline exclaimed: BREWERY WHO COULDN'T ORGANISE A P*** UP IN THE PUNJAB .

Meanwhile, the England management aired complaints about the 9.30am Test starts (which had been requested by the TCCB), about the foul smell emanating from the canal next to the Madras Test ground, about the bedlam of the Indian cricket crowds. Off-spinner Chauhan was accused, anonymously, of 'chucking'. Fletcher remained unimpressed by any of the Indian spinners: 'They are good bowlers but not outstanding ones.' A gala celebrating sixty years of Test cricket between England and India was held at the elite Cricket Club of India in Bombay. The England players failed to show, despite an appeal from Sunil Gavaskar.

For the third Test in Bombay, India were unchanged again. Gooch was back. Emburey was recalled and Salisbury dropped. Blakey was retained, despite a poor match in Madras, so that Stewart could open with Gooch. Atherton came in at three. Gooch finally won a toss but was soon out to Kapil for 4. Not long after, Stewart and Atherton found themselves at the same end. After mutual hesitation, Stewart walked. When Blakey was out for one, England stood at 118 for 6. Thanks to Graeme Hick's 178 – his long-awaited first Test century – England were all out for 347.

In the field, England were inept. Blakey missed a stumping chance. Emburey bowled without variety and Tufnell without control. Kambli exploded before his home-town crowd. Dropped by Gooch at slip on 119, he went on to make 224, the highest score by an Indian batsman against England. While he was at the wicket with Tendulkar, Azharuddin, Amre and Kapil, the Indians scored at one run a minute. To cap it all, the tail-enders Kumble and Chauhan both clouted sixes off the tiring Emburey. India were all out for 591, their highest score against England in a home Test.

England were left a day and a half to score 244 to avoid an innings defeat. Prabhakar removed Stewart, Gooch and Atherton to reduce England 34 for 3. The spinners dealt with Gatting, Smith and Hick, all of whom resisted for a period only to succumb when they seemed well set. The luckless Blakey went for a duck, again. England were all out for 229, India won the Test by an innings and 15 runs, and the series 3-0.

'Shame of Bombay whitewash' ran the back-page headline in the *Sun*, which dubbed the England squad 'Bombay Potatoes'. The *Mirror* lead was 'Cowboys and Indians'. Lander called on Fletcher and Dexter to resign. Gooch confessed, 'It's not just that we have lost but that we have lost badly,' then added, 'I am not prepared to accept defeat and failure.' It was hard to see that he had much choice. India had won every match in a Test series for the first time in its history.

Four one-day internationals remained. England won the first in Bangalore and the second in Jamshedpur, where someone in the crowd threw a nail at Devon Malcolm. 'It's now become dangerous for players fielding anywhere near the boundary,' said Fletcher. The flight back to Delhi was even more perilous. The pilot had to negotiate a safe landing after detecting a brake failure. 'Miracle escape for England stars as plane is crippled', announced the *Mirror*.

The two final one-day matches were at Gwalior, heartland of Scindia's patrimony. In the first, England scored 256, including 129 from Robin Smith. Sidhu responded with 134 and Azhar with 74, enabling India to win by three wickets. A stone was thrown at Stewart; police with lathis waded into the crowd. The *Mirror* construed this as 'Battered Stew stops a riot'. In the final match, Hick scored a century and England made 265 for 4, but thanks to Azhar's 95 off sixty-three balls, India passed them with two overs remaining. The one-day series, which at one point England had led 2-1, was drawn 3-3.

Overall, this was possibly the worst ever performance by a touring team in India and certainly the worst ever performance by England against India. Following the collapse of its professional strategy, the England Committee fell back on a parody of the old amateurism, with its obsessive concern for appearances. 'We have to look at the whole matter of facial hair,' Dexter commented when he left the TCCB meeting held at the end of the series. Gooch's trademark stubble had offended the county chairmen, as had England's casual attire at post-match ceremonies.

Nothing reveals the essence of English insularity like the spectacle of Englishmen abroad. In India in 1993, the England squad set what Gavaskar described as a 'world record' for excuses. Indian food, pitches, umpires, transport, even the Indian air were all cited as reasons for English failure. The Indian cricket crowds were too noisy and too big. The firecrackers were distracting. The banners were intimidating. The Indian wicket-keeper put off the English batsmen by encouraging his bowlers with repeated cries of 'shabash!' (well done).

From the beginning, the English media portrayed the Indian tour as an ordeal. David Hopps in the *Guardian* called it 'an extreme test of forbearance'. In the *Independent*, Martin Johnson prepared readers for the Indian experience with a series of diarrhoea jokes. Of course, complaints about diet and illness have long been common among

Western travellers in India. But the English are not the only ones to suffer this kind of disadvantage away from home. Food in Britain often makes visiting Indians and Pakistanis ill. It is not only the work of local microbes to which foreign visitors have little tolerance; it is also a hazard of eating without local guidance at restaurants in strange towns. The isolation of the English players in first-class hotels meant that when they did expose themselves momentarily to Indian conditions, they were vulnerable. In future, the English might consider going to India early (they already do this for tours of the West Indies) so that they have time to adjust to the sheer physical and cultural strangeness of the place. They might even try to *enjoy* the country.

Tufnell's verdict on India summed up the collective derision in which the host country was held by the visiting English: he told reporters he had 'done the elephant and done the poverty and might as well go home'. Bennett and Fletcher restricted extra-curricular social activities to a minimum. In India, Gooch explained with a resigned shrug, you are mostly 'confined to your hotel'. It was as if they were travelling in a country at war.

The complaints about 'designer' pitches and lost tosses were a futile protest against the game's autochthony. These had always been the chances of cricket, in England as elsewhere. When they came England's way in the course of the series, they were not taken. England simply failed to adapt to overseas conditions - though visiting players succeed in doing this in England every summer, displaying more resilience and ingenuity than the English players showed in India.

Fletcher's all-round suspicion of India and things Indian, above all its umpires, imbued his players with an inhibiting paranoia. He let the media know that he wanted to play an extra batsman as 'insurance against debatable umpiring decisions'. Emburey alleged that Indian batsmen were never given out LBW in India, hardly an encouragement to English bowlers. At the third Test in Bombay, one of the BBC radio commentators sagely assured listeners in Britain, 'Tendulkar will not be leg before in this match'. Soon after, he was LBW to Tufnell for 78.

Most Indian cricket supporters are happy to admit that some of their umpires are useless, just as they are willing to tell any visitor who shows an interest how corrupt and incompetent their politicians are. In the past, the Indian complaint against Indian umpires was that they bent over too far to favour the visiting side, especially if that side came from the MCC. It was said that the umpires were overawed by the English amateurs and were therefore out of step with the spirit of independence. All that has changed. England now have to take their chances like other visiting teams.

As with the complaints about the violence and the politics, the assumption behind the whining and whinging about food, travel, pitches and umpires was that England and English cricket were normative. India was treated as a land of fathomless mystery and deceit. Peter Roebuck spelled out the mundane reality: 'There is no secret to winning games here, or anywhere else. To win, a team must take wickets quickly and score runs quickly.'

England did neither. Critics of the tour selection felt vindicated. Gower and Russell had been sorely missed. Stewart's play suffered as ever greater responsibilities were heaped on him. The vaunted professionalism championed by the England Committee wilted under pressure. Outside the controlled conditions of the Lilleshall laboratory, it disintegrated. Fielding was sloppy and field placings defensive and unimaginative. For all the expert coaching, the England cricketers displayed lack of technique in both batting and bowling on turning wickets. Unlike John Lever in 1976-77, the medium-pacers failed to swing the ball. The decision to take along Geoff Arnold, a seamer, as the squad's bowling coach, in preference to Norman Gifford or another spinner, was an indication that Fletcher and Gooch wanted to play cricket in India as if India were England. When it turned out not to be, they complained.

What marked the English players out was not so much their failure to adapt to India as their making such a drama out of it. It was as if this was the only way they could assert their Englishness. In begrudging the home side credit for its achievement, they betrayed a profound loss of English confidence in striding the world stage. They seemed unaware that in belittling the Indian success, they belittled themselves.

The frustrations of the side were embodied in Gooch and Fletcher, the Essex men abroad. Before the tour, Gooch had said, 'Fletch is the overriding reason I want to go to India.' Fletcher had been his captain in India in 1981-82, when plans were finalized for the rebel tour to South Africa. Among Gooch's reasons for going to South Africa were what he called the 'unspeakably tedious cricket and endless dull evenings' of the Indian tour. During that tour (England lost the six Test series to India 1-0), Fletcher had knocked down his stumps after being given out and been forced to apologize. Not surprisingly, with this background, the captain and team manager became the 1993 tour's chief whingers and whiners, setting the tone for the rest of the squad.

Ill and bored, Gooch failed where he had succeeded in previous series:

leading from the front. His image as the no-nonsense NCO of English cricket was never in keeping with reality. In 1986, he had wanted to withdraw from the England party in the West Indies after he became the focus of anti-apartheid demonstrators. A few years later, he resigned the Essex captaincy because it was affecting his batting form. Far from being a modest servant of the game, seeking fair treatment and nothing else, Gooch was self-involved and self-pitying. India brought out the worst in him. He explained: 'Tours today have three priorities: playing cricket, preparing to play cricket and travelling to play cricket.' Unlike Greig in 1976-77 or Phil Edmonds on the 1984-85 tour, Gooch displayed none of the humour to which Indian crowds so readily warm.

As they went down to defeat after defeat, Fletcher and Gooch seemed bereft of ideas or inspiration. From the beginning, their tactics were predicated on damage-limitation. Over the course of the Test series, England scored their runs at 2.35 an over. India scored at 3.17 an over. In the field, India's over rates were faster than England's. The English needed to take risks to win, but refused to do so. At the same time, they refused to take responsibility for defeat.

Gooch and Fletcher had shared, with many in Britain, a blind belief that only rigorous professionalism could overcome hostile world conditions. Instead, it led to a siege mentality. Failure left Gooch, Fletcher and Dexter bewildered. That is why they took refuge in feeble distractions: smog, prawns and facial hair.

In their self-imposed isolation, their sullen conviction that they were being hard done by, the England side in India were a projection of the embattled majority abroad - a bizarre historical inversion of empire. The media, which had gleefully assisted in creating this negative English identity, now turned against its standard-bearers. The demonization of the Pakistanis gave way to a kind of delirious national self-flagellation. The *Sun* gloated: 'Gooch and Co crack up when chips are down.' Botham called for the return of Lamb, Gower and himself to 'restore pride' in the upcoming Ashes. Boycott complained, 'We should have had more fire in our bellies, more passion.' The England side in India became not only the apt representatives of a small nation bewildered by the larger world, but also the ideal object for its self-disgust.

In contrast, India was rejuvenated. Its captain was a Muslim from Hyderabad, in the south. One of its openers, Sidhu, was a Sikh from the Punjab, in the north. Kambli, its new batting star, was a Dalit from Bombay, in the west. In their elan and unity on the field, the Indian team transcended the country's dithering politicians and repudiated the demagogues of its embattled majority. And it did so through a return to traditional Indian strengths on the cricket field: spin bowling and attacking strokeplay, all of which looked handsome on Star TV. This was the first Test series to be covered solely on satellite in both domestic and overseas markets.

In February 1994, Javed Ansari in *India Today* looked back over India's highly successful year in international cricket. He saw the England tour as a turning point: 'The jousting of egos, the sulks, the groupism have abated, even if temporarily. The crux surely is that this Indian team, tired of abuse, frustrated by defeat, has eventually understood that a common collective purpose is the basis of any success.'

But he warned that India's future in an unprotected world market remained uncertain:

> Squashing Sri Lanka, Zimbabwe and a pathetic England doesn't really mean that the Indian team has qualified to sit alongside Zeus in Mount Olympus. Countries like South Africa, Pakistan, the West Indies and Australia are further up and India not only needs to pass them but to do so without the benefit of home crowds, tailor-made pitches and neighbourhood umpires.

In February and March of 1993, two nations, India and England, had passed each other on the cricket field in a fog of mutual self preoccupation. For me, England's defeat brought to mind Marx's remarks on the role of the Sepoys (Indian soldiers trained by and serving under the British) in the Indian Mutiny: 'There is something in human history like retribution; and it is a rule of historical retribution that its instrument be forged not by the offended but by the offender himself.'

In 1993, cricket, not for the first or last time, was such an instrument.

Coda: England in Sri Lanka

'How peaceful things are here, in complete contrast to the three Tests in India,' the BBC radio commentator observed at the start of the one-off Test against Sri Lanka at the Sinhalese Sports Club. 'There are only a few thousand spectators here today in Colombo, hardly any banners and the wicket is green, just like home.'

The small crowd at the Test was the result of a scheduling clash. The same day, 20,000 spectators packed another Colombo cricket ground to watch Royal College v. St Thomas, the island's equivalent to Eton v. Harrow. Strangely, Sri Lankan cricket was still swathed in a Victorian ethos. On a tour of Australia in 1989, captain Arjuna Ranatunga objected to racist sledging: 'There is no abuse for players in Sri Lanka; we play like gentlemen. We came here as gentlemen, we play as gentlemen and we want to go home as gentlemen.'

In eleven years of Test cricket, Sri Lanka had won three out of forty-three Tests. Since its admission as a full member of the ICC, it had been shabbily treated by some of the longer-established Test countries, notably England, which had granted it only infrequent one-off Tests. Because of civil war and the accompanying terror and counter-terror, no Test cricket was played in the country between 1987 and 1992.

But 1992-93 had already been Sri Lanka's most successful international season ever. In August, they had won two out of three internationals against Australia and drawn all three Tests, coming within sixteen runs of winning the first. In December, after a Tamil suicide bomb had killed five people in Colombo, half the New Zealand touring party had returned home. Sri Lanka beat the depleted side in the one-day series and won one and drew one of the two Tests.

The Sri Lankans were looking forward to the England visit, but the same could not be said of the English. Gooch had bailed out, as planned, after the last one-day match in India. Stewart led the ragged party on to the final leg of the tour. As well as captaining the side, he was asked to open the batting and keep wicket.

In the first one-day international, Sri Lanka compiled 250 for 5 in forty-seven overs. The English bowling was sloppy. DeFreitas went for 25 in three overs. There were 25 extras. The fielding was described in the press as 'shoddy and petulant'. The last ball of the innings produced three byes: Stewart rolled at the stumps, missed, and then Jarvis, following through, also rolled and missed. England were then dismissed in their first innings for 170 in 36.1 overs.

In the Test match, having won the toss, England batted unadventurously in high temperatures. After their Indian trauma, the batsmen seemed wary of the most innocuous balls. Scyld Berry thought the 'England team seem programmed, rather than prepared'. He could detect 'little sign of wit or will to win'. Smith's 128 – his first century for England overseas – was a painful effort, coming in 338 balls and 448 minutes. England reached 316 for 4 but were then all out for 380. The spinners, Warnaweera and Muralitharan, took four wickets each.

The Sri Lankan openers, Hathurusinghe and Mahanama, made 99 together in 102 minutes. The top six batsmen all scored between 43 and 93. Tillekeratne and Muralitharan put on 83 for the ninth wicket. Sri Lanka were all out for 469.

England's second innings was inept and bad-tempered. Gatting and Stewart both objected to being given out caught. Fairbrother, run out for three, also protested. The bails were already off when Warnaweera knocked out the middle stump. Under Law 28.1.c, the umpire correctly gave the batsman out. Emburey and Lewis grafted for the team's top scores. Caught down the leg side off Warnaweera, Tufnell ended the English innings with another show of dissent.

Sri Lanka were left the best part of a day to score 140. Emburey and Tufnell had them worried at 61 for 4, but Tillekeratne and Ranatunga, batting with dash and assurance, took the side nearly home. With four runs still needed, Ranatunga was caught at short leg. Jayasuriya came in and hit Tufnell first ball for six over midwicket. Sri Lanka had won their first Test victory over England.

'THIRD RATE' was the *Mirror's* verdict on 'another day of England shame'. Lander described it as 'one of the blackest days in England's 116-year Test history'. During the Test, he reported, 'England degenerated from a team of honest tryers into a rabble'. But the *Mirror* could not leave it at that. Lander claimed that Alex Stewart was 'on the war path' over Sri Lankan 'chucking'. Pressed on the allegation, Fletcher failed either to clear or condemn the Sri Lankans: 'I cannot tell you how they do it, or why our spinners cannot make the ball fizz and go the way they seem to be able to.'

By this time, most of the cricket press had grown weary of Fletcher's whinging. Lander alone was persuaded that England had been 'sorted out by a pair of "chuckers". They were victims, too, of some sub-standard international umpiring.'

Warnaweera's quick off-cutters were widely suspect in Sri Lanka and had already been queried by Martin Crowe at the end of 1992. He had been called for chucking five times in Sri Lanka, but not once on his tours of India and New Zealand. Muralitharan, the only Tamil in the team, also came under suspicion. When he bowled, his elbow appeared bent, but that is not the same as 'chucking', which is notoriously difficult to define. When he had toured England in 1991, no one had objected to his action and he had never been called in Sri Lanka.

According to *Counterpoint*, a local English-language magazine which campaigns for human rights and a peaceful solution to the island's internal strife, Warnaweera's 'chucks did not account for any dismissals in this Test – but chucks there certainly were'. Only Tufnell's dismissal in the second innings, the magazine felt, was due to umpiring error. It praised the 'superb team effort' that had brought Sri Lanka this historic triumph, but also noted that Sri Lanka had yet to win a Test away from home. It called for neutral umpires and asked: 'Why are we so desperate to win no matter what? With the talent at our disposal we don't need to have to resort to cheating ...'

In the final one-day international in Moratuwa, down the coast from Colombo, neither Muralitharan nor Warnaweera played. Sri Lanka won the toss and inserted England on a turning pitch. The left-hander Jayasuriya, known mainly as a batsman, took 6 for 29. England were all out for 180. Sri Lanka raced to 183 for 2 in 35.2 overs. Towards the end of the innings, Aravinda de Silva hit Salisbury (who had not played since Madras) high over his head. Smith ran round and called for the catch. He missed, slid, damaged his knee and had to be carried off. De Silva then hit two fours and a six off the next three balls. He finished the match with a fourth six. England's humiliation was complete.

Sri Lanka's demands for a three-Test series in England now seem undeniable.* Their cricketers had batted in the classical mould, with nimble footwork and straight bats. Their captaincy, bowling and fielding made the best of limited resources, exposing England's failure to do the same. The writing was on the wall for the England Committee. The Ashes defeat the following summer simply put it up in neon for all to see.

In London, I listened to the news of England's demise on the morning radio. Meditating on this extreme inversion of the imperial order, I ate breakfast, read the paper and set off for the House of Commons, where I had an appointment with Dennis Skinner to talk about the current state of the Labour Party. Skinner was cheerful, which isn't always the case. I asked him what was up. 'Sri Lanka beat England,' he snorted.

Skinner is well known as a republican and class fighter. Rooted in the miners' culture of Derbyshire, caustic, irascible, uncompromising, Skinner seems a quintessentially English figure. He is that, but he is also a figure of opposition, and an internationalist who insists: 'I would go anywhere to fight for the workers of the world, but I won't put on a uniform to fight for the Queen and the ruling class.'

Knowing he was a cricket aficionado who in his youth had bowled in the Bassetlaw League, and intrigued to see how he would fare on the Tebbit test, I asked him whom he supported in Test cricket.

'Anyone but England,' he replied, without a moment's hesitation.**

---

* But in 1998 have yet to be granted.

** Some critics accused me of insinuating that it was 'politically incorrect' to support England (a kind of reverse Tebbit test). On the contrary, what I was arguing

Between 1878 and 1980, England played 554 Tests, winning 36 per cent, losing just over 25 per cent and drawing just under 35 per cent. Between 1980 and 1993, England played 141 Tests, winning 21 per cent, losing 38 per cent and drawing 39 per cent. In the same period, they lost five series to Australia, five to West Indies, three to Pakistan and three to India. Up till 1980, England had lost only one Test to New Zealand; between 1980 and 1993 it lost three more, and won only six. Of Test-

– and still believe – is that everyone should be at liberty to support, or not support, the teams of their choice. No one should seek to impose his sense of 'nationhood' on another or use sport to test another's patriotism.

Of course there is nothing wrong with supporting England and being vociferous and enthusiastic about it – as long as this passion does not lead to abusing or excluding others. Sport without partisanship would be a dry spectacle. But sporting partisanship that fuels hatred ruins the sporting occasion.

In any case, partisanship is a peculiar beast. As the American comedian Jerry Seinfeld noted, "People come back from the game yelling, 'We won! We won!!' No: *they* won; *you* watched." This leap of imagination, this widening of the definition of the self, is indeed comic – precisely because it is so wonderfully human. I am the last person to want to keep it out of cricket, but I do believe that when it is applied to nations (as opposed to cities or towns) it becomes incendiary material and has to be handled with caution. 'England' is clearly a far more complex and resonant entity than Arsenal or Manchester United, Somerset or Northamptonshire.

Cricket's historic tragedy is that Test cricket was formalised before domestic competition (not only in England). Compared to any of its rival team games, cricket places greater relative emphasis on international encounters; being a top cricketer means being a Test or one-day international cricketer. As a result partisanship in cricket is pre-eminently national partisanship, with all its burdens and ambiguities. We cannot go back in time, take the course adopted by football, and thereby undo the damage done by the high Victorian institutionalisation of 'English cricket'. But we can take a leaf from football's book. In all the talk about reforming the county game, why are there no proposals for a UEFA Cup-type competition that would bring together the top first-class sides from around the world? I'd love to see Warwickshire take on Bombay, or Surrey up against Western Australia, or Glamorgan battle it out with Karachi or Barbados. This globalisation of the domestic game would enhance the 'competitiveness' of county cricket, and in the long run could prove a major money-spinner. However, it would entail a relative reduction in the overweening prestige of Test cricket and a blurring of national boundaries (especially as English counties would employ their overseas stars to maximum advantage). At the moment, the ECB seems unable even to contemplate such horrors.

playing nations, only Sri Lanka and Zimbabwe have poorer playing records over the same period. India may not have won as many Tests as England, but it has lost far fewer, and not only at home.

English cricket neatly mirrors the decline of Britain as an economic and political power, but it does more than that. It also encapsulates the neurotic struggle to come to terms with that decline.

The game became English in the late eighteenth century because it embodied the profound changes taking place in England at that time. It became imperial because while being English it was also universal and adaptable. English remains the language of world cricket. It peppers the Hindi and Urdu Test commentary. Cricket English has the charm of a world jargon, excluding the uninitiated but including all cricket lovers, of whatever nation. Cricket values, above all, fair play, are supposed to be international, yet they are also supposed to be English.

And there's the rub. Defeat at the hands of former colonies, getting 'beaten at our own game', explodes what Benedict Anderson calls 'the fundamental contradiction of English official nationalism, i.e. the inner incompatibility of empire and nation'.

Unlike its Scottish or Welsh cousins, English nationalism has few popular icons, and nothing like the USA's Fourth of July. England may have the first national anthem, 'God Save the King', but it is a hymn not to a nation, but to a sovereign monarch. The country's flag is a 'jack', something stuck on the mast of a boat to signal the national presence on the high seas and in foreign lands. It has never had the popular potency of the tricolour or the stars and stripes. It is a projection of imperial power, not the symbol of a people. What kind of England can it evoke? Mainly, it seems, an England whose identity consists in dominating others. Take that away and what is left? The projection of empire becomes a projection of loss of empire. The Union Jack becomes a token of vanished dominance, which is why the British National Party has appropriated it with such ease. Similarly, the England flag flown at Test matches, the red cross of St George, has become not the emblem of Spenser but of the National Front and a gaggle of cranky right-wing English nationalists. The fascists have been able to purloin these national symbols so easily because they do not really belong to anyone else. It has always been much harder for the far right in America to get exclusive possession of the flag, though it has tried.

In the days of Shakespeare and Milton, English nationalism spoke in revolutionary tones. But with its adaptation by empire, it was purged of all democratic content. The English Revolution, the English Jacobins, the Chartists were all swept from popular memory. English nationalism became the cult of a dynastic, imperial state.

Gutted of democracy, English nationalism rested on a sense of moral superiority underpinned by the crude reality of military and economic dominance. The hierarchy of empire was seen as a natural one, with the English at the top, and top among them, the landed elite. Other nationalisms formed during the nineteenth century embodied aspirations for change, for a transformation in the nation's internal life and its relations with other peoples. English nationalism embodied a veneration of the status quo.

Cricket proved the ideal vehicle for the national/imperial ideology which crystallized at the end of the nineteenth century. This was not 'by accident', as Rowland Bowen thought. Because of the game's early origins, cricket combined an egalitarian premise with a deeply hierarchical culture. Its transitional nature made it a peculiarly suitable vehicle for an 'Englishness' in transition from the native heath to world dominance. As it spread through the empire, it provided the English with a global image of themselves. It was an index of English supremacy, just as it later became an index of English decline.

The 'sporting' pretensions of the British empire were to shape the resistance to it. In the long run, they also rebounded on English nationalism and English cricket themselves. If the nation is defined as the ruler of an empire, and this empire is justified as the embodiment of universal civilized values, including the rule of law and cricket, what happens when that empire collapses, when others lay claim to those values? What is left of 'England' and 'Englishness'?

All this helps explain the inner weakness and brittleness of English chauvinism today. It rests on a national identity with a hole in the centre. This hollowness is only enlarged when 'England' is used as a trope for the United Kingdom (as it is in cricket). Once again, it becomes a cypher for a state, not the name of a people.

Paradoxically, the empire cut Britain off from the world. It raised insularity to a transcendent virtue, and reinforced native empirical traditions, while stripping them of radicalism. Fair play and the unwritten constitution became the highest expressions of a pragmatic nation. Empiricism may have saved the English, as Orwell thought, from irrational authority and mysticism, but it also confined all arguments to an appeal to 'common sense', which often proves as arbitrary as any religious cult.

The legendary English insularity has become a way of relating to the outside world. Where the solipsism of Americans makes it hard for them to know where their own country ends and others begin, the English are intensely conscious of national borders, and intensely self: conscious about being 'English' in foreign lands. Here the crusty cricket commentator muttering about the food in India and the lager swilling lad donning Union Jack shorts in Spain are at one. Beer cans and baked beans became totems of identity in an alien land.

Once the world ceases to reflect the 'natural' superiority of the English, 'Englishness' passes into a kind of permanent crisis. Without empire, little is left but an assertion of racial continuity. This is why national decline has been accompanied by increasingly racist and exclusivist invocations of 'England' and 'Britain'. Under its impact, English nationalism has become much more unrestrained and vulgar.

In the absence of other expressions of national identity, sport takes on a special importance. The imperial cult of 'manly' games has become the last redoubt of English national identity in a world that doesn't give a damn about England. The violent machismo of the football nationalists is simply the old public-school cult, denuded of middle-class hypocrisies and cool, imperial confidence. The old racists were smugly superior; the new ones are riddled with fear and anxiety.

England and English cricket do not much like David Richards's 'shrinking world'. The island experience has become a cross to bear. It only makes the larger world look more menacing as it closes in. The angst of this experience is all too apparent in England's recent Test performances.

With its defensive forward prod and its seam-up trundlers, its pragmatic professionalism and resentment of decline, its endless hesitancy and crippling fear of failure, English cricket is a mirror of what Englishness has become. It epitomizes the shift from a nationalism based on dominance to one based on insecurity.

The amateur legacy has become an instrument of self-torture. English masochism is indulged by endlessly measuring present realities against a largely fictional past. Instead of giving strength and purpose, the national past – felt now only as a sense of loss – saps confidence and feeds self-doubt. This is one good reason for a sweeping reassessment of the English past, including the past of English cricket.

The neurosis of English cricket – visible in selection, in captaincy, in the whole approach of a generation of English players – is rooted in the trauma of national decline. Where players from other countries often find positive inspiration in representing their nations, for English players, national representation is an inhibiting burden. What haunts English cricketers is not so much the insatiable demand for national success, as the sheer pregnancy of meaning in national failure.

It seems as if history exerts a double squeeze on English cricket, top and bottom: lumbering the national side with a heavy burden of representation, while narrowing the game's popular base.

I sat in the 800-year-old ruins of a Native American ball court in Arizona, wearing my New York Yankee baseball cap (made in Korea) and thinking about cricket.

The ball game played here had a pedigree that makes cricket look like a parvenu. For some 2,000 years it was played over a one-million square-mile area, stretching from the isthmus of Panama to the south west of today's United States. It was played by both kings and commoners. At the height of its popularity, 16,000 rubber balls were imported every year from the coastal jungles to the Aztec capitals in central Mexico. Only a few days before my visit to the ruin, the descendants of the ancient Mayan rubber tappers had staged an armed rebellion against the Mexican state. Their anger was directed at the North American Free Trade Agreement, a symbol of the global market which threatened to destroy what was left of their traditional economy and enslave them, as surely as the conquistadors had done, to the economic priorities of a foreign elite.

When they first encountered the ancient game, the Spanish, to whom rubber was unknown, were awed by the bouncing balls, which seemed to have a life of their own. Players struck the ball with their hips, buttocks or knees (all of which were padded). The object was to direct the rapidly moving ball through the iron hoops attached to the side walls of the stone court.

The elite constructed ball courts for their own and for public use. They hired and played with professionals. Because of the complex scoring method, games were long. There was gambling on results. Sometimes, the game was used as an augury, a way of divining the will of the gods. It served also as a substitute for war or a means of settling civil conflicts. Rulers played it to acquire territory or tribute. Over the centuries, it also acquired a hieratic significance. It became the centrepiece of numerous religious rites, some of which involved human sacrifice.

The imagery of decapitation is carved all over the Central American ball courts. The ancient myths make clear that the ball game was a means of linking life on earth with the underworld where the deities resided. The ball symbolized the severed head, which was seen as animated and autonomous, forever seeking reunion with its headless body, often represented by the ball court itself. Both ball and head evoked the movements of sun and moon, rising out of and setting into the underworld.

As a game of constant motion (made possible by the rubber ball) it not only evoked the change of seasons, it was actually held responsible for them. Playing the game and performing its accompanying ritual were essential to appease the gods and preserve universal order.

What a terrible burden for a ball game!

The ball-game cult was a common denominator through otherwise diverse societies. Though its meaning changed over time and space, it remained a single recognizable game. It was the game itself that the people of pre-Conquest Central America must have loved, not its political and religious encumbrances.

Sitting in the ruins, I felt sorry that any game should be so bowed down. I felt convinced that the Central American ball game had a lesson for cricket: sport becomes more beautiful, more human, the more it liberates itself from ritual and tradition, the more it becomes itself without apologies.

I started to wonder: what if there were no cricket? What if it passed into history, as Rowland Bowen said it would, as the Central American ball game had? There are so many things I would miss.

A leg-spinner leaving a batsman floundering (the Schadenfreude of the googly), the arc of a straight six, the crisp, dismissive sound of a square cut, the sudden savagery of a stump uprooted by pace. The unredeemable tragedies of the dropped slip catch or mistimed hook. The humour of the game. The hapless tail-ender flat-footedly hoiking the unplayable fast bowler for six over midwicket. Sitting in the stands, missing the fall of a wicket, distracted by an article in the newspaper or some movement in the clouds, looking up, embarrassed, and wondering what has happened.

The solace of an empty county ground on a bright weekday morning.

What I would miss most of all would be the sublime waste of an entire day on something with no redeeming purpose whatsoever. The more I thought about it, the more I became convinced that this whole book was nothing but an elaborate attempt to justify that waste.

It seems that cricket will never be left to be just cricket. It is always asked to 'stand for' something more than itself. Here the anti-colonialist CLR James and the imperialist Lord Harris were in agreement. James was, in the end, a cricket traditionalist, for all his revolutionary commitment. His tortuous celebration of the public school games ethos tells us much about James, but also much about the contradictory role of cricket in colonial society. His highest claim on behalf of Frank Worrell was that he was a worthy disciple of the master who inspired *Tom Brown's School Days*.

Cricket is its own end. It is not, nor should it be, a means to an end: to private profit or national aggrandizement. The baggage of higher purpose, a telltale sign of English capital's perennial need to seek a noble rationale for its beastliness, weighs down on the game, suppressing its delightfully pointless beauty.

Benedict Anderson argues that the power of nationality lies in the fact that you cannot choose it. It elevates a personal destiny to a cause. My experience has made me wary of and fascinated by all nationalisms. I admit to having no loyalty whatsoever to the spirits people invoke when they pronounce the sacred names of 'England' or 'America'. So I suppose my loyalty, in the end, is to cricket, the game itself, that marvellous universal. It is a loyalty I never chose, which is why I am helpless in its grip.

Maybe I wind up at one with the old amateur ideologists, believing that what matters is playing the game, not winning or losing, not taking sides. Orwell defined 'serious sport' as 'war minus the shooting'. For that reason, he detested it, though for the same reason, many others love it. But the whole idea of sport as a substitute for war seems to me profoundly degrading. The equation trivializes both activities. Cricket is superior to war, not a substitute for it. It is self-evidently a more rational and mutually beneficial species of inter-national interaction. Those who would reduce it to war, or use it for warlike purposes, betray it. And nations which would use it to aggrandize themselves at the expense of others, will find, in the end, that the game itself springs surprising revenges. For all the tensions that run through it, cricket is an affirmation of a shared world. At times, its level playing field even points to a higher democracy, beyond nation and market.

Some will say that I have been as guilty as anyone of imposing my own prejudices on the game. But as the black cricketers in South Africa have taught us, it is impossible and undesirable to compartmentalize our lives, to separate our love of the game from our other loves (or hates). One of cricket's genuine claims is that it engages the whole human being, body, mind and heart. Much as we might like the game to become, once again, merely a game, any human activity as complex as cricket will always carry meanings and invite interpretation. Our aim should be to ensure that those meanings and interpretations are not a burden on but an extrapolation of the game's democratic essence. We cannot return to a pristine cricket which never existed. Instead, we should see in the game's inclusive premises, its autochthonous open-endedness, a rich realm of human possibility – a realm in which even England can find a place.

I do not believe that English cricket is doomed or that English Test teams will know only failure. But the revival of English cricket will have to mean a lot more than winning Test matches. Indeed, I suspect that learning new ways of losing Test matches will be part of the road to salvation. Revival is about more people playing the game, getting more joy out of it, seizing and remaking it for their own purposes, just as the elite seized and remade the peasant game in the eighteenth century. It is about playing the game to a higher standard, a standard not judged by winning or losing, but by degrees of invention and imagination. It is about exploring the limits of the game, and transgressing them.

I do not feel I have wandered far from cricket in this book. It was cricket itself which took me on all these excursions, which asked the questions, then contradicted the answers. The multiform, polysemous nature of the game kept slipping through my fingers. I have often felt as if I was trying to take a snapshot of a creature forever on the wing. I have come back again and again to the triangle of cricket, nation, market. For two hundred years, nation and market have nurtured and guided, pummelled and cudgelled cricket. Often, they have squabbled over it. And sometimes, gloriously, cricket has burst the boundaries they try to impose on it.

8

Cricket, Nation, Market
1994-1998

● *Cricket in a 'young country'* ● *The unequivocal Englishman*
● *Race, class, and libel* ● *The ostrich syndrome* ● *Radical status quo*
● *Tesco-isation* ● *The search for success and the re-branding*
of Britain ● *Home but not alone*

'We are not old duffers. We are a young, vibrant, modern and forward-looking organisation, made up of people with energy and vision.' Thus said Tim Lamb, Chief Executive of the England and Wales Cricket Board in March 1998, shortly after an industrial tribunal had ruled that this forward-looking organisation had sexually discriminated against Theresa Harrild, its former receptionist.

Lamb's *cri de coeur* was understandable. Over the last few years English cricket had been making belated but strenuous efforts to adapt to what it took to be the modern world. Even as he spoke, plans were afoot to stage floodlit matches at selected county grounds, only 20 years after Kerry Packer introduced floodlights in Australia and 42 years after English football adopted them. The old TCCB had been replaced by the new, stream-lined ECB, headed by Lord MacLaurin, the man who had put the Tesco chain at the top of the retailing heap. And although radical reform of the county championship seemed as far off as ever, at least the ECB had recognised that something had to be done about it.

Only weeks before the industrial tribunal Lamb had taken great pains to distance the ECB from the MCC's refusal, once again, to admit women to membership. On the eve of the MCC vote, the recently remodelled *Wisden Cricket Monthly* had observed: 'Cricket has a major image problem ... Football is perceived as vibrant, modern, youthful; cricket is not. The image is not entirely fair, but it is there and it will be massively reinforced if this vote goes the wrong way ...' The vote went the wrong way; although the exclusionists were reduced to a minority of voting members, they carried the day thanks to the MCC's requirement for two thirds support for rule changes. Speaking for the ECB, Tim Lamb disowned the MCC ('it is merely a private club') and assured the public that nothing would be allowed to stand in the way of the long-promised modernisation of the English game.

Now all Lamb's hard work to transform the image of English cricket had been suddenly torpedoed, and from such an unexpected source, a mere employee, and a woman at that. Harrild had told a tale straight out of a nineteenth century novel. Seduced and abandoned by a junior executive, pressed into having a abortion, she plunged into suicidal depression, only to find herself dismissed by an ECB official with a surreptitious pay-off and a final attempted grope. It's never easy for an employee to win an industrial tribunal, but in this case the panel declared unanimously that Harrild's account of life among the overgrown lads at Lord's was 'truthful'. Once again, English cricket was being made to look antediluvian by the people charged with preserving and promoting it. 'These Lord's cads should be run out,' fulminated the *Mirror*, which also observed that 'the sort of people who run this sport ... live in the past where women were there just for sex and acting as servants.' Even the *Daily Mail* got in on the act, running Harrild's confessions under the front page banner headline 'My sexism ordeal at Lord's'. Feminists noted it was the first time the *Mail* had ever been able to bring itself to use the word 'sexism' without scare quotes. So things were certainly changing, but not, it appeared, at Lord's, or at least not very quickly.

Industrial tribunals, unlike judges or juries, are charged not merely with ruling in favour or against a plaintiff but with uncovering the truth of the matter at hand; they have an inquisitorial role and they pursue it vigorously. Harrild and her witnesses were cross-examined in detail by the panel, who were also in possession of a written submission from the ECB's solicitors. The ECB declined to attend the hearing. Unlike Theresa Harrild, Lamb and his team were not prepared to subject themselves to cross-examination, nor to present any evidence that would corroborate their version of events. That didn't stop the ECB insinuating that, had they condescended to appear in the tribunal and play by the rules of the game, they would have won. With help from friendly journalists, Lamb launched a damage limitation exercise – airily dismissing the tribunal's findings, impugning Harrild's veracity – which as a species of unfair play seemed a lot more egregious than ball-tampering.

It seems that in English cricket the only people who are ever held to account for their mistakes are the players. A fortnight after the tribunal's ruling, Mike Atherton resigned from the England captaincy following his team's loss of another Test series to the West Indies. Atherton's reign had coincided with a generational change-over, both among players and selectors (indeed, the retiring generation of players quickly became the new generation of selectors.) It had survived the forlorn experiment with curmudgeonly autocracy under Ray Illingworth, and new manager David Lloyd and new chair of selectors David Graveney had placed training, coaching, and psychological preparation on a more scientific footing. Everyone agreed that things were much better than in the dark days of 1993, when Atherton had taken over from Gooch, but still, victories remained rare and consistency elusive. Indeed, under Atherton, England demonstrated a mercurial volatility that had it appeared in Pakistani, Indian or West Indian teams would have elicited familiar generalisations about other people's 'national character'. Atherton's four and a half year tenure at the top had been littered with false dawns and abject disasters. In the end, the harvest was just too meagre. Out of 52 tests, he had won only thirteen. Worse yet, out of 12 Test series he had won only three – against New Zealand home and away, and against India in England. On top of that there were dire one-day performances in Australia, South Africa, the World Cup, and Zimbabwe. Along the way, the England team managed to lose two major sponsors (Whittingdale and Tetley) and irritate their hosts in south Asia and southern Africa.

In the future, I suspect students of the game will be puzzled by Atherton's record-breaking hold on the captaincy. When he called it a day, there was hardly a whimper of regret in the media, and not one article urging him to soldier on, yet from his school days he had been hailed as a 'natural leader'. Like most cricket fans I found him an enigma. I enjoyed his batsmanship – there was always a lot happening when he was at the crease, if you watched carefully – and sympathised with his fuck-you attitude to the media. But too often he seemed grudging in defeat and insensitive to his hosts overseas. On the field, his tactical caution was understandable, but it didn't leave much for the fans to talk about. Although his fellow players backed him throughout, he seemed unable to inspire them in moments of crisis, and unable to get the best out of mavericks and loners. Despite occasional acrimony, he enjoyed a relatively benign press, and unlike his immediate predecessors received support throughout from nearly all the major broadsheet reporters and BBC commentators. There were a number of reasons for this, but one was simply the growing awareness that what was wrong with English cricket could not be put right by a single individual, and that the resources available to the England captain and selectors were limited. Since 1980, England have won only four of sixteen overseas series (two of those wins were against New Zealand). And they have not won a five Test series anywhere since 1987.

By 1998, nearly everyone in English cricket had had enough of the old ways and wanted something new. Modernisation became the mantra. Too many years of failure, too many empty promises had taken their toll on even the staunchest traditionalists. However, although it was widely conceded that some kind of radical change was needed, consensus on the details remained elusive. The discussion was haunted by a sense of *déja vu*. We have passed this way before: when the TCCB was formed to replace the MCC in 1968, when Ted Dexter and Micky Stewart established their England Committee in 1989. And still the dilemmas seem as far from being resolved as ever: do we need more or less 'professionalism'? What is the balance between the classic two-innings contest and the limited-overs one-day game? What is the 'England' represented by the England team, and where does it fit in cricket's new world order?

Somehow modernity seems to remain problematic for the English, and Tony Blair's strenuous grasping at its totems and tokens only confirms this uncomfortable fact. Like the New Labour Government, the MacLaurin regime has so far proved stronger on the rhetoric of national renewal than the reality. And like England itself, English cricket has found the high road to modernisation speckled with potholes and elongated by unexpected detours.

The Saturday of the Lord's Test against West Indies, 1995. I was sitting high up in the Mound Stand with my friend, Suresh Grover, perusing the July issue of *Wisden Cricket Monthly*, which had just hit the news-stands. Keith Arthurton was nursing the West Indies tail, pushing the first innings total past England's 283, and the atmosphere was somnolent. West Indies supporters were few and far between, as they were to be throughout that summer, driven from England's Test grounds by bans on banners and musical instruments, advance credit card bookings, and exorbitant prices. In the *Guardian*, drama critic and cricket-lover Michael Billington bemoaned the 'vaguely apartheid atmosphere' which had descended upon the venerable headquarters of cricket.

As the full-time Co-ordinator of the Southall Monitoring Group, Suresh spends his days working with people who have suffered racial harassment, domestic violence, or unjust treatment at the hands of police, housing authorities, employers or immigration officials. He is used to standing up to bullies and bureaucrats. And he has never been afraid to speak out against those people within his own community who would divide it along religious or communal lines. Although his parents came from the sub-continent and he grew up in Bradford, he's a West Indies fan. Not merely because his experience in this country has led him to subscribe to the 'Anyone but England' theory, but because he had been won over by the style, success and cohesion of the great West Indies teams of the 70s and 80s.

David Frith, the editor of *WCM*, had been an outspoken critic of those teams and their fast-bowling strategy. In the latest issue, reviewing *Real Quick*, a tribute to the great west Indies pace masters by Alastair McLellan and Michelle Savidge, he disparaged the famous four-prong attack as 'morally indefensible'. His verdict on the achievements catalogued in the book was tersely dismissive: 'Holding was usually magnificent – as was Wes Hall before him – and Garner and Ambrose were fortunate to be endowed with such long limbs. That will suffice.'

I had been reading *WCM* since its launch in 1979. Back then, it was a welcome alternative to *The Cricketer*, brighter, sharper, and more up-to-date. Sadly, over the years, the magazine had been soured by Frith's increasingly cranky approach not only to West Indies quicks, but also towards Pakistanis (fans as well as players) and the South African question. Nonetheless I had remained a loyal reader. On my way to my seat, I had picked up a copy of the new issue at the Lord's shop, noting the cover headline *'Racism and National Identity'*, and fearing the worst.

Now, as the West Indies tail wagged, I turned to page nine, and found an article entitled 'IS IT IN THE BLOOD?'. The author was Robert Henderson (a name that meant nothing to me) and his text was illustrated with photos of Geoff Greenidge (captioned 'the last white player to represent West Indies') and Phil DeFreitas (captioned 'to England at 10'). I read its 2000 words with growing disbelief and when I had finished, went back to the start and read the whole piece again. Disbelief turned to anger. I handed the article to Suresh, whose head twitched in irritation as his eyes ran up and down the columns. 'My god, how can they get away with that crap?' he asked, handing me back the magazine as if it was a piece of rotten meat. We talked for a while about the arguments in the article, why they were pernicious, and what we should do about them. Reading Henderson so inflamed Suresh's bias against England that he refused to be impressed by Darren Gough's amazing, near horizontal leap to catch Arthurton at long leg and put an end to the West Indies innings at 324.

The following Monday, England bowled out West Indies a second time to level the series. Dominic Cork took 7-42, the best England Test debut ever, and became the latest in English cricket's long line of media-elevated messiahs, a burden which would nearly crush him in the coming years. As I listened to Test Match Special, I made photocopies of the Henderson article and sent them, along with a covering letter, to about twenty individuals whom I knew shared a love of cricket and a commitment to racial justice. Most were people active in anti-racist organisations or community groups, some were MPs and trade unionists, and a few were journalists. I urged them to write to *WCM* about the Henderson article, as well as to Mike Atherton (who was a member of the *WCM* Editorial Board), and suggested it was time we did something about challenging racism in cricket. I also wrote a letter to *WCM* myself, in which I argued that 'Is it in the blood' was 'illogical, ignorant, and bigoted.' I had no idea that it would prove only a drop in the postal torrent which *WCM* was to receive in response to the article. Frith admitted it was by far his biggest mailbag ever, running 9-1 against Henderson.

Later, it was often reported that Henderson's piece had precipitated a furore because it suggested that 'foreign-born' players lacked commitment to England. Frith claimed his critics had not read the article, or had misrepresented it. This was wishful thinking. Those who studied Henderson's contribution in its entirety were the most likely to be concerned by the decision to publish it.

Frith's stand-first labelled it an examination 'from a cricketing viewpoint – of the sensitive matters of racism and national identity.' The author commences his treatment of a topic he describes as 'long overdue for honest discussion' with complaints about the West Indies board's alleged discrimination against Asians and whites. Promptly stretching credulity to breaking point, he asserts that 'those who control the first-class cricket of the white Test-playing nations are drawn from the liberal elites'. Under their aegis, 'only one public line on racism in cricket is tolerated, namely that only whites may be racist.' Why was South Africa singled out when so many other nations 'do not have clean racial hands'? 'How many non-Muslims have played for Pakistan, or Tamils for Sri Lanka? ... How many untouchables have played for India?' (By the way, the answer in all three cases is a few, but not enough). For Henderson, 'racially and culturally determined selection' is ubiquitous and those who deny it are hypocrites.

But does he object to such policies? Apparently not, because the rest of his article tries to make a case for England practising the most rigorous 'racially and culturally determined selection'. Addressing a *WCM* correspondent who had argued that it was wrong to lump DeFreitas and Ramprakash in with cricket migrants from southern Africa like Smith and Hick, Henderson boldly nails his colours to the mast:

> 'If I were to take the coward's way, I could point out that DeFreitas came to England at quite an advanced age (around 10) ... I could say, of course, I was not referring to Ramprakash ... because he was born and bred here. But those would be weasel words.'

Henderson then quotes Matthew Engel's observation in the 1995 *Wisden*: 'It cannot be irrelevant to England's long-term failures that so many of their recent Test players were either born overseas and/or spent their formative years as citizens of other countries.' He omits Engel's crucial caveat ('It is not a question of race') and explicitly rejects his inclusiveness: 'An Asian or a negro raised in England will, according to the liberal, feel exactly the same pride and identification with the place as a white man. The reality is entirely different.' Most of the rest of the article is dedicated to proving that blacks and Asians, wherever born or raised, can never be 'culturally' English and can never feel 'a deep, unquestioning commitment to England'.

> 'Norman Tebbitt's cricket test is as pertinent for players as it is for spectators. It is even possible that part of a coloured England-qualified player feels satisfaction (perhaps subconsciously) at seeing England humiliated, because of post-imperial myths of oppression and exploitation.'

Henderson points to 'the generally resentful and separatist mentality of the West Indian-descended population in England, and urges doubters to cast their minds back to the riots of the 1980s, take a stroll around Brixton, Deptford, Hackney, Moss Side, St Paul's *et al*, and think of Haringey Cricket College which has had few if any white members ... There would seem to be no obvious reason why players such as DeFreitas and Lewis should not share the mentality [of] the general West Indian derived population.' Worse yet is the negative impact 'the interlopers have on the unequivocally English players and consequently on team spirit'. Henderson is quite certain that 'mixed groups' can never 'develop the same camaraderie as 11 unequivocal Englishmen.' In sum, 'the problem for the England selectors is perhaps similar to that facing England as a nation.' The establishment has 'conspired' to 'remove any sense of pride or sense of place in the hearts of those who are unequivocally English ... Indeed, perhaps even some of the unequivocally English players lack a sufficient sense of pride in playing for England.' In a closing peroration which should have set alarm bells ringing the moment it crossed the *WCM* editorial desk, Henderson asserts:

> 'For a man to feel the pull of 'cricketing patriotism' he must be so imbued with a sense of cultural belonging that it is second nature to go beyond the call of duty ... is that desire to succeed *instinctive* [Henderson's italics], a matter of biology? There lies the heart of the matter.'

Later, Matthew Engel described the Henderson article as 'densely argued'. Dense it certainly was – crammed with small evasions and Big Lies, stereotypes and sneers – but where was the argument? The only logic underpinning the article's twists and turns, its piling of non-sequitor upon innuendo, was the logic of racism, and the leap in the last paragraph from culture to biology – highlighted in the headline chosen by Frith – was characteristic of the piece as a whole, as of so much far right rhetoric. To me, the article seemed a veritable catalogue of exhausted racist casuistries, bristling with resentment, stuffed with the pseudo-sociological paranoia of the bigot at sea in the modern cosmopolis, and replete with the venerable fascist mantra about the 'liberal elite' betraying the national heritage.

I had sent the Henderson article to Kevin Mitchell, the *Observer* sports writer, whom I had met the year before and whose gutsy and compassionate features I admired. Kevin told me he found the piece pretty outrageous, wanted to know who this Henderson bloke was (I couldn't help him there) and said he was going to do a news story about it the following Sunday. He also told me that the article had caused a stir in the Derbyshire dressing room, and that Adrian Rollins, the county's opening bat (and Haringey Cricket College graduate), had written an angry letter to *WCM*. When the story appeared on the *Observer's* front page under the headline 'Cricket world divided by 'negro' loyalty row', I was taken aback. I thought the publication of the article in *WCM* was important, but not that important, which probably just showed how inured even I had become to the appearance of dubious racial propaganda in the cricket media. Kevin reported that the *WCM* office had been 'inundated with calls and letters'. Frith was surprised by the reaction but defended the article: 'Some people are scared [of this issue]. It's healthier out in the open ...' Kevin had also sought a comment from Matthew Engel, editor of *Wisden Cricketers' Almanack* and a member of the *WCM* editorial board:

> 'I can't go along with everything that Mr Henderson says, as I'd never heard of
> him before. But the question of nationality and sport is a legitimate one, as
> anyone observing Wimbledon or Test cricket can see. There is a problem of
> how you marry the wider question of race and nationality into the narrow
> issue of sporting patriotism. I'm not sure it helps if you scream 'racist' when
> someone make a contribution to that debate.'

So far the only public statements about the issue had come from Frith
and Henderson. So just who was doing the 'screaming'? In the next day's
Guardian, Paul Foot (to whom I had also posted the Henderson piece)
decried Henderson's case as 'quack segregationist 'science' of the type
which flourished under the Third Reich.' Responding to Engel's
statement in the *Observer*, he added, 'I'm not sure it helps either if liberal
journalists respond to the most blatant racialism by covering up for it.'
Extraordinarily, Engel had seen Foot's column before it went to press and
was able to reply in his own column in the same paper on the same day.
Here he defended Frith's right to 'edit as he sees fit'. The Henderson article
was 'a curious one'. It was 'strange that he should use the word 'negroes',
which is now widely regarded as offensive outside far right wing political
circles.' Engel dismissed Henderson's mutterings about 'instinct' and
'biology' as 'drivel', but went on to argue that there is a 'difference
between team games and individual sports'. Foot had derided
Henderson's claim that a dressing room of 'six Englishman, two west
Indians, two southern Africans and a New Zealander' could not develop
'the same camaraderie as 11 unequivocal Englishmen'. Here, insisted
Engel, it was Foot who was 'talking drivel'. He argued that 'teams that
flog their guts out for their country habitually do better than collections
of individuals whose sole aim is to further their own careers. This is one
of the reasons England cricket teams lose more often than they win.'

For Engel, this failing was one facet of a broader problem with British
identity. Recalling the way Michael Slater kissed the Australian insignia
on his helmet after scoring his maiden Test century at Lord's in 1993,
Engel declared: 'It is hard, no, impossible to imagine either Graeme Hick
or Phil DeFreitas doing the same – in the unlikely event of them
summoning the resolution to produce a similar performance.' In the
Financial Times, Michael Spinaker responded: 'DeFreitas has lived in
England since the start of secondary school. Are these not a cricketer's
formative years? And if it is the years before that are formative, would

Engel accept as English a player who had lived in Australia since, say, the age of ten? I doubt it.'

I've puzzled for some time over what Engel meant by insisting on the division between individual and team sports. The implicit argument seemed to be that a 'foreigner' (however defined) might well succeed in English or British colours at the 100 meters or singles tennis or boxing, but as a member of a football or cricket or rugby team (hard to say where Britain's 4x400 relay team would fit in) he or she would be likely to detract from the cultural cohesion necessary for victory. The only practical upshot of Engel's analysis (one which I assume he would oppose) would be a programme to screen out players with insufficient commitment to the national cause. To many people, national identity and national commitment are self-evident phenomena, but the impossibility of devising an unbiased measurement of either quality suggests that, as so often, the self-evident is merely the illusory.

The saddest aspect of the Engel analysis is its assumption that diversity – racial, cultural, national, even linguistic – is an insuperable obstacle to the forging of a common purpose on the field of play. Across western Europe all the big football clubs are not only multi-racial, but multi-national, and often polyglot. This has not inhibited them on the field nor has it diminished the fervour of supporters. The great West Indies sides of the 70s and 80s comprised players from as many as seven different countries, as well as players with diverse racial, cultural and religious associations. Of course, there were tensions among them. But when the tensions were transcended, the unity in diversity of the team was clearly a source of inspiration. It has been to the West Indies team's advantage that it represents an aspiration towards West Indian unity, a desire to fashion a broader, more inclusive identity. It has been to the England team's disadvantage that just about the only time English national identity is invoked, as in the Henderson Affair, it is with the purpose of excluding someone because of his colour or country of origin.

Engel insisted that the 'legitimate debate' he sought was one arising from professional sportspersons competing under flags of convenience, people like Greg Rusedski, Zola Budd, Graeme Hick or Robin Smith. 'Like many people in cricket, I am concerned that it is too easy for players to choose which Test team they will represent, even if their connection with the country is marginal.' But by yoking together DeFreitas and Hick, Engel himself blurred the critical dividing line between these two very different 'debates'. And it was surely telling that in the 'debate' which ensued there was not a single specific proposal for an amendment to the existing eligibility rules. In the absence of such a proposal, what was the point of this 'legitimate debate'?

Personally, I think it's a shame people give the Lambs, Smiths and Hicks such a hard time. Certainly cricket fans have no reason to complain. They came to England because of the exceptional conditions which faced top class southern African cricketers in the 70s and 80s. Out of loyalty to their families and a natural desire to make the most of their talents, they committed their working lives to England. Mostly, they did so without fanfare or false ardour. They escaped the personal consequences of the international boycott of apartheid, but, unlike the English players who travelled in the opposite direction, they did not break sanctions or aid the apartheid regime. South Africa's loss was England's gain.

Of course, there is a fundamental distinction between these 'mercenaries' and DeFreitas or Malcolm or the vast majority of Asian and black cricketers earning a living in the English first-class game. These players were either born in Britain or came here with their parents as children. They did not come to England to play cricket. But as soon as 'Englishness' is defined not by simple quantifiable rules of birth or residence, the line dividing these two groups gets blurred. The search for 'cultural cohesion' opens a Pandora's Box, releasing an army of demons. And the demand that the England Test team show itself to be truly English (and for some commentators the only way they can do that is by winning more often) merely succeeds in saddling English cricket with yet another sentimental-cum-moral burden.

As someone who had relished Engel's sardonic coverage of cricket's South African imbroglio, I was disappointed with his apparent inability to grasp the malice and menace implied in Henderson's article, and aghast at his efforts to justify its publication in a cricket magazine. I wrote a piece in the *Guardian* saying as much, and Engel retorted that I had distorted his views 'in order to have a simple target'. I am afraid I remain convinced that the confusions permeating Engel's views on race and nationality were his own responsibility, not mine. The simple target would have been Robert Henderson, but I was more concerned with the real question raised by the article: how such dangerous, divisive and downright silly ideas had come to be treated with respect within the cricket world.

Outside that world, condemnation of Henderson's views was virtually unanimous. Black sports stars found nothing ambiguous in the article, and could see no justification for printing it. 'It's not part of a legitimate debate,' said Victor Ubogu, 'It's crap.' Rightly, they saw no reason why their commitment to the sides they played for should be questioned or why they should have to prove their national loyalty. Even Norman Tebbit was quick to draw a clear distinction between Henderson's views and his cricket test, whose aim was 'to promote national integration'. He called Malcolm and DeFreitas 'nothing but a credit' in their efforts for the national side. In an editorial, *The Times* deplored the 'ugly article' and 'the irresponsibility of the magazine's editor' in giving credence to an analysis as 'impoverished and execrable' as Henderson's.

Within a week of the *Observer* article, Henderson's tortured logic had been dissected and denounced across the political spectrum. Malcolm and DeFreitas threatened to sue for libel. Mike Atherton told journalists during the truncated third test at Edgbaston (on an uneven pitch, West Indies bowled England out twice within two days) that he had resigned from the *WCM* Editorial Board. 'I disapprove not only of the views expressed in the article but also its inclusion in the magazine.'

Frith found himself at the centre of a national controversy, his editorial policy under a type of scrutiny with which he was entirely unfamiliar. On 7th July, in a statement issued through the Press Association, he admitted publication of Henderson's article was an 'error of judgement' and offered 'unreserved apologies to all whose sensibilities have been offended'. He had hoped the article would be 'a springboard for beneficial debate' and blamed the furore it had caused on 'distortions in certain sections of the media'. He told Kevin Mitchell, 'I've been up there like a dart board on Henderson's behalf and I've had enough of it.' The August issue of *WCM* included two pages of letters critical of Henderson and articles by Brearley and Gower debunking Henderson's unreal view of top-class sporting competition. 'The unconscious is a hybrid and elusive beast,' wrote Brearley, 'Mr Henderson's attempts to expose it in others reveal more about his than theirs.' Gower was equally derisive. 'Without being unpatriotic, I think the notion of 'national pride' has been over-rated ... Motivation comes from many sources, and a player's determination to do well is an individual quality.'

Frith's editorial was headlined 'Who needs ancestors?' (a reference to Voltaire: 'Whoever serves his country well has no need of ancestors'). It struck a defensive posture from the beginning and never abandoned it. 'Robert Henderson's article did not place a question mark beside foreign-born England cricketers. It was already there. Reservations have rumbled round the cricket grounds and in the sports columns of the newspapers for several years.' His purpose in publishing the Henderson article, Frith now claimed, was to 'dismiss' these reservations so that 'so that cricketers and other sportsmen could be cleansed of suspicion about commitment.' He attributed the negative public reaction to 'the somewhat cold nature of Mr Henderson's language' and blamed the press for shifting 'the grounds of debate from national identity exclusively to race' (though it was Henderson himself who had told the *Evening Standard*, 'Personally I would not select Asians or blacks. It is a particular problem with team sports.') Frith then quoted with approval Bill Deedes, the high Tory former *Daily Telegraph* editor, who had loftily declared that the commentators had all got 'the wrong end of the stick' in the Henderson affair. Sounding increasingly like a *Private Eye* parody of himself, Deedes explained, 'It is cosmopolitanism, not colour, which dilutes loyalty.' Neither Deedes nor Frith seemed to be aware that 'cosmopolitanism' was the charge levied by Nazi propagandists against Jews and leftists, whose loyalties, they claimed, were not exclusively to the German nation-state.

The Henderson Affair fascinated the media. It had all the elements: race and national identity, Englishness and cricket, the hallowed name of Wisden. Pundits had a field day. Within the cricket world there was shock and confusion. No one wanted to be associated with Henderson, and very few were prepared to defend Frith's editorial choices. But the overall tone was defensive. Many writers, commentators, administrators and players were deeply uncomfortable at the sudden and unexpected spotlight thrown on their little world, a world in which assumptions about race and nation had hitherto remained unexamined. Tim Rice turned apoplectic when he received an appeal from Hit Racism for Six, a group founded in the wake of the Henderson Affair to campaign against racism in cricket. Rice accused the group of creating a problem where none existed. Cricket, he claimed, was 'one of the least racist features of British society.' Most cricket correspondents I spoke to during that summer were at pains to insist that Henderson was merely an aberration and had received far too much attention.

So how did 'Is It In The Blood?' end up in *WCM*? An indefatigable correspondent, Henderson had for some time been bombarding the good and the great of the cricket world with essays expounding his views and statistical tables purporting to support them. According to Henderson, it was Frith who had first made contact with him, after seeing one of his broadsides, and had asked him to contribute to *WCM*. The result was an article, published in 1991, entitled 'A Fundamental Malaise', in which Henderson argued that cricketers ought to possess 'an instinctive allegiance to a culture' and questioned Nasser Hussain's right to play for

England because of a statement he had made to the effect that he felt 'Indian'. Responding to a letter of complaint from Nasser's mother, Shireen Hussain, Henderson explained, 'It is essentially an aesthetic judgement. The inclusion of south Africans, west Indians and an Indian in recent XIs offends my sense of rightness or proportion, just as a badly-drawn picture or self-conscious acting performance does.' In 1993, he sent out an analysis of 'England Qualified Interlopers Test records', sub-divided into 'colour players' (Cowans, DeFreitas, Hussain, Ramprakash, Small, Malcolm, Lawrence) and 'white players' (Caddick, Hick, Lamb, Smith). He provided a further county-by -county breakdown of 'foreign personnel', among whom he classified 'White players with little or no British childhood experience' and 'those with Negro or Asian blood wherever born.' He was also careful to segregate 'white south African' from 'coloured south Africans' (Nigel Felton and Damien D'Oliveira).

I suspect if most people found this sort of material in their letter box their response would not be to write to Henderson politely expressing 'interest' or 'sympathy' with his arguments or averring 'I agree with you up to a point'. But that is exactly what a surprising number of cricket writers and commentators did. Henderson claimed that 'two thirds of all the national newspaper cricket writers' shared his views and was enraged at what he saw as their pusillanimity in not coming to his aid in his hour of need. Of course, he was wildly over-eager to snatch at any sign of approbation or even mere forbearance as proof that his views had been endorsed in full. Nonetheless, the inability of so many educated people to spot a rank racist crank when confronted with one was testimony to the myopic insensitivity that still afflicts the cricket establishment, especially when it comes to issues of race or nation.

In 1994 Frith had written to Henderson: 'How can a true Englishman ever see this as his representative side despite all the chat about the commitment of the immigrant?' As Frith himself has noted with some irritation, this sentiment was by no means confined to contributors to *WCM*. Reporting England's victory over West Indies in the Lord's Test, the *Independent* commented: 'What made it additionally pleasing was that England's attack did not for once look like a United Nations strike force. Not since the Old Trafford Test of 1989 ... have England fielded five bowlers (or any amount come to that) with undiluted allegiance to the country they were representing.'

The vexed question of allegiance swirled around the six-hitting exploits of young Gloucestershire batsman Andrew Symonds throughout the summer of 1995. Symonds, black and Birmingham-born, had moved to Australia at 18 months of age. Under ICC rules he was eligible to play for England, but earlier in the year he had told British journalists, 'I'm a fair dinkum Aussie.' There was much debate about whether he should or should not be selected to play for England. Graham Gooch, that part-time patriot, was vociferously opposed. Symonds had no commitment to 'the English way of life', unlike Gooch's friend Lamb, whose commitment was evinced, Gooch argued, by his love of fishing and hunting. Symonds wanted to keep his options open (not least so that he could continue to play for Gloucestershire, which would become difficult if he were reclassified as an overseas player), but by selecting him for that winter's England A-tour, Ray Illingworth forced him to choose. The *Guardian's* cricket writers described the choice as a matter of 'conscience', as if it would have been somehow immoral or dishonest for Symonds to opt to play for England.

Once again a player's inner motivations, his sense of self and his social identity were being scrutinised from the outside in a search for impurities. In the end, Symonds rejected Illingworth's offer and returned to Australia. In December, the TCCB altered its eligibility rules. From now on players with dual nationality would have to sign a declaration that they had no 'desire or intention to play cricket for any country outside the European Community'.

In the face of a globalised economy and migrant workforces, loyalty oaths are unlikely to resolve English cricket's self-induced crisis of national identity. But the cricket authorities were not alone in seeking to re-enforce the line of divide between the English and the not-English. Even as the Henderson Affair was rippling through the sports pages, the National Curriculum chief Nick Tate was voicing concerns about the dilution of British national identity. 'We've become apologetic about the majority mainstream culture ... we belong to one country and if membership of it is to mean anything we have to have a common culture' – a culture which in his view was explicitly Christian. Chris Woodhead, the Chief Inspector of schools, agreed. 'A clear sense of national identity gives a country collective strength'. Like Henderson, Bill Deedes and many others, Woodhead proclaimed himself strongly opposed to 'some watered-down cosmopolitan mish-mash'.

As in cricket, so in politics; the quest for national identity merely revealed national insecurity. Tate, Woodhead, Frith, Deedes (not to mention Henderson): none of them could grasp the underlying truth that the unresolved conflicts within the nation are the nation, and the only vigorous nation is one that is in formation, merrily borrowing from all and sundry.

During that summer of 1995, West Indian pace bowlers were variously described by British newspapers as 'muggers' and 'savage'. Glyn Woodman, then Surrey's Chief Executive, explained why he expected relatively few black faces at this year's Oval Test, in decades past West Indies' home away from home: 'Twenty years ago parts of this ground were almost no-go areas. They could sit wherever they liked and all get together and they can't do that now because of pre-selling of tickets.' At the Test itself, private security guards confiscated miniature flags and whistles from West Indian supporters while allowing white spectators to bring in champagne bottles. During the Headingley Test, commentator Henry Blofeld referred on air to people watching the match from buildings outside the ground as occupying the 'Jewish seats' (he apologised and was officially reprimanded). At the NatWest semi-final between Yorkshire and Northamptonshire, Anil Kumble was subjected to prolonged and raucous racial abuse (which, a steward reported, emanated as much from the executive boxes as the notorious Western Terrace).

As always, it is impossible to understand events in the backwater of cricket without considering the broader ebb and flow of the times. And during the summer of 1995 the Henderson Affair was only one among many reminders that racism is alive and well in modern Britain. In May, Brian Douglas, a black man, died after being struck on the head by police using new US-style batons in Kennington, not far from the Oval. In June, Asian youths in the Manningham district of Bradford took to the streets for three days following the wrongful arrest of teenagers playing a noisy game of football. An enquiry later blamed the riot on the 'arrogance and ignorance' of local police. In July, the Commissioner of the Metropolitan Police singled out black youths as 'muggers', relying on statistical evidence nearly as spurious as Henderson's, and launched Operation Eagle Eye – a police sweep explicitly aimed at a particular section of the community, defined by colour.

The Tory Government announced yet another crackdown on illegal immigrants and launched their Asylum and Immigration Bill, which sought to deny welfare benefits to asylum seekers. According to the British Crime Survey, there had been a 50% increase in racial incidents over the previous five years. A TUC report revealed that blacks with university degrees remained twice as likely to be unemployed as whites with the same qualifications, and that 66% of black employees were being paid a lower hourly rate than white workers doing similar jobs.

Another report showed that black children were being excluded from state schools at a rate six times that of whites. Meanwhile, Childline, the children's charity, revealed that racial abuse was a common experience for children from ethnic minority backgrounds, and a major cause of mental illness. It seemed that all over the country, an awful lot of people were paying a heavy price for not looking like Robert Henderson's idea of an unequivocal Englishman.

Frith's half-hearted apology did not deter Malcolm and DeFreitas, and in September *WCM's* lawyers read out a statement in court in which they apologised for printing the article, disassociated the magazine 'entirely from the allegations' made by Henderson, and agreed to pay 'substantial damages' to both plaintiffs. Damages were also subsequently paid to Chris Lewis.

David Graveney, Secretary of the Professional Cricketers' Association, had advised Malcolm and DeFreitas not to sue. Undeterred, the two players sought and received assistance from the Professional Footballers' Association, a body both more independent of management and less frightened of the issue of racism than the PCA. 'I felt strongly that this sort of thing must be brought out into the open and dealt with before it takes root,' said Malcolm. 'Look at the problems football has with racism. I had a chance to do my bit to stop that happening in cricket. Too many things have been swept under the carpet in the past but the problem is eventually the bump under the carpet gets so big you fall over it.'

Malcolm started playing cricket seriously only after his move from Jamaica to Sheffield at the age of 15. Not surprisingly, at every stage of his subsequent career, he has been a late starter. Thanks to Sheffield's Caribbean Sports Club, he was able to progress into the local leagues, but because of Yorkshire CCC's 'Yorkshire-born only' rule, he ended up signing for Derbyshire. His 9 for 57 against South Africa at the Oval was often cited during the Henderson Affair as some kind of scientific and therefore decisive refutation of Henderson's arguments. But the triumphant flourishing of Malcolm's match-winning effort raised more questions than it answered. It still harked back to the quaint notion that people's loyalties can be tested and proven, as if by some inquisitorial trial: throw him in at the Pavilion end and see if he takes wickets. If he does, he's a loyal black, but if he doesn't? Is the 'Englishness' of those who fail to deliver on the big occasions somehow 'equivocal'?

As so often in this debate, people were desperately seeking some measurement, some standard, of that notorious will o' the wisp, national identity. And as ever, when people seek certainty in a realm of ambiguity, their attempts to impose standards merely reveal their own prejudices. In his autobiography, Frith agrees that at the Oval Malcolm 'was totally committed to England's cause, even though he was Jamaican born and even though he told *The Cricketer* in an April 1995 interview that his heroes were Viv Richards, Michael Holding and Richard Hadlee, and that his favourite music was rhythm and blues, soul, funk and reggae.' The latter preference, of course, is one Malcolm shares with millions of white English youths, and Frith's assumption that it was somehow alien to Englishness merely confirmed what a poor view of contemporary reality you get from the comfort of a cricket press box.

After winning the apology and damages from *WCM*, Malcolm set off with the England party to South Africa, where he was lionised in the townships and greeted by Nelson Mandela with the words, 'So you are the destroyer.' But the man most feared by the South African batsmen fell out with Ray Illingworth and bowling coach Peter Lever, who staged a press conference by the side of their hotel pool to tell the world that 'the destroyer' was useless. Apparently they had been trying to change the bowling action with which the 32-year old Malcolm had already taken more than 100 Test wickets and were peeved at his resistance to their directions. Dropped from the side for most of the series, Malcolm was called back for the final match at Cape Town, where he was expected to come up with the goods at a moment of crisis. Unable to dismiss the tail-enders with the new ball, he was blamed for England's loss of the Test and with it the series. 'If you can't bowl out the last pair with the new ball you don't deserve to win,' declared Illingworth, but surely the point was that if you can't score more than 153 runs on a good pitch in the first innings of a Test, you ought not to blame your bowlers for losing the game.

Having endured what he later described as 'the worst three months of my life', Malcolm aired his grievances in the *Daily Express*. For the first time, he wondered aloud (as had many in the black community) whether his shabby treatment by the England management might have anything to do with his colour. The cricket media – which had been appalled at Illingworth's inept man management, and had largely defended Malcolm against Lever's charges – now turned as one to dismiss the idea out of hand. David Gower suggested that Malcolm had been 'got at' by people from outside the game. No one stopped to ask why the usually cautious Malcolm, hitherto highly reluctant to discuss the question of race in public, should feel driven to make such a statement. And nobody paused to answer the serious question he posed: would he have been treated the same if he were white? Neither the cricket authorities nor the press was prepared even to consider the possibility that the answer might be 'no'. Certainly, Dermot Reeve's account of the South African tour, published some months later, would have done nothing to relieve Malcolm's suspicions:

> 'All I can say is that Illy referred to Devon as 'Nig-nog' in the nets in Port Elizabeth. It came after Devon had bowled out of turn. It wasn't directed at Devon, but I heard Illingworth utter the word in exasperation. That may appear a racist comment when set down on paper, but possibly Illingworth didn't realise the significance of what he was saying. He is not a subtle man.'

It should go without saying, but in the cricket world it doesn't, that allegations of racism ought to be treated seriously and investigated objectively; and if any truth is found in them appropriate action should be taken. Instead, Malcolm was punished by the TCCB for breaking the gagging clause in his contract, as was Illingworth when he responded to Malcolm's claims.

Malcolm's up-and-down career with England seems to have endeared him to fans of all colours. Like Phil Tufnell, he is seen as fallible, vulnerable, and something of an outsider. When Northamptonshire signed him up for the 1998 season, in one of the highest pay deals ever secured by a county cricketer, club officials justified the expense by explaining that Malcolm was now 'the most popular cricketer in the country.'

In January 1996 Frith was sacked by the *WCM* management. In his autobiography he portrays himself as the victim of 'a collaborative manoeuvre'. As one of many individuals singled out for rough treatment in this pained and profoundly aggrieved book, I'd like to make clear that I think it's a pity the cricket establishment effectively embargoed it, refusing even to review a major effort by one of the game's leading historians. However, the autobiography does confirm the obsessive character of Frith's self-declared 'fascination' with questions of national identity. He proudly quotes from the letter of complaint he sent me in the midst of the Henderson Affair: 'My father and two uncles fought the Nazis, while German bombs fell close to my childhood home. Your native land was still pondering the options.' I had replied that since I was born in 1953, I could hardly be held responsible for the vagaries of US foreign policy 1939-41! The obvious point – that the merits of an argument do not rest on the national (or racial or religious) background of the individual who is making them – seemed to be lost on Frith. Bizarrely, he speculated that I may have conspired against him with my 'compatriot', J Paul Getty, *WCM's* proprietor.

In his editor's notes to the 1996 *Wisden Cricketers' Almanack* (also owned by Getty), Matthew Engel reported that *WCM* had 'made the mistake' of publishing Henderson's article. Nonetheless, he still insisted that 'it is reasonable to believe that not everyone who has chosen to regard himself as English has done so out of any deep patriotic commitment'. Therefore, 'the qualification rules should be tightened'. He did not say how. As for Robert Henderson, who felt he had been crucified merely for saying what others were thinking, in early 1997 he was investigated by police for sending 'race hate' letters to Tony and Cherie Blair. Officers from the Met told the *Mirror*, 'the language is very basic, direct and insulting.'

'No one can deny that this case is emotionally charged. Issues of race, class and country move in and out of it like black clouds.' Thus George Carman QC, summing up for the defence in the High Court, five days after Pakistan had bowled out England (taking the last eight wickets for 75 runs) to win the 1996 Lord's Test.

It was the first Test encounter between the two sides since the ball-tampering summer of 1992. Of all the after-shocks of that episode, none caused more media uproar, and none was more curious, than the libel action brought by Ian Botham and Allan Lamb against Imran Khan. For the English cricket authorities, and most cricket commentators, the case was a distressing embarrassment. 'Old coals that have been raked over too often,' in the words of Christopher Martin-Jenkins. Everyone was keen to avoid any rehearsal of the unpleasantness of 1992. Cricket relations between the two countries were to be placed on a fresh footing, epitomised by the amicable entente between the two captains, Lancashire team-mates Akram and Atherton, regarded as more worldly operators than their 1992 predecessors, Javed Miandad and Graham Gooch.

Imran, who had retired from cricket shortly before that series, was distressed by the accusations levelled against his countrymen, and defended them in a series of newspaper articles and television appearances. From the beginning, he argued that the laws on ball-tampering were ill-defined, that the practise in one form or another was commonplace in professional cricket and that it was therefore invidious to single out the Pakistanis as offenders. Then, in a biography by Ivo Tenant published in May 1994, he admitted that in a forgotten English county match in 1981 he had used a bottle top to scratch the surface of the ball so that it would swing. In making this confession, Imran's aim had been to widen the debate, to highlight its ambiguities and double standards, but he succeeded only in inflaming the controversy, and indeed, to many, his remarks suggested that Allan Lamb had been right all along. Certainly Lamb himself saw it this way. In the *Sun*, he accused Imran of 'teaching' Wasim and Waqar how to 'cheat'. In the *Mirror*, Ian Botham called on the ICC to discipline Imran and demanded his resignation from the newly-established ICC advisory committee of leading former Test cricketers (a course which Imran was to follow, for his own reasons, in the days ahead).

A week later, Imran hit back in the *Sun*. In an interview, he claimed that 'all the biggest names' in cricket had somehow tampered with the ball – a practise which, he made clear once again, he did not regard as cheating. Nowhere in the article did he name Ian Botham. Then, in June, in a lengthy interview in *India Today*, Imran said that 'racism' had helped shape English attitudes towards Pakistani bowlers, and observed:

> 'Look at the people who have taken the rational stand in the controversy, Tony Lewis, Christopher Martin-Jenkins, Derek Pringle. They are all educated Oxford types. Look at the others, Allan Lamb, Ian Botham, Fred Trueman. The difference in class and upbringing makes a difference.'

When the interview was picked up by the British press, Imran was quick to disavow the remarks, and wrote to Botham and Lamb to assure them that in his view they were 'outstanding sportsmen'. On 8th July, he received his reply: a letter from solicitors acting for Botham and Lamb demanding a public apology, not only for the *India Today* remarks, but also for the interview in the *Sun*, which, Botham claimed, had defamed him as a cheat. Imran drafted a statement insisting he did not regard either man as a 'racist', a 'cheat' or 'uneducated' and offered to publish it as a letter to the *Times*. Botham and Lamb rejected the offer and chose to sue for libel. Thus the case began its long, slow, expensive journey towards that confrontation in the High Court.

Two years later, on the eve of the trial, and only days before the Lord's Test, the millionaire entrepreneur Jim Slater tried to intervene to resolve the dispute – and save cricket further public embarrassment. Imran agreed that the three men would shake hands on the court steps while he delivered a statement stressing not only that he had never regarded either Botham or Lamb as 'racist' or 'uneducated' but also that he considered all Botham's Test wickets to have been taken legitimately. Slater offered to pay the legal costs incurred by all three litigants. Once again Botham and Lamb rejected the offer. They demanded 'an apology' from Imran for making offensive remarks. But Imran insisted he had not made the remarks, that he had never called the men racists or uneducated or cheats, and, as he later explained, 'I could not let them make me apologise for something I hadn't said. I would rather die than apologise for something I did not do.'

The 13 day trial in the High Court attracted more publicity than anything that happened on a cricket pitch all summer. It became not only the 'clash of the cricket giants', the 'race and class trial', but also a contest between sharp-witted silks (both sides employed big name QCs at £3000 a day), and a 'battle of the wives', in which fashion correspondents and feature writers poured over the dress-sense and courtroom demeanour of Kathy Botham, Lindsay Lamb (both of whom seemed possessed of more common sense and clearer minds than their husbands) and the six months pregnant Jemima Khan, who took the palm from the older women in the young, pretty and passive stakes.

Much to their annoyance, Mike Atherton and David Lloyd were called as witnesses for the defence the day before the Test was to begin. They were followed by more than a dozen English Test cricketers, past and present, who took the witness stand to give evidence about the theory and practise of ball tampering. Carman interrogated Derek Pringle about the use of lip salve by Essex players to polish the ball (an illegal practise). When asked, 'Was that done on a regular basis?', Pringle replied, 'Every day.' The argument had its comic moments. A surly Brian Close questioned Geoff Boycott's probity, and when, in response, an agitated Boycott prepared to demonstrate Close's alleged hypocrisy with the aid of a training shoe, he was forced to step down by the judge, concerned that 'this witness' evidence is getting out of hand'.

Both sides produced their experts and their video footage, but the only conclusion that could be drawn was that when it came to ball tampering there was simply no consensus, either as to the nature of the offence, its frequency or its seriousness. However, the very fact that there was no consensus supported Imran's original argument, which was that ball-tampering was ill-defined, and that therefore the attack on the Pakistanis in 1992 had been discriminatory.

Much was made in the press of Imran's mid-trial abandonment of his plea of 'justification', i.e. that the allegedly libellous remarks pertaining to 'all the big names' tampering with the ball were true. Imran's lawyers had earlier introduced a video of a 1982 Test match in which Botham appeared to prod the ball with his fingers. Botham's briefs insisted it 'showed him manipulating, quite legally, a ball that had gone out of shape', and that it therefore supported their client's case. On the witness stand, Botham insisted he had never illegally tampered with the ball in any way. Since Imran had always been willing to accept Botham's good faith in this regard, and since he was not seeking to prove that Botham (or anyone else) was a cheat, he dropped that particular part of his plea (and as a result was later compelled to bear part of the legal expenses). He conceded to Botham what Botham refused to concede to the Pakistanis: that it was wrong to accuse anyone of unfair play on the basis of this kind of ambiguous evidence. The jury of seven women and five men seemed to have no difficulty grasping the argument, elusive as it appeared to many cricket scribes.

Although much of the testimony at the libel trial pertained to ball-tampering, the jury was not asked to rule on this vexed conundrum. They were asked to decide whether or not Botham and Lamb had been libelled by Imran. In law, this meant that the plaintiffs had to show that Imran had published statements likely to lower their standing in the eyes of reasonable persons.

It is important to remember who started the name-calling here. Since August 1992, Lamb and Botham, in print and on the airwaves, had repeatedly dubbed the Pakistani cricketers 'cheats'. Imran's allegedly libellous remarks were made in response to those accusations, which neither Botham nor Lamb has ever withdrawn or qualified. Indeed, Botham had a history of making derogatory remarks about all things Pakistani, beginning with the famous 'mother-in-law crack' of 1987, which he happily owned up to when cross-examined in the High Court. According to the *Sunday Mirror*, one of the highlights of his 1990 'roadshow' was this joke: 'How do you improve Pakistani umpiring? Shoot them!' To illustrate how untrustworthy and conspiratorial the Pakistanis were, he regaled audiences with a description of Abdul Qadir appealing to a local umpire, 'Howzat ... uncle?'. In both Pakistan and India, 'uncle' is a respectful form of address to elder males.

That Botham would mistake it for a telltale sign of nepotism betrayed the extent to which his prejudices about Pakistan had been shaped by sheer ignorance. He made no effort to conceal his bitterness about England's defeat by Pakistan in the 1992 World Cup final, and suggested repeatedly that it was secured by illegitimate means. An interview with the *Mirror* in 1993 began with the statement: 'Botham has never made any secret of the fact that he does not like Pakistan ... country or cricketers ...' In 1995, he and Lamb took their 'Beef and Lamb in a stew' cabaret act to riot-torn, bomb-ripped Bombay, where they treated well-healed punters to sarcastic quips about Pakistan's food, weather, prohibition of alcohol and behaviour on the cricket pitch. Apparently, the barbs were well-received among supporters of Shiv Sena, a Bombay-based right-wing political movement violently hostile to Muslims and Pakistanis.

Under questioning from Carman about his attitude towards sportsmanship and the Laws of Cricket, Botham made a revealing admission. 'You can stretch the laws to a point. You can nick it or you can walk. If you're playing against the Australians, you don't walk.' Of course, it was a joke. But the point of the joke was that, in practise, 'fair play' is defined in the context of national affiliation, which was what Imran had been trying to say all along.

In the end the most striking feature of the 'race and class trial' was how little light it shed on either race or class, their relationship to each other or their impact on cricket. If Imran did imply to the *India Today* reporter that racist irrationality was confined to the 'lower classes' then it would seem he had learned little from his years of residence in this country. And if he does consider Botham, Lamb or Fred Trueman representative members of the 'uneducated' working class, then his view of England must be as cartoon-like as their view of Pakistan.

Botham, Lamb and Trueman are all wealthy men (and all three are said to vote Conservative). Lamb hails from a prosperous farming family in the Cape, where he still owns land. As an expatriate South African, he was particularly vulnerable to allegations of racism, and his wife made it clear in court the hurt and embarrassment these had caused. On the witness stand, Lamb himself explained, 'I left South Africa because I was against anti-apartheid' (sic). The comic verbal muddle apart, you had to feel sorry for Lamb; he was being forced to cloak his legitimate personal and financial reasons for moving to England in the rhetoric of anti-racism, something he had wisely avoided doing in the past. As a cheerful mercenary, he had played for England with huge success and without pretence. He had no need to cite a higher motive, but in the High Court, he was locked into a symbolic battle where perceived social identities – the badges of nation, class, race, religion – obscured individual human realities.

Botham's father was a career military man before leaving the service to run a small business. With pride the great all-rounder and populist hero informed the court that he hailed 'from a working middle class background' – a statement which demonstrated just how bewildering class self-definition can be in a society which embraces egalitarian values while at the same time producing vast inequalities in personal wealth. For me, one of the sadder spectacles of English cricket in the last twenty years has been the transformation of Ian Botham from cheeky, exuberant, anti-establishment tyro into sanctimonious, self-regarding super-patriot. But even here Botham was merely re-enacting one of English cricket's archetypal scenarios: yesterday's fiery rebel becoming today's miserable old fogey.

In an article on the libel case in *The Spectator*, Tunku Varadarajan told his readers what they wanted to hear: that the masses of the sub-continent held the English gentlemen, the officer class, in deep respect, but hated the subalterns. 'There is no one in the world so boorish, coarse and offensive as the English lower orders,' he declared, and no one more illustrative of this 'type' than Ian Botham (the author also had harsh words for Imran Khan). How revealing that Spectator readers, usually so quickly enflamed by any instance of 'reverse racism', accepted this article without protest, and how strange that Botham chose not to sue. After all, this was a far more derogatory comment than anything Imran was alleged to have said.

As for Imran himself, he is not a 'Pathan aristocrat' but an upper middle class Punjabi, the son of an engineer. His wife, of course, is the debutante daughter of a millionaire. Nothing surprising there. Cricket has for many decades been a means of upward mobility, both in England and the sub-continent, and few cricketers have been as adept at constructing and reconstructing their identity as Imran. In the two years running up to the libel trial, the one-time Playboy of the Western World, suave, libertine and supremely self-confident, had recreated himself as a devout Muslim, critic of Western imperialism and humble servant of the Pakistani people, much to the irritation of the British media, which could not fathom such an apparent volte-face. His donning of *shalwar kameez* – standard male dress in Pakistan – was (incorrectly) reported as a symbol of his conversion to fundamentalist Islam, and his attacks on the 'brown sahibs' – wealthy Pakistanis obsessed with western consumer culture – were denounced as arrant hypocrisy. Imran seems blessed with an ability to believe passionately in whatever he's arguing at the moment, and is never more sincere than when he is contradicting himself. But the apparently limitless facility for self-deception which carried him through one crisis after another during his cricket career proved a disaster when he turned to politics.

Imran's electoral ambitions grew out of the remarkable fund-raising effort he mounted on behalf of the cancer hospital he was building in Lahore in memory of his mother. Threatened by his mounting prestige, alarmed by the enthusiastic crowds he drew across he country, Benazir Bhutto's Government banned him from the airwaves, harassed and smeared him. In April 1996, a bomb in the cancer hospital killed six patients. In November, after the dismissal of the Bhutto government, Imran launched his election campaign, promising to 'bowl out' corruption and injustice. The Western media followed him everywhere (sceptics dubbed him 'the candidate of the BBC'), but seasoned Pakistani observers always insisted he would find it difficult to convert his cricketing popularity into votes.

Covering the elections in early 1997, I watched with fascination Imran's efforts to tip-toe between religious orthodoxy and secular liberalism, democracy and authoritarianism, big business and the poor masses. In the end he proved as pathetically unable to reconcile the contradictory claims of tradition and modernity as his antagonists in English cricket. It became obvious in the closing days of the campaign that his fledgling party was doomed to humiliating defeat. On television he appeared genuinely bewildered by the stubborn refusal of the Pakistani people to respond to his call. Lashing out at media bias and criticism of his political inexperience, he snapped at a reporter: 'I went to Oxford too! I was there before Benazir!'. But when pressed to spell out his specific policies on the major issues – the economy, women, the military, education – all Imran could offer was a fervent pledge to do 'whatever is good for the people of Pakistan'. In this case, the people of Pakistan weren't having it. His party received a derisory share of the vote and failed to win a single seat. The largely illiterate masses revered Imran as a great cricketer, but they were smart enough to know that this did not automatically make him a great national leader.

This came as a surprise to many western commentators, whose treatment of Imran, and of Pakistani affairs in general, is coloured by a view of Pakistan, and more broadly of Islam, as irredeemably alien. Imran and his countrymen and women are the eternal Oriental 'other', governed by irrational norms and fundamentally unknowable to the western mind. Here the English cricket media is at one with Harvard professor Samuel Huntingdon, whose fashionable 'clash of civilisations' thesis has elevated long-held western prejudices to the level of global strategic theory. 'The time has come for the West to abandon the illusion of universality and to

promote the strength, coherence and vitality of its civilisation,'
Huntingdon declared 'Western peoples have far more in common with
each other than they have with Asian, Middle Eastern, or African people.'
The professor singled out Islam, in particular, as inimical to Western
values and consciousness, and warned that no common understanding
could be forged with a culture so intrinsically alien.

This 'east is east and west is west' philosophy crops up regularly in
cricket writing, a handy if rather tautologous way of explaining perceived
differences. Commenting on the 1995 Benson and Hedges final in *The
Times*, John Woodcock compared Mike Atherton's 93 off 141 balls for
Lancashire (who batted first and won) to Aravinda DeSilva's 112 off 95
balls for Kent (who lost):

> 'English commitment and Sri Lankan artistry were on show ... vigilance and
> genius, the Occident and the Orient ... two contrasting cricketing cultures...
> you really need to be born on the sub-continent to play exactly as De Silva
> does, with eyes that flash and wrists that are naturally supple and feet that
> need no telling ... Englishmen have to work harder to break the mould.'

Woodcock's admiration for DeSilva was heartfelt, but his praise was,
unintentionally, double-edged. It was the old duality of nature and
nurture, spontaneity and deliberation, and it obscured far more than it
revealed. Cricket writers relish archetypes - the beefy fast bowler, the
diminutive keeper, the phlegmatic opening batsman, the cavalier
strokemaker, the temperamental left arm spinner - but, when transferred
to the international arena, these archetypes all too easily degenerate into
mere racial or national stereotypes. And the tragedy of the stereotype is
that it occludes our view of reality. It severs us from the glorious
unpredictability of human diversity. De Silva's batsmanship, even in the
frenetic one day arena, is for the most part correct, classical and every bit
as calculated and crafted as Atherton's. And his daring shot-making in
that B and H final owed far more to the fact that his team were chasing a
sizeable target than to genetic or cultural factors. Woodcock is an
immensely knowledgeable observer of the game, but in this case he was
so besotted by the lure of the cricketing Orient that he simply could not
see what was in front of his eyes.

I suspect the same was true of those cricket writers who professed
astonishment at the High Court jury's majority verdict in favour of
Imran, which left a shell-shocked Botham and Lamb with an estimated
£500,000 legal bill. Preoccupied with fashion statements, stereotypes,

old grudges and bad cricketing puns, the media had not been paying as much attention to the rigour of the legal arguments as the jury. These citizens were required to measure what material damage Imran's alleged remarks were likely to have on the two plaintiffs' reputations, and on that score it's hard to deny they came to a reasonable conclusion. They may have been influenced by the knowledge that Imran's proffered positive statement would have had far wider circulation – and far less ambiguity – than either of the negative articles which were the subject of the action. And they may also have wondered why Botham and Lamb were so determined to pursue this grievance, when Botham, in particular, had refrained from taking action against perpetrators of much more damaging allegations. Just what was the purpose of this suit, and exactly what kind of 'apology' were Botham and Lamb trying to squeeze out of Imran?

The jury's decision was the lead front page story in every national newspaper. The *Mirror*, which had done more than anyone else to keep the ball-tampering saga alive, devoted its first three pages plus a four page special pull-out to the courtroom encounter, which, declared Henry Blofeld, was 'as dramatic, tense and breathless as anything I have ever experienced on a cricket field'. Imran thanked 'the Almighty' and insisted once again, 'I've never called anyone a racist or a cheat … I'm sad that this has had to come to the court. It was not because of me.' He called on the ICC to clarify the Laws on ball-tampering and declared, 'The Pakistani cricketers have been vindicated,' which might well have come as a shock to the jury, who had never been asked to make a judgement on Pakistani cricketers.

The verdict caused consternation among English observers, and even the Master of the Rolls observed that something would have to be done about such 'perverse decisions' (only days before, a Merseyside jury had acquitted women peace activists who had vandalised a Hawk fighter aircraft bound for repressive Indonesia). One of the many ironies of the libel trial was that those who normally spring to the defence of British traditions, who see democracy, human rights and 'fair play' as distinctively western, were found scoffing and sputtering at that ancient and irreplaceable English institution, the jury, while Imran, that icon of the Orient and self-appointed scourge of the West, commented: 'the verdict has filled me with admiration for British justice and especially for the fairness of the jury system whereby ordinary citizens have a God-given sense to be able to sift through the legal arguments and see the truth. I hope one day in Pakistan, we, too, can have a jury system.'

After the high court decision, the three tired, prickly, self-important middle aged men left the summer's stage, and the Test series moved on to Headingley, headquarters of Yorkshire cricket, epicentre of some of the most fraught, and certainly the most well-publicised of English cricket's racial dilemmas.

So far it had been a harmonious series, and in comparison to 1992 the tabloids had been restrained. There were jokes about 'getting out the prayer mats' and 'facing Mecca from the pavilion end', and complaints about excessive appealing (which had also been made earlier in the summer against the Indian bowlers, Srinath and Prasad), but no accusations of 'cheating'. Waqar, Wasim and Mushtaq Ahmed were recognised for what they were: three of the most inventive and effective attacking bowlers in the world, which was no more than what the average English cricket fan had believed for many years. Perhaps events surrounding the hugely successful Euro 96 football championship held in June had made the tabloids think twice about embarking on another bout of Paki-bashing. In the run-up to England's semi-final against Germany at Wembley the *Mirror* had declared 'war' against the Germans and abused the nation's footballing rivals and erstwhile enemies as 'krauts', 'Huns' and 'Fritzes'. Commentators in the 'quality' press tut-tutted, but more significant was the backlash among the fans, who for the most part welcomed visiting supporters and eschewed xenophobia. Sheepishly, senior executives at the *Mirror* conceded they had misread the popular mood.

On the eve of the Test, the Pakistani squad were unable to practise in the indoor nets, which had been commandeered by the corporate hospitality organisers to store the vast amounts of food and drink to be consumed by their clients. Wasim could not help but wonder how the English would have reacted had they been similarly inconvenienced while on tour in Pakistan. The first two days of the Headingley test passed off without incident. I attended the Thursday and Friday, and spent time chatting with Pakistani supporters scattered across the Western Terrace. The mood was relaxed, despite the officious stewards, hired by a private security firm, who ejected spectators dressed up as a pantomime horse and a giant carrot. In a feature article examining racial divisions in Yorkshire club cricket, Matthew Engel wrote: 'Stand-offishness is the right word, certainly more apt than racism. There are people in Yorkshire on both sides of the racial cricketing divide – and it is a divide – who are quick to take offence, and too slow to make allowance for different ways of doing things.'

I didn't attend the Saturday of the Test, but my friend, the educator and author Chris Searle, did, accompanied by his 11-year-old son and his son's Pakistani friend. His account of their day on the Western Terrace was published in the *Observer* the following week. What he and his young companions witnessed was not some 'cultural divide' or 'clash of civilisations', but an assault on the civil rights of cricket spectators, and the Asian community as a whole, by a vocal racist minority:

'At lunchtime the atmosphere was friendly and interactive: someone had brought a bunch of large beach balls which were slapped around the terraces. It was good humoured and brought the crowd together – until, one by one, the balls were captured by the stewards to a unity of booing from almost all the spectators ... Just after tea, an elderly white man managed to defeat the cordon of stewards blocking the main route through the terrace. He was cheered by everybody, white and Asian. Then a youth in a Pakistan shirt tried, failed and was held by three white stewards. Suddenly, in a second, scores of white spectators were on their feet, hurling abuse – now not at the stewards, but at the restrained Asian youth ... In an instant, it was as if a boil had been pricked and the pus of four centuries of Empire was pulsing out. White spectators behind me and the boys were screaming, 'Stab the Pakis!' Abuse was coming from all directions ... beer was thrown over Pakistan supporters in the front rows.

As a group of middle-aged Asians protested half way back up the terraces, they too were pounced upon and led away by stewards and police. White spectators around them chanted their support for the police: 'Take them out! Take them out!' This was not blind yobbery. It was the spillage of racism, incontrovertible and putrid. My son's friend sat through it all, apparently bemused, but with who knows what happening inside him. As Asian woman walked past with a small child. 'Let's have a look at yer chapatti, love.' Shouted out a young man to my left, as a group of other Englishmen dressed as spoof Moslems screamed abuse and made fey bows towards the Pakistani supporters.

A Pakistan supporter, dubbed 'Omar Sharif' by the spectators in front of me, made a harmonious gesture by going round groups of white supporters with a bowl of cooked chicken pieces. Some accepted them, thanking him – others took them and thrust them back at him, hostilely and insultingly. As for me I had seen and heard enough, and I am sure my son and his friend had too. I felt angry all the way home: there was the customary racist partiality of the police and private security firms, the failure of senior England players sitting on their balcony 100 yards away to come down and use their influence with the crowd

– and the shameful behaviour of hundreds of young Englishmen. ... No other event in a lifetime of playing cricket and 40 years of watching first-class and test cricket has persuaded me so much of the imperative need for anti-racist campaigns like Hit Racism for Six...'

Although BBC commentators chose to veil it in silence, the outbreak of racial abuse had been reported by several newspapers, and condemned by Leeds MP Derek Fatchett, who was present on the day. Yorkshire president Lawrence Byford investigated the trouble first hand and when asked by a journalist if it had 'racial undertones', replied, 'Use your own eyes.' However, the club's Chief Executive, Chris Hassell, was quick to repudiate the suggestion, insisting, 'It is a drink problem, not a race problem.' Not surprisingly, this was the line taken by Yorkshire's official report into the disturbances, published eight months after the event, in March 1997. 'The media hype painted a very distorted picture,' the report complained. The problems on the Western Terrace were 'drink-related' and in this regard 'there was in fact a significant improvement from the previous year'. Although acknowledging that 'stewarding standards must be improved', club officials insisted 'the correct approach had been adopted in 1996'. Suggestions that racism was a specific problem requiring a specific response were dismissed out of hand.

In the *Observer*, Kevin Mitchell condemned the report as a 'monument to sophistry'. Hit Racism for Six noted that no attempt was made to solicit independent evidence or representative testimony on the events under study. Nor was any effort made to advertise the compilation of the report or to secure responses from a cross-section of spectators or black and Asian community organisations. Instead, club officials had relied entirely on unsolicited letters from a handful of spectators touching on a variety of topics. The report conceded that six of these complained of racial abuse, but chose to quote at length only a single letter, which came from an unnamed 'distinguished senior civil servant' who insisted there was no racial abuse on the day he attended. Strangely, the authors of the report seem not to have noticed that the day he attended was the Friday of the Test. The outbreak of racial abuse occurred on the Saturday.

What extraordinary contortions some people will perform to blind themselves, and others, to painful home truths! When it comes to racism, English cricket's real problem is its culture of complacency and denial, which expresses itself in a knee-jerk defensiveness whenever the touchy topic rears its ugly head. The burden of the case against the cricket establishment and cricket media is not that they are racist but that they are unable and unwilling to recognise the reality of racism and the problems it poses for the game. Commentators who huff and puff about Mexican waves or Barmy Army chanting seem oblivious to outbursts of racial abuse. Ground authorities seem unable to distinguish between genuinely anti-social, insulting or dangerous behaviour and behaviour that is merely different, unexpected, or eye-catching. The carrot and the horse were ejected, but on the Saturday not one spectator was removed or punished for the specific offence of racial abuse. (Ironically, Headingley is the only Test ground in the country which explicitly bans such abuse.) The clamour against the alleged 'reverse racism' or 'separatism' of black and Asian leagues always exceeds the nearly inaudible protest against the far more numerous instances of exclusion, prejudice, discrimination and sometimes overt racism practised by all-white clubs, white-dominated leagues, white officials or white cricket commentators.

A Yorkshire and Humberside Sports Council Report commented in 1995: 'Mention racism and some club representatives say they would prefer to talk about cricket.' And that attitude is reflected at the game's higher echelons. It took the TCCB/ECB two years to respond to letters sent to it by Hit Racism for Six, and when officials finally agreed to meet representatives of the group, they refused to concede that racism was any kind of problem in the game (outside the Western Terrace) or that it in any way might be inhibiting the game's future development. Among the reams of evidence they disregarded was the testimony of Mike Atkins, who had helped found the Sheffield Caribbean Sports Club in the mid-70s. Despite many successes on the field and a strong record of promoting young talent (including Devon Malcolm), the Sheffield Caribbeans found themselves effectively barred from all the established top quality leagues in South Yorkshire. They were told they needed a better ground; after a Herculean fund raising effort they procured one. They were told they needed to prove their playing credentials; they did so on the field, with aplomb. Yet repeatedly their application for admission was voted down by senior clubs. Within a week of purchasing a ground from an engineering firm, the clubhouse door and windows were smashed; later the store room, garage and part of the pavilion were burnt; glass was sprinkled on the pitch. Yet, like so many other black and Asian cricket clubs around the country, they persevere, evincing a commitment to the game that ought to be the envy of the English authorities.

In May 1998, Roehampton Institute's Centre for Sport Development Research published the first major academic study of the issue. In preparing 'Anyone for Cricket? Equal opportunities and changing cricket cultures in Essex and East London', researchers interviewed club cricketers, secretaries, and umpires to try to find out why so many clubs (some 41% in the area) failed to affiliate to the Essex Cricket Association. The report's authors, Ian McDonald and Sharda Ugra, concluded that there were 'two distinct but related cultures of cricket'. One is mainly black and Asian, urban, and confined to council-maintained public pitches; in this culture, cricket is 'primarily a competitive sporting occasion, and largely exists outside the official structures'. The other is white, rural, and endowed with well-kept private facilities; here cricket is 'primarily a social occasion based on the traditional rituals of English cricket, and exists largely as part of the official structure'.

The report repeatedly stresses that, in practise, these two cultures 'are not equal'. Black and Asian cricketers, despite their formidable hunger for the game, simply do not enjoy the same facilities, access to leagues, and opportunities to compete as their white counterparts. What's more, their way of playing cricket – overtly competitive, sometimes highly vocal – is sometimes frowned upon by white players or officials. This is not merely a question of cultural difference, what Matthew Engel called 'stand-offishness'. The report showed that Asian and Afro-Caribbean clubs, despite the radical differences between their respective cultures (not to mention racial, religious and national affiliations), play together without strife, and without the disputes over drinking, praying or 'excessive' appealing which mar the much more infrequent interaction with white clubs. 'Most black and Asian players argued that the mainstream leagues hide behind league regulations and cultural stereotypes of black and Asian cricket, to prevent the admission of black and Asian clubs into the official leagues.' As a result, the report concluded, 'many young people are being lost to the game'.

The researchers unearthed a startling degree of insularity among white players and their clubs. One club secretary, also chairman of an Essex League, commented, 'It isn't that we consciously don't encourage any ethnic minorities ... we'd be delighted to have a West Indian fast bowler or something like that.' The exclusion of black and Asian cricketers from the mainstream was seen by many whites as self-inflicted and by others as inevitable. Some even viewed racial abuse as a 'natural' response to the presence of black or Asian players. Intriguingly, it was the black and Asian cricketers who seemed most preoccupied with standards of play, competitiveness, and technique. In contrast, the white players emphasised the game's cultural mystique.

'For many predominantly white clubs, the traditional 'English' way of staging cricket is the 'norm' to which black and Asian players should adapt or with which they should integrate ...The majority of white cricketers linked cricket to Englishness, but it was a specific notion of Englishness – rural, traditional, and civilised – which they linked to a specific kind of cricket – 'genteel', non-aggressive, village cricket.'

Whether or not this view of the village game is realistic – and in my experience it is not – it is clearly a powerful element in defining the game for many of its participants. The Englishness of English cricket thus becomes a means of exclusion, and therefore a barrier to the game's development. The report sums up: 'Whilst the culture of English cricket may not be explicitly racist, it can lead to a culture of racial exclusion, racial stereotyping and to a lesser extent racial abuse of black and Asian cricket players.'

The cricket establishment's 'hear no evil see no evil' approach to racism seems at odds with its super-vigilance when it comes to drug use. Although the authorities correctly insist that drugs are not a problem in the game, they have imposed severe penalties on players found to have ingested cannabis or cocaine. People like Ed Giddins and Keith Piper were punished for an activity undertaken in private, with no bearing on either their performance on the field or their public behaviour. They didn't thump their wives or cheat on their taxes or drink and drive. The crimes they committed were victimless, and no one would have heard of them had they not been publicised by the cricket authorities themselves, the very people who happily allow the game to be used to promote alcohol and tobacco, two drugs which wreak far more havoc in our society than coke, grass or hash. Just what code of morality is supposed to be at work here? As ever, the authorities' principal concern is with 'the image of the game' – the image they seek to market to media, sponsors and advertisers. Their fond belief that a drug-free image is more important than an anti-racist image proves just how remote they are from the British youth whose interest they need to attract if English cricket is ever to flourish anew.

However, all is not lost. The Roehampton researchers interviewed 62 eight-to-eleven year olds from six east London schools – girls and boys, white, black and Asian – and found their perceptions of the game largely free of the familiar stereotypes and their attitudes towards national affiliation refreshingly relaxed. Most of the children did not think you had to play either for the country you lived in or the one you or your parents came from. 'It's your choice,' said one, 'like in football'. 'The example of Hussain and the Hollioakes was used by some students to illustrate their belief that one's choice of cricket team was independent of one's ethnic background or indeed original nationality.' All the students were asked whether they agreed with the statement, 'cricket's an Asian game, football's a white game and basketball's a black game'. Hearteningly, every single student disagreed. Many dismissed the formula as 'racist'. 'While making strong ethnic identifications with cricket and cricketers themselves, the students nevertheless expressed clearly the opinion that cricket was a sport for all.' These kids are way ahead of Tebbit and Henderson and indeed many of our leading cricket writers.

Significantly, 'there was no association made between cricket and its English origins and only three students stated that the sport was invented in England.' I know this revelation will distress the self-appointed guardians of England's heritage, but personally I see it as a sign of hope for the future. The best thing that could happen to English cricket is for young people to forget the 'English' part and rediscover the game itself: awkward and graceful, fluent and lapidary, tantalisingly complex, endlessly engrossing.

After England's hapless performance in the 1996 World Cup, TCCB chairman Dennis Silk, public school headmaster and former MCC president, asked in high dudgeon: 'Are we a degenerate nation that cannot be bothered to make the effort?' In January 1997, after the 'best prepared England team ever' had drawn the inaugural Test series against Zimbabwe 0-0 and lost the one day series 3-0, Tim Lamb, chief executive of the newly-established ECB, declared, 'It's a defining moment. I just ask England's fans to bear with us because we're determined to get things right.' His boss, Lord MacLaurin, promised to 'take the game apart bit by bit and put it back together again.' Eight months later, they unveiled their 'blueprint' for the salvation of English cricket, 'Raising the Standard'. It was the most comprehensive and ambitious plan for reform ever contemplated by the English cricket establishment.

The basic thesis of the MacLaurin blueprint was that the future of the game depended on a 'successful and vibrant England team', and that to produce such a team English cricket at all levels needed to be made more 'competitive'. Above all, what was needed was a 'a seamless progress for the most talented cricketers from school, through club, into representative and international cricket'. Towards that end a variety of structural changes were proposed affecting club and county, recreational and professional cricket.

Howls of protest greeted the Murray Report of 1993, a modest document compared to Raising the Standard, but this time dissent was surprisingly muted. The modernisers appeared to have crushed – or co-opted – the traditionalists. Welcoming the ECB proposals in an editorial, the *Times* denounced English cricket as 'flabby', 'overweight' and 'uncompetitive.' This from the organ which twenty years before had greeted Kerry Packer as an anti-Christ. It seemed the national side's repeated humiliations on the field had overcome the qualms of conservatives. In order to compete in a global marketplace, English cricket, like so many other public institutions, from the BBC to the welfare state, was to be made 'lean and mean', and (as Kerry Packer once said) the devil take the hindmost.

While the blueprint was widely hailed both for its 'radicalism' and 'balance', there was little enthusiasm for its centrepiece, a new and somewhat arcane format for the venerable county championship. The first-class counties would be divided into three conferences; each team would play each side in the other two conferences once, after which all teams would engage in a series of play-offs to determine the final placings. This byzantine scheme satisfied neither the modernisers – pushing for a simple two-division system, with promotion and relegation – or the traditionalists, who insisted on an all-play-all season. In September, the ECB's First Class Forum – bringing together the 18 first class counties plus the MCC – rejected both the MacLaurin plan and a proposal for two divisions promoted by the richer counties (mainly those with Test match grounds). Instead, they opted for a hybrid half-way house: the county championship as at present, with a 'Super Cup' of one day play-offs among the top teams in September. With a straight face, the ECB proudly dubbed the new arrangement 'the Radical Status Quo'.

The media pilloried the county chairmen as backward-looking feudal barons, unwilling to sacrifice their own petty interests for the good of the nation. For the *Economist*, the good of the nation was, as ever, primarily a matter of sound business practise. The magazine argued that without a successful national side cricket would not earn the money needed to subsidise the counties. Since their 'crowds will stay small come what may', the counties should abandon the current system and its unearned privileges and submit themselves to MacLaurin's modern 'pyramid of excellence'. For failing to do so, 'they deserve a loud raspberry'.

It was rumoured that MacLaurin had only advanced the implausible three conference idea in order to force the counties into opting for two divisions. Although it was hard to see how the proposal met any of the stated aims of Raising the Standard, its illogic was less the product of Machiavellian manipulation than of the contradictory forces driving the re-casting of English cricket. 'Any format needs not only to produce a very competitive championship but also the right quantity of first class cricket,' the blueprint declared, but squaring that circle proved easier in theory than practise. All the report's objections to a two-division system – that it would penalise counties with Test players, make counties less likely to agree to rest Test players and 'less inclined to take a chance on youth when old stagers seem a safer bet with promotion and relegation at stake' – could be levelled at any system which increased the 'competitiveness' and therefore the status of county fixtures. The more attractive the domestic schedule, the more intractable will become the county v country conflict for leading players. It may be that the demands of increased 'competitiveness' in the domestic and international spheres are simply irreconcilable. Of course, at least part of the dilemma could be resolved by sharply reducing the number of matches played, but that would undermine the counties' effort to 'generate maximum revenue', as required of them by the blueprint. 'Counties must be encouraged to become more financially independent and must therefore have opportunities to stage a programme of cricket which has wide public appeal'; it was essential that all counties be given 'more opportunity to stage highly pressurised, entertaining and competitive one day cricket.' Hence it was not merely for tradition's sake that MacLaurin specified one non-negotiable parameter for reform: 'any changes ... must ensure the preservation and well-being of 18 first class counties as a centre of excellence, a focus for local cricketing interest and as an outlet for selling the game.'

The blueprint promised not only to 'raise standards of play' but also to 'raise the amount of income coming into the game'. Indeed, it presented these two aims as complementary facets of the search for increased 'competitiveness'. But the report's tangled, contradictory proposals for the professional game demonstrated that they are by no means always compatible. One of the principal aims of the whole exercise was to redress the long-standing problem of 'too much cricket'. More time was needed for practise and preparation, and, crucially, the amount of cricket played by England's top stars needed to be reduced. However, the plan ultimately adopted by the ECB provides for only five fewer cricket playing days per season, and, thanks to the two-division 50-over National League which will replace the Sunday League, the mad dash round Britain's motorways, so detested by county cricketers, will be exacerbated. While pledging the ECB to 'maintaining the primacy of Test cricket', Raising the Standard proposed an increase in the number of one day internationals and in the total number of one day domestic matches. The high profile of the new National League and the revamped NatWest, along with the increasing specialisation of England's one day international squad, seems destined to make a nonsense of MacLaurin's pyramid of excellence – the purpose of which is to breed Test cricketers.

One proposal to which the counties readily acceded was to cut staff numbers 'substantially with almost immediate effect'. In a marvellous specimen of Orwellian Newspeak, the ECB declared its intention to 'reduce first class county staff sizes to allow more cricketers the opportunity to progress further in the game'. So no more 'fat and flabby' county pros taking up places that should got to young England wannabes. But was this measure designed to improve competitiveness or merely to cut labour costs? While big business regards the two as synonymous, sport is a different matter. The assumption that the national side will improve if it is drawn from a smaller pool of full-time players is, at best, speculative, and it seems unlikely that productivity in cricket can ever be measured as it is in a capitalist enterprise.

The much derided 'comfort zone' of county cricket amounts to nothing more than a modest degree of financial security, acquired by players after many decades of forelock-touching supplication. MacLaurin, like Blair, is a believer in 'flexible labour'. Fewer full-time staff, it is argued, will leave more room for part-timers and amateurs to come through. 'I still think it realistic that a stock-broker who is a gifted cricketer should play at a sufficiently competitive recreational level that he can make the step to the county game,' explained MacLaurin (as the late lamented *Inside Edge* observed, MacLaurin did not reveal his plans for non-stock brokers). Precisely how anyone is supposed to hold down a job, no less build a career, and maintain the sort of readiness needed to parachute into the first class scene as and when required, remains a mystery. Promising young cricketers will be compelled, like under-funded British pole vaulters, high jumpers or discus throwers, to rely on sympathetic employers and individual sponsorship from small firms. And it's hard to see how late bloomers would ever get a chance, even at the higher levels of amateur cricket, where an under-25s quota will operate. Don't the has-beens and the hacks, the players the *Times* would dismiss as 'flabby', also contribute to the sum of our summer's entertainment? Is the only cricketer we should value the one who might one day play for England?

Even as Australian cricketers, a more independent and assertive breed than their English counterparts, challenge the part-time arrangements prevalent in Shield cricket, the ECB seems eager to revert to semi-amateurism. England's cadre of professional cricketers look set to join further education lecturers, sub-editors and designers, social workers and health care staff in the less-than-wonderful world of casualised labour, a world without job security or protection from arbitrary dismissal, and with little room for the occasional loss of form. The assumption here is that insecurity improves performance. It's worth noting, however, that this nostrum is applied somewhat selectively, and certainly not to English cricket's ever-swelling army of administrative and marketing officials.

It is not hard to see why county committees would welcome a cut in labour costs, but why on earth was the Professional Cricketers Association prepared to endorse a proposal that could lead to one quarter of its membership losing their jobs? At the very least, in exchange for such a heavy haemorrhage, the PCA ought to have demanded free agency, a transfer system, and the replacement of the benefit system with portable pensions. Such innovations would seem to be in keeping with MacLaurin's philosophy, but would, of course, immediately upend the contrived economic equation which sustains the whole edifice of the first class game, and which Raising the Standard was determined to preserve. The ECB's terror of a transfer market, with its upward pressure on wages, clearly outweighs its commitment to the free market. The counties and the ECB, unlike the players, are to remain cushioned, protected from the impact of unfettered 'competitiveness'. Cricketers will not be allowed to sell their services to highest bidder. Surely, if MacLaurin's thesis is to be taken seriously, this must be seen as a major inhibition on 'competitiveness' and a disincentive to improved performance.

Matthew Engel put Lord MacLaurin's claims succinctly. 'Above all what English cricket needs is something that Lord MacLaurin is better qualified than anyone to provide. It needs Tesco-isation. The game needs to become an attractive product sold in an imaginative manner at competitive prices.'

Under MacLaurin's leadership, Tesco overtook Sainsbury's as the industry leader in sales and profits. It did so by closing half its stores, reducing wage costs, changing its image to attract more upmarket custom (no more plebeian Green Stamps), expanding abroad, diversifying its outlets (Superstores, Express, Metro, Compact) and its interests (the future for retail, according to MacLaurin, lies in 'a move away from one's core business into other forms of stores'). How can the lessons of this experience be applied to English cricket? To the extent that Tesco-isation means anything, it is a cure that may well prove worse than the disease.

Anyone who has studied the rise and fall of national sporting teams – not only in cricket – will conclude that it is a process complex to the point of mystery. Australia's recent success has been variously ascribed to its national academy, the discipline of Grade cricket, the strength of the Sheffield Shield, and the patriotic élan of its players. Pakistan's domestic cricket is chaotic and ill-equipped, but it does seem to be a highly effective conveyor belt of raw talent. Sri Lanka's triumphs owe much to its remarkable infrastructure of quasi-Victorian schools cricket, the by-product of a peculiar history and geography which could not be reproduced elsewhere. In the West Indies, two decades of world dominance coincided with a decline in the base of the game in the islands, disproving MacLaurin's key assumption: that a winning national side automatically strengthens the game at the grass roots.

What seems to count most in the making and unmaking of great international sides is the place cricket occupies in the national culture. The most significant difference between cricket in England and cricket in its major rivals is that the game's social base in England is proportionately smaller and less representative in relation to the population as a whole. Although cricket is of huge symbolic importance in England (hence the media fixation with the Test side), in the active life of the people it is relatively a minor recreation. Its niche in the national culture is a high-profile one, but it is a niche which both confines and warps the game, and nothing MacLaurin proposed is likely to alter this.

English cricket's attraction to advertisers, sponsors and media is the high concentration of ABC1s among its followers. It is their purchasing power which sells advertising time on Sky's Test and one day international coverage, and which draws in the likes of Vodaphone and NatWest. But this social profile is also the game's principal burden, inhibiting its promotion among less well-healed but larger constituencies. And economic developments are pushing cricket, along with sport in general, even further upmarket. The 1998 Social Trends report revealed that watching spectator sport (along with drinking in pubs) has become a leisure activity mainly for the better off (unlike betting, fun fairs, and bingo). During a three month period in 1996, one third of all ABs had been to a spectator sports event, in contrast to only 18% of Ds and 7% of Es. With its huge popular base, football can survive this long-term trend, but it leaves cricket in a quandary. The measures needed to expand the game's social base – the only plausible recipe for long-term renewal – are by no means the same as those required to maximise its short-term revenue potential.

Tesco-isation presumes that market forces can only invigorate and renew. It presumes that cricket must aim to enlarge or at least retain its share of Britain's £10 billion a year sports industry. But the pressures market forces exert on English cricket may well only hasten the sport's demise as a genuinely popular pastime. The parts of the MacLaurin Report most likely to whet a fan's appetite – floodlit one day games, regional matches against touring teams, more one day internationals – appeared as mere afterthoughts. The assumption seems to be that all the English cricket fan wants is for the national side to win, even if he or she can't see them doing it. Spectators have already been purged from the grass verges by the ubiquitous boundary boards. Ticket prices for international matches have become exorbitant. Advance credit card booking excludes millions. The corporate hospitality industry has usurped more than its fair share of the best seats, transforming the appearance and culture of many grounds. As county out-grounds have been culled, there has been a sad reduction in the diversity and accessibility of playing venues. This has affected not only charming festival sites like Weston-Super-Mare and Harrogate, but also major conurbations like Sheffield, Bradford, Liverpool and, soon perhaps, Swansea.

Though stymied in their attempts to re-organise county cricket, MacLaurin and Lamb proved more successful in their campaign to persuade the new government to remove home Test matches from the list of prestigious sporting events 'of national importance' (the FA Cup Final, Olympics, Grand National, etc.) which must be telecast free on terrestrial television. Though 'de-listing' was met with only perfunctory resistance, it is likely to have far greater and more lasting impact on the future of English cricket than anything contained in Raising the Standard.

ECB officials lobbied effectively for the right to sell their product in the open market, where Rupert Murdoch's Sky Sports is bound to outbid the BBC. At the moment, fewer than one in five households subscribe to Sky Sports, and they are concentrated in the upper income brackets. In 1997, BBC's live Test match telecasts were watched by 2-3 million every day. Sky's coverage of one day internationals attracted 500,000. And these 500,000 had to pay an average £20 a month extra for a service which used to be provided for nothing more than the license fee.

Had it not been for the live telecast of home Test matches on the BBC, I would probably never have succumbed to the charms of cricket, and I suspect millions of others would say the same. De-listing will radically circumscribe the casual but widespread involvement with the fluctuating real-time drama of Test cricket, and along with it, cricket's place in the public eye. (Surely the argument that penniless punters can watch Sky down the pub cannot apply to a five day Test!). This is not to say that cricket fans have no grievances with the BBC, nor to deny that Sky has improved the technical quality and range of international cricket coverage. For me, the BBC's foibles are amply compensated by the absence of adverts and especially of Sky's relentless, hyperbolic self-promotion. But more important, public service broadcasting must remain a major player, and standard-setter, in the cricket market if there is to be any counter-weight to Murdoch's power. Despite its present eagerness to emulate all things Australian – from cricket academies to the Grade format – the ECB seems to have overlooked the success of Australia's policy on sports broadcasting, which since 1992 ensures that free-to-air channels are given first option on no fewer than 41 sporting events, including every rugby and cricket international involving Australia, home or away.

Cricket needs money, but how much does it need, and at what cost to the future of the game as a whole? Between 1990 and 1994 the price the BBC paid for Test cricket rose by more than 645 per cent. Even with the continued listing of home Test matches the ECB would still receive substantial sums from the BBC and have a wide range of fixtures left over which it could sell to Sky for further millions. Ironically, de-listing will reduce the status of Test matches in comparison to one day internationals, which flies in the face of everything the ECB says it stands for. As ever, the guardians of England's cricketing traditions are highly selective about which traditions they'll fight to preserve, and which they're happy to hawk to the highest bidder.

It's not as if cricket is being starved of funds, commercial or public. Between 1995 and 1998, the game received nearly £50 million from the national lottery – a larger share of lottery capital awards than any other sport. More money may be required for future developments – the ECB produced a figure of £300 million - but what ought to be considered first is where and how the ECB allocates the resources it already has. What is desperately needed is investment at the base, but that requires a radical redivision of the pie, and MacLaurin and Lamb seem as averse to the notion of economic redistribution as Tony Blair and Gordon Brown.

Promotion and development of the game at the grass-roots was effectively ignored by Raising the Standard. The base of the pyramid exists, it seems, only to provide a means of ascent to the top. The report rightly talked of the need to 'bridge the gap between the recreational and first class game', but what was offered was not so much a bridge between neighbouring realms as the invasion of one by the other. All minor county, club, schools and youth cricket will now come under the aegis of the ECB's cricket committees. Recreational cricket will be subject to a dictatorship of the professionals (or rather, of the professional administrators), and will be shaped and reshaped to fit their priorities. In contrast to the caution and respect for tradition which marked MacLaurin's approach to reforming first-class cricket, his proposals for the recreational game were grandiose and uninhibited. By 2000, minor counties and second XI cricket will be replaced by 'a regional/divisional fully integrated 38 county championship which will act as the principal feeder for first class cricket'. In this 'county board' competition, cricketers contracted to the counties will play (on Sundays and Mondays) side by side with non-professionals. The ECB also aims to consolidate and streamline the current hodge podge of league and club cricket into a 'network of premier leagues' providing a 'greatly enhanced standard of competition for the top 2,000-plus recreational cricketers'. The premier leagues will be supervised by the ECB, which will control everything from playing conditions to disciplinary codes and registration rules, and which has promised to 'exercise quality control in granting premier status'. In other words, the ECB will run the premier leagues the way they have run first-class cricket: carefully controlling admission to the inner circle.

The ECB wants both county board and premier league competitions to adopt the format favoured in Australian Grade cricket, which is believed to be more 'competitive' and to provide better preparation for the stern examination of Test cricket. However, it is not at all certain that Grade cricket's two-day one-innings format leads 'naturally' (as the ECB claimed) to five-day two-innings matches. Besides, if people enjoy certain forms of cricket competition - minor counties, club friendlies, regional leagues – why should they be coerced into playing or watching a different form merely because the ECB believes this will be of benefit to the national side? The northern leagues, certainly, need no lectures from the heirs of the MCC about making cricket either popular or 'competitive'.

'Raising the Standard' offered no strategy and no money for the popularisation of the game among young people or in the inner cities, and no measures to span the gulf between the 'two cricket cultures' identified in the Roehampton report. Local authority cutbacks and the sell-off of playing fields have turned many urban areas into cricket deserts, and a massive, carefully planned and democratically controlled injection of resources will be needed to revive it there. The priority for the ECB should be providing facilities – pitches, practise nets, bats, balls and pads – in cities, towns and villages, and material support for the legion of committed volunteers whose efforts keep cricket alive at the grass-roots, like the Rose in Spanish Harlem: 'coming up in the streets, right up through the concrete ...' Despite the ECB's grandiose plans for restructuring recreational cricket, it offered a measly annual grant of £1000 to the 200 top clubs it was trying to prod into forming premier leagues. The share of Test and one day international profits allocated to each first class county is only slightly less than the share allocated to the whole of recreational cricket. And the insistence that funds are channelled only through the established county boards tends to exclude independent community projects, like the London Community Cricket Association or the Sheffield Caribbean Sports Club.

The blueprint was supposed to embrace the national game as a whole, but it contained only a single sentence on women: 'The WCA will be integrated into the ECB administrative structure' (a somewhat arrogant assertion, given that the WCA itself, an independent organisation for more than half a century, only voted to merge into the ECB eight months after the report was published). And, apart from the increased focus on representative youth cricket (England under-15s, etc.) it offered nothing of substance to universities, colleges, or schools (though it preserved the Oxbridge special status). The report did propose the development of a new variant of cricket especially designed for secondary schools. It would be a step up from KwikCricket but still played with a soft ball – an idea that betrayed little understanding of the dynamic appeal of competitive sport to adolescents and little faith in the intrinsic attractions of the game of cricket. Like the ECB's World Cup slogan, 'It's not just cricket', it is a gimmick rooted in the belief that cricket must be candy-coated for the masses, a belief which reveals more about the ECB than it does about cricket or the masses.

Like New Labour, the MacLaurin blueprint sought reform and renewal without threatening entrenched privileges. The ECB, which subsumed the old TCCB, as well as the NCA and the (largely defunct) Cricket Council, was meant to provide the game with a modern, centralised decision-making structure and effective management from above. But claims that it was a 'new organisation' should be taken with a pinch of salt. Most of its leading personnel were inherited from the TCCB. They have been supplemented with new appointments – accountants, PR technicians and former players. There has been acerbic comment on the rapid growth of this new cricket bureaucracy, but little interest in the principal question that must be asked of any bureaucracy: who appoints its members, what interests do they represent, and to whom are they accountable?

Under the ECB's new constitution, the First Class Forum, comprising representatives of the 18 first class counties plus the MCC, retains an effective veto over all major developments affecting the game. Indeed, through the ECB, commercial cricket has acquired more power than ever over recreational. The FCF reserves the right to nominate the ECB chairman. Its own chairman serves *ex-officio* as the ECB's deputy chair. The FCF also directly elects the chairmen of the ECB's major committees – cricketing, finance, marketing, and the England Management Committee. These chairmen, in turn, are voting *ex-officio* members of the ECB management board, on which the FCF is also directly represented, along with the Recreational Cricket Forum (representing club, league, university and schools cricket), which is consigned to a permanent minority. The England Management Committee, a discreet resuscitation of Ted Dexter's much lampooned England Committee, is comprised of ECB officers and committee chairmen. The whole set up is effectively self-selecting and self-perpetuating.

Intriguingly, the architects of the new ECB constitution passed up the opportunity to do away once and for all with the anomaly of the MCC, the self-styled 'private club with a public role', just as Blair's plan for a renewed London democracy and elected mayor managed to leave intact the ancient prerogatives of the Corporation of the City of London. Like the MCC, the Corporation owns priceless community assets by virtue of historical precedent rather than capital investment. For all Tim Lamb's insistence that the ECB has nothing to do with the MCC, the fact is that the MCC enjoys a vote on the FCF (MCC Secretary Roger Knight is one of its representatives on the ECB management board) and still casts a vote for the England Test selectors. Lord MacLaurin himself came to the ECB chairmanship via his activity in the MCC. Indeed, the ECB and MCC share a website ('Lord's – the home of cricket') where you can click on to the 'England's heritage' page and the 'virtual' tour of the Long Room. So the old boys of English cricket trek the byways of cyberspace, dragging with them centuries of reflexive elitism.

Feudal-style authority may have been replaced by the modern ethos of managerialism (half quack science and half quasi-religious ritual), but the ECB remains loftily indifferent to the niceties of accountability and representation. How many other public bodies would permit the kind of flagrant conflicts of interest which the ECB takes in its stride? David Graveney is both chairman of selectors and chief executive of the PCA – something like being shop steward and personnel manager at the same time. And only a year after signing a major sponsorship deal with Vodaphone in his capacity as ECB representative, MacLaurin was appointed the company's chairman. Presumably he will enjoy negotiating with himself when the current sponsorship deal expires. Like other British institutions, cricket has long been governed by a network of clubby inter-connections, a tradition which ensures that the existing parameters of debate and action remain unexamined, and that anyone outside the magic circle of influence and access remains voiceless. 'We've never had a vote,' MacLaurin once boasted of his 12 years as Tesco chairman, 'the board directors are very carefully chosen.' Tesco-isation, it is clear, will do nothing to shrink English cricket's chronic democratic deficit.

Like Tony Blair, the mandarins of the ECB set themselves above 'special interests' in order to govern for the general good. Tim Lamb spelled out what they had in mind when he said the game had to be 'de-democratised'. But in the absence of democracy, who defines the 'general good'? Who determines, and how, what is or is not in 'the national interest'? At least special interests are accountable, defined, negotiable. The counties may be selfish and backward-looking, but we know what interests they represent. Without them, where is the ECB's mandate? Who else will scrutinise or restrain power at the centre? County committees are often incompetent and narrow-minded, but they are what they are not because they represent special interests, but because they have emerged in an environment shaped first by the MCC and later the TCCB. Their financial dependence, their cacooned conservatism are the result of English cricket's long tradition of top-down rule by an elite acting in what it claims is 'the national interest'. This historic inhibition on the development of English cricket will only be exacerbated by 'Tesco-isation'. Far from transcending 'special interests', it promotes them, not least the interests of big business, the most powerful and unaccountable of the 'special interests' in cricket, as in society at large.

According to Richard Peel, the ECB's corporate affairs director (i.e. image-maker and spin-doctor in chief), 'The aim is to get some powerful messages across about the success of cricket, from schools right up to international level.' The ECB's strategy, it seems, is to 'sell success' because 'success sells' – and never mind selling the game itself, its spectacle, humour, frustrations and fun.

Of course, most cricket fans want to see their team win, but that is not their sole reason for going to the cricket. Attendance at Test and one-day internationals in Britain has climbed steadily during the nineties, regardless of England's fortunes in the field. But Peel, who had previously worked for John Birt at the BBC, was clearly referring to something more – or other – than an improved won-lost record. Britain, like the United States, has increasingly become a winner-take-all society. Rewards at the top have multiplied many times over, while the living standards of the majority have stagnated. 'Success' has become a fetish, a value in itself, regardless of how it is achieved or its cost to others. Increasingly, it is treated as a transferable trait: fashion models become novelists, novelists become TV presenters, TV presenters become politicians, politicians become health gurus, supermarket magnates become cricket administrators, and Test cricketers become cricket commentators, whether or not they demonstrate a facility with the English language.

MacLaurin's appeal to 'competitiveness', a shibboleth invoked throughout *Raising the Standard*, echoed the prevailing go-getting rhetoric of 'success'. It also harped on a long-established theme in the debate about Britain's identity in the modern world. Like Tony Blair, and before him, Margaret Thatcher (and before her, Harold Wilson), MacLaurin promised to shake-up old institutions to make the country once again 'competitive' in a global market. Despite the deregulation of the eighties, despite the long public celebration of economic individualism, there remains the nagging suspicion that the English are just not 'tough' enough to cut it with the big players of the cut-throat new world order, that they are, as Dennis Silk suggested, 'a degenerate nation which cannot be bothered to make the effort.' It seemed there were just too many English people, from county cricketers to single mothers, who thought they were entitled to a cushioned passage from cradle to grave.

In an interview with broadcaster Martyn Lewis for a book entitled *Reflections on Success*, Mike Atherton complained, 'There is a lot of envy of success. Sometimes I'm sure there is a real desire to see the national team do badly. It is a typically British attitude.' The notion that the English suffer from a debilitating antipathy towards 'success' (in contrast to the no-holds-barred Americans) has been knocking around for the best part of a century, so it's not surprising that it should so imbue the self-consciously English (but deeply competitive) world of English cricket. For many commentators, lack of 'competitiveness' is a flaw in the national character, the result of a soft and spoiled national life, and the cause of England's demise as a great cricket power.

In August 1997, Nasser Hussain opined that England had lost the Ashes to Australia (again) because English cricket wasn't 'nasty' enough. 'This softness comes from playing county cricket, which is all very matey and lovey-dovey. No one is sledging anyone, we are all mates out there and it's about a few cups of tea and maybe a Pimms or two afterwards.' The next day, during a tense NatWest semi-final in Chelmsford, a verbal exchange between Mark Ilott and Robert Croft led to a brief bout of mutual chest-prodding (and supplied the most frequently replayed cricket highlight of the summer). The authorities came down heavily, and the prophets of 'competitiveness' were quick to insist that this was definitely not the kind of 'competitive' behaviour they had in mind. The incident revealed not only cricket's lingering uneasiness about the unfettered will-to-win, but just how difficult it is in practise to distinguish between unstinting competitive zeal (approved by all) and boorish aggressiveness (condemned by all). Everyone thought they knew what Hussain was talking about, but the Illott-Croft confrontation showed that what he was talking about was impossible to define to anyone's satisfaction.

Sport provided economics with a model of competition; now, sadly, the economics of competitiveness seems to have become a model for sport. The ethos of the two are radically different; victory or defeat in cricket is not comparable to success or failure in the economy. Sport is founded as much on co-operation as competition (co-operation among members of a team, co-operation between teams), and most spectators want to see both of these qualities on display. The ECB, however, appears to believe that the purpose of cricket is to forge (and flog) a national identity of 'success'.

In reducing the fortunes of cricket in Britain to the fortunes of the England side, the MacLaurin report defined the nation as a competitive entity. Here, the Tory peer found himself at one with the New Labour Prime Minister. In the heated prelude to Euro 96, Blair told football fans he looked forward to a national triumph, and observed: 'For true supporters, victory is all. In sport as in politics, a well-fought campaign for second place means nothing.' Leaving aside the casual disregard for the virtues of principle in politics, Blair showed little insight into the psyche of the 'true supporter', whose support for his or her side does not waver in defeat.

He also seems to have missed the ambivalence which runs through the discussion of 'competitiveness' in English life and sport. The dose of ruthlessness prescribed for the English malaise by so many English nationalists seems to involve a drift away from the very 'Englishness' which nationalists like to celebrate. In a survey of *Daily Telegraph* readers, respondents defined 'English character' as 'tolerant, reserved, self-deprecating, cheerful in adversity, having a strong sense of fair play and prone to side with the underdog.' Above all, 'an Englishman will appreciate and understand the game of cricket' (most, of course, do not). Asked to list 'cultural items' characterising Englishness, *Telegraph* readers ranked the top five as: fish and chips, cricket on the village green, pubs, church bells, and the last night of the Proms. Hardly 'Cool Britannia'!

The ECB has announced plans to jazz up the one day National League with pop music, mascots, parachutists, jugglers, prizes and give-aways. For some this is anathema; for others, a long overdue shot in the arm. For me, the ECB's rather quaint notions of 'razzmatazz' are largely an irrelevance. Whenever they get the chance, children and their parents (and some eager adults without children) swarm over the outfield during lunch or tea intervals to improvise miniature cricket matches on the high-quality turf. This custom has now been institutionalised in the KwikCricket displays at international matches. But it isn't the same. What's missing are spontaneity and participation. The arrival of the Barmy Army during England's tour of Australia in 1994-95 seemed to herald a new type of English cricket spectator, but its subsequent evolution – into 'official' and 'unofficial' wings, each repudiating the antics of the other – and its rapid commercialisation suggested that it will take more than the odd bout of massed chanting to invigorate England's cricket culture.

Because of its peculiar historical evolution, cricket in England, unlike cricket in south Asia or the West Indies or Australia, lacks a living link to the popular culture of the day, and blasting out M People's 'Search for the Hero' as the batsman walks to the wicket is no compensation. The social conditions which have made British youth innovative world-shakers in popular music, bursting out of the inner cities and the suburbs in wave after wave, have also made them largely indifferent to cricket. Rather than licensing the corporate hospitality racket, let's revive crowd spontaneity and diversity by reserving a section of seats for sale on the day and dropping the ban on banners and musical instruments. So far, English cricket's notion of populism seems to be subjecting the entire crowd to a succession of over-familiar middle-of-the-road chart-toppers programmed in advance by a marketing executive. Let the spectators make their own music (as in the West Indies and Sri Lanka) and the administrators concentrate on making them comfortable. What's needed are the conditions in which spectators themselves, through tolerant interaction, can shape the atmosphere and draw their own boundaries. You cannot artificially create a new cricket culture any more than you can a national identity.

Not that any such thoughts have inhibited the architects of New Britain. Launching his plans for the Millennium Dome, Peter Mandelson declared, 'We want to forge for Britain a new identity as a modern, forward-looking nation. For too long we have been seen by too many people as having had our day, on the decline, a country with a great history but little to offer the future.' Unfortunately for Mandelson, the designer of the Dome's 'British' theme zone – dubbed the 'UK@Now' project – happened to be a Frenchman. But, of course, the business of national identity is itself a globalised phenomenon. In a report called 'Britain TM: Renewing our Identity', the think-tank Demos outlined how countries could adopt the techniques used by companies to 'manage their identities'. The shop-worn, introverted 'United Kingdom' could be re-launched as an 'outward-looking, diverse, creative hub in an increasingly open, global economy.' The Spice Girls PR man put the same idea more crudely. 'Britain's image was being re-established around the world and there were three key factors: Tony Blair, the England football team, and the Spice Girls. The message is, come on everybody, let's support our team.'

Cricket was notably absent from his list, as it was from other catalogues of what the Design Council called Britain's 'creativity in lifestyle' – fashion, music, adverts. However, the underlying lesson of the 're-branding of Britain' is that, in today's global economic order, national identity is a commodity which can be packaged and re-packaged. 'New Britain' is an artificial construct designed to sell products and promote politicians. It is as remote from the wellsprings of genuine popular culture as the theme park Englishness of the ECB/MCC website. Even county cricket, in its own way, can claim a more intimate link with popular feeling, and a loyalism bred not by a contrived marketing strategy but through the complexities of lived experience, not least, the experience of watching your team lose more often than it wins, something the ECB mandarins seem to regard as an indulgence. The making of New Britain has been an exercise in post-modern political manipulation, a triumph of representation over reality. Rather than tamper with the patterns of investment and ownership which really make the nation what it is, our New Labour elite offers national renewal through repackaging. And English cricket appears to be pursuing a parallel course. Tesco-isation means combining an upmarket economic base with downmarket presentation – the worst of both worlds. In its preoccupation with individual and national 'success', and its assumption that English national identity can only thrive if the nation is seen to be beating other nations, it should fit in all too neatly with the elite vulgarity which is the hallmark of New Britain.

English cricket will survive as long as the cash tills keep ringing, and that they will continue to do, whether or not more people are given the chance to play and watch the game. The political economy of modern sport, with its niche marketing and addiction to corporate sponsorship, makes it possible to increase revenues while alienating the bulk of the population. If nothing else, the history of English cricket in the last twenty years surely proves that.

Lord's, July, 1997. Middlesex v. Australia. The sun is shining and I am trying to explain why Shane Warne is the Michael Jordan of cricket to my American niece and nephew. They're both sports nuts, and I had been eagerly anticipating our day at Lord's and my chance to show off my adopted game. I knew that unless they sat high up at the nursery end, it would be hard for them to make sense of the play, so I was left with no alternative but to fork out £50 for five tickets in the Compton Stand Upper Tier. There were no discounts for Middlesex members or for juveniles. Hannah, who was nine, was startled to learn that women were not admitted to the lovely brick pavilion at the far end of the ground. Perhaps England really was the semi-medieval place of Walt Disney fantasy. Eleven-year-old Alex stared long and hard and silently at the men in white on the green field. Eventually, he got it, noting how Mark Taylor had moved 'the guy standing next to the catcher' (the slip fielder next to the wicketkeeper) to a remote corner of the field. 'It's more defensive.'

Two sessions were sufficient for them, but they enjoyed the game enough to insist we spend another £30 on a mini-cricket set. For several days after I repeatedly endured the humbling experience of being clean bowled by an 11-year-old American. Alex and Hannah didn't know or care about Lord's or England's heritage. It was a three day game, played in whites, with no razzmatazz and no league points or cup place at stake. But it was cricket, and they liked it.

The lessons are obvious. First, the game does not belong to any one country or culture; there's no more reason to find it strange that an American kid likes cricket than that a British kid takes to basketball or a Samoan to rugby or a Japanese to baseball.

Secondly, the game sells itself, if people are given a chance to watch and play it.

Alas, there is no pristine cricket. There is only the cricket history has given us. However, practical reform is certainly possible. I can think of a host of things I'd like to see the ECB do to expand the base of the game and enfranchise the players and the punters. But all would require money and control flowing away from Lord's, and somehow I can't see them ever reaching the top of the ECB's agenda.

I've lived in England more than a quarter of a century. With each passing year, the balance between the American and English parts of my life shifts inexorably towards the latter. When I'm abroad I miss English breakfasts, British TV and radio, the NHS, my squalid, beautiful, mixed-up inner city neighbourhood, and the chance to escape from it into the rumpled greenery of the Marches. And enthralled as I am by the great modern sports stadia in North America, south Asia, and Europe, I miss Chelmsford, Hove, Taunton, Canterbury, Ilford, Abergavenny, Cardiff, and, yes, Lord's, though I still think it should be nationalised. I'm not worried about whether I'm American or English. National identity is not natural or god given or genetic or even 'cultural'. It is constructed and reconstructed, contested and disputed, and usually more divisive than uniting. For generations, English cricket and the England team have provided a vehicle through which that identity is discussed. It is as though history has magnetised English cricket, making it a pole of attraction for powerful feelings about the past and uncertainty about the future. That has been to the detriment of the game in this country. The thrust of *Anyone But England* was that, in the modern world, the search for a homogeneous national culture or unchanging national identity was both futile and dangerous, and an historic burden on English cricket. With cricket, as with the country, what's needed is a democratic redistribution of power and resources, a change in substance, not merely in image.

Bibliography

Allen, David Rayvern (ed.), *Cricket's Silver Lining: 1864-1914*, Willow Books, London, 1987

Allison, Lincoln (ed.), *The Politics of Sport*, Manchester University Press, 1986

Allison, Lincoln (ed.), *The Changing Politics of Sport*, Manchester University Press, 1993

Altham, H.S. and Swanton, E.W., *A History of Cricket* (third edition), George Allen & Unwin, London, 1947

Anderson, Benedict, *Imagined Communities: Reflection on the Origin and Spread of Nationalism*, Verso, London, 1983

Anderson, Perry, *English Questions*, Verso, London, 1992

Bailey, Jack, *Conflicts in Cricket*, Kingswood Press, London, 1989

Bailey, Phillip; Thorn, Philip; Wynne-Thomas, Peter, *Who's Who of Cricketers*, Hamlyn, London, 1993

Baloch, Khadim Hussain, *Summer of Swing*, Essex, 1993

Beckett, J.V., *The Aristocracy in England, 1660-1914*, Basil Blackwell, Oxford, 1986

Berry, Scyld, *Cricket Wallah, with England in India 1981-2*, Hodder & Stoughton, London, 1982

Berry, Scyld (ed.), *The Observer on Cricket*, Unwin Hyman, London, 1987

Birley, Derek, *The Willow Wand: Some Cricket Myths Explored*, London, 1979

Birley, Derek, *Sport and the Making of Britain*, Manchester University Press, 1993

Blunden, Edmund, *Cricket Country*, 1944; reprinted by Pavilion Books, 1985

Bose, Mihir, *A Maidan View: the Magic of Indian Cricket*, George Allen &
Unwin, London, 1986

Bose, Mihir, *A History of Indian Cricket*, Andre Deutsch, London, 1990

Bose, Mihir, *Cricket Voices*, Kingswood Press, London, 1990

Bowen, Rowland, *Cricket: a History of Its Growth and Development
Throughout the World*, Eyre & Spottiswoode, London, 1970

Bradley, James, 'The MCC, Society and Empire: A Portrait of Cricket's
Ruling Body, 1860-1914', in *The Cultural Bond: Sport, Empire,
Society*, James A. Mangan (ed.), Frank Cass, London, 1992

Bright-Holmes, John (ed.), *The Joy of Cricket*, Martin Secker & Warburg,
London, 1984

Brodribb, Gerald (ed.), *The English Game, a Cricket Anthology*, Hollis &
Carter, London, 1948

Brooke, Robert, *A History of the County Championship*, Guinness
Publishing, London, 1991

Callinicos, Luli, *Gold and Workers: 1886-1924*, Ravan Press,
Johannesburg, South Africa, 1980

Cannadine, David, *The Decline and Fall of the British Aristocracy*, Picador,
London, 1992

Cardus, Neville, *English Cricket*, Collins, London, 1945

Chandler, Joan M., *Television and National Sport: the United States and
Britain*, University of Illinois Press, Chicago, 1988

Corbett, Ted, *Cricket on the Run*, Stanley Paul, London, 1990

Cowdrey, Colin, *M.C.C., the Autobiography of a Cricketer*, Hodder &
Stoughton, London, 1976

Crace, John, *Wasim and Waqar: Imran's Inheritors*, Boxtree, London,
1992

De Selincourt, Hugh, *The Cricket Match*, Jonathan Cape, London, 1924

Dobbs, Brian, *Edwardians at Play, Sport 1890-1914*, Pelham, London,
1973

D'Oliveira, Basil, *The D'Oliveira Affair*, Collins, London, 1969

Edmundson, David, *See the Conquering Hero: the Story of the Lancashire
League, 1892-1992*, Mike Mcleod Litho Ltd, Altham, Lancashire, 1992

Evans, Richard, *The Ultimate Test*, Partridge Press, London, 1990

Gatting, Mike (with Angela Patmore), *Leading from the Front*, Queen
Anne Press, London, 1988

Gilroy, Paul, *Small Acts*, Serpent's Tail, London, 1993

Gooch, Graham (with Alan Lee), *Out of the Wilderness*, Willow Books,
London, 1985

Gothaskar, M.V., *The Burning Finger - an Indian Umpire Looks Back*,

Marine Sports, Bombay, 1992

Gould, Stephen Jay, 'The Creation Myths of Cooperstown', in *Bully for Brontosaurus*, Hutchinson Radius, London, 1991

Green, Benny (ed.), *The Wisden Papers, 1888-1946*, Stanley Paul, London, 1989

Green, Benny (ed.), *The Wisden Papers, 1969—1990: Mixed Fortunes*, Stanley Paul, London, 1991

Greenidge, Gordon (with Patrick Symes), *Gordon Greenidge: the Man in the Middle*, David & Charles, Newton Abbot, 1980

Guha, Ramachandra, *Wickets in the East: an Anecdotal History*, Oxford University Press, Delhi, 1992

Guttmann, Allen, *From Ritual to Record: the Nature of Modern Sports*, Columbia University Press, New York, 1978

Hain, Peter, *Don't Play with Apartheid*, George Allen & Unwin, London, 1971

Hammond, Dave, *Foul Play: a Class Analysis of Sport*, Ubique Books, London, 1993

Hargeaves, John, Sport, *Power and Culture*, Polity Press, Cambridge, 1986

Harte, Chris, *A History of Australian Cricket*, Andre Deutsch, London, 1993

Hobsbawm, E.J., *Industry and Empire: an Economic History of Britain Since 1750*, Weidenfeld & Nicolson, London, 1962

Hobsbawm, F.J., *The Age of Revolution: 1789-1848*, Weidenfeld & Nicolson, London, 1962

Hobsbawm, E.J. and Ranger, Terence (eds), *The Invention of Tradition*, Cambridge University Press, 1983

Holt, Richard, *Sport and the British: a Modern History*, Oxford University Press, 1989

Howat, Gerald, *Learie Constantine*, George Allen & Unwin, London, 1975

Howat, Gerald, *Cricket Medley*, Sports History Publishing, 1993

Khan, Imran, *All Round View*, Chatto & Windus, London, 1988

Kynaston, David, *W.G.'s Birthday Party*, Chatto & Windus, London, 1990

Kynaston, David, *Bobby Abel, Professional Batsman*, Martin Secker & Warburg, London, 1982

James, C.L.R., *Beyond a Boundary*, Stanley Paul, London, 1963

James, C.L.R., *Cricket*, Allison & Busby, London, 1986

Jameson, Frederic, *Postmodernism, or, the Cultural Logic of Late Capitalism*, Duke University Press, Durham, North Carolina, 1991

Lemmon, David, *For the Love of the Game: an Oral History of Cricket*, Michael Joseph, London, 1993

Lemmon, David (ed.), *Benson and Hedges Cricket Year*, 12th edition, Headline Books, London, 1993

Lewis, Tony, *Double Century: the Story of MCC and Cricket*, Hodder & Stoughton, London, 1987

McDonald, Trevor, *Viv Richards, the Authorised Biography*, Pelham Books, London, 1984

Manley, Michael, *A History of West Indies Cricket*, Andre Deutsch, London, 1988

Mason, Tony (ed.), *Sport in Britain, a Social History*, Cambridge University Press, 1989

Moers, Colin, *The Making of Bourgeois Europe*, Verso, London, 1991

Moorhouse, Geoffrey, *The Best Loved Game*, Michael Joseph, London, 1979

Orr-Ewing, Ian (ed.), *A Celebration of Lords and Commons Cricket: 1850-1988*, Kingswood Press, London, 1989

Orwell, George, *The Collected Essays, Journalism and Letters of George Orwell*, Penguin Books, London, 1970

Oslear, Don, *The Wisden Book of Cricket Laws*, Stanley Paul, London, 1993

Powell, William, *The Wisden Guide to Cricket Grounds*, Stanley Paul, London, 1992

Pugh, Martin, *The Making of Modern British Politics: 1867-1939*, Basil Blackwell, Oxford, 1982

Pycroft, James, *Cricketana*, London, 1864; reprinted by Tyre Industry Publications Ltd, Clacton-on-Sea, Essex, 1987

Rader, Benjamin G., *Baseball, a History of America's Game*, University of Illinois Press, Chicago, 1992

Richards, Viv, *Hitting Across the Line*, Headline Books, 1991

Roberts, Cheryl, *Don't Deny My Dreams: Stories of Black Youth Playing Sport in Apartheid South Africa*, Township Publishing Co-operative, Cape Town, South Africa, 1992

Roberts, Cheryl (ed.), *Challenges Facing South African Sport*, Township Publishing Co-operative, Cape Town, South Africa, 1990

Roberts, Cheryl (ed.), *Reconstruction of South African Sport*, NOSC, East London, South Africa, 1992

Roebuck, Peter, *Tangled Up in White*, Hodder & Stoughton, London, 1992

Ross, Alan (ed.), *The Kingswood Book of Cricket*, Kingswood Press, London, 1992

Said, Edward, *Culture and Imperialism*, Knopf, New York, 1993

Scarborough, Vernon L. and Wilcox, David R. (eds), *The Mesoamerican Ballgame*, University of Arizona Press, Tucson, Arizona, 1992

Scott, Neville and Cook, Nick, *England Test Cricket: the Years of Indecision, 1981-1992*, Kingswood, London, 1992

Senan, Chandra, *Spin Washed and Kumble Dried, the 1993 England Cricket Tour of India, or the Sub-continental Spinquisition*, Preposterous Publications, Chester, 1993

Sissons, Ric, *The Players: a Social History of the Professional Cricketers*, Kingswood Press, London, 1988

Sproat, Iain (ed.), *The Cricketers' Who's Who, 1993*, Queen Anne Press, London, 1993

Steen, Rob, *Spring, Summer, Autumn*, Kingswood, London, 1991

Steen, Rob, *Desmond Haynes, Lion of Barbados*, Witherby, London, 1993

Swanton, E.W., *Gubby Allen, Man of Cricket*, Hutchinson Stanley Paul, London, 1985

Swanton, E.W. (ed.), *Barclays World of Cricket*, Collins, 1980

Vamplew, Wray, *Pay Up and Play the Game: Professional Sport in Britain, 1875-1914*, Cambridge University Press, 1988

Warner, Sir Pelham, *Lord 's: 1787-1945*, George G. Harrap and Co., London, 1946

Williams, Marcus (ed.), *The Way To Lord's: Cricketing Letters to the Times*, Willow Books, London, 1983

Williams, Raymond, *Culture and Society 1780-1950*, Chatto and Windus, London, 1958

Woods, Donald, *Cricket World: Reflections on the 1992 World Cup*, Broadcast Books, Bristol, 1992

Wright, Graeme, *Betrayal: the Struggle for Cricket's Soul*, H., F. & G. Witherby, London, 1993

Plus: Works of Marx, Engels, Trotsky, *Wisden Cricketers' Almanack*, Indian Cricket (annual - Kasturi & Sons Ltd, Madras, India), *The Cricketer International*, *Wisden Cricket Monthly*, *Cricket World*, *Inside Edge*, *JM96**, *SportsStar*, *Caribbean Cricket* and the much lamented *Cricket Life International*.